Chinese Politics

Written by a team of leading China specialists, this updated 2nd edition of *Chinese Politics* explores the dynamics of state power and politics in contemporary China, focusing on the Xi Jinping era.

Through its multi-disciplinary contributions, this book explores the extent to which Xi has reshaped the political, economic, socio-cultural, and demographic terrains of the PRC, as well as Beijing's foreign policy. The book will help readers to think productively about the trajectory of these aspects of Chinese politics and society through Xi's current term and beyond. The book also highlights the potential role outside countries and non-state actors might play in shaping China's trajectory as the PRC's economic rise may be stalling. Through each exploration of these issues, the book addresses the central question of what *The Xi Jinping Difference* has been, and will likely continue to be, in Chinese politics.

Key subjects covered in this new edition include:

- Law and the political system
- Socialization of youth
- The fate of the private sector
- Technology and digital authoritarianism
- The Belt and Road Initiative
- Population aging

Chinese Politics continues to be an essential textbook for all students of contemporary China as well as scholars interested in the dynamics of political and social change.

Stanley Rosen is Professor of Political Science and International Relations at the University of Southern California, USA.

Daniel C. Lynch is Associate Dean of the College of Liberal Arts and Social Sciences and a Professor of Public and International Affairs at the City University of Hong Kong.

Asia's Transformations
Edited by Mark Selden
Cornell University, USA

The books in this series explore the political, social, economic and cultural consequences of Asia's transformations in the twentieth and twenty-first centuries. The series emphasizes the tumultuous interplay of local, national, regional and global forces as Asia bids to become the hub of the world economy. While focusing on the contemporary, it also looks back to analyse the antecedents of Asia's contested rise.

National Identity, Language and Education in Malaysia
Search for a Middle Ground between Malay Hegemony and Equality
Noriyuki Segawa

Japan's Future and a New Meiji Transformation
International Reflections
Edited by Ken Coates, Kimie Hara, Carin Holroyd and Marie Söderberg

Dangerous Memory in Nagasaki
Prayers, Protests and Catholic Survivor Narratives
Gwyn McClelland

Popular Culture and the Transformation of Japan – Korea Relations
Rumi Sakamoto & Stephen Epstein

The Making of Modern Korea, 4th Edition
Adrian Buzo

Literature After Fukushima
From Marginalized Voices to Nuclear Futurity
Edited by Linda Flores and Barbara Geilhorn

Chinese Politics, 2nd Edition
The Xi Jinping Difference
Edited by Stanley Rosen and Daniel C. Lynch

For more information about this series, please visit: www.routledge.com/Asias-Transformations/book-series/SE0401

Chinese Politics
The Xi Jinping Difference
Second Edition

**Edited by Stanley Rosen and
Daniel C. Lynch**

LONDON AND NEW YORK

Designed cover image: Marcos Corrêa/PR (CC BY 2.0 DEED)

Second edition published 2024
by Routledge
4 Park Square, Milton Park, Abingdon, Oxon, OX14 4RN

and by Routledge
605 Third Avenue, New York, NY 10158

Routledge is an imprint of the Taylor & Francis Group, an informa business

© 2024 selection and editorial matter, Stanley Rosen and Daniel C. Lynch; individual chapters, the contributors

The right of Stanley Rosen and Daniel C. Lynch to be identified as the authors of the editorial material, and of the authors for their individual chapters, has been asserted in accordance with sections 77 and 78 of the Copyright, Designs and Patents Act 1988.

All rights reserved. No part of this book may be reprinted or reproduced or utilised in any form or by any electronic, mechanical, or other means, now known or hereafter invented, including photocopying and recording, or in any information storage or retrieval system, without permission in writing from the publishers.

Trademark notice: Product or corporate names may be trademarks or registered trademarks, and are used only for identification and explanation without intent to infringe.

First edition published by Routledge 2010

British Library Cataloguing-in-Publication Data
A catalogue record for this book is available from the British Library

Library of Congress Cataloging-in-Publication Data
Names: Rosen, Stanley, 1942– editor. | Lynch, Daniel C. (Daniel
    Christopher), editor.
Title: Chinese politics : the Xi Jinping difference / edited by Stanley Rosen
    and Daniel C. Lynch.
Other titles: Xi Jinping difference
Description: Second edition. | Abingdon, Oxon ; New York, NY :
    Routledge, 2024. | Series: Asia's transformations | "First edition published
    by Routledge 2010." | Includes bibliographical references and index.
Identifiers: LCCN 2023051133 (print) | LCCN 2023051134 (ebook) |
    ISBN 9781032191515 (hbk) | ISBN 9781032191522 (pbk) |
    ISBN 9781003257943 (ebk)
Subjects: LCSH: China—Politics and government—2002– | Xi, Jinping. |
    China—Economic conditions—2000– | China—Social conditions—2000–
Classification: LCC DS779.46 .C472 2024 (print) | LCC DS779.46
    (ebook) | DDC 951.06—dc23/eng/20231228
LC record available at https://lccn.loc.gov/2023051133
LC ebook record available at https://lccn.loc.gov/2023051134

ISBN: 978-1-032-19151-5 (hbk)
ISBN: 978-1-032-19152-2 (pbk)
ISBN: 978-1-003-25794-3 (ebk)

DOI: 10.4324/9781003257943

Typeset in Times New Roman
by Apex CoVantage, LLC

Contents

List of figures	*vii*
List of tables	*viii*
List of contributors	*ix*
Acknowledgments	*xi*

	Introduction	1
	STANLEY ROSEN AND DANIEL C. LYNCH	
1	**Law and the Political System in Xi Jinping's China: The Decline of the Party/State Distinction**	17
	DONALD CLARKE	
2	**Educating the Next Generation: Propping up the Party and Undermining Alternatives**	44
	KARRIE J. KOESEL	
3	**The Private Economy Under Party-State Capitalism**	67
	MARGARET M. PEARSON, MEG RITHMIRE, AND KELLEE S. TSAI	
4	**Xi Jinping's Partnership with Technology Companies and Social Media Platforms**	83
	DANIELA STOCKMANN AND TING LUO	
5	**Technology Policy Under Xi Jinping, 2012–2022**	105
	DOUGLAS B. FULLER AND RICARDO L. KOTZ	
6	**Chinese Urban Poverty: Negligence or Disdain?**	125
	DOROTHY J. SOLINGER	
7	**How to Think Xi Jinping Thought**	142
	JEAN CHRISTOPHER MITTELSTAEDT AND PATRICIA M. THORNTON	

8 The 20th Party Congress: Toward Personalistic Autarky? 161
JOSEPH FEWSMITH

9 The Evolving Leadership in Xi's PLA: Factionalism, Weak
Coalition, or Military Preparedness? 178
VICTOR C. SHIH

10 The BRI Under Xi Jinping: Fragmented Authoritarianism
Beyond Water's Edge 193
ANDREW MERTHA

11 Chinese Foreign Policy Under Xi Jinping 217
JUNE TEUFEL DREYER

12 Who Is Blamed for the Pandemic? Survey Findings and
Implications for the China Model 239
YUEN YUEN ANG, TWILA TARDIF, AND WENJIA SONG

13 Implications of the Reformation of China's Demographic
Structure 262
WANG FENG

Index *281*

Figures

2.1	Chinese Leaders and Party Mention by Decade, 1951–2022	58
3.1	Registration and Deregistration of Small and Microenterprises, 2016–2021	77
4.1	Percentage of Internet Users in China, 2000–2021	85
4.2	Percentage of Internet Users Using Social Media Platforms	86
7.1	Chaohu City Mass-Volunteer Integration	150
12.1	"Yes, I Blame China for COVID-19"	245
12.2	"Yes, I Blame the U.S. for COVID-19"	246
12.3	Global Distribution of Blame	247
12.4	Who in China Is Blamed?	248
12.5	Who in the U.S. Is Blamed?	251
12.6	Do Americans and Chinese Blame the Government, the Leader, or the People?	252
12.7	Who in China Is Blamed by the Respondents from Mainland China, Hong Kong, and Taiwan?	253
13.1	Convergence to Very Low Fertility	264
13.2	Parity Progression Ratios from Birth to First Child	265
13.3	Proportion of Women Who Never-Married by Age, China, Selected Years	267
13.4	Four Decades of Educational Expansion in China, 1982–2020	268
13.5	Life Expectancy at Age 65, China, Japan, and South Korea	270
13.6	Three Urbanizations in China, 1978–2020	272
13.7	Shares of Population by Main Source of Living, Urban China, 2020	274
13.8	Shares of Population by Main Source of Living, Rural China, 2020	275

Tables

1.1	Rank of Leader of Political-Legal Institutions, 2002–2022	22
5.1	Domestic Market Share Goal for Products Made by Chinese Firms	113
8.1	Politburo Standing Committee	167
8.2	The Rest of the Politburo	168
8.3	The Secretariat	169
8.4	Central Military Commission	170
9.1	Key Military Region-Level Officers and Their Factional Ties with Xi, 2016 Versus 2022	183
9.2	Mean and Standard Deviation of the Number of Current and Total Ties MR-Level Officers Had with Army-Level or Above Officers, 2016 Versus 2022	185
9.3	The Most and Least Networked MR-Level Officers Active in 2022	186
9.4	Full MR Commanders, Their Branch, and the Number of Fighting Unit Commands, 2016 Versus 2022	188
12.1	Survey Questions on Blame in Existing Surveys	242
12.2	Number of Respondents in Each Country	243
12.3	Number of Respondents in Mainland China, Hong Kong, and Taiwan	252

Contributors

Yuen Yuen Ang is the Alfred Chandler Chair of Political Economy at Johns Hopkins University

Donald Clarke is Professor of Law and the David A. Weaver Research Professor at the George Washington University Law School

June Teufel Dreyer is Professor of Political Science at the University of Miami, Coral Gables and a senior fellow at the Foreign Policy Research Institute.

Joseph Fewsmith is Professor of Political Science and International Relations, Pardee School of Global Studies, Boston University

Douglas B. Fuller is Associate Professor at Copenhagen Business School

Karrie J. Koesel is Associate Professor of Political Science at the University of Notre Dame

Ricardo L. Kotz is a Ph.D. candidate in the Department of Public and International Affairs, City University of Hong Kong

Ting Luo is Senior Lecturer of Political Communication at Manchester Metropolitan University

Daniel C. Lynch is Associate Dean of the College of Liberal Arts and Social Sciences and a Professor of Public and International Affairs at the City University of Hong Kong

Andrew Mertha is the George and Sadie Hyman Professor of China Studies, Johns Hopkins School of Advanced International Studies

Jean Christopher Mittelstaedt is Departmental Lecturer in Modern Chinese Studies in the Faculty of Asian and Middle Eastern Studies at the University of Oxford

Margaret M. Pearson is the Horace V. and Wilma E. Harrison Distinguished Professor of Government and Politics at the University of Maryland

Meg Rithmire is the F. Warren MacFarlan Associate Professor of Business Administration at Harvard University

Stanley Rosen is Professor of Political Science and International Relations at the University of Southern California

Victor C. Shih is the Director, 21st Century China Center, and Ho Miu Lam Chair Associate Professor in China and Pacific Relations at the School of Global Policy and Strategy at the University of California, San Diego

Dorothy J. Solinger is Distinguished Emerita Professor of Political Science, University of California, Irvine

Wenjia Song is a Ph.D. candidate in the Department of Political Science, Tsinghua University

Daniela Stockmann is a Professor of Digital Governance and Director of the Centre for Digital Governance at the Hertie School, Berlin

Twila Tardif is Professor of Psychology at the University of Michigan

Patricia M. Thornton is Associate Professor in the Department of Politics and International Relations at the Dickson Poon China Centre at the University of Oxford and a Fellow of Merton College

Kellee S. Tsai is Dean of the College of Social Sciences and Humanities and Distinguished Professor of Political Science at Northeastern University

Wang Feng is Professor of Sociology at the University of California, Irvine

Acknowledgments

This volume can be viewed as the third volume in a series of co-edited books examining the current state of Chinese politics. The first two volumes – *State and Society in 21st Century China: Crisis, Contention, and Legitimation* (2004) and *Chinese Politics: State, Society and the Market* (2010) – were co-edited by Peter Hays Gries and Stanley Rosen. This new volume is co-edited by Stanley Rosen and Daniel C. Lynch. In the fourteen years since the second volume appeared, China has undergone many changes, with the most significant change being the ascension of Xi Jinping to the top of the Chinese political system in 2012. Now that it has become clear that Xi will likely be retaining the top three positions in the Party, the state, and the military into the indeterminate future, the co-editors felt the need for a book that would examine the impact Xi has had and will continue to have on Chinese politics.

We would especially like to thank Dorothy J. Solinger and Patricia M. Thornton, who have contributed chapters to each of the three volumes, and to Andrew Mertha, who also contributed a chapter to the 2010 volume. We would also like to welcome the first-time authors of ten chapters to this volume, in the order of their chapters: Donald Clarke; Karrie J. Koesel; Margaret M. Pearson, Meg Rithmire, and Kellee S. Tsai; Daniela Stockmann and Ting Luo; Douglas B. Fuller and Ricardo L. Kotz; Jean Christopher Mittelstaedt (who has co-authored the chapter by Patricia M. Thornton); Joseph Fewsmith; Victor C. Shih; June Teufel Dreyer; Yuen Yuen Ang, Twila Tardif, and Wenjia Song; and Wang Feng.

We wrestled with the issue of whether to use pinyin, Chinese characters, or both pinyin and Chinese characters for the Chinese terms and names in the book. In the end, given the prominence of our contributors, we made some suggestions but allowed each of them to decide which of these options to choose. Thus, Chinese characters, sometimes with pinyin as well, are used in the text, but not always in the footnotes or bibliography.

Stanley Rosen would like to acknowledge the Dornsife College of Letters, Arts and Sciences at the University of Southern California for financial support.

Daniel C. Lynch would like to express his gratitude for intellectual stimulation to colleagues in the Department of Public and International Affairs at the City University of Hong Kong.

Finally, Rosen and Lynch would both like to collectively thank the many people at Routledge who have greatly improved the final manuscript. Thanks in particular go to acquisition editor Stephanie Rogers; editorial assistant Andrew Leach; production editor Gillian Steadman; copyeditor Elizabeth Guinn-Miller; and project managers Indumathi Sambantham and Rajalakshmi Ramesh. Rosen and Lynch would also like to thank Daniel Lewis, who designed the cover graphic.

Introduction

Stanley Rosen and Daniel C. Lynch

The year 2022 marked multiple watersheds in Chinese politics and society. Most famously, Chinese Communist Party (CCP) General Secretary Xi Jinping shattered the norm established by Deng Xiaoping in the 1980s by having himself anointed, at the October 2022 20th Party Congress, to a third five-year term of office. Deng had set a requirement that general secretaries only serve two consecutive five-year terms as head of the Party, except in unusual circumstances. Not only would Xi serve a third term, but he also signaled that he would even serve a fourth term after 2027 because he did not reveal a successor at the 20th Party Congress. Under the expectations laid down by Deng, the successor is always revealed at the end of a general secretary's first five-year term. By still not naming or even hinting at a successor halfway through 2023, Xi would appear to be planning to remain the Party's top leader all the way until 2032 and perhaps beyond.

Xi's appointment to a third five-year term was accomplished under conditions of extremely stringent repression, a direct consequence of the "zero-Covid" policy the general secretary had put in place nearly three years earlier after the initial Wuhan outbreak quickly threatened to spread nationwide in January-February 2020. The zero-Covid policy exacted an economic toll and a human rights toll by sharply restricting people's ability to travel into or out of China from 2020 through to late 2022, but it did prove successful in keeping Covid deaths and long-term injuries to multiple bodily systems down to extraordinarily low levels relative to other countries. Indeed, no country had a better (published) Covid record than China from early 2020 to early 2022, at least when the metric used was the sheer physical toll. Gradually over those two years, zero-Covid became intermingled with the China Model or "Chinese Solution," on which the CCP never quite fully elaborated but did hint broadly that, whatever its precise content, suggested a superior developmental blueprint for lower- and middle-income countries to consult seriously if not necessarily imitate in full. Even the other leading great powers of the international system might be encouraged to follow China's approach to Covid, various Chinese writers and party-state spokespeople suggested. Just look at how relatively disastrous the Covid performance was in China's chief systemic rival, the United States, as well as key U.S. allies such as the United Kingdom.

But while zero-Covid certainly achieved some laudable goals in 2020–2022 by keeping vulnerable people alive and healthy, its utility and its ethical acceptability

DOI: 10.4324/9781003257943-1

both came crashing to a halt after the arrival in China of the extremely transmissible Omicron subvariants in the spring of 2022. Shanghai and other large cities were thrown into unthinkably restrictive lockdowns – *genuine* lockdowns, of a severity and length unknown in almost every other part of the world. Angry online expressions of resistance increased throughout the spring and into the summer of 2022. Possibly, resistance to lockdowns was one reason that a Ministry of Public Security official announced in September 2022, in connection with preparations for the 20th Party Congress to be held in mid-October, that "the authorities had arrested more than 1.4 million criminal suspects nationwide since the end of June, helping to 'create a safe and stable political and social environment' for the successful convening of the 20th Party Congress" (Wang 2022).

Within this context, a CCP report issued during the week of the Congress in mid-October "used the word 'security' 91 times, up from 55 mentions in 2017 and 36 in 2012" (Shepherd and Li 2022). Moreover, Xi's "comprehensive national security concept" – a slogan urging the active detection and management of threats in all areas of policymaking – was allocated a separate section in the programmatic Congress report for the first time. This obsession with security and insecurity – this "securitization" of potentially anything – traces its history to the earliest days of Xi's rule and can be considered a bedrock, foundational principle of Xi governance. Indeed, one of the co-editors of this volume found in a 2022 *Modern China* article that Xi's radical reconcentration of party-state power in his own hands – already basically accomplished by the beginning of the "New Era" (新时代) in 2017 – should be interpreted from an international relations perspective as a complex "securitization move" in which an elite figure defines some trend, tendency, or other development as a security threat so severe that it becomes necessary to deploy special, extraordinary measures to address it. What in China's case was the perceived threat or configuration of threats that Xi could use to justify his reconcentration of power right on through to the 20th Party Congress of October 2022 and possibly all the way to 2032 and beyond? The answer would seem to be an obsession with a threat to the stability and integrity of the political order itself resulting from the dislocations caused ultimately by trying to fuse a Leninist political system with what was, by the early 2010s – when Xi became General Secretary – already a well-developed network society inextricably bound up with globalization (including of dangerous microbes) and inescapable, unpredictably disruptive technological advance (Lynch 2022).

In choosing to securitize the various risks perceived to be threatening China's authoritarian political system, and to mobilize even stronger and tighter party-state clampdowns on society, Xi showed no sign of yielding to the pressures building in society to relax the increasingly onerous Covid restrictions and resume some modicum of economic liberalization. It became increasingly obvious during the summer of 2022 that signaling an eventual end to zero-Covid would be necessary if young people, in particular, were to continue holding out any hope of finding decent jobs after the crisis ended and of consuming pleasurably again, including by traveling internationally. Absent any party-state promise to lift zero-Covid sooner rather than later, the outlook for life and career looked bleak to many young people. Yet through the party congress and on into November 2022, the party-state refused to budge. The economic damage continued to mount, as 2022 would end with a full-year GDP growth rate of only 3.0 percent, the lowest rate since 1976 except for the first full Covid year of 2020, when the GDP growth rate was 2.2 percent. The goal for 2023 would be a still-anemic (for "rising China") 5 percent (Hale and Sun 2023).

Nor did the new Politburo and Politburo Standing Committee lineup that emerged from the party congress suggest a particular Xi interest in reinvigorating the economy by relaxing restrictions on the sort of market forces which had played such a critical role in fueling historically rapid growth from the early 1990s to the mid-2010s. Xi was more concerned with pursuing his vision of achieving "common prosperity," which seasoned China economics reporters Keith Bradsher and Alexandra Stevenson termed "a vaguely defined, egalitarian campaign of redistributing wealth that has unnerved investors and could be a signal of higher taxes to come" (Bradsher and Stevenson 2022). Xi's stress on common prosperity was a cold shower for private entrepreneurs and others who had hoped market forces could be unleashed again to help power China out of the severe economic doldrums in which the country was now mired as a consequence of the radical zero-Covid policy. At one time, Chinese people had supported the policy as health-protecting, but after the arrival of the Omicron subvariants, zero-Covid appeared to have exhausted all imaginable utility and was actively harming not only the economy but fundamental social and political stability.

The problem was that there was no one left in Zhongnanhai who could tell Xi Jinping "no." He had expelled all of his known potential opponents from the top of the Chinese political system by removing every single individual who might potentially act as a factional rival, in the process throwing another Deng Xiaoping norm out the window as Deng had preferred to rule collegially and to allow a certain respect and authority over particular policy realms for factional (to use the term loosely) rivals. Deng and his immediate lieutenants would in normal circumstances act as first among equals and attempt to achieve consensus in policymaking. But at the October 2022 20th Party Congress, Xi swept aside *all* of the remaining Hu Jintao (r. 2002–2012) proteges, "including Premier Li Keqiang, and installed a new top leadership entirely dominated by his own loyalists" (Bradsher and Stevenson 2022). In a shocking move, during the closing ceremony of the Party Congress, Xi even had Hu Jintao physically ushered from the Great Hall of the People after Hu began acting erratically. As reported by AFP:

'We still don't know what caused Hu's actions, such as whether it was opposition to Xi's power or simply an unfortunately timed senior moment,' said Neil Thomas, a senior China analyst at the Eurasia Group consultancy. 'So without more information it's hard to draw solid conclusions about how this incident relates to Chinese politics.'

(Chen and Ramirez 2022)

But there was certainly one conclusion that could be drawn. At the time of the party congress, 96-year-old Jiang Zemin lay on his deathbed in Shanghai, suffering from leukemia and other severe diseases. Jiang would die on 30 November 2022. At that point, with Hu Jintao now also out of the picture, the institution of elder revolutionaries that had emerged by the late 1970s to watch over and advise the younger generation of general secretaries and their lieutenants was now gone from history. The only remaining senior elder, Zhu Rongji, would turn 95 years old in October 2023, and he had remained publicly silent for years. With the institution of elder revolutionaries first allowed to atrophy and then apparently shoved from history, Xi neither had to contend with significant opposition from inside the Politburo nor from revolutionary uncles looking over his shoulder. Xi's power appeared absolute.

But then, seemingly out of nowhere yet in fact simmering for many months, came a series of small-scale (yet consequential) socio-political explosions from society in the form of mass student-led protests against Covid restrictions, depressed economic conditions, and political repression. These protests suddenly made Xi's rule seem not quite so absolute. To some observers, it even appeared to become *shaky*.

Fully six weeks after the 20th Party Congress ended, onerous Covid restrictions were still in place and were only being relaxed gradually, in line with the ironclad rules imposed from on high. Anger was simmering throughout urban China, especially among younger people desperate to get their lives and careers back on track after nearly a full year of extraordinarily tough and in some cases even absurd restrictions. With tensions at the boiling point, suddenly during the last week of November 2022, a tragic fire broke out in an apartment complex in Urumqi, Xinjiang. Ten people were reported smothered to death through smoke inhalation, either because – according to rumors – they had been locked in their apartments by overzealous zero-Covid enforcers, or else because rescue vehicles could not penetrate the maze-like roadblocks put in place to prevent people from circulating freely. The rescue vehicles could not reach the apartment complex in time to save people's lives (Buckley et al. 2022).

Apparently spontaneous protests now erupted in multiple major Chinese cities simultaneously, nearly all led by young people, suggesting that the protests were driven by a complex combination of volatile factors that had finally boiled over. A team of *New York Times* journalists reported on 10 December 2022 that the mass discontent which had been brewing for many months finally "bubbled over in recent weeks as throngs of students, job seekers, and young professionals stormed the streets in major cities across China to protest the government's iron-fisted Covid rules" (Wakabayashi et al. 2022). Social stability was at stake, and possibly even political stability. To the surprise of most observers, almost as soon as the protests began, Xi turned on a dime and instantly ended nearly all zero-Covid policies. What policies he chose not to end by fiat were ended by the citizens themselves when they took matters into their own hands. "The relatively small-scale protests and vigils that received the most attention – generally involving dozens or hundreds of people – masked a much broader rebellion at tens of thousands of residential compounds across the country" (Mitchell et al. 2022). The zero-Covid policies then suddenly disappeared, but in an under-vaccinated population, the virus was free to run rampant. If half of the PRC population became sick with Covid during the winter of 2022–2023, and the death rate were comparable to Hong Kong's in the winter of 2022 or Taiwan's in the spring of that same year, some 1.5 million Mainland Chinese people would have died from Covid between December 2022 and March 2023.

In the midst of all the protests and then the sudden volte-face on zero-Covid, the discourse of just a few weeks prior which had presented Xi as an all-knowing or even nearly omnipotent strongman who had locked down iron-fisted control over the world's most uncompromisingly authoritarian political system (at least among the wealthy countries) was jettisoned and replaced with something entirely new. Opined the highly respected *New York Times* journalist Chris Buckley on 1 December 2022:

> [T]he flash flood of defiance suggests that Mr. Xi's next years in power could be more contested and turbulent than had seemed plausible even a month ago. His hold on the party elite seems unassailable; his hold over parts of society, especially the young, seems less sure.
>
> (Buckley 2022)

In late January 2023, the *Financial Times* even published a report quoting several prominent specialists on elite Chinese politics speculating on the imminent return of *factions* within the top Chinese political elite (White 2023). So much for the certainty of an unassailable new Xi Jinping hegemony which looked likely to be locked into place for at least a decade, and perhaps for much longer.

The Big Questions We Will Address in This Book

How much power does Xi Jinping have to shape the political, economic, sociocultural, demographic, and foreign policy trajectories of the probably still-rising (albeit at a much slower rate) People's Republic of China (PRC)? How much power did he exert to alter China's developmental path(s) during the first decade of his rule (2012–2022), and how much power will he likely be able to exert over the next ten-year trajectory through 2032? How and why does this vary by policy or issue-area? What role, if any, can outside countries and non-state actors play in shaping this trajectory? Why does it matter so much within the context of world history?

Answering questions such as these definitively would be an impossible task for anyone, but we have assembled a diverse and multi-talented group of some of the sharpest minds and keenest observers of varying aspects of contemporary China to analyze and explain the contexts associated with these issues ultimately for the purpose of answering the question of what *The Xi Jinping Difference* has been, and will likely continue to be, in Chinese politics.

In Chapter One, Donald Clarke examines the role of law in China's political system and documents the decline of the Party/state distinction and the distinction between law and politics, a trend that began a few years prior to the Xi era but has been greatly accelerated under the Xi administration. Not only are concepts such as judicial independence, separation of powers, and constitutionalism rejected, but it is also clear that wherever the rule of law might be thought to be inconsistent with Party leadership, it is the rule of law that must yield. He details the progressive merger of Party with state in, for example, the issuance of legal norms by Party bodies, the granting of legal authority to Party institutions, and the merger of Party and state institutions. Although the downgrading of the Party/state distinction *in fact* is familiar going back to the Mao era, Clarke points to the trend to downgrade the effort to maintain the distinction *in form* as well, which appears to signal an abandonment of any expectations of an eventual separation of Party and state, or even a reduced role for the Party, as former General Secretary Zhao Ziyang had envisioned on October 14, 1987, when he noted, "it seems that in socialist countries the separation of party and government is a big trend" (Gewirtz 2022). In short, what had been viewed, both in China and elsewhere, in the early post-Mao era as a hopeful, liberalizing trend, has been decisively halted.

Chinese leaders, famously starting with the public concerns raised by Chairman Mao, have always put a strong emphasis on the political education of Chinese youth, including both the cultivation of new generations of leaders for the CCP and the political socialization of youth more generally. While recent studies have documented how the CCP seeks to replenish its ranks (Doyon 2023; Tsimonis 2021), in Chapter Two Karrie J. Koesel addresses the larger issue of socialization for those who are not contemplating political careers. Examining the politics subject-test on China's entrance examination for university, commonly known as the *Gaokao*, from 1951–2022, Koesel uses the exam as a window into how political legitimacy is articulated and maintained over time. She finds that the exam questions reveal two narratives: an accountable and responsive CCP, and an effort to erode any support for alternatives to communist party rule by posing questions that focus on Western imperialism and aggression, the exploitative nature of capitalism, and the hypocrisy of American elections. By adopting such a long timeframe, Koesel is able to demonstrate changes in the questions at different points in PRC history, and how the questions have become more nuanced, sophisticated, and worldly. For example, more recently the questions have become less ideologically dogmatic and CCP accomplishments less sensational. Western imperialism has shifted to Western protectionism, and capitalist democracy is seen as less responsive and less representative than socialist democracy. The "Xi Jinping factor" exerts itself by having the personification of Xi included among the exam questions. Although Koesel ends her analysis with the 2022 exam, the Xi factor was not only expanded for the 2023 exam, but it apparently has now become pronounced enough to be discussed in Western media accounts (Leahy and Sun 2023). While acknowledging the difficulty of determining whether political education is being internalized successfully by the student end-users and promoting regime stakeholders, Koesel offers her informed analysis on this important question in her conclusion.

Indeed, the regime is well aware of this issue, and at the time of this writing, there is draft legislation on "patriotic education" that is being submitted to the National People's Congress for review and discussion. While the general content is similar to the patriotic education movements of the 1990s, the new legislation expands both the scope and the jurisdictions by encompassing new technologies and including Hong Kong, Macau, Taiwan, and overseas Chinese as the targets for the new law. It requires Internet content and service providers, as well as broadcasters and publishers, to strengthen the creation and dissemination of patriotic content and to develop new platforms and products to actively promote patriotism online. The nine "main content points" of the proposed legislation include Marxism, Maoism, and the theories of Xi Jinping, making it clear that, while not yet an "ism," Xi's theories have supplanted the contributions of all other post-Mao leaders, including Deng Xiaoping, long considered the "architect of the reform program" (Kilpatrick 2023; Carter 2023). As multiple chapters in this volume make clear in a variety of issue areas, much will depend on how the policy is implemented; however, it does strongly suggest that the space for independent decision-making by content providers continues to narrow.

Margaret M. Pearson, Meg Rithmire, and Kellee S. Tsai begin Chapter Three on the role of private enterprise in reform-era China by noting the importance of the private sector to the Chinese economy in terms of tax revenues, GDP, technological innovation, urban employment, and the generation of new jobs and firms. However, they also note that the private sector's contribution to China's GDP declined by over 15 percent under Xi Jinping (2012–2019) as state-owned enterprises became larger, more indebted, and less profitable, and the role of the CCP in the economy grew. They document how a state capitalist model evolved into the more politicized variant they label "party-state capitalism," under which the boundaries between private and state firms become blurred, not unlike the blurring of party/state boundaries described by Donald Clarke in his chapter on the role of law. The prioritization of political goals over economic growth under this variant of capitalism during Xi's tenure is redefining both the incentives and the challenges for private entrepreneurs and the government actors who interact with them. While there remains a certain degree of mutual dependence and even cooperation in government-business relations in industrial sectors identified as critical for China's future, businesses operating in industries that have experienced regulatory crackdowns have a greater sense of uncertainty.

Daniela Stockmann and Ting Luo begin Chapter Four on China's technology companies and social media under Xi Jinping by boldly asserting that they will be taking issue with the "conventional wisdom" that often depicts Xi as having centralized control over nearly every dimension of Chinese governance, including Internet governance. They use empirical evidence to argue that China's governance of the Internet is best understood as a corporate management model, where by the Chinese state engages in a partnership with the key technology companies. While Xi assumes a leadership role enforced by state instruments of control and cooptation strategies, at the same time the state remains dependent on these companies due to their platform power, expertise, and knowledge. Moreover, offering a detailed analysis comparing Internet governance under Hu Jintao and Xi Jinping, the authors demonstrate that the foundations for this management model were rooted in the Hu Jintao years, although it fully evolved into a mutually beneficial relationship under Xi. They conclude that while state control clearly increased under Xi's policies, cooptation strategies were perhaps even more significant, noting the preferential treatment given to a select group of tech companies for funding, licensing, and support to expand business abroad.

Chapter Five, by Douglas B. Fuller and Ricardo L. Kotz, continues the focus on the crucial area of technology and, in its discussion of a series of pre-Xi policy initiatives, argues, as Stockmann and Luo did, that Xi's technology policy can be best understood as a continuation, as well as amplification, of policies that began under the administration of Hu Jintao and Wen Jiabao, with an "explosive" growth in funding and goals beginning in 2006. Fuller and Kotz offer a detailed analysis – covering semiconductors, electric vehicles, and artificial intelligence – of the largest technology effort under Xi, the well-known "Made in China 2025" policy, which set off alarm bells in Washington and has been a key factor in U.S. policies targeting Chinese technological ambitions. The chapter concludes that Xi's ambitious pursuit of technological policies without reforming the institutions and practices through which such policies are pursued sets distinct limits on China's prospects for success, particularly given the foreign backlash in such critical sectors as semiconductors.

Chapter Six, by Dorothy J. Solinger, who has previously written extensively and sympathetically about China's urban poor, reveals an important aspect of Xi Jinping's "vision" for the Chinese society of the future in terms of which social forces are included and which are excluded. She begins by addressing a common misconception in writings about efforts to root out poverty in China, viz., that China has abolished poverty, a claim widely reported in China and abroad after Xi declared "complete victory" in February 2021, although he later clarified that the victory was confined to rural China, and others, including Solinger, have questioned even that claim. But the concern with rural China is genuine. By contrast, as Solinger notes, the marginalized urban poor have been caught between the lofty ambitions and limited funds of the localities and Xi's and the Central government's focus on the "Dream of Modernization," which includes speedy economic growth, technical superiority, and world prominence. Despite Xi's championing of "common prosperity," a slogan advanced in August 2021, Solinger suggests that he has been much more concerned about the nurturing of an ever-expanding middle class. Concluding with Xi's speech at the 20th Party Congress in October 2022, where he noted that China was committed to "cultivating a large workforce of high-quality talent," with "no effort . . . spared . . . to bring together the best and brightest from all fields for the cause of the Party and the people," the detailed data and lucid analysis Solinger provides leaves little doubt that the alleviation of urban poverty has no place in Xi's vision.[1]

Chapter Seven, by Jean Christopher Mittelstaedt and Patricia M. Thornton, moves us from the city to the countryside, and focuses on the construction and management of "New Era Civilized Practice Centers" and "Integrated Media Centers," a project from 2018 to propagate and disseminate Xi Jinping Thought at the county level and below. While such projects are commonly seen in Western analyses as the fostering of a Xi "personality cult," Mittelstaedt and Thornton suggest an alternative reading that views the establishment of these "two Centers" as a form of infrastructural state building, with the more lasting impact that comes with this extension and transformation of the Party-state's role at the social grassroots. They conclude by noting that even though the evidence to date shows that the most ambitious aim of these pilot projects – increasing the power and popular appeal of Xi Jinping Thought at the local level – has thus far not been successful, the Centers have allowed the Party-state to leverage digital technology and platform governance to better respond to the needs of the masses, allocate resources more efficiently, and improve the overall quality of their services, thereby expanding the infrastructural power of the Party-state at the county level.

Chapter Eight, a comprehensive analysis of the 20th Party Congress of October 2022 by Joseph Fewsmith, brings us solidly into the arena of elite politics. As had Stockmann and Luo in their discussion of Internet governance, Fewsmith takes issue with the standard interpretation in the Western media that Xi won an "unprecedented" third term at the Party Congress. Fewsmith suggests that rather than breaking with an increasingly institutionalized system, Xi was reverting to the tradition of staying in power as long as a leader was physically and politically able to do so. Critical of what he viewed as corrosive trends within the Party, Xi centralized power, imposed greater discipline on the Party, and quelled signs of an emergent civil society. Fewsmith provides a detailed analysis of personnel changes that came out of the Party Congress, where the Politburo Standing Committee was packed with allies of Xi, as well as such changes at the first session of the 14th National People's Congress, held in March 2023, noting that these changes make it clear that Xi intends to rule in a personalistic manner, reversing the norms that Deng Xiaoping put in motion four decades ago. Fewsmith also notes that Xi remade the military at the 19th Party Congress and again at the 20th Congress, which is likely to make the military highly responsive to Xi's decision-making, an issue that is addressed in the chapter by Victor C. Shih. Fewsmith concludes that Xi's efforts to concentrate power in his own hands have "clearly moved China into a post-reform era" under which the CCP has moved toward the kind of personalism not seen since the Maoist period. In this sense, it is interesting to compare Fewsmith's analysis of Xi's concentration of power with the "corporate management model" Stockmann and Luo describe where Xi is compelled to engage in a partnership with key technology companies. Both analyses can certainly be correct since the two chapters are examining very different issues.

While Fewsmith noted Xi's wholesale changes in leading military personnel at the two most recent party congresses, Victor C. Shih in Chapter Nine examines the changes which took place from 2016–2022 and what they suggest about Xi's strategy in civil-military relations. Examining the scholarly literature, Shih notes that a key issue for both democratic and authoritarian countries is how to prevent a coup while maintaining military effectiveness. He assesses whether Xi is pursuing a factional strategy, a coalition of the weak strategy, or a strategy that maximizes military professional expertise. He finds clear evidence that while Xi initially sought to control the military through factionalism, that tendency had weakened by 2022, also finding little evidence that Xi is pursuing a coalition of the weak strategy; rather, he is appointing more officers with combat and command experience in frontline units to senior positions, while specialists and loyalists have been placed in command of strategic branches of the PLA. He concludes that this suggests, ominously for China's potential rivals, that the party leadership under Xi has focused its military personnel policy on achieving results.

Chapter Ten, Andrew Mertha's take on the Belt and Road Initiative (BRI), shows us the difficulty of separating domestic politics from foreign policy, and reveals the fragmentation of Chinese politics as well as, in his words, how all politics is ultimately local. He presents a "China Model" far removed from much of the scholarly and policy discourse that often focuses on a centralized state inexorably rising and reveals how China's domestic political structures are being internationalized, suggesting that the effectiveness of Chinese foreign investment and aid is only as good as the domestic institutions that manage the relationship. Since the vast majority of BRI actors are subnational, Mertha shows the necessity, at both vertical and horizontal levels, for bargaining and consensus-building, something also suggested in Chapter Three on private enterprise, and Chapter Six on technology and social media, but that can just as often lead to bureaucratic infighting and conflict. Using case studies of BRI projects in Nicaragua, Myanmar, Ghana, and Cambodia, he argues that the politics embedded in China's domestic bureaucratic and institutional landscape, and their "attendant pathologies," are increasingly becoming a key factor in explaining China's international behavior. Although BRI is an important component of "the Xi Jinping difference," Xi appears either unwilling or unable to overcome China's domestic fragmentation, even when it manifests itself in China's foreign initiatives.

Chapter Eleven, by Yuen Yuen Ang, Twila Tardif, and Wenjia Song, reports the detailed and disaggregated results of a fifteen-nation online survey conducted from May to June 2020, during the early days of the Covid pandemic, and focused on who within China and the US was to blame for the problems associated with the less-than-successful Covid policies of the two nations. They find that overall, China is blamed more (56.9 percent) than the US (49.3 percent), but for those who blame China more, Xi Jinping is blamed less than the Chinese government and the Chinese people, whereas for those who blame the US the most, Donald Trump receives the most blame. However, their analysis goes beyond their survey and examines China's zero-Covid strategy and its dismantling and the likely effects on Xi Jinping's popularity, concluding with some key takeaways on China's model of domestic governance. First, they suggest that since Xi made zero-Covid a core part of his argument about the "institutional advantage" of centralized authoritarian rule, its abject failure has damaged not just Xi's narrative, but likely also his popularity. Second, the failure of zero-Covid demonstrated the gap between the top-down mobilization model that is promoted as a success by China's propaganda apparatus and the actual "China Model" instituted by Deng Xiaoping that enabled economic success during the reform era, suggesting that Xi's insistence on maintaining zero cases stood in opposition to Deng's principles of pragmatism and flexibility, and prevented the leadership from getting the kind of timely feedback necessary to alter a policy that had gone off the rails.

While Chapters Ten and Eleven had clear foreign policy implications, Chapter Twelve, by June Teufel Dreyer, is devoted solely to Chinese foreign policy under

Xi Jinping. Dreyer begins her chapter with a discussion of China's assertiveness, noting that while it has frequently been associated with Xi's tenure, it had clear antecedents, although Xi's initiatives have clearly accelerated this earlier post-Deng trend. A study of all aspects of foreign policy and a discussion of all countries and regions is not possible in a single chapter, but Dreyer is admirably able to cover foreign economic policy, for example the BRI familiar from Mertha's chapter, and China's relations with Russia, the US, Japan, Europe, North and South Korea, India and Pakistan, Southeast Asia, and Africa. Her conclusion notes that while recent public opinion polling has shown a decline in favorability ratings toward China in nations with more advanced economies, this drop in soft power has been offset by large gains in Chinese hard power, which are considered to be much more important in China's calculus. Thus, it can be argued that Xi's foreign policy has succeeded, in the sense that China has garnered substantial support from countries with less developed economies for many of its international positions, and some of these countries have welcomed Chinese investment. Moreover, efforts led by the US to counter China's expanded reach have been cautious, inadequate, and in some cases nascent. China's recent more active role in international diplomacy has led to the brokering of a peace agreement between Saudi Arabia and Iran, but its efforts to mediate in the conflict in Ukraine have been stillborn, given its close association with Putin and Russia.

Chapter Thirteen, on China's changing demographic structure, by Wang Feng, presents a wealth of data related to China's demographic transition, with valuable comparisons to Japan and South Korea, other nations that have been dealing with a similar transition. Wang takes issue with those who focus almost solely on the stark population numbers, important as they are, arguing instead that what is most important is an examination of the institutional conditions that have allowed for past economic successes but now present daunting challenges. The challenges are economic and ultimately political and include the necessity to transform the nation's economic growth model, complete urbanization, and provide social benefits that are compatible with those of an upper-middle income society. Wang devotes a great deal of attention to the continuing inequalities of life and life chances, a long-lasting legacy from China's socialist planned economy era, among which are crucial differences between urban and rural China, and the social divide among populations residing in cities, particularly the need to "digest" the hundreds of millions of city residents who suffer from having a secondary citizenship status. As with Solinger's chapter on the urban poor, the issue of a population stratified by social status looms large in Wang's chapter as well, and the designation by Chinese officials and the official media of migrants living in poverty conditions in Beijing as a "low-end population" unworthy of a great city (CMP Staff 2017) strongly suggests that such social stratification will continue. While Wang applauds Xi Jinping, unlike his immediate predecessors, for recognizing China's shifting demographic landscape and taking bold actions, including the lifting of the one-child policy in 2015, he also notes that other items on the ambitious reform agenda of 2013 have been long forgotten, or even reversed, echoing Fewsmith's depiction that China has entered the "post-reform era."[2] Yet without a new economic growth model for the era of population decline, Wang concludes, China will be unable to sustain increased living standards.

A recent article by sociologist Andrew Walder, also focused on Chinese inequality, reminds us that such a new model would be exceedingly difficult not only to implement but perhaps even to imagine as possible by Xi and his lieutenants, as they pursue an agenda that features multiple contradictions. Similar to Wang, Walder highlights China's highly distinctive political and economic structures which still retain many features of the pre-reform state socialist model. These structures were designed to preserve CCP control over financial resources and the direction of economic activity, enforce the priorities of the central party-state, promote an investment-driven growth model, and prevent the formation of autonomous private actors with resources sufficient to weaken or undermine the party's control. Adding to the difficulties, the reforms have created beneficiaries of rapid economic growth, including members of the immediate and extended families of serving party-state officials, some of the regime's most committed supporters. Taking serious steps to implement Xi's signature common prosperity initiative, to take one example of a policy contradiction, by documenting private wealth for taxation purposes, would be divisive and damaging to party unity and therefore to the political stability that is the underlying basis of Xi's entire agenda (Walder 2023). Thus, we have the paradox of the necessity to initiate structural reforms to respond to current economic problems and move China toward a more sustainable growth model and the political difficulty of doing so without undermining the basis of the party's and therefore Xi's control. In that sense, although a number of the chapters suggest that Xi has built on policies initiated during the Hu Jintao/Wen Jiabao years (2002–2012), Walder argues that Xi is constrained much more by the continuing legacies established during the Maoist period and further complicated by the effects of reform era policies on Chinese social forces.

On the Horizon

Wang Feng's concluding chapter, building on themes interwoven through all of the preceding chapters, also invites us to reflect on the implications of the probably under-recognized fact that half or more of the world's currently living population was born after 1990 (Ritchie and Roser 2019). Why should this be important in the context of a book analyzing Xi Jinping's impact on China's developmental trajectory? It is important because it means that 4 billion people have only ever known a world in which China is "rising." The concept of China rising refers not only to the material reality of rapid economic growth, increased comprehensive national power relative to that of other countries, and the full panoply of other positive outcomes associated with "development," broadly defined, but also with a *narrative* which has often implied that China's rise would inevitably continue indefinitely into the future. Among many other things, this narrative suggests, for those who still accept it, that China will eventually – perhaps as soon as the late-middle of the 21st century – surpass the United States to become the world's most powerful country. Such a fundamental transformation in the global power structure would generate a huge array of implications not only for the nature of the international system, but also for what kind of political regimes (democratic? authoritarian?) would become dominant globally, and even for the content of world popular culture. It would then have follow-on secondary and tertiary consequences that are exceedingly difficult to think through because of the inherent complexity of such large-scale historical processes. We want therefore to reflect not only on the many specific important issues raised by chapter contributors in this book, but also on what they imply separately and collectively for the fate of China's rise.[3]

The professional China analyst who first fully elaborated the contemporary concept of the rise of China was the (at the time) Hong Kong-based investment banker and current Harvard Kennedy School professor William Overholt, who first proposed the rise idea in talks he presented when traveling through Asia for business meetings during the 1980s.[4] Overholt himself was not a "hype-ster," as many later popularizers of the rise of China narrative would become. He even waited several years before systematizing his observations and insights and writing a book. Overholt published *The Rise of China: How Economic Reform Is Creating a New Superpower* on the first day of January 1993 in hardback form and in October 1994 in paperback.[5] Nicholas D. Kristof slightly beat Overholt to the punch with the first known publication using the term "the Rise of China" when he published an article under that title in *Foreign Affairs* just weeks before the first edition of Overholt's book would appear (Kristof 1992). Whether as empirical social science forecasting or as unintentional creator of a new narrative, Overholt's book would quickly become hugely influential in diffusing the idea of a rising China worldwide, which in turn reinforced the confidence of foreign investors and many other observers and actors that such a rise could succeed, or would indeed be inevitable, encouraging the investment and state policies that quickly began to fuel and then sustain that very rise.

But consistent with the findings of many of this book's chapters – and all of the chapters that address the issue directly – Overholt himself now considers that the rise of China is challenged in myriad ways as a direct consequence of the CCP leadership's own unwillingness or inability to respond to what Overholt calls "China's crisis of success," by which he means the crucible at which all late developers eventually arrive: Will the authoritarian state that successfully directed economic development adapt creatively to the radically changed society and economy that have resulted from the success, or will it fail to do so and watch the economic miracle and socio-cultural flowering come to a halt? (Overholt 2018). Taiwan, South Korea, and others succeeded in decades past. How would the PRC respond? Overholt's assessment in the late 2010s was that the PRC under Xi Jinping was not responding successfully.

Indeed, the Chinese government was inadvertently exacerbating the crisis, Overholt found – a point he elaborated in a commentary article for *Barron's* published in May 2023 (Overholt 2023). In this article, Overholt goes straight to the concern of many of the contributors to this book when he writes that "instead of accommodating complexity through a market economy and elections," as the earlier Asian dragons Taiwan and South Korea had done, perpetuating their prosperity, "under

President Xi Jinping, Beijing is fighting the tide of a diverse society with redoubled hierarchy and centralization." Overholt continues that Xi Jinping's obsession with security is blocking needed reforms. "In the global financial crisis, China benefited from central control of banks and major companies. Leaders concluded that central political control was superior to Western models. Yes, superior for crisis management, but inferior for normal times" (Overholt 2023).

This tendency – discussed above in the context of Covid and other challenges – for the CCP state to almost automatically attempt to securitize any risk or uncertainty which will inevitably appear in an increasingly complex and globally-connected society suggests a paradox: Xi may indeed be making an enormous *difference* in affecting the trajectory of China's rise, exerting massive power, but inadvertently using that power in such a way that he creates the unintended consequence of slowing the rise and aggravating many of the other problems this book's contributors discuss in the individual chapters. Overholt now expects China's GDP to be growing at less than 3 percent a year by the late 2020s, which would probably mean at rates equal to or lower than the growth rates of China's systemic rivals, the US and the European Union. If that happens, the rise of China in relative power terms will have stalled or even ended. To be sure, the material quality of life of Chinese people can and probably will continue to improve, the important point which Wang Feng emphasizes in his chapter on demography. But the rise of China in the sense of the PRC's comprehensive national power increasing relative to that of the US and its allies would be *over*. A master narrative will have been eclipsed. We would be in uncharted territory: "post-the-Rise-of-China." Especially for the world's 4 billion people born after 1990, an entire new paradigm would be needed to understand China and to think about its place in the world. What would this new paradigm be?

The end of China's rise in relative power terms would in turn raise another critical question: If the determination to increase wealth and strength, both in absolute and relative terms, has been a central driving force in Chinese history for the past 150 years, how would the PRC under Xi Jinping respond to conclusive evidence that China's relative rise has stalled? Would it respond by reversing the trend toward massively increasing party-state control and repression, as explained in such rich detail by Donald Clarke? Would it abandon this strategy in favor of relaxing controls over society including through the legal system and pursuing some form of limited liberalization, if liberalization would be necessary to rekindle the national rise? Or would the party-state instead double down on defining nearly all emerging new risks as security threats and using the new technologies at its disposal to intensify repression across multiple sectors and fields?

Notes

1 Poorer migrants are another urban social group that has been stigmatized and marginalized. The Chinese media and official documents on urban policy in Beijing have referred to them as the "low-end population" (低端人口), reportedly with the aim of "optimizing the city's development composition," with some critics suggesting that the authorities see poorer migrants as "an eyesore for a modern city that wants to be taken seriously." See CMP Staff (2017).

2 Addressing problems associated with the cost of raising children and gender inequalities would be an important component of any new policy initiatives. See, for example, Hong and Wang 2023.
3 To be sure, few professional China specialists ever flatly asserted that China's rise would inevitably succeed. Indeed, one of the earliest specialists to warn of the specifically demographic challenges which threatened to slow the rise was Wang Feng himself, writing in an influential 2011 article analyzing the results of the 2010 Chinese census (Wang 2011). Meanwhile, economists such as Michael Pettis were warning early in the aftermath of the 2007–2009 global financial crisis and Great Recession that China's policy responses to those events were aggravating the worst features of the PRC's debt-driven economic development model and threatening to lock the country in a middle-income trap (Pettis 2013). But especially after China entered the World Trade Organization at the end of 2001, and well into the late 2010s, much of the world's mass media and certainly social media were full of exaggerated and sometimes lurid predictions about China's rise and its likely "inevitable" success, which would either be wonderful or terrible for the world, depending on the "analysis" of the person or entity making the prediction.
4 Overholt explained this process of how he developed the rise of China concept and refined it based on feedback from his audiences in a private communication at an October 2019 conference in Macau.
5 The 1994 edition is still in print as of this writing (Overholt 1994).

References

Bradsher, Keith, and Alexandra Stevenson. 2022. "Xi Tightens His Grip on China at a Difficult Economic Moment." *New York Times*. October 23.

Buckley, Chris. 2022. "After Xi's Coronation, a Roar of Discontent against His Hard-Line Politics." *New York Times*. December 1.

Buckley, Chris, Vivian Wang, Chang Che, and Amy Chang Chien. 2022. "After Daily Blaze, Surge of Defiance against China's Covid Policies." *New York Times*. November 27.

Carter, Cindy. 2023. "Online Responses to New Draft Legislation on 'Patriotic Education'." *China Digital Times*. July 3.

Chen, Lauren, and Leo Ramirez. 2022. "Former Chinese President Hu Removed from Congress." *Agence France-Presse*. October 22.

CMP Staff. 2017. "The Making of the 'Low-End Population'." *China Media Project*. November 30.

Doyon, Jérôme. 2023. *Rejuvenating Communism: Youth Organizations and Elite Renewal in Post-Mao China*. Ann Arbor: University of Michigan Press.

Gewirtz, Julian. 2022. "China's Road Not Taken: How the Chinese Communist Party Rewrites History." *Foreign Affairs*. September 22.

Hale, Thomas, and Sun Yu. 2023. "China's Economy Expands 3% in 2022 after Zero-Covid Policies Hit Growth." *Financial Times*. January 17.

Hong, Nicole, and Zixu Wang. 2023. "Why China's Young People Are Not Getting Married." *New York Times*. July 10.

Kilpatrick, Ryan Ho. 2023. "Legislating Love for the Ruling Party." *China Media Project*. June 30.

Kristof, Nicholas D. 1992. "The Rise of China." *Foreign Affairs* 72: 59–74.

Leahy, Joe, and Sun Yu. 2023. "China's University Entrance Exam Promotes Xi Jinping's Cult of Personality." *Financial Times*. June 18.

Lynch, Daniel C. 2022. "Xi Jinping Confronts the Network Society." *Modern China* 48(2): 231–252.

Mitchell, Tom, Thomas Hale, Sun Yu, and Edward White. 2022. "The Humbling of Xi Jinping." *Financial Times*. December 3.

Overholt, William H. 1994. *The Rise of China: How Economic Reform Is Creating a New Superpower*. New York: W.W. Norton & Company.

Overholt, William H. 2018. *China's Crisis of Success*. Cambridge and New York: Cambridge University Press.
Overholt, William H. 2019. "Private Communication." October Conference in Macau.
Overholt, William H. 2023. "The Era of Chinese Supergrowth Is Over." *Barron's*. May 26. www.barrons.com/articles/china-economy-growth-slowdown-gdp-fc7aa994?refsec=other-voices&mod=topics_other-voices.
Pettis, Michael. 2013. *Avoiding the Fall: China's Economic Restructuring*. Washington, DC: Carnegie Endowment for International Peace.
Ritchie, Hannah, and Max Roser. 2019. "Age Structure." *Our World in Data*. https://ourworldindata.org/age-structure.
Shepherd, Christian, and Lyric Li. 2022. "Under Xi, China Wants Absolute Security [and] It's Making the World Nervous." *Washington Post*. October 21.
Tsimonis, Konstantinos D. 2021. *The Chinese Communist Youth League: Juniority and Responsiveness in a Party Youth Organization*. Amsterdam: Amsterdam University Press.
Wakabayashi, Daisuke, Claire Fu, Isabella Qian, and Amy Chang Chien. 2022. "Even as China Eases Covid Rules, Some Youths Still Fear a Grim Future." *New York Times*. December 10.
Walder, Andrew. 2023. "China's Extreme Inequality: The Structural Legacies of State Socialism." *The China Journal* 90(July): 1–26.
Wang, Feng. 2011. "The Future of a Demographic Overachiever: Long-Term Implications of the Demographic Transition in China." *Population and Development Review* 37(Supplement): 173–190.
Wang, Vivian. 2022. "'We're All Over This Place': Building a Fortress for Beijing's Moment." *New York Times*. October 15.
White, Edward. 2023. "China's Palace Politics: Xi Jinping Loyalists Compete for Power." *Financial Times*. January 25.

1 Law and the Political System in Xi Jinping's China

The Decline of the Party/State Distinction

Donald Clarke

Introduction

The first ten years of the Xi Jinping era have been marked by seemingly contradictory movements in the relationship between the legal system and the political system. On the one hand, the line between the legal and the political, between the state and the Party, has become increasingly blurred – indeed, to speak of a line at all is arguably to impose a distinction that the system itself does not recognize.[1] The "absolute leadership" of the Party over legal institutions has been repeatedly stressed, and the idea that the Party would withdraw in favor of the state has been decisively rejected.

On the other hand, this era has seen increased efforts to professionalize the judiciary and strengthen the court system. While few scholars argue that such efforts will lead to, or are even aimed at, establishing "rule of law" in the sense of a government accountable to legal institutions, a number have viewed the reforms through the lens of the concept of "authoritarian legality"[2] – a broadening of the scope of (for example) genuinely independent adjudication, with a progressively smaller number of cases being subject to political intervention (the ultimate potential for which is not denied). These reforms are better viewed, however, through the lens of centralization, which in other fields of governance has been a signal feature of the Xi era. The aim is greater central control, not more judicial independence, even though we may observe what appears to be increasing judicial independence as a byproduct.

This chapter begins with a brief review of the role of the legal system in the Mao era as well as the post-Mao legal system on the eve of the Xi era. Having thus set the stage, it looks specifically at developments in the Xi era, addressing in particular the question of whether China has, in the words of Carl Minzner (2011), "turned against law." First, it discusses the administrative structure of the legal system. This will aid in understanding the significance of policy changes. Second, it looks at two important Xi-era reforms within the legal system: the establishment of Supervisory Commissions and efforts to professionalize the judiciary. Third, it discusses the broader relationship between politics and the legal system, mapping the decline of the distinction between politics and law, between the Party and the state. It concludes by arguing that we may be seeing *in utero* what will turn out to be fundamental changes in the role of the legal system in the Chinese polity.

Background: The Legal System Before the Xi Era

Law in the Mao Era

The role of law in the political system of the People's Republic under Mao's leadership was minimal. Although China had a formal constitution from 1954, that document played no role in the legal system – its provisions were not enforceable by courts – and virtually no role in the political system. As Mao remarked, "I took part in the drafting of the constitution, but even I don't remember it."[3] It is hard to imagine similar sentiments from the drafters of the Declaration of Independence or the U.S. Constitution.

Nor was the state or the citizenry meaningfully regulated by statutes passed by state bodies. During the entire period from their establishment in 1954 until the death of Mao in 1976, the National People's Congress (NPC) and its Standing Committee, the highest law-making bodies in China, passed only five enactments formally labeled "law" (法 fa) in addition to the 1954 and 1975 constitutions. They did pass a number of law-like documents – that is, rules of general application to all or large portions of the population – that were not labeled "law"; depending on what counts as a "law-like document," there were about three dozen between 1954 and 1958 inclusive, but only two thereafter. Between 1967 and 1974, there appears to have been no legislative activity of any kind under any name by either body (OLP 2019). They did not pass a criminal law, a law on contracts, or a law on torts (non-criminal wrongs such as negligent infliction of damage). At the top, political infighting among the elite was carried on without reference to law; rivals could be deposed and imprisoned without serious regard to legal standards and institutions.[4] At the bottom, ordinary citizens could be imprisoned or executed without any determinate legislative basis (Cohen 1968; Wu 2017).

When one thinks of the role law could play in a political system – regulating the timing of elections, terms of office, or the transfer of power; imposing norms of transparency on government operations; controlling corruption and other abuses of office by officials – it is clear that it was doing nothing of the kind in Mao-era China.

Law in the Post-Mao Era

Law in the post-Mao era has experienced a significant revival. Law faculties shuttered during the Cultural Revolution were re-opened and their professors recalled from exile in rice fields and factories. The state itself promoted the idea that law should replace internal administration as a primary tool of governance. The civil caseload of courts rose dramatically as they were called on to handle disputes in the growing private sector of the economy as well as in the publicly owned sector, and the judiciary itself became increasingly professional and well-educated. The NPC, its Standing Committee, and the State Council became active in the promulgation of laws and regulations. The 300-odd lawyers at the beginning of the reform era grew to some 250,000 by the end of 2013, at the beginning of the Xi era (Chen 2020, 247). Such was the wave of activity that by 2008, Wu Bangguo, the chairman of the NPC Standing Committee, could declare that the formation of the Chinese legal system was "basically complete" (Xinhua News Agency 2008).

Perhaps equally important were changes in the discourses of law and legality. In the Mao era, law meant coercion; it was spoken of as a tool of dictatorship and as a means for handling antagonistic contradictions, i.e., those between the people and the enemy. To deal with a person "according to law" meant putting them in jail, not reading them their rights. In the post-Mao era, by contrast, law was increasingly spoken of as a tool for the protection of rights and as a set of norms to apply to government as well as to citizens.

Has the Xi era seen a halt in, and perhaps even a reversal of, those trends? To a certain degree, analysts are divided. Some, such as Peerenboom (2014), Chen (2016), and Zhang and Ginsburg (2019) see a continuation of previous trends. While generally not predicting a transition to anything like the rule of law in the sense of significant legal constraints on the state, they find an increasing legalization of government operations and social relations and a growth in the importance of legal institutions such as courts.

On the other side, analysts such as Minzner (2011), Liebman (2011), Liebman (2014), Chen (2020), Zhang (2021), Pils (2022), and Clarke (2022) find, in Minzner's phrase, a turn against law, in which the fundamental post-Mao consensus on the direction of legal reforms has been replaced by an increasing turn to non-legal mechanisms and discourse in matters of governance.[5]

As these works cover the issue, this chapter, while tending toward the latter school, will not revisit the debate in detail. What seems unmistakable is that under Xi, the idea that the Party should operate behind the scenes has been rejected. It is being put front and center in a number of fields, from national security to corporate governance (Milhaupt and Lin 2021). While a number of high-level documents on legal institutions have been issued, and an entire Central Committee Plenum devoted to legal issues, there has been no backtracking on the core concept of the supremacy of the Party and its "absolute leadership" (*juedui lingdao* 绝对领导) over the legal system.[6] Constitutionalism, judicial independence, separation of powers, and checks and balances have been explicitly rejected (ChinaFile 2013). The role of political-legal committees as the basic organizational form for Party leadership over legal institutions has been endorsed as something that should persist for a long time to come (Chinese Communist Party Central Committee 2014b).

Moreover, some Mao-era concepts that had seen declining visibility in public discourse have been resurrected. An important 2019 Party directive on political-legal work, in addition to asserting the Party's "absolute leadership" over legal institutions (thereby, in Ling Li's (2019) words, indicating "a complete and unambivalent severance from the judicial independence framework"), stressed the theory of the people's democratic dictatorship and the two kinds of contradictions as set forth by Mao (1969) in his famous speech of 1957. Under this theory, certain contradictions (conflicts) are antagonistic – between the people and the enemy – and cannot be resolved except through coercion. Other contradictions are non-antagonistic – occurring within the ranks of the people – and should be resolved through education and persuasion. Under the Maoist theory, "law" and its institutions were reserved for the handling of antagonistic contradictions.

If this concept is taken seriously, it indicates a rejection of legal institutions for the governance of ordinary civil matters and a return of the centrality of criminal proceedings in court work. To date, there is no indication that anything like this is happening. Thus, it is probably best to understand the theory of contradictions not as a dominant philosophy that explains everything about the Chinese legal system, but rather as a live alternative paradigm that exerts a kind of gravitational pull on existing institutions, depending on the degree to which it is stressed by the government at any given time.

Administrative Structures and Key Institutions

The first ten years of the Xi era saw a great deal of lawmaking in a number of areas, particularly in the realm of national security in the latter years. But the best way in a short survey to understand the role of law in the political system is to look at major institutions of the legal system. Indeed, the first lesson here is that it is misleading to speak simply of a "legal system" as if it existed apart from politics. Chinese discourse and actual governance structures themselves speak of the "political-legal system" (*zheng-fa xitong* 政法系统), and it is that way of categorizing institutions that itself helps to define the categories.

The Political-Legal System

From its first experiences in governing a territory until today, the Party has seen courts, prosecutors, police, and other institutions conventionally considered part of the legal system as dealing with the same task: the maintenance of order and the protection of the Party's rule (Lötveit 1979; Liu 2012). They are therefore subject to unified management by the Party-state, and they are considered part of the same "system" (*xitong* 系统), a technical term in Chinese administration (Yu 2010).[7] This management was originally done through a body that was formally part of the state, but that body was soon superseded by a Party body that I will henceforth refer to generally as a political-legal committee (PLC), regardless of its actual name.[8]

Over the years, PLCs have generally governed the courts, the procuratorate, the public security organs, the judicial administration (*sifa* 司法) organs, and most recently the state security organs (Jing et al. 2016), although at one time or another the political-legal *xitong* "has run the court system, the prosecutors, the labor camps, the prisons, the fire departments, the border guards, the uniformed police, the secret police, and issuance of passports, among other things" (Lieberthal 2004, 224). This governance has often included the power to dictate specific actions and outcomes.

Although the power of PLCs has waxed and waned over time (Wang and Minzner 2015, 342–345), the existence of the political-legal *xitong* demonstrates a particular approach to order. It is the institutional manifestation of a view that the Party-state has a number of coercive institutions that show at most a division of labor in pursuit of a common task. This view is clearly visible in the fact that judges wore military-style uniforms right up until the early 2000s (Trevaskes 2004, 12).

Another more significant consequence of this view is that there is much more mobility of personnel within a *xitong* than across *xitong*. Just as it is normal for a senior bank official (in the finance and economics *xitong*) to cross over to a post in the Ministry of Finance or the People's Bank of China, so it is normal for officials to move among the police, procuratorate, and court bureaucracies. As Ng and He (2017, 88–89) write:

> Moving in and out of the judiciary is rather common for those who move up the ladder. Many of the most senior judges in the system today have worked in other Party-state organs before returning to, or simply landing in, a senior position.

A case in point is Wang Shengjun, who after a twenty-year career in the Party political-legal bureaucracy and a brief stretch as a provincial police chief was made President of the Supreme People's Court, despite his lack of any legal education.[9]

Perhaps even more revealing is the case of Sun Hongshan. As of June 2021, Sun served concurrently as both the president of the provincial-level court in Shanxi and the Party secretary – the most powerful official – of the provincial police department (Yun 2021).[10]

The unified management of legal institutions in the service of larger political goals is an approach that is not going away. The Fourth Plenum of the Party's 18th Central Committee in 2014, dedicated to legal matters, made it clear that the political-legal *xitong* governed by PLCs at various levels would be around for some time to come (CCPCC 2014a). Even were PLCs to disappear, the principle of Party management of this particular class of institutions is to remain (Jing et al. 2016, 123).

For a long time, PLCs were generally headed by those with a public security background; at the local level, typically the head of the police at the same administrative level. Put simply, the police dominated the courts.[11] After the 18th Party Congress in 2012, however, this pattern began to change, with police chiefs no longer dominating the leadership of local PLCs. At the central level, whereas the Central PLC (CPLC) had traditionally been chaired by a member of the PBSC, from 2012 onward it was chaired by a regular Politburo member only. At the same time, however, the CPLC chair still reports directly to the General Secretary of the Party, Xi Jinping (ZGXWW 2014).

A further change in the status and orientation of the CPLC occurred at the 20th Party Congress in October 2022. Although the rank of the CPLC and its leader did not change, the nature of its leadership did. As noted earlier, in previous years the CLPC was often headed by someone with a public security background, such as a former Minister of Public Security like Zhou Yongkang. For the first time, the CLPC is now headed by a former Minister for State Security, Chen Wenqing.[12] (He was briefly in both posts between the time of his appointment at the 20th Party Congress and the time of the appointment of his replacement at the Ministry of State Security at the end of the same month.) The current Minister for State Security, Chen Yixin, is the Secretary General of the CPLC, a senior position (Lau 2022). These appointments highlight the overwhelming national security (or Party

22 Donald Clarke

security, if you will) orientation of the Xi Jinping administration, and legal institutions such as the courts will necessarily fall into line.

Legal System Institutions and Their Ranks

A revealing lens through which to understand the role of legal institutions in the political system is that of rank. Rank is a key concept in Chinese politics (Lawrence and Martin 2013; Nie and Gu 2015; Singapore Chamber of Commerce in China n.d.). Individuals in executive positions in the Party or state, broadly defined to include state-owned enterprises and institutions such as universities, all have a rank that can be compared with the rank of other such individuals so that everyone knows who is senior and junior. Institutions also have ranks in the sense that leadership of a particular institution generally implies a certain rank, and an individual leading an institution generally lends that rank to the institution. The top three ranks are, in descending order, National (*zheng guo ji* 正国级), Vice National (*fu guo ji* 副国级), and Minister (*zheng buzhang ji* 正部长级).

A key element of the rank system is that institutions and individuals generally cannot give orders to others of equal or superior rank.[13] Institutions do not obtain authority by virtue of their assigned subject matter jurisdiction; they get it by their rank. By the same token, an institution often has the practical power to exceed its formal subject matter jurisdiction simply by virtue of its ability to impose its will on those inferior in rank.[14] Conflicts are resolved by a common superior, not by courts.

Table 1.1 shows a rough approximation of the political importance of various institutions within the political-legal *xitong*. Importance is assumed to be indicated

Table 1.1 Rank of Leader of Political-Legal Institutions, 2002–2022[15]

	Central Commission for Discipline Inspection (CCDI)	*Central Political-Legal Commission (CPLC)*	*Ministry of Public Security (MPS)*	*Supreme People's Court (SCC)*	*Supreme People's Procuratorate (SPP)*	*National Supervisory Commission (NSC)*
National (正国级)	2002–22	2002–12				
Vice National (副国级), Politburo		2012–22	2002–07			2018–2022
Vice National, Central Secretariat, not on Politburo			2022–			2022–[16]
Vice National, not on Central Secretariat or Politburo			2007–22	2002–2022	2002–2022	

Source: Author

by the rank of the leading official, and an official of Vice National rank who sits on the Politburo is assumed to be more important than an official who has Vice National rank for any other reason.

As can be seen, the Central Commission for Discipline Inspection (CCDI), a purely Party body discussed later in this chapter, is clearly the most important of the listed institutions. Its head has the highest possible political rank – National rank, the same rank as Xi Jinping – and that has been so for the full twenty years surveyed and no doubt beyond that. The Central Political-Legal Commission (CPLC) comes in a clear second. In the ten years of the Hu Jintao era, its head was a member of the Politburo Standing Committee (PBSC), giving him National rank, but in the Xi era – that is, since 2012 – its head has been on the Politburo but not on the Standing Committee, giving him Vice National rank.

The political rank of the Supreme People's Court (SPC) and the Supreme People's Procuratorate (SPP) have been clear and stable over time: their heads have held Vice National rank, but not Politburo seats. This puts them clearly below the CCDI and the CPLC, and even, during Zhou Yongkang's time in office, below the Ministry of Public Security. Others who rank higher than the heads of the SPC and the SPP include every member of the PBSC, including of course the General Secretary, Xi Jinping; the state chairman (often translated "President"; a ceremonial and powerless position); the head of the NPC Standing Committee; the Premier; the head of the Chinese People's Political Consultative Congress; and the Chairman of the Party's Central Military Commission.

The Ministry of Public Security has always been more important than most other ministries in the State Council. From 2002 to 2007, it was headed by the formidable Zhou Yongkang, who also had a Politburo seat. When he was promoted to the Standing Committee of the Politburo, he relinquished his post of Minister of Public Security. Since then, the Ministry has remained powerful – the successive ministers have only briefly (at the very beginning of their tenure) held only ordinary Minister rank, but have instead held Vice National rank (although without a seat on the Politburo). In other words, the Minister of Public Security and his ministry have generally held the same rank as the president of the SPC and the court itself (ditto, *mutatis mutandis*, the head of the SPP), even though the SPC is directly under, and its president is appointed by, the NPC. The current minister, Wang Xiaohong, appointed in 2022, continues this tradition. As a member of the Central Secretariat, he holds Vice National rank.

The National Supervisory Commission (NSC), discussed more fully later in this chapter, is not yet old enough to have established a clear pattern. From its inception in 2018 until 2022, its head had Vice National rank and was a member of the Politburo, thus putting it ahead of the SPC and the SPP, even though they are all formally directly under the NPC. But as of 2022, the new head does not have a Politburo seat, thus downgrading the NSC to the level of the SPC and the SPP. This does not necessarily mean that the substantive work of the NSC is affected, since that work can be carried out by the CCDI, which maintains its unambiguous supremacy of rank over all other institutions.

Within the court system itself, the effect of rank is pervasive. Both courts and their presidents rank lower than the Party and government organizations and their respective leaders at the same administrative level and thus are subordinate to them (Li 2023, 23; Ye 2023, 13). Certain jurisdictional rules look to the administrative ranks of the disputants in order to determine which level of court should hear the case (Li 2023, 29). Thus, in any given case, the extent to which "the law will be distorted by the political order varies from case to case, depending on the power dynamics between the litigants," their allies, and other interested parties (Li 2023, 42).

Reforms in the Xi Era

National Supervisory Commission and the Central Commission for Discipline Inspection

The Central Commission for Discipline Inspection, established in its modern form in 1978, is the Party's chief anti-corruption body. Its importance has expanded greatly since the 2012 launch by Xi Jinping of an anti-corruption campaign that has seen literally millions of officials investigated and hundreds of high-ranking cadres brought down (Carothers 2021). In recent years its apparent jurisdiction has expanded to cover political offenses as well. Commissions for Discipline Inspection (CDI) were established and empowered at the central and local levels because state anti-corruption bodies, such as the Ministry of Supervision (formally dissolved in 2018, although it had essentially been merged with the CCDI since 1993) and specialized departments housed within the procuracy simply did not have the clout to deal with powerful Party figures. A powerful Party body was needed.

The CCDI and its local counterparts were and are extremely powerful. As explained here, until recently they have had the power to investigate and detain coercively, called "double designation" (*shuanggui* 双规) from its formal character as an order to appear at a designated time and place to answer questions. *Shuanggui* is by no means a pleasant experience; reports of torture and attempted suicide by detainees are common (Human Rights Watch 2016).

Should the investigation lead the CDI to believe that criminal prosecution is warranted, the evidence gathered in their investigation, regardless of whether the investigation conformed to the rules of evidence gathering under the Criminal Procedure Law, can be turned over to prosecutors.

Two problems with *shuanggui* emerged over time. First, *shuanggui* never had a proper legal footing. Both the Chinese constitution and China's Law on Legislation state that any restriction of physical liberty must be authorized under legislation passed by the NPC or its Standing Committee. No such legislation was ever passed authorizing *shuanggui*, and the consensus among Chinese academics was that it was therefore unlawful (Dui Hua 2013).[17] As China's leaders continued to promote legality and to claim the mantle of the rule of law, this anomaly became increasingly obvious and embarrassing.

Second, the CDI's jurisdiction by its nature did not extend beyond Party members. But not only could corruption occur among non-Party members, but the CDI investigators often needed evidence and other forms of cooperation from witnesses and relatives of those being investigated, and if those persons were not Party members, exercising coercive powers over them was on even weaker legal ground than *shuanggui* itself.

The National Supervisory Commission (NSC) is intended to be the answer to these problems.[18] In March 2018, the Law on Supervision came into effect, establishing organs called "Supervisory Commissions" at each main level of state administration. The content of the law and the surrounding publicity make it clear that the activities of Supervisory Commissions are intended to be a replacement for the *shuanggui* system (Xi 2017), although neither this nor any other law formally abolished coercive *shuanggui*.

In practice, it appears that Supervisory Commissions are little more than a legal cloak thrown over the work of the CCDI and its local counterparts, who will continue working much as before. The Law on Supervision in effect both legalizes and broadens *shuanggui*. It broadens *shuanggui* by giving the Supervisory Commissions jurisdiction over everyone, not just Party members. In theory, coercive *shuanggui* was limited to Party members. Despite occasional exceptions, by and large that principle seems to have been followed. But the Supervisory Commissions have jurisdiction over "all public employees exercising public power." (This includes officials at so-called "autonomous mass organizations," revealing just how autonomous these organizations really are.)

How about legalization? The Law on Supervision legalizes the Supervisory Commission system only in the most formal sense of the term. It is a document passed by the NPC with the clear intention of giving the system an appropriate legislative basis. But what exactly is the system that now has a legislative basis? Essentially, it means that anything done by the Supervisory Commission system is now lawful as long as it is a Supervisory Commission that is doing it. But the law says little that limits the Supervisory Commissions' powers. All the rules we see in the Law on Supervision describing what Supervisory Commissions can and cannot do, and how they can do it, are not even in theory enforceable by any outside body. It is entirely up to the Supervisory Commissions themselves as to whether they want to follow those rules.

In summary, although *shuanggui* as a formally lawless exercise of Party-state coercion is apparently in the past, its successor is law-governed only in the most formal sense: there is now a statute about it. But the statute governing it imposes no standards or accountability mechanisms. In particular, the Supervisory Commissions are not accountable to courts; like the court hierarchy, the Supervisory Commission hierarchy is as a formal matter directly under the People's Congresses at various levels. It runs parallel to the courts, not under them. Indeed, it has been formally designated a political body, and not part of the legal system at all.

Although the creation of the NSC saw the elimination of the Ministry of Supervision and the anti-corruption departments within the procuratorate, the CCDI has by no means been abolished; far from it. The CCDI and the NSC have been amalgamated in a complex way, while retaining a formal separateness. They share a website, and the official literature describes them as "two signs with a single team" (Chen and Lu 2022). They are said to be operating in a single office but not merged.[19] It is difficult to find accounts of the two institutions that make clear what exactly the practical distinctions are, but presumably officials wear one hat or the other, depending on what is convenient and appropriate in particular circumstances, in order to avoid constraints on their work.

Despite their considerable overlap in jurisdiction and personnel, the two institutions are still headed by different people, and here is where the relative importance of each – the CCDI dominating the NSC – becomes clear. The CCDI is headed by Li Xi, a protege of Xi Jinping appointed to the Politburo Standing Committee at the 20th Party Congress in October 2022. This means he is of full National rank (Nie and Gu 2015). The head of the NSC, Yang Xiaodu, is a member neither of the Politburo Standing Committee nor even of the larger Politburo, having lost his Politburo seat at the 20th Party Congress. This confirms reports that while the NSC, like the Supreme People's Court (SPC) and the Supreme People's Procuratorate (SPP), has Vice National rank (Duowei 2018), it is not fully equal to other organizations with Vice National rank headed by higher-ranking officials such as full Politburo members, and is far behind the CCDI. The Party body remains vastly more important. On the other hand, the NSC still outranks the SPC and the SPP, since even its deputy head, Li Jinguo, slightly outranks their leaders – as well as, curiously, his own – by virtue of his membership in the Central Secretariat.

Reforms in the Court System

China's courts have undergone two important reforms in the Xi era. Both have been characterized by scholars as increasing the autonomy of courts and the professionalism of judges. But when we ask, "Autonomy from whom?" and "Professionalism for what?", it becomes clearer that these reforms are about increasing the responsiveness of courts to central authority, and that central authority is increasingly that of the Party directly or of the increasingly merged Party-state.

Prior to the reforms, Chinese courts and judges were responsible to political power at the same administrative level. Judges were formally appointed by the local People's Congress or its Standing Committee, but the actual power – as with any important governmental position – resided in the local Party committee. Funding for courts came from the local government (*renmin zhengfu* 人民政府), which in turn was also under the control of the local Party committee. In effect, a court was not much, if anything, more than just another office of local administration, governed according to the principles of the traditional work unit (*danwei* 单位).

This structure led to a number of problems, most notably local judicial protectionism. Local courts, being accountable to local government, would do their bidding when local interests were at stake.[20] More generally, tight local control meant that local officials could intervene for any reason, not just to protect local businesses.[21] One of the chief aims of the reforms was to eliminate or at least reduce local officials' ability to intervene in court activities.

The Judge Quota Reform

Between 2014 and 2017, China implemented what was called the "quota reform" (*yuan'ezhi gaige* 员额制改革) in the court system.[22] In this reform, all those with the title of judge (*faguan* 法官), regardless of rank, were required to re-apply for their positions, with about 57 percent (120,000 out of 212,000) able to requalify (Sun and Fu 2022, 866).

The guiding purpose behind the reform was to make courts less like what they had traditionally been – just another government bureaucracy, organized hierarchically with lower-level officials reporting to, and taking orders from, more senior officials – and to devolve more decision-making power (as well as responsibility) to individual judges, who would now be better qualified. The title "judge" would be mostly reserved for those who actually decided cases.

The requalification process does not, however, seem to have been a serious attempt to screen out unqualified candidates. As Sun and Fu (2022, 876) describe the written exam, "[T]he questions were drafted in such a way that [the examinations] were hard to fail." The oral exam asked questions such as, "What do you do to be a good judge against the backdrop of socialist rule of law?" And what really mattered, and counted for the most, was an opaque and unaccountable holistic performance evaluation by court leaders: "All the evidence indicates that it was the Party group in a court that decided which judges were in and which were out."

Whether the reforms have actually changed much is open to question. In 2002, there were approximately 210,000 people with the title of judge, of which about 150,000 were frontline judges actually hearing cases (Sun and Fu 2022, 971). In 2014, out of 212,000 with the rank of judge prior to the reform, 120,000 requalified to serve as frontline judges (Sun and Fu 2022, 866). Thus, the number of frontline judges has remained about the same, although they now have more judicial assistants than before (Sun and Fu 2022, 873). But after the reform, it is more likely that someone with the title of judge is someone who decides cases.

Reforms in Appointments

More notable have been accompanying reforms in the career path of judges and the funding of courts. All of these affect the incentives of courts as institutions and judges as individuals, and to understand behavior we need to understand incentives.

As discussed earlier, prior to reform, courts were heavily dependent upon local government, and a judge's entire career path might be within a single court. They would start at the bottom, perhaps as a clerk (and perhaps without any training in law) and work their way up.[23] Those with impressive degrees from elite universities would still start out at the bottom, but at a higher-level court. There was no established system for identifying capable judges in lower-level courts and promoting them up to higher-level courts, certainly not across jurisdictional boundaries. As Sun and Fu (2022, 876) write,

> Before the reform, higher courts routinely, if not exclusively, appointed judges from within their own pool of judicial assistants or clerks. A court

clerk at a HPC would become a justice of the HPC upon appointment . . . . [E]very court, regardless of level, effectively internally appointed its own judges who then literally served in the same court for their entire judicial career.

Moreover, the career goal of a judge in the traditional system was to get out of judging, a low-status job, and get promoted into an administrative position in the court (Sun and Fu 2022, 871).

The Xi-era reforms aimed to change all that. As noted, the reforms aimed to enhance the status of judges by reducing their number and making the title fit the job. In addition, the reforms attempted to make the judiciary more like a self-contained civil service with clear career paths and criteria for advancement. The Law on Judges was revised in 2019 to formally institutionalize a policy whereby new judges would have to start their career at a Basic-Level People's Court, and higher-level courts would select their judges from lower-level courts.

A Judges and Procurators Selection Committee (*faguan jianchaguan linxuan weiyuanhui* 法官检察官遴选委员会) (JPSC) was established at the provincial level to oversee and approve all judicial selections for all courts in each province.[24] But its role seems to be largely ceremonial, with the Party groups at each level of court playing the decisive role (Li 2016, 67; Sun and Fu 2022, 877–878). As a result, although appointment power has in form been centralized up to the provincial level (and even then, the form is not complete: local People's Congresses and their Standing Committees must still formally appoint and dismiss), in substance local courts, and the powers to whom they answer, are at least in some places still calling the shots about their own appointments in the way they have always done.

A little-known feature of the personnel appointment reforms is that judges and procurators are, unlike in the past, now part of a professional management system separate from that of government officials generally. This means that their ranks cannot be readily converted in civil service ranks, which in turn has for them the discouraging result that

> the prospect of upward career mobility – which is what "really" counts in China's political reality – is drastically limited, since it has become much more difficult and rare for them to be transferred or promoted from a judicial institution to a political one closer to the core of the party-state.
>
> (Ye 2023, 10)

Reforms in Funding

When courts depend on local government for funding – whether for judicial salaries or for more infrastructural needs such as buildings, vehicles, and computers – they are not free to ignore the wishes of local government. Consequently, Xi-era reforms have sought to diminish the reliance of courts on local governments for funding.

The funding reform was launched in 2013, with a Party Central document that called for the unified management at the provincial level of personnel, finances, and property of courts and procuratorates at and below that level (CCPCC 2013). These reforms, whose implementation began in 2014, have made some progress, but it would be a mistake to view them as substantially accomplished, let alone complete.[25] The conclusion of a 2021 Chinese study was that "after five years of practice in pilot projects, provincial-level unified management has by no means achieved its goals of 'delocalization,' 'de-administrativization,' and 'balancing judicial supply'," even going so far as to call it a "failure" (*shibai* 失败) (Fan 2021, 72). According to the study, of 741 courts that had already undergone reform (not all have), 249 still relied in significant measure on local (subprovincial) governments at their administrative level for funding (Fan 2021, 72–73). Needless to say, courts that had not undergone reform would have even greater reliance. A major reason for the failure of reform is that provincial governments, now theoretically responsible for funding all courts within the province, simply do not have the funds to fulfill this new responsibility (Fan 2021, 74).

A 2023 study came to a similar conclusion, finding that "the vertical centralization of the judicial system has largely failed. The institutional dependence of local courts upon same-level Party committees and governments has been perpetuated or even exacerbated" (Ye 2023, 3). Lower-level governments now tell courts to look to the provinces for funding,[26] but the provinces do not provide adequate funds. About one-third to one-half of a judge's income can come from bonuses, which are funded by local government, not the province (ibid., 6). As a result, courts find themselves more dependent on local governments than before (ibid., 8). In the words of one judge, "What we used to take for granted has now become something that we have to beg for" (ibid., 7).

Current Status

Whatever the institutional reforms, any talk about Chinese courts being "independent" must be heavily qualified. As Sun and Fu (2022, 870) write,

> The Leninist system is predicated on the notion that the court is just one cog in the wheels of the larger political machine. Within that political-legal complex, judges are not distinct from prosecutors, police officers or prison wardens and are commonly referred to as cadre-police (*ganjing* 干警), a generic term that the Party uses to categorize all personnel within the political-legal establishment . . . who are appointed and monitored by, and accountable to, the Party.

That the primary orientation of that machine is political is hardly a secret or an accident. A typical statement comes in 2018 from Guo Shengkun, then a member of the Politburo and the chairman of the Central Political-Legal Committee:

> Political-legal organs [which includes courts] . . . are first and foremost political organs, they have no professional work that is separate from politics, we must forthrightly speak of politics as the basic demand, to take care of and

resolve problems in order to prevent political risks.... [We must] ensure that the "knife handle" is firmly in the hands of the Party and the people.

(Zhao 2018)

Moreover, the courts, as part of the political-legal system, are subject to the "absolute leadership" of the Party (CCPCC 2019, art. 6; Chen 2020, 259). As always, however, "Party leadership" can be interpreted in different ways. To Zhang and Ginsburg (2019, 336), it is meant to apply only to the central Party leadership: "All things considered, the Party leadership now seems strongly committed to shoring up the judiciary's institutional independence vis-a-vis all state and Party entities, but with the major exception of itself." But once the language of absolute Party leadership is released into the wild, as it were, it is not necessarily controllable by its creators. Local Party leaders can use it to justify their own actions and orders, and who can challenge them? The very political system sanctified by the central Party leaders is what gives local Party leaders their power.

Unsurprisingly, therefore, the picture gleaned from empirical research is complex. A study of administrative litigation against police departments (most at the sub-provincial level) found that the reform, in theory reducing the influence of local governments on courts, did not increase plaintiffs' win rates (Zhou et al. 2021). (It could be, of course, that local governments exercised no influence before the reform as well as after it, which would account for the lack of any observed effect, but such an explanation seems unlikely.)

On the other hand, Lei and Li (2022) and Liu et al. (2022) found a decline in judicial local protectionism following the reforms, and Sun and Fu (2022, 879) write that judges they have interviewed report being freer to decide cases according to legal standards, with less interference from local Political-Legal Committees.

The long-term effects of the reform on judicial morale will bear watching. As the number of judges has gone down, caseloads have gone up, both absolutely and of course on a per-judge basis (Chen and Li 2020, 28–29). The judiciary seems to be afflicted by a wave of resignations (Zhou 2016; Li 2016; Luo 2020).[27] Judicial evaluation by means of objective indices unrelated to the merits of decisions, such as cases closed (good) or appeals made (bad), continues. Pressure to mediate cases, thus avoiding legal judgments and appeals, continues (Chen and Li 2020, 32–33 et seq.), suggesting that the "turn against law" identified by Minzner (2011) is still in action.

Politics and Law in the Xi Era

Decreasing Importance of Party/State and Law/Politics Distinctions

A characteristic feature of the Xi era has been a decline in the importance of the distinction between the Party and the state, and the distinction between law and politics. It is tempting to speak of a *blurring* of the line, but to do so assumes the objective existence of such a line, and such an assumption may misread the Chinese polity. It is fair to say, however, that various participants in the system have themselves asserted the existence of these distinctions in the past, and that such assertions and arguments based around them have become conspicuously weaker in the last decade, while at the same time institutions and practices that appear to be inconsistent with such distinctions have become more visible.

Having long since rejected Zhao Ziyang's vision of a Party that withdrew almost completely from day-to-day government administration, the Party now increasingly rejects as inefficient the model of duplicative Party and state bodies in all facets of administration. Thus, mergers and the elimination of overlapping jurisdictions have become more common. As one orthodox law professor put it, "The party is a key part of the state system, forming a constitutional foundation for political reform that is aimed at integrating party and government functions." (Tian 2018) The rise of explicitly political Party governance at the expense of a separate state has particular salience in the realm of law, where, no less than in central banking, some degree of independence from the political power of the day is usually beneficial.

Perhaps the most visible sign of the absence of the Party/state distinction was a Party pronouncement in 2014 (CCPCC 2014b) that "the leadership of the Party and socialist rule of law are completely consistent" (党的领导与社会主义法治是一致的). The phrase appeared in the Resolution of the Fourth Plenary Session of the 18th Central Committee, a meeting specifically dedicated to matters relating to China's legal system (Clarke 2015). From the Party's continued rejection of concepts such as judicial independence, separation of powers, and constitutionalism, it is clear that to the extent that rule of law might ever be thought to be inconsistent with Party leadership, it is rule of law that must yield. Some two-plus decades following the relaxation of the post-June 4th crackdown, we see again language describing legal institutions as "swords of the Party" and an important tool of the people's democratic dictatorship (Chen 2020, 267).

The progressive merger of Party with state can be seen in a number of areas:

Issuance of Legal Norms by Party Bodies

In 2014, the Central PLC issued an opinion on criminal sentencing (Xinhua 2014), drawing complaints even at the time that such an action violated China's constitutional structure (e.g., Gao 2014). The following year, the Central Office of the CCP and the State Council jointly issued an opinion on the disposal of property in criminal cases (Xinhua 2015; see also Chen 2020, 257 n.60).

Granting of Legal Authority to Party Institutions

A number of laws specifically designated a role for Party institutions on matters both minor and major. The 1986 Regulations on the Administration of Geographic Names (State Council 1986) were completely revised in 2022 (State Council 2022), with the revisions including among other things a requirement that some names must be approved by the Party Center. Article 44 of the State Security Law, enacted in 2015, grants an unnamed "central state security leading organ"

(中央国家安全领导机构) – by which is meant the Party's State Security Commission, established in 2014 – the power to establish and coordinate a national security system, and Article 63 gives it the power to deploy state resources in emergencies (NPCSC 2015). And both the Law on Public Servants (NPCSC 2018) and the Constitution (NPC 2018) were amended in 2018 to name Xi Jinping personally in their text – in Article 4 and the Preamble respectively.

Although the Party's leadership over the military was already stated in Article 19 of the 1997 National Defense Law (NPCSC 1997) (and there being an acknowledgment of reality, not a grant of power), the People's Armed Police went from joint state/Party control to sole Party control (under the Central Military Commission) in 2020 (NPCSC 2020, art. 20).

Merger of Party and State Institutions

A number of Party and state institutions were merged in the Xi era. The 13th National People's Congress of March 2018 was the occasion for a massive restructuring of government and Party bodies. Most prominently, anti-corruption efforts were in effect merged with the creation of the National Supervisory Commission, a new state body directly under the National People's Congress but defined as "political," not administrative or judicial. As discussed elsewhere in this chapter, it operates co-extensively with the Central Commission for Discipline Inspection, with which it shares offices and a website.

A new Central Party School was established that merged the existing Central Party School with the Chinese Academy of Governance. The latter's mission was premised on the idea that there was a set of managerial skills needed by officials independent of politics. The merger represents the rejection of that idea.

The State Administration of Press, Publication, Radio, Film, and Television was abolished, with many of its functions brought directly under the authority of the Party's Propaganda Department. The heads of the three successor agencies – the State Administration of Radio and Television, the State Administration of Press and Publications, and the State Bureau of Film – were concurrently Deputy Ministers of the Propaganda Department (Stratford et al. 2018).

The Central Organization Department, which formerly had formal management jurisdiction only over Party personnel, took over the functions of managing all civil servants from the State Administration of Civil Service, although the latter title was retained to facilitate international exchanges. And the United Front Work Department took over ethnic, religious, and overseas Chinese affairs.[28]

What is the significance of this downgrading of the Party/state distinction? In one sense, not much. The Party/state distinction has never mattered very much. This was clear in Mao-era China. The first three-plus decades of the post-Mao era saw efforts by some insiders to promote the separation in form in the hope that it might one day lead to the separation in substance. But there is little evidence that the latter has occurred to any significant degree.

What current trends mark is not so much the downgrading of the Party/state distinction in fact as the downgrading (while not yet the total abandonment) of the effort to maintain it in form. The Party's leadership simply seems less interested than before in trying to run China – and to present it to the outside world – as a state structured in the standard fashion, with a state separate from the ruling party and a relatively apolitical civil service. No longer operating behind the scenes, the Party has outed itself. The *Global Times* proclaimed, rather than denied, the fact that the Chinese Communist Party is not really a political party in the ordinary sense of the word, saying that the CCP "is substantially different to Western-style parties in scale, goals, operating mechanism and the role it plays in society.... No English word can really describe it" (Editorial 2020). What the downgrading signals, then, is that it is past time to abandon essentially teleologically-driven expectations of an eventual separation between Party and state, and not simply assume it will happen eventually in the absence of strong evidence.

Does Law Matter? The Amendment of the Constitution

A fundamental question often asked by observers is whether law matters in China at all. One partial way of looking at the question is to examine a recent amendment to China's constitution.

In March 2018, the National People's Congress amended the constitution to remove the limit of two five-year terms previously imposed on the office of State Chairman (国家主席, often translated as "President") of the People's Republic of China. The consensus of observers was that this was done in order to allow the then-holder of the office, Xi Jinping, to continue as State Chairman (a state office) after receiving an expected third five-year term as General Secretary of the Party at its 20th Congress in the fall of 2022 (ChinaFile 2018).[29] The question to be examined here is what this event reveals about the role of law in the Chinese political system.

One school of thought views the amendment as a sign that law does matter, at least sometimes, even in matters of high politics (Zhang and Ginsburg 2019). According to this view, if Xi wanted a third term as Chairman, it was not an option for him simply to take it and to ignore the constitutional term limit. In an earlier era, by contrast, it had been possible for the leadership to simply ignore (for example) the constitutional requirement (NPC 1954, art. 20) that the Third National People's Congress, formed in 1964, be replaced four years later by a Fourth National People's Congress – which was not organized until 1975.[30]

While counterfactuals are treacherous, it is indeed hard to imagine that Xi could have had himself named State Chairman for a third term without the appropriate constitutional amendment. It does not necessarily follow, however, that law now matters in high politics. The key question is *why* Xi could not ignore the constitutional rule.

Certainly it is not because there exists in China any specific institution capable of making the constitutional rule matter. If Xi had had himself named to a third term as State Chairman without amending the constitution, there is no body (other than a Party body) before whom a disgruntled citizen or political rival could have brought a complaint, and which then could have declared Xi's State Chairmanship invalid. It is unthinkable.

But a rule – any rule – can have force without it necessarily being part of a legal system. Its having force does not make it *ipso facto* a *legal* rule. The term limit was specifically and unambiguously spelled out in a document to which Xi himself proclaimed, and demanded, fealty. A violation could not have been hidden or explained away even by the most specious logic. Thus, even though he could have had himself named to the office in spite of the term limit, there would have been a cost – in legitimacy among the public, in respect and deference among his colleagues in the leadership, or in some other form not adequately captured by these terms. That cost is the force behind the rule.

At the same time, amending the rule was a relatively low-cost option. It was not a *no*-cost option; it publicly signaled Xi's intention to seek a third term as General Secretary perhaps earlier than he would have liked, and the fact that the amendment was announced and accomplished quite suddenly, without any significant advance notice or opportunity for public commentary, suggests that opposition was anticipated. But since the cost of amending the rule was lower than the cost of openly violating it, we saw the rule amended.

The general principle at work here is that in high politics, legal rules are not fundamentally different from Party rules, the rules of a religious order, or even rules of etiquette. A suitably powerful individual has the actual ability to decide simply to ignore the rule. But they will not necessarily do so. They will compare the excess of benefit over cost of ignoring the rule with the excess of benefit over cost of amending the rule and act accordingly.

Conclusion

One of the clearest indications of the legal system's role in the political system is what it does not do: regulate the exercise of political power. This has been so since the founding of the People's Republic. The Party's political supremacy may be written into the constitution, but that is a symptom, not a cause, of that supremacy. At the most basic level, the Party's supremacy is not rooted in law (Zhang 2022b). One of the most basic features of governance of any large country, for example – the relationship between the central government and regional governments – is not regulated by law at all. It is instead regulated through the Party's internal personnel appointment system (Wang 2021, 157). Indeed, critical questions such as central-local relations, Party-state relations, and power relations among the top public offices are not only absent from the constitution, but have been deliberately left out in order to allow the Party to maintain its exclusive regulatory authority over such matters (Li and Zhou 2019).

While this element of the political system has remained remarkably stable in the almost half-century of the post-Mao era and the almost three-quarters of a century from the founding of the People's Republic, other elements such as economic policy have been quite unstable. It is therefore difficult and perhaps unwise to make long-term predictions or identify long-term trends.

What one can say, however, is that what many both inside and outside of China saw, correctly or not, as a hopeful, liberalizing trend beginning in the early post-Mao era has been decisively halted. Both the discourse and the reality of meaningful judicial independence and legal constraints on government have been firmly rejected.

This rejection is not solely attributable to the Xi administration; Minzner (2011) dates it to several years before. But there can be little doubt that the Xi administration has doubled down on it and affirmed the absolute primacy of politics and the Party over legal institutions and legal standards. When the Party-state wants to do something, the law does not stand in its way.[31]

Notes

1 One commentator suggested using "government" instead of "state," and reserving "state" for the whole package of Party and (formal) government. The general usage at present, however, is to use "state" to refer to formal organs of government as opposed to the Party, and to use the term "Party-state" to refer to the whole package, and indeed to affirm the existence of such an undifferentiated package. In order to avoid confusion, I will stick with the general usage.
2 On the concept of authoritarian legality in China, see generally Gallagher (2017), Fu and Dowdle (2020), Wang (2022), and Whiting 2023 (forthcoming).
3 "宪法是我参加制定的, 我也记不得." Quoted in Liu (2002, 43).
4 Consider, for example, the case of Pan Hannian (潘汉年), who was arrested and imprisoned in 1955 in connection with the purge of Gao Gang and Rao Shushi (Xiao-Planes 2010; Zhang 2012). After seven years in prison, in 1962 he was brought before the Supreme People's Court for a formal trial, all elements of which, including the sentence, had been decided on before the trial by the top Party authorities. The written verdict was carefully proofread by Premier Zhou Enlai. Peng Shuhua, one of the three judges assigned to the case, provided a fascinating memoir (Li 2011) in which he repeatedly speaks of the way in which the case was entirely dictated by outside political authorities, in spite of the consensus of those in the court that the charges were unsupported by the evidence. That was irrelevant to the proceedings.
5 Regrettably, space considerations forbid a discussion of the question of whether, and to what degree, the government seeks and can obtain legitimacy through presenting itself as, and perhaps actually, operating legalistically. On this issue, see, among others, Epstein (1994), Gallagher (2006), Lee (2007), Landry (2008), Stockmann and Gallagher (2011), Michelson and Read (2011), Liebman (2014), Whiting (2017), and Fu et al. (2021).
6 While the concept of Party leadership over the legal system is older than the PRC itself, the addition of the modifier "absolute" gained currency only in 2019.
7 For an extensive list of what constitutes the political-legal system and what it should be doing, see CCPCC (2019), art. 6.
8 See generally Liu (2010, 9); Hou (2013, 2).
9 Wang's résumé up to the time of his appointment is available at https://news.sina.com.cn/c/2008-03-16/110915159271.shtml [https://perma.cc/GCU5-GWHK].
10 As of the time of this writing (February 2023), it appears that Sun no longer heads the court.
11 On the subordination of courts to political authority generally, see "Reforms in the court system" later in this chapter.
12 The Ministry of Public Security is responsible chiefly for what may be considered ordinary police matters – everyday crimes and social security, as well as sundry other matters including household registration and the issuance of passports. The Ministry of State Security is the chief civilian agency responsible for the security of the regime itself. It is in charge of intelligence and counterintelligence and is active in foreign influence operations. See generally Mattis and Brazil (2019) and Joske (2022).

13 Ma and Ortolano (2000, 81) present some almost comical examples, including a case in which environmental protection agency staff in Guangzhou were blocked from inspecting the Retired Air Force Personnel Club because many members had a higher Party rank than the Party secretary of Guangzhou.
14 In the fall of 2022, for example, the Artists' Communist Party Branch for Songzhuang, an artists' colony in the Beijing suburbs, issued a notice declaring that no artists in art institutions or enterprises were permitted to engage in shows of their work without the permission of the Party Branch (Zhang 2022a). It did not specify a sanction for disobedience, but in any case a Party body does not have the authority to issue this kind of order.
15 Brief anomalies have been omitted for clarity of presentation.
16 I have placed the NSC in this row because its deputy head holds the indicated rank.
17 For an interesting meditation on the issue of *shuanggui*'s lawfulness, see Sapio (2015).
18 The following account draws on my discussion in Clarke (2022, 564–569). For an excellent account of the Party's anti-corruption efforts leading up to the birth of the NSC and its current status, see Fu (2022, 89–95).
19 On the distinction between merger and joint operations, see Zhang (2018).
20 This problem has been noted by Chinese and non-Chinese analysts alike for decades. See e.g., Clarke (1996, 41–49); Zhang (2003, 80–83); Pan et al. (2015); Wang (2018); Huang (2019).
21 See Chang and Liu (2018); Ang and Jia (2014).
22 The reform was kicked off with the 2014 issuance by the Central Party Leading Small Group on Comprehensively Deepening Reform of the "Framework Opinion on Several Issues in Judicial System Reform Pilots" (Mu 2016). It was considered finished in 2017 (Luo 2017). For details, see Song (2016) and Sun and Fu (2022).
23 A 1998 study of several basic courts found that the "great majority" of judges had held other positions within the court such as bailiff, clerk, or driver before being promoted to judge (Li 1998).
24 The Guangdong JPSC was chaired by the vice president of Guangzhou University, but the rest of the eight standing members appear to be from the political-legal system. There are also 60 non-permanent members (Zhang and Yue 2015).
25 Zhang and Ginsburg (2019, 339), for example, write somewhat prematurely that "the Party leadership has implemented a number of measures designed to substantially reduce this influence, primarily through removing all judicial budgetary decisions to the provincial level or above."
26 Ye (2023, 8) quotes a judge as saying, "The same-level party-state thinks that 'financially you are no longer our business.'"
27 The problem of recruiting and retaining judges has been highlighted in several Supreme People's Court work reports – in 2017, 2018, 2019, 2021, and 2022. A modest dissent is raised by Liu (2019), who argues that because the statistics do not show *why* judges leave the judiciary, it is premature to state that it is because of unsatisfactory working conditions.
28 These and other changes are discussed in detail in Chan (2022, ch. 13).
29 The role of State Chairman is ceremonial; the office is one of the few in China where the actual power and the formal power roughly coincide. It is, however, a convenient office for the Party leader to hold, because it allows him to represent the Chinese state formally as well as actually in a state-centric international order and minimizes protocol problems.
30 Even the Third National People's Congress was over a year late under the constitutional rule.
31 A recent telling, albeit trivial, example is the case of American-born Olympic skier Eileen Gu, who competed on the Chinese national team in the 2022 Winter Olympics. According to the International Olympic Committee, which viewed her Chinese passport in order to confirm her eligibility to represent China, she acquired Chinese citizenship in 2019 (Feng 2022). Chinese law forbids dual citizenship, and requires any foreign citizen acquiring Chinese citizenship to give up the foreign citizenship (NPC 1980, art. 8). There is no public record of Gu having renounced her U.S. citizenship, and there would be if she had done so (Peng 2022). Neither she nor the Chinese government have stated that

she has done so. It is therefore clear that the Chinese government, which has no constitutional authority to simply ignore legislation passed by the National People's Congress, nevertheless did so in issuing a passport to Gu.

References

Ang, Yuen Yuen, and Nan Jia. 2014. "Perverse Complementarity: Political Connections and the Use of Courts among Private Firms in China." *The Journal of Politics* 76(2): 318–332.

Carothers, Christopher. 2021. "Xi's Anti-Corruption Campaign: An All-Purpose Governing Tool." *China Leadership Monitor* (67). www.prcleader.org/carothers [https://perma.cc/CQ6L-2J2X].

CCPCC [Chinese Communist Party Central Committee]. 2013. "Zhonggong Zhongyang Guanyu Quanmian Shenhua Gaige Ruogan Zhongda Wenti de Jueding" (中共中央关于全面深化改革若干重大问题的决定) [Decision of the Chinese Communist Party Central Committee on Several Important Issues in Comprehensively Deepening Reform]. November 12. www.gov.cn/jrzg/2013-11/15/content_2528179.htm [https://perma.cc/R3R4-ZYUZ]; English translation at http://chinacopyrightandmedia.wordpress.com/2013/11/15/ccp-central-committee-resolution-concerning-some-major-issues-in-comprehensively-deepening-reform/ [https://perma.cc/YBL4-SPUX].

CCPCC [Chinese Communist Party Central Committee]. 2014a. "Communiqué of the Fourth Plenary Session of the 18th Central Committee of the Communist Party of China." October 23. www.china.org.cn/china/fourth_plenary_session/2014-12/02/content_34208801.htm [https://perma.cc/4VMM-JGQ7].

CCPCC [Chinese Communist Party Central Committee]. 2014b. "Zhonggong Zhongyang Guanyu Quanmian Tuijin Yi Fa Zhi Guo Ruogan Zhongda Wenti de Jueding" (中共中央关于全面推进依法治国若干重大问题的决定) [Decision of the Chinese Communist Party Central Committee on Several Important Questions Relating to Comprehensively Promoting Ruling the Country According to Law]. October 28. http://politics.people.com.cn/n/2014/1029/c1001-25926893.html [English translation at https://perma.cc/XHF4-CXYM].

CCPCC [Chinese Communist Party Central Committee]. 2019. "Zhongguo Gongchandang Zheng-Fa Gongzuo Tiaoli" (中国共产党政法工作条例) [Regulations of the Chinese Communist Party on Political-Legal Work]. January 18. www.xinhuanet.com/politics/2019-01/18/c_1124011592.htm [https://perma.cc/R24X-N8YX].

Chan, Alfred L. 2022. *Xi Jinping: Political Career, Governance, and Leadership, 1953–2018*. New York, NY: Oxford University Press.

Chang, Yanlong (常延龙), and Yiming Liu (刘一鸣). 2018. "Zhengfu Xingzheng Jibie, Sifa Ganyuli He Fayuan Panjue" (政府行政级别、司法干预力和法院判决) [Government Administrative Ranks, the Power to Interfere in Judicial Proceedings, and Court Judgments]. *Guangdong Caijing Daxue Xuebao* (广东财经大学学报) *[Journal of the Guangdong University of Finance and Economics]* 2018(2): 99–111.

Chen, Albert H. Y. 2016. "China's Long March towards Rule of Law or China's Turn against Law?" *Chinese Journal of Comparative Law* 2016(4): 1–35.

Chen, Benjamin Minhao, and Zhiyu Li. 2020. "How Will Technology Change the Face of Chinese Justice?" *Columbia Journal of Asian Law* 34(1): 1–58.

Chen, Binghui (陈炳蕙), and Zhixin Lu (卢佐鑫). 2022. "Jingji Fanfu Zhong Ji Jian Jiancha Heshu Bangong Zhidu Ji-Fa Xianjie Xietiao Yanjiu" (经济反腐中纪检监察合署办公制度纪法衔接协调研究) [A Study of the Linked Coordination between Discipline and Law in Economic Anti-Corruption Activities of the Joint Operations System of the Central Commission for Discipline Inspection and the Supervisory Commissions]. *Xiandai Shangmao Gongye* (现代商贸工业) *[Modern Business, Trade, and Industry]* 2022(16): 143–145.

Chen, Jianfu. 2020. "Chinese Law and Legal Reform: Where to from Here?" *Hong Kong Law Journal* 50(1): 243–273.

ChinaFile. 2013. "Document 9: A Chinafile Translation." *ChinaFile*. November 8. www.chinafile.com/document-9-chinafile-translation [https://perma.cc/5U2L-X66E].

ChinaFile. 2018. "Xi Won't Go: A Chinafile Conversation." *ChinaFile*. February 25. www.chinafile.com/conversation/xi-wont-go [https://perma.cc/X82V-PXUX].

Clarke, Donald. 1996. "Power and Politics in the Chinese Court System: The Enforcement of Civil Judgments." *Columbia Journal of Asian Law* 10(1): 1–92.

Clarke, Donald. 2015. "China's Legal System and the Fourth Plenum." *Asia Policy*. July 16. www.nbr.org/publication/chinas-legal-system-and-the-fourth-plenum/.

Clarke, Donald. 2022. "Order and Law in China." *University of Illinois Law Review* 2022(2): 541–595.

Cohen, Jerome Alan. 1968. *The Criminal Process in the People's Republic of China, 1949–1963: An Introduction*. Cambridge: Harvard University Press.

Dui Hua. 2013. "Corruption, Shuanggui and Rule of Law." *Dui Hua Human Rights Journal*. June 27. www.duihuahrjournal.org/2013/06/corruption-shuanggui-and-rule-of-law.html [https://perma.cc/68SX-88BD].

Duowei. 2018. "Liang Hui Sudi: Jianchawei Zhuren Guige Gao, Yang Xiaodu Huo Timing" (两会速递：监察委主任规格高 杨晓渡获提名) [Bulletin from the Two Meetings: Chairman of Supervisory Commission Has High Rank, Yang Xiaodu Secures Nomination]. *Duowei Xinwen (多维新闻) [Duowei News]*. March 17. http://news.dwnews.com/china/news/2018-03-17/60046523.html [https://perma.cc/V2AB-YABY?type=image].

Editorial. 2020. "What Is the CPC? US Needs to Be Taught." *Global Times*. July 17. www.globaltimes.cn/content/1194854.shtml [https://perma.cc/DXH4-RTT9].

Epstein, Edward J. 1994. "Law and Legitimation in Post-Mao China." In *Domestic Law Reforms in Post-Mao China*, ed. Pitman B. Potter. Armonk, NY: M.E. Sharpe, 19–55.

Fan, Lisi (范丽思). 2021. "Shengji Tongguan Hou Fayuan Jingfei Baozhang Jizhi Zaizao" (省级统管后法院经费保障机制再造) [Reconstructing the System of Guaranteeing Court Expenses after Implementing Unified Management at the Provincial Level]. *Renmin Sifa (人民司法) [People's Judicature]* 2021(22): 72–78, 105. https://mp.weixin.qq.com/s/z8UquZTSEMNPOfxPQ0q9uA [https://perma.cc/8QXC-DSRG].

Feng, Emily. 2022. "For Some Athletes, What Is Chinese Is Not So Simple." *NPR*. February 13. www.npr.org/2022/02/13/1080059720/for-some-athletes-what-is-chinese-is-not-so-simple [https://perma.cc/RSA8-7E8G].

Fu, Hualing. 2022. "Between the Prerogative and the Normative States: The Evolving Power to Detain in China's Political-Legal System." *Law & Ethics of Human Rights* 16(1): 61–97.

Fu, Hualing, and Michael Dowdle. 2020. "The Concept of Authoritarian Legality: The Chinese Case." In *Authoritarian Legality in Asia: Formation, Development and Transition*, eds. Weitseng Chen and Hualing Fu. Cambridge: Cambridge University Press, 63–89.

Fu, Yiqin, Yiqing Xu, and Taisu Zhang. 2021. "Does Legality Produce Political Legitimacy? An Experimental Approach." https://papers.ssrn.com/abstract=3966711.

Gallagher, Mary E. 2006. "Mobilizing the Law in China: 'Informed Disenchantment' and the Development of Legal Consciousness." *Law & Society Review* 40(4): 783–816.

Gallagher, Mary E. 2017. *Authoritarian Legality in China: Law, Workers, and the State*. Cambridge: Cambridge University Press.

Gao, Hongming (高洪明). 2014. "Zhongyang Zheng Fa Wei Chutai Shifa Zhidao Yijian Weixian Weifa" (中央政法委出台释法指导意见违宪违法) [The Issuance by the Central Political-Legal Committee of a Guiding Opinion Interpreting Law Is Unconstitutional and Illegal]. *Boxun Xinwen Wang (博讯新闻网) [Boxun News Net]*. February 26. https://news.boxun.com/news/gb/pubvp/2014/02/201402261232.shtml [https://perma.cc/K6E2-UA7K].

Hou, Meng (侯猛). 2013. "'Dang Yu Zheng-Fa' Guanxi de Zhankai ("党与政法"关系的展开) [The Development of the Relationship between the Party and Political-Legal Institutions]. *Faxue Jia (法学家) [The Jurist]* 2013(2): 1–15.

Huang, Li. 2019. "Local Protection in Chinese Securities Litigation: A 20-Year Empirical Study of Securities Cases in China." *Hong Kong Law Journal* 49(3): 1089–1138.

Human Rights Watch. 2016. *"Special Measures": Detention and Torture in the Chinese Communist Party's Shuanggui System*. New York, NY: Human Rights Watch.

Jing, Yuejin (景跃进), Mingming Chen (陈明明), and Bin Xiao (肖滨). 2016. *Dangdai Zhongguo Zhengfu Yu Zhengzhi* 当代中国政府与政治 *(Government and Politics in Contemporary China)*. Beijing: Zhongguo Renmin Daxue Chubanshe.

Joske, Alex. 2022. *Spies and Lies: How China's Greatest Covert Operations Fooled the World*. Richmond, Victoria: Hardie Grant Books.

Landry, Pierre. 2008. "The Institutional Diffusion of Courts in China: Evidence from Survey Data." In *Rule by Law: The Politics of Courts in Authoritarian Regimes*, eds. Tom Ginsburg and Tamir Moustafa. Cambridge, UK; New York: Cambridge University Press, 207–234.

Lau, Jack. 2022. "China Names Chen Yixin as New State Security Minister in Leadership Shake-Up." *South China Morning Post*. October 30. www.scmp.com/news/china/politics/article/3197778/china-names-chen-yixin-new-state-security-minister-latest-leadership-shake [http://bit.ly/3KBztal].

Lawrence, Susan V., and Michael F. Martin. 2013. "Understanding China's Political System." *Congressional Research Service*. www.fas.org/sgp/crs/row/R41007.pdf.

Lee, Ching Kwan. 2007. *Against the Law: Labor Protests in China's Rustbelt and Sunbelt*. Berkeley: University of California Press.

Lei, Zhenhuan, and Yishuang Li. 2022. "Judicial Independence through Recentralization: Evidence from China." March 12. https://papers.ssrn.com/abstract=4052769.

Li, Anthony H. F. 2016. "Centralisation of Power in the Pursuit of Law-Based Governance: Legal Reform in China under the Xi Administration." *China Perspectives* 2016(2): 63–68.

Li, Ling. 2019. "Ling Li Analysis of Chinese Communist Party's Political-Legal Work Directive." *ChinaLawTranslate*. January 22. https://perma.cc/Z8JS-KBEK.

Li, Ling. 2023. "Order of Power in China's Courts." *Asian Journal of Law and Society* (forthcoming). https://ssrn.com/abstract=4406016.

Li, Ling, and Wenzhang Zhou. 2019. "Governing the 'Constitutional Vacuum' – Federalism, Rule of Law and Politburo Politics in China." *China Law and Society Review* 2019(4): 1–40.

Li, Qing (李菁). 2011. "Pan Hannian an Shenpan Qinli" (潘汉年案审判亲历) [Personal Experience of the Trial of the Pan Hannian Case]. *Shenghuo Zhoukan (生活周刊) [Life Weekly]*. May 11. http://old.lifeweek.com.cn//2011/0511/32313.shtml [https://perma.cc/PGF4-3NWZ].

Li, Xiaobin (李晓斌). 1998. "Shenpan Xiaolü Ruhe Neng You Da Fudu Tigao?" (审判效率如何能有大幅度提高？) [How Can There Be a Large Increase in the Efficiency of Adjudication?]. *Faxue (法学) [Jurisprudence]* 1998(10): 52–54.

Lieberthal, Kenneth. 2004. *Governing China: From Revolution through Reform*. 2nd ed. New York: W.W. Norton.

Liebman, Benjamin L. 2011. "A Return to Populist Legality? Historical Legacies and Legal Reform." In *Mao's Invisible Hand: The Political Foundations of Adaptive Governance in China*, eds. Sebastian Heilmann and Elizabeth J. Perry. Cambridge, MA: Harvard University Asia Center, 165–200.

Liebman, Benjamin L. 2014. "Legal Reform: China's Law-Stability Paradox." *Daedalus* 143(2): 96–109.

Liu, Ernest, Yi Lu, Wenwei Peng, and Shaoda Wang. 2022. "Judicial Independence, Local Protectionism, and Economic Integration: Evidence from China." August. https://ssrn.com/abstract=4205091.

Liu, Quane (刘全娥). 2012. "Shaan-Gan-Ning Bianqu Sifa Gaige Yu 'Zheng-Fa Chuantong' de Xingcheng" (陕甘宁边区司法改革与"政法传统"的形成) [The Judicial Reform in Shensi-Kansu-Ningsia Border Region and the Formation of the "Political-Legal Tradition"]. Ph.D. thesis. Faculty of Law, Jilin University, Changchun, Jilin, PRC. June.

Liu, Yong (刘勇). 2010. "Zheng-Fa Wei Zhidu de Lishi Yange" (政法委制度的历史沿革) [The Historical Evolution of the Political-Legal Committee System]. Master's thesis. Institute of Marxism, China University of Politics and Law, March.

Liu, Zheng (刘政). 2002. "1954-Nian Xianfa Shixing San Nian Hou Weishenme Bei Zhujian Qifei" (1954 年宪法施行三年后为什么被逐渐弃废) [Why the 1954 Constitution Was Gradually Set Aside Three Years after Coming into Effect]. *Zhongguo Renda (中国人大) [National People's Congress of China]* 2002(14): 42–43.

Liu, Zhong (刘忠). 2019. "Zhongguo Fayuan Gaige de Neibu Zhili Zhuanxiang – Jiyu Faguan Cizhi Yuanyin de Zaifenxi" (中国法院改革的内部治理转向 – 基于法官辞职原因的再分析) [The Direction of Internal Governance of China's Court Reforms: A Re-Analysis Based on Reasons for Resignations of Judges]. *Fa Shang Yanjiu (法商研究) [Studies in Law and Business]* 2019(6): 75–88.

Lötveit, Trygve. 1979. *Chinese Communism, 1931–1934: Experience in Civil Government*. London: Curzon Press.

Luo, Sha (罗沙). 2017. "Woguo Fayuan Faguan Yuane Zhi Gaige Shidian Gongzuo Jiben Wancheng" (我国法院法官员额制改革试点工作基本完成) [Work on China's Court and Judge Quota Reform Pilots Is Basically Complete]. *Xinhua Wang (新华网) [Xinhua Net]*. February 13. https://perma.cc/NG93-A937.

Luo, Xiaojing (罗晓静). 2020. "Fayuan Rencai Liushi Yanzhong, Weiyuan Jianyi Shidang Yanchang Faguan Tuixiu Nianling" (法院人才流失严重 委员建议适当延长法官退休年龄) [Problem of Talent Outflow from Courts Is Serious; Delegate Proposes Appropriately Extending the Age of Retirement for Judges]. *Xin Jing Bao (新京报) [New Beijing News]*. January 15. https://ishare.ifeng.com/c/s/7tG2hTwNzp9 [https://perma.cc/97NC-A46C].

Ma, Xiaoying, and Leonard Ortolano. 2000. *Environmental Regulation in China: Institutions, Enforcement, and Compliance*. Lanham: Rowman & Littlefield.

Mao, Zedong. 1969. "On the Correct Handling of Contradictions among the People" (speech of Feb. 27, 1957). In *The Political Thought of Mao Tse-Tung*, ed. Stuart R. Schram. New York: Praeger, 236–244.

Mattis, Peter L., and Matthew J. Brazil. 2019. *Chinese Communist Espionage: From the Revolution to the People's Republic*. Annapolis, MD: Naval Institute Press.

Michelson, Ethan, and Benjamin L. Read. 2011. "Public Attitudes toward Official Justice in Beijing and Rural China." In *Chinese Justice*, eds. Margaret Y. K. Woo and Mary E. Gallagher. Cambridge: Cambridge University Press, 169–203.

Milhaupt, Curtis J., and Lauren Yu-Hsin Lin. 2021. "Party Building or Noisy Signaling? The Contours of Political Conformity in Chinese Corporate Governance." *Journal of Legal Studies* 50(1): 187–217.

Minzner, Carl F. 2011. "China's Turn against Law." *American Journal of Comparative Law* 59(4): 935–984.

Mu, Ke (木可). 2016. "'Guanyu Sifa Tizhi Gaige Shidian de Kuangjia Yijian' Chutai" (《关于司法体制改革试点若干问题的框架意见》出台) ["Framework Opinion on Several Issues in Judicial System Reform Pilots" Is Released]. *Zhongguo Faxue Zhuanjia Wang (中国法学专家网) [Chinese Legal Expert Network]*. January 12. www.ilawchina.com/home/xueshu/sifagaige/1120.html [https://perma.cc/Q7Z8-XFKU].

Ng, Kwai Hang, and Xin He. 2017. *Embedded Courts: Judicial Decision-Making in China*. Cambridge: Cambridge University Press.

Nie, Huihua, and Yan Gu. 2015. "Zhongguo Guanyuan Jibie de Zhengzhi Luoji" (中国官员级别的政治逻辑) [The Political Logic of Official Ranks in China]. *FT Zhongwen Wang (FT 中文网) [Financial Times Chinese Network]*. September 7. www.ftchinese.com/story/001063796?full=y&archive [https://perma.cc/GR6R-C2RR].

NPC [National People's Congress]. 1954. "Zhonghua Renmin Gongheguo Xianfa" (中华人民共和国宪法) [Constitution of the People's Republic of China]. September 20. www.law-lib.com/law/law_view.asp?id=343215 [https://perma.cc/CUE5-R8WE].

NPC [National People's Congress]. 1980. "Zhonghua Renmin Gongheguo Guoji Fa" (中华人民共和国国籍法) [Nationality Law of the People's Republic of China]. September 10. www.law-lib.com/law/law_view.asp?id=2143 [https://perma.cc/3GAL-6NA7].

NPC [National People's Congress]. 2018. "Zhonghua Renmin Gongheguo Xianfa" (中华人民共和国宪法) [Constitution of the People's Republic of China]. March 11. www.law-lib.com/law/law_view1.asp?id=613902 [https://perma.cc/4DGV-LQN4].

NPCSC [National People's Congress Standing Committee]. 1997. "Zhonghua Renmin Gongheguo Guofang Fa" (中华人民共和国国防法) [People's Republic of China National Defense Law]. March 14. www.law-lib.com/law/law_view.asp?id=324 [https://perma.cc/89ET-5PC8].

NPCSC [National People's Congress Standing Committee]. 2015. "Zhonghua Renmin Gongheguo Guojia Anquan Fa" (中华人民共和国国家安全法) [People's Republic of China State Security Law]. July 1. www.law-lib.com/law/law_view.asp?id=506526 [https://perma.cc/X3EZ-V6X7].

NPCSC [National People's Congress Standing Committee]. 2018. "Zhonghua Renmin Gongheguo Gongwuyuan Fa" (中华人民共和国公务员法) [People's Republic of China Law on Public Servants]. December 29. www.law-lib.com/law/law_view1.asp?id=637395 [https://perma.cc/3GTE-NE94].

NPCSC [National People's Congress Standing Committee]. 2020. "Zhonghua Renmin Gongheguo Renmin Wuzhuang Jingcha Fa" (中华人民共和国人民武装警察法) [People's Republic of China Law on People's Armed Police]. June 20. www.law-lib.com/law/law_view.asp?id=692270 [https://perma.cc/P46R-5U72].

Nie, Huihua, and Yan Gu. 2015. "Zhongguo Guanyuan Jibie de Zhengzhi Luoji" (中国官员级别的政治逻辑) [The Political Logic of Official Ranks in China]. *FT Zhongwen Wang (FT 中文网) [Financial Times Chinese Network]*, September 7. www.ftchinese.com/story/001063796?full=y&archive [https://perma.cc/GR6R-C2RR].

OLP 2019: Quanguo Renda Changweihui Fa Gong Wei Lifa Guihua Shi (全国人大常委会法工委立法规划室) [National People's Congress Standing Committee Legislative Affairs Commission Office of Legislative Planning], ed. 2019. *Zhonghua Renmin Gongheguo Lifa Tongji 2018-Nian Ban (中华人民共和国立法统计2018年版) [Legislative Statistics of the People's Republic of China 2018 Edition]*. Beijing: Zhongguo Minzhu Fazhi Chubanshe (中国民主法制出版社) [China Democracy and Legal System Publishing House].

Pan, Yue (潘越), Jianping Pan (潘健平), and Yiyi Dai (戴亦一). 2015. "Gongsi Susong Fengxian, Sifa Difang Baohuzhuyi Yu Qiye Chuangxin" (公司诉讼风险、司法地方保护主义与企业创新) [Corporate Litigation Risk, Judicial Local Protectionism, and Enterprise Innovation]. *Jingjin Yanjiu (经济研究) [Economic Research]* 50(3): 131–145.

Peerenboom, Randall. 2014. "The Battle over Legal Reforms in China: Has There Been a Turn against Law?" *Chinese Journal of Comparative Law* 2(2): 188–212.

Peng, Michelle. 2022. "Eileen Gu Didn't Have to Choose between China and the U.S. I Wasn't So Lucky." *Time*. February 15. https://time.com/charter/6148188/eileen-gus-identity/ [https://perma.cc/L2HG-3DU7?type=image].

Pils, Eva. 2022. "The New Tyranny of Rule by Virtue: Normalising Alternatives to Law as the Legitimate Basis of Power." *European Institute for Chinese Studies Briefs | Analysis* 2022(22). https://perma.cc/5N45-7VHT.

Sapio, Flora. 2015. "On the Legality of Shuanggui." *Forgotten Archipelago*. May 23. http://florasapio.blogspot.com/2015/05/on-legality-of-shuanggui.html [https://perma.cc/V2AC-M8MQ].

Singapore Chamber of Commerce in China. "Zhongguo Ganbu Jibie" (中国干部级别) [Ranks of Cadres in China]. www.singcham.com.cn/index.php?m=content&c=index&a=show&catid=81&id=3 [https://perma.cc/AXQ2-C3X3].

Song, Yongpan (宋永盼). 2016. "Fayuan Yuanezhi Gaige Jiqi Peizhi Jizhi Wenti Yanjiu" (法官员额制及其配置机制问题研究) [A Study of the Court Judge Quota Reform and Issues of Institutional Configuration]. *Zhongguo Fayuan Wang (中国法院网) [China Court Network]*. March 23. www.chinacourt.org/article/detail/2016/03/id/1827042.shtml [https://perma.cc/82S2-JQY4].

State Council. 1986. "Diming Guanli Tiaoli" (地名管理条例) [Regulations on Administration of Geographic Names]. January 23. www.waizi.org.cn/law/9400.html [https://perma.cc/4M7S-L9TG].

State Council. 2022. "Diming Guanli Tiaoli" (地名管理条例) [Regulations on Administration of Geographic Names]. March 30; effective May 1, 2022. www.law-lib.com/law/law_view.asp?id=747939 [https://perma.cc/2YL6-WF7Q].
Stockmann, Daniela, and Mary E. Gallagher. 2011. "Remote Control: How the Media Sustain Authoritarian Rule in China." *Comparative Political Studies* 44(4): 436–467.
Stratford, Tim, Jason Goldberg, Christopher Adams, Nicholas R. Francescon, and Grace Gao. 2018. "More Officials Appointed to Lead Film and Media Authorities in China." *National Law Review*. July 21. www.natlawreview.com/article/more-officials-appointed-to-lead-film-and-media-authorities-china [https://perma.cc/F65R-H2E9].
Sun, Ying, and Hualing Fu. 2022. "Of Judge Quota and Judicial Autonomy: An Enduring Professionalization Project in China." *China Quarterly* 2022(251): 866–887.
Tian, Feilong. 2018. "China's Revised Constitution Befits a Nation on the Rise." *South China Morning Post*. March 24. 14.
Trevaskes, Susan. 2004. "Propaganda Work in Chinese Courts." *Punishment and Society* 6(1): 5–21.
Wang, Shucheng. 2022. *Law as an Instrument: Sources of Chinese Law for Authoritarian Legality*. Cambridge: Cambridge University Press.
Wang, Yuedan. 2021. "Laboratories of Authoritarianism." *Stanford Journal of International Law* 57(2): 137–190.
Wang, Yuhua. 2018. "Relative Capture: Quasi-Experimental Evidence from the Chinese Judiciary." *Comparative Political Studies* 51(8): 1012–1041.
Wang, Yuhua, and Carl Minzner. 2015. "The Rise of the Chinese Security State." *The China Quarterly* 2015(222): 339–359.
Whiting, Susan H. 2017. "Authoritarian 'Rule of Law' and Regime Legitimacy." *Comparative Political Studies* 50(14): 1907–1940.
Whiting, Susan H. 2023. "Authoritarian Legality and State Capitalism in China." *Annual Review of Law and Social Science* 19: 357–373. Available at: https://doi.org/10.1146/annurev-lawsocsci-111622-063635.
Wu, Guo. 2017. "Outsourcing the State Power: Extrajudicial Incarceration during the Cultural Revolution." *China: An International Journal* 15(3): 58–76.
Xi, Jinping. 2017. "Secure a Decisive Victory in Building a Moderately Prosperous Society in All Respects and Strive for the Great Success of Socialism with Chinese Characteristics for a New Era." Speech delivered at the 19th National Congress of the Communist Party of China, October 18. https://perma.cc/8R8L-NV93 (English); https://perma.cc/QKW9-W6WT (Chinese).
Xiao-Planes, Xiaohong. 2010. "The Pan Hannian Affair and Power Struggles at the Top of the CCP (1953–1955)." *China Perspectives* 2010(4): 116–127.
Xinhua. 2014. "Zhongyang Zheng Fa Wei Chutai Zhidao Yijian, Qieshi Fangzhi Sifa Fubai" (中央政法委出台指导意见 切实防止司法腐败) [Central Political-Legal Committee Issuues Guiding Opinion to Effectively Prevent Judicial Corruption]. *Xinhua Wang (新华网) [Xinhua Net]*. February 24. http://news.xinhuanet.com/politics/2014-02/24/c_119476695.htm [https://perma.cc/GD6H-BHQM?type=image].
Xinhua. 2015. "Zhong Ban Guo Ban Yinfa Yijian, Jinyubu Guifan Xingshi Susong Shean Caiwu Chuzhi Gongzuo" (中办国办印发意见 进一步规范刑事诉讼涉案财物处置工作) [Office of the Central Committee and Office of the State Council Publish Opinion, Further Standardize the Work of Disposing of Assets Connected with Criminal Litigation]. *Xinhua Wang (新华网) [Xinhua Net]*. March 2. http://news.xinhuanet.com/legal/2015-03/02/c_1114492360.htm [https://perma.cc/R3TB-2JYX?type=image].
Xinhua News Agency. 2008. "China Basically Forms Socialist Legal System." *Beijing Review*. March 10. www.bjreview.com/NPC&CPPCC2008/txt/2008-03/10/content_103596.htm [https://perma.cc/7N3K-82FJ].
Ye, Meng. 2023. "The Limits of Judicial Reforms: How and Why China Failed to Centralize Its Court System." *The China Quarterly* (forthcoming). https://doi.org/10.1017/S0305741023000358.
Yu, Yifu (于一夫). 2010. "'Yi Dang Zhi Guo' Mianmian Guan ("以党治国" 面面观) [An All-around Look at "Ruling the Country by the Party"]. *Yan Huang Chunqiu 炎黄春秋*

(Annals of the Yellow Emperor) 2010(7). www.yhcqw.com/31/7662.html [https://perma.cc/5J7S-H8VY].

Yun, Tianrun (云天润). 2021. "Shanxi Jingjie 'Yibashou' Liangxiang: Sheng Fayuan Yuanzhang Jian Shang Gongan Ting Dangwei Shuji" (山西警界 "一把手" 亮相：省法院院长兼任省公安厅党委书记) [The Chief of the Shanxi Police World Is Revealed: The President of the Provincial Court and Simultaneously the Party Secretary of the Provincial Police Department]. June 1. https://mp.weixin.qq.com/s/h6TeN0eewefvDdyclReRKA [https://perma.cc/54QH-TURX].

ZGXWW. 2014. "Zheng Fa Wei Gaige Jiasu, Jianshao Anjian Ganyu" (政法委改革加速 减少案件干预) [Reform of Political-Legal Committees Speeds Up; Interference in Cases Is Reduced]. *Zhongguo Xinwen Wang (中国新闻网) [China News Network]*. www.chinanews.com.cn/gn/2014/10-23/6707403.shtml [https://perma.cc/9DT9-NTSL].

Zhang, Li (张力). 2018. "Dang-Zheng Jiguan Heshu Bangong de Biaozhun, Gongneng, Wenti Yu Chonggou" (党政机关合署办公的标准：功能、问题与重构) [The Standard, Functions, Problems, and Reconstruction of Party and State Organs' Joint Operations]. *Zhengzhi yu Falü (政治与法律) [Politics and Law]* 2022(8): 72–81.

Zhang, Lifan. 2022a. "@zhanglifan (Twitter)." October 26, 8:24 PM. https://t.co/mz7K4XBGSO [https://perma.cc/HRS6-GC8N].

Zhang, Luyao (张璐瑶), and Zhengxuan Yue (粤政宣). 2015. "Guangdong Sheng Chengli Faguan Jianchaguan Linxuan Weiyuanhui, Lin Shaochun: Cong Yuantou Shang Bahao Faguan Jianchaguan Rukouguan" (广东省成立法官检察官遴选委员会 林少春：从源头上把好法官检察官入口关) [Guangdong Province Establishes Judges and Procurators Selection Committee; Lin Shaochun: Get a Good Grasp on the Entry of Judges and Procurators from the Point of Origin]. *Xinlang Xinwen (新浪新闻) [Sina.com News]*. October 12. https://news.sina.cn/gn/2015-10-12/detail-ifxirmqz9991343.d.html [https://perma.cc/2T2R-KAHT].

Zhang, Min (张敏). 2012. "Jiemi: Shuobuqing de Pan Hannian Yuanan Zhongde Pingfan Shimo" (揭秘：說不盡的潘漢年冤案終得平反始末) [Secret Revealed: The Complete Story of the Rehabilitation of the Mysterious Unjust Case of Pan Hannian]. *Zhongguo Gongchandang Xinwen Wang (中国共产党新闻网) [Chinese Communist Party News Network]*. June 26. http://dangshi.people.com.cn/BIG5/n/2012/0626/c85037-18380519-4.html [https://perma.cc/7RHP-TFW7?type=image].

Zhang, Qianfan. 2003. "The People's Court in Transition: The Prospects of the Chinese Judicial Reform." *Journal of Contemporary China* 12: 69–101.

Zhang, Qianfan. 2021. "The Communist Party Leadership and Rule of Law: A Tale of Two Reforms." *Journal of Contemporary China* 30(130): 578–595.

Zhang, Taisu, and Tom Ginsburg. 2019. "China's Turn toward Law." *Virginia Journal of International Law* 59: 313–393.

Zhang, Zhong. 2022b. "Ruling the Country without Law: The Insoluble Dilemma of Transforming China into a Law-Governed Country." *Asian Journal of Comparative Law* 2022 (preprint): 1–24.

Zhao, Enze (赵恩泽). 2018. "Zhongyang Zheng-Fa Gongzuo Huiyi: Shizhi Bu Yu Zuo Shehuizhuyi Fazhi Guojia Jianshezhe" (中央政法工作会议：矢志不渝做社会主义法治国家建设者) [Central Political-Legal Work Conference: Unswervingly Commit to Being a Constructor of a Socialist Rule of Law Country]. *Renmin Ribao (人民日报) [People's Daily]*. January 23. http://legal.people.com.cn/n1/2018/0123/c42510-29782366.html [https://perma.cc/ZP64-6BRF].

Zhou, Dongxu (周东旭). 2016. "Zuigao Fayuan Gongzuo Baogao Lianxu Shinian Ti 'Rencai Liushi'" (最高法院工作报告连续十年提 "人才流失") [Supreme People's Court Work Report Raises the Issue of Outflow of Talent for Ten Years Running]. *Caixin (财新) [Finance News]*. March 13. http://topics.caixin.com/2016-03-13/100919588.html [https://perma.cc/34A7-MQ55].

Zhou, Hui, Junqiang Liu, Jiang He, and Jianxin Cheng. 2021. "Conditional Justice: Evaluating the Judicial Centralization Reform in China." *Journal of Contemporary China* 30(129): 434–450.

2 Educating the Next Generation

Propping up the Party and Undermining Alternatives[1]

Karrie J. Koesel

Chinese leaders tend to blame contentious youth on failures in education. In the wake of the Tiananmen Square demonstrations in 1989, Deng Xiaoping directed responsibility at ideological and political training: "Our worst omission of the past 10 years was in education. What I meant was political education, and this doesn't apply to schools and students alone, but to the masses as a whole."[2] What followed was an elaborate campaign to bolster political education among youth, including teaching that patriotism was inseparable from love for the Chinese Communist Party (CCP) (Zhao 1998; Action Plan for Patriotic Education 2006 [1994]; State Education Commission 2006 [1995]; Hayhoe 1992, 1993; Yan 2014; Liu and Ma 2018). Youth mobilization in Hong Kong twenty-five years later received a similar reaction from Beijing, which blamed the 2014 Umbrella Movement and subsequent anti-extradition protests on the absence of political education in Hong Kong's schools (Vickers and Morris 2022; Morris and Vickers 2015; Baldwin and Li 2015). This led to the introduction of National Security Education, new compulsory courses that resemble political education in the Mainland and seek to cultivate regime stakeholders (Vickers and Morris 2022, 193; Education Bureau 2021).

This chapter explores the role of political education in contemporary China – how the party-state teaches popular legitimacy among the nation's youth and how it socializes young people to be supportive of communist party rule. It examines political education through the lens of the National College Entrance Exam (NCEE), commonly called the *Gaokao*. The Gaokao is a nationwide standardized examination that high school seniors must take to gain admission to universities and colleges in China. This high-stakes examination covers multiple subjects, including one section devoted to politics. Students must answer questions on Marxism-Leninism and Socialism with Chinese Characteristics, identify political institutions and economic reforms, and provide correct interpretations of current events. All of these topics are covered extensively in political education coursework.

The Gaokao is not only a benchmark for political correctness in China, but also opens a window onto how the party-state articulates legitimacy in its own words. Examination questions are written and vetted by regime representatives and reflect the political knowledge and ideological orientations that the party-state deems as most important and wants to transmit to its younger generations. Encoded within the questions are recurring narratives that reinforce CCP rule. The communist party is depicted as benevolent and selfless, confident and capable, and advancing China. These pro-Party narratives are not terribly surprising considering that one of the goals of political education is to socialize students to accept and support the CCP. However, the examination includes a more subtle narrative to orient students away from potential competitors, especially the West. Questions point to the flaws and threats of other political and economic systems in an attempt to instill in young people the superiority of communist party rule.

In developing this argument, the chapter focuses on political education in China as a long-term tool to socialize young people into regime stakeholders. It draws on seven decades (1951–2022) of the politics subject-test of the Gaokao to illustrate how Party authority is claimed and maintained over time, as well as how the examination questions seek to undermine political and ideological alternatives. The chapter concludes with a consideration of the small yet significant shifts in "thought work" under Xi Jinping, including his growing presence on the examination and positioning as the center of the communist party.

Political Education in China

Political education is often dismissed as brainwashing or indoctrination, but in its most basic form it is the day-to-day teaching of official political knowledge and the guidelines for model citizenship. It is designed to instill in young people a strong appreciation of their country, its political and economic systems, and leaders. The goals are twofold. One is to mold youth into good citizens who will accept and abide by the political rules. The other is to cultivate diffuse support for the political system (Easton 1965). Diffuse support can be understood as generalized trust and confidence citizens attach to the political regime. Often it appears as positive associational support, such as high levels of trust and regime satisfaction, but "may appear as blind loyalty or unshakable patriotism" in more extreme forms (Easton and Dennis 1969, 63; Easton 1965; Truex 2020). Diffuse support is beneficial because it adds an outer layer of defense for the regime and "forms a reservoir upon which a system typically draws in times of crises, such as depressions, wars, and internecine conflicts" (Easton and Dennis 1969, 62–63).

To cultivate diffuse support, political education begins in a student's formative years, when they are assumed to be the most impressionable. It attempts to build legitimacy by teaching the grounds on which political authority is claimed and socializes students around shared values within and across generations (e.g., Easton and Dennis 1969; Easton and Hess 1962; Rosen 1983; Merelman 1986; Fairbrother 2003; Li et al. 2004; Rosen 2010; Law 2011; Vickers 2009; Paglayan 2022). Although the content of political education may be repackaged over time, each generation is taught to identify as part of the nation and the regime, and to share its worldview. Generations are also taught to recognize the inherent dangers of political or ideological alternatives. In this way, political education operates as a long-term guardian – it legitimizes current political authority and steers young people away from the competition.

In China, political education has long functioned as a guardian for the communist party. Before coming to power, literacy at rural bases was taught using pamphlets on the basic tenets of Marxism-Leninism to transform peasants into revolutionaries and build New China. Textbooks and teaching materials often introduced lessons through a political lens. Statistics, for example, was taught by "counting how many houses were torn down and how many people were killed by the Japanese army" and music lessons focused on anti-Japanese war songs, such as the "March of the Volunteers" and the "March of Saving China" (Law 2011, 61). Practical knowledge, thus, was heavily steeped in politics and patriotism to build a base for the communist party.[3]

After the founding of the People's Republic of China (PRC), political education was further integrated into Chinese schools. The goals were to teach the expectations of socialist citizenship, unify thinking around communist party ideology, and build diffuse support for the new regime. Mao Zedong argued that "thought control is the first priority in maintaining overall leadership" and Party leaders have consistently used political education to orient youth (quoted in Zeng 2016, 115; Doyon and Tsimonis 2022). Under Jiang Zemin, for example, the Ministry of Education emphasized that political education should teach

> ideology, moral character, general knowledge of Marxism-Leninism and Mao Zedong Thought, and the theory of Socialism with Chinese Characteristics [in order to] nurture the entire body of students as citizens who love the socialist Motherland, who have social morality and civilized behavior, and who observe discipline and obey the law.
> (State Education Commission 2006 [1995], 22, 27)

Hu Jintao strengthened political education at colleges and universities to correctly orient Chinese youth to the challenges at home and coming from abroad (Xinhua 2008, 2010). Xi Jinping likewise prioritizes political education, describing it as "irreplaceable" and necessary "for training generations of socialist builders and successors" (Xinhua 2020; Li et al. 2022). According to Xi, "ideological and political courses are key to implementing the fundamental task of cultivating people" (Xinhua 2020, 2019; Xi 2014; Implementation Outline of Patriotic Education in the New Era 2019). Thus, political education has been and remains a crucial tool to socialize students to accept and support CCP rule.

To ensure Chinese youth develop the "correct" orientation, political education occupies a central role in the national curriculum from primary to graduate training. In primary school, Chinese students spend a minimum of one hour per week in political education courses. Children learn to sing the national anthem, identify the national flag and capital, and learn key facts about the founding and leadership of the CCP (Law 2011, 101). This curriculum expands in junior high school, where nearly all students spend at least two hours weekly surveying core political doctrines and positions of the CCP. Political education intensifies in senior high school, where students take compulsory courses, such as *Thought and Politics* (思想政治), that instruct them on political ideology and philosophy, moral character, and current political events (Vickers 2009, 524; Li et al. 2004). Political education training even extends into university and graduate studies as well as into schools of religious training (Ministry of Education of the PRC 2018; Cantoni et al. 2017; Reinoso and Koesel forthcoming).[4] All of this reflects the importance placed on the political education of young people. Indeed, by the time Chinese students complete their studies, 10–20 percent of coursework has been dedicated to political education training (Hayhoe 1993, 26; UNESCO 2009). Of course, these estimates do not take into account political education exposure outside of classrooms, including extracurricular activities (Communist Youth League), patriotic museums, popular media or politically oriented APPs, such as "Study [Xi], Strong Nation" (学习强国) that tests users' knowledge of Xi Jinping Thought.

The Gaokao

Chinese political education is further distinctive in that it is tested on the National College Entrance Examination (NCEE, 普通高等学校招生全国统一考试). The NCEE, more commonly known as the *Gaokao* (高考) or "high exam," is the gatekeeper of higher education in China.[5] The Gaokao is somewhat equivalent to the U.S.-based SAT (Scholastic Aptitude Test) and ACT (American College Testing) or the Japanese National College Entrance Examination (*Nyugaku shiken)*, but it is far more formidable. The Gaokao spans two days and questions include essay, short answer, multiple choice, and fill-in-the-blank across multiple subjects, including politics.[6]

The politics subject-test evaluates command of basic socialism, working knowledge of political institutions, government policies and laws, and awareness of contemporary political and economic events – all subjects covered at length in political education coursework (see e.g., Cantoni et al. 2017; Law 2011; Wang 2008; Zhao 1998; Hayhoe 1993, 1992). The politics subject-test additionally evaluates how well students can reproduce the worldview of the party-state. It tests the ability to correctly interpret politics and current events and whether students "express the right emotions, attitudes and [political] values they should have."[7] The Gaokao is a high-stakes examination and questions require a correct and measured response (Howlett 2021). Expected answers are not intended to reflect creativity and individuality, but an opportunity for students to demonstrate their "good political thinking" as the party-state understands it. Students who reproduce the expected thinking receive more points and increase their prospects for university admission – the main gateway for upward social mobility.[8] Thus, the examination incentivizes students to learn and repeat the worldview of the party-state.

The Design and Content

The importance of the Gaokao in the educational system means that Chinese authorities oversee the design and content closely.[9] Each year distinguished experts in their related fields prepare new questions for the upcoming exam. Generally, these experts are selected from universities and key high schools in early spring.

However, if an invited expert has a relative taking the Gaokao that year, they are prohibited from participating (Huang 1992). Experts are divided into teams to draft the questions following the Gaokao's annual guidelines and current curriculum standards for the subject-test. Drafted questions go through a series of reviews before approval, teams do not know whether their questions are selected, and the content of the examination is guarded as a "state secret" (Ye 2013).

Jiali Luo and Frederick Wendel (1999, 62) describe the exam drafting process in the following way:

> Question-writers are gathered in a special place. From the day they are called upon to construct exam items, they must stay in the designated place for almost a month without any form of contact with family members, relatives, or friends.

One former exam designer likened the experience as being held in a "penitentiary," where soldiers and security dogs regularly patrol the grounds and even the garbage is carefully scrutinized before being sent out for incineration (Ye 2013). Another lamented that mobile phones were confiscated and all communications monitored until the end of the examination (interview with former exam writer, Guangdong, September 2016).

All of this suggests that the party-state takes the political education of youth extremely seriously. It is woven into the national curricula from primary through higher education and carefully tested on the Gaokao. Students (and future elites) are evaluated on the political knowledge covered in political education courses and rewarded for reproducing the worldview of the party-state on the examination. Of course, this sidesteps the thorny issue of whether or not students are actually internalizing the lessons of political education or parroting the expected answer on the Gaokao to increase their point total. Nevertheless, it is evident that the party-state views political education as a long-term investment with significant returns. This investment is built on the premise that political education is an effective tool to socialize youth and orient them toward the CCP. It instills in young people a strong appreciation of the Party's core political values, policies, and leadership. It fosters political legitimacy not by preventing young people from rebelling against the CCP, but by teaching them that there is no need to do so.

Propping Up the Party and Undermining Alternatives

The politics subject-test goes to great lengths to legitimize the CCP. Questions emphasize the CCP's accomplishments, minimize its flaws, and repeatedly signal strength. The Party is portrayed as benevolent and selfless, confident and capable, and able to advance China. This pro-Party narrative is to be expected, as political education is intended to socialize young people – through intellectual and emotional appeals – favorably toward communist party rule. At the same time, the legitimation of the party-state is also built on creating distance between the PRC and alternative political systems and ideologies. The questions focus on the failures and threats of different political and economic systems, including the imagined past. They accentuate the weaknesses of Old China, highlight foreign aggression, and point to the hypocrisy of Western economic and political institutions. This undermining narrative complements the pro-Party message by diminishing demand for potential alternatives.

To illustrate how these narratives work in tandem, the discussion now turns to the examination questions. This draws on seven decades of the politics subject-test (1951–2022), which includes 1,268 questions and the corresponding answer keys that provide explanations and model answers for students to emulate.[10] When available, I also draw on the grader guidelines used to award points.

Propping Up the Party

The CCP plays a prominent role on the politics subject-test. The questions test a student's comprehension of Party ideology, institutions, and current policies.[11] Often they are designed so that students must explain why the CCP must lead. Within the first few years after the founding of the PRC, candidates were tested on their understanding of the Party's revolutionary mandate and why "Party leadership must be strengthened" (Question 9, 1954; Question 1, 1957). Here, the questions signaled that only a strong CCP could "change China from a backward agricultural country to an advanced socialist industrial country" (Answer key, Question 10, 1957). For instance, students needed to stress that the CCP "led the people of the whole country to overthrow the reactionary rule of imperialism, feudalism, and bureaucratic capitalism" (Answer key, Question 10, 1957). Questions also underscored the importance of loyalty. A 1953 question asked: "Why did the Central Committee of the Soviet Union remove Beria from the communist party?" Students should explain that Beria was a traitor because he put the Ministry of Internal Affairs (NKVD) above the Party and government (Answer key, Question 5, 1953). The lesson is clear: The Party is above all.

By the 1960s, students were tested on some of the early accomplishments of the Party, such as uniting peasants during the socialist revolution, advancing people's communes, fighting corruption, and leading the fight against imperialism, feudalism, and bureaucratic capitalism (Question 2, 1960; Question 1, 1964; Question 2, 1964; Question 3, 1963). Of course, the examination questions excluded any mention of Party failures, such as the Great Leap Forward. When the Gaokao was reinstated after the Cultural Revolution, the examination again returned to the narrative of a strong communist party advancing China. Questions and model answers stressed that without the Party "nothing in current China would exist" (Answer key, Question 14, 1980) and that Party leadership is essential for developing the national economy (Question 6, 1978; Question 7, 1978; Question 2, 1979). To reinforce that only the communist party must lead China, students were asked to refute the following fallacy: "Our country can realize the four modernizations without the leadership of the communist party" (Question 14, 1980). The expected answer notes that only the CCP is capable of modernizing China's agriculture, industry, science and technology, and national defense.

In the 1990s, students needed to explain why the "Party is key" in constructing a socialist spiritual civilization, why the Party is the choice of the Chinese people, and that only the Party can lead the people to "overthrow the three big mountains," a reference to conquering imperialism, feudalism, and bureaucratic capitalism (Question 18, 1991; Question 8, 1997). The emphasis on the Party as essential for advancing China is again underscored on the 2000 exam, which quoted General Secretary Jiang Zemin as saying: "To make China great, the key point lies in our Party" (Question 12, 2000).

The CCP is also consistently described in favorable ways on the examination, such as modest, hardworking, and brilliant, to generate diffuse support for communist party rule. The 2011 examination, for example, described Chinese communists as "selfless," "committed," "loyal," and "dedicated" and asked students to explain the "fundamental reason why the CCP can attain [such] brilliant achievements" (Question 18, 2011). The expected answers generally require students to focus on the "hard work" of Party members and of the commitment of the CCP to "wholeheartedly serve the people" – a slogan attributed to Comrade Lei Feng, a propaganda icon from the 1960s used to inspire youth (Question 31, 2007; Question 38, 2003; Question 34, 2001; Question 35, 1990). The image of a selfless and driven Party has also continued under Xi Jinping. In celebration of the 100th anniversary of the CCP, one question noted that the Party's mission is "to seek happiness for the Chinese people and the rejuvenation for the Chinese nation" (Question 15, 2021).

However, not all questions use such exuberant language to describe the Party and its promises. To grossly inflate the Party's deeds or disconnect it from day-to-day life would likely be interpreted as overt propaganda (not political knowledge) and seed doubt that the Party is neither as strong nor as accomplished as it claims, as it did in the Soviet case (see e.g., Yurchak 2005; Houn 1961; Huang 2018). Therefore, to ensure the examination supports but does not subvert the legitimacy of the CCP, the questions attempt to connect the Party to current issues in a credible way. In the post-Mao era, questions introduce minor shortcomings of the Party but do not suggest incompetence or corruption, especially among top leadership. They also highlight the CCP's ability to learn from its own mistakes – self-correction is "a manifestation of our Party's strength" (Answer key, Question 14, 1980).

More generally, the Party is portrayed as addressing contemporary challenges head-on, such as leading soldiers and civilians to fight back against floods and obtain historic bumper crops (Question 29, 1992), addressing rural poverty (Question 48; 1988; Question 15, 2017; Question 40; 2018), providing clean drinking water (Question 18, 2022), advancing rural democracy (Question 25, 1999; Question 40, 2018), and building a self-reliant, patriotic, and culturally powerful China (Question 53, 1990; Question 38, 2013). In one case, students were asked about the Party's response to the ecological and economic crisis at Lake Dongting, China's second-largest freshwater lake (Question 29, 2002). The answer key is telling: Students should highlight an accountable and responsive CCP managing the crisis, a message that Party elites are keen for youth to internalize.

Examination questions also do not shy away from politically sensitive topics but address them in such a way that again highlights a problem-solving CCP. For example, China has one of the deadliest rates of coal mining accidents, and the

2010 examination addressed mining accidents that have caused "serious casualties and property losses" in the country (Wang et al. 2011; Question 13, 2010). In this case, students should organize their answers around a responsive party-state that is "serving the people" and correcting unsafe mining practices.

As these examples illustrate, the politics subject-test is far from neutral in its portrayal of the party-state; it is rather an opportunity to elevate the leadership and its accomplishments. The questions consistently depict an accountable and responsive Party, one that is confident and capable, serving the people, and addressing even the most challenging obstacles head-on. This narrative is intended to favorably orient students toward the CCP.

Undermining Alternatives

The pro-Party message is reinforced by a second narrative that identifies potential threats to communist party rule. This undermining narrative highlights external threats and foreign aggression toward China; it points to the flaws and failures of the Western countries' economic and political systems with the goal of limiting outside influences and diminishing demand for alternative models of development. Over time, the nature of the external threats and competitors identified on the Gaokao has followed shifts in Chinese politics. Western imperialism has given way to criticism of Western economic protectionism; condemnation of capitalism has shifted to failures of Western elections. However, across the seven decades, there remains one constant: The United States is the primary threat.

IMPERIALISM

In the Maoist era, foreign aggression was largely framed through the lens of imperialism. Students were expected to identify the major characteristics of imperialism (Question 11, 1952; Question 8, 1954; Question 4, 1965), know that Old China's ruling class was imperialistic (Question 6, 1952), and recognize imperialist aggression globally (Question 3, 1952; Answer key, Question 1, 1959; Question 2, 1963). For example, candidates needed to complete the following sentence about American aggression: "Recently, American imperialism bombed the _____ power plant, which caused people from all over the world to _____" (Question 3, 1952). The blanks should be filled with "Yalu River" and "protest," which reinforced the point that American imperialism is condemned globally. Another question emphasized global protest against the execution of Ethel and Julius Rosenberg – two Americans convicted of espionage for selling secrets to the Soviet Union. The question described the Rosenbergs as "peace warriors" and asked: "Who were the peace warriors the American government conspired against and murdered this June, despite protests from people all over the world?" (Question 4, 1953).

More generally, questions prompt students to explain how they can "frustrate American imperialistic plans of invasion and war" (Question 4, 1963). Indeed, the link between imperialism and Western aggression is well-developed. Students must discuss the inevitability of war between imperialist countries (Question 8,

1954) and the impending threat of imperialism for the socialist world (Question 2, 1963). The model answers warn that imperialist aggressors will attempt "not only to politically subvert and militarily invade socialist countries, but also to infiltrate and erode socialist countries ideologically and culturally, scheming to realize the 'peaceful evolution' within socialism" (Answer key, Question 2, 1963). Thus, students must be vigilant and communicate in their answers that imperialism is the "root of modern war. The aggressive nature of imperialism is never going to change, [and] American imperialism is the most vicious and most aggressive imperialism of modern times" (Answer key, Question 4, 1960).

The threat of American imperialism was particularly evident on the Gaokao in the 1960s. Students needed to explain: "Why can the Kennedy Administration only be worse, and not better, than the Eisenhower Administration?" (Question 8, 1961). American imperialism is also referenced with regard to the Vietnam War, asking why "the Vietnamese people's struggle of fighting against American imperialism to save their country must succeed and American imperialism fail?" (Question 2, 1965). The expected answers should focus on American actions as "unjust, reactionary, barbaric and extremely unpopular" and American imperialism as a "paper tiger" (Answer key, Question 2, 1965). Again, the question and expected answer is far from neutral, but mirrors the worldview of the party-state and reveals the level of sophistication in global affairs expected of students.

In the reform era, imperialism became less prominent on the examination, but never completely left. A question in the 1980s described imperialism as "monopolistic, parasitic or rotten, and dying capitalism" (Question 14, 1987). Another referred to the legacies of Japanese imperialism, including a few Japanese "right-wing forces" that deny the Nanjing Massacre (Question 6, 2000). More commonly, however, the examination focused on foreign aggression, especially as instigated from the United States. In 1990, one question detailed four decades of external pressures on China:

> As our country was founded, the United States sent troops to invade North Korea, coveted our land, and invaded and occupied our country's Taiwan province; at the same time [the U.S.] imposed isolation, containment, blockade, and embargoes on us in an attempt to stifle the new China in its cradle.
> (Question 53, 1990)

As the question suggests, the United States is portrayed as a long-standing adversary seeking to contain China. In that same year, students were also required to read short passages by American presidents and discuss them in light of the "counter-revolutionary rebellion that occurred in Beijing in 1989" – a veiled reference to the Tiananmen Square student demonstrations (Question 52, 1990). It is worth quoting the passage at length because it shows how students are taught to understand the scope of U.S. interference. The passage reads:

> The Voice of America is an enormous non-military force. It is a force that will light a fire in the darkness of communist society.
> (Reagan 1987)

> With regard to the Soviet system, one of the greatest dangers is that their thinking, people, [and] society come in contact with us; because these kinds of contacts can sow the seeds of discontent and these seeds may one day bear the fruit of peaceful evolution.
>
> (Nixon 1984)

> After World War II, the West tried to force communism into a dilemma under the policy of 'containment'. I wish to go beyond this policy. The New World we seek is a federation of free nations that act in accord with one another – In this New World, there will be more and more countries entering the ever-expanding circle of freedom.
>
> (Bush 1989) (Note: The "New World" or "the circle of freedom" that Bush speaks of is the capitalist system of the West.) (Question 52, 1990)

In using statements from Presidents Reagan, Nixon and Bush, the question reinforces the idea of threats coming from the United States. It also signals to students how they should understand the "counter-revolutionary rebellion" that occurred in Beijing the previous summer – that is, it was instigated from hostile external forces attempting to contain China.

The message of hostile external forces is again reinforced, but with more explicit language, in the following year. One question stated:

> The international reactionary forces have never given up their fundamental position of hostility and subversion of the socialist system. Since the late 1950s, after the failure of their single-handed armed intervention, they shifted their policy to focus on peaceful evolution; use all kinds of methods, utilize all kinds of opportunities, and go through all kinds of channels to combine with domestically hostile forces and conduct subversive activities. This indicates that:
>
> A The international reactionary forces have changed their subversion from two hands to one hand
> B Peaceful evolution and anti-peaceful evolution are an important form of struggle between modern capitalism and socialism
> C The strategy of imperialist peaceful evolution is the external condition for the evolution in socialist countries
> D International class struggle and domestic class struggle are intimately linked.
>
> (Question 29, 1991)

Here, the expected answers are B, C, and D – that international reactionary forces are actively seeking to subvert socialism and therefore hold back China. The answer key notes that choice A is incorrect because "it conceals the aspect of armed interventions carried out by international reactionary forces" (Answer key, Question 29, 1991). In other words, foreign forces continue to use all methods to subvert China. These questions are important because they disclose that in moments of existential crisis, such as the Tiananmen Square movement and collapse of communism outside of China, political education blames foreign forces.

By the 2000s, the discussion of external threats and aggression again shifted toward the global economy. The United States is described as a destabilizing force that seeks to disadvantage China economically. The U.S. is linked to meddling with China's economic cooperation with Asian and African countries (Question 39, 2005), associated with irresponsible economic practices that trigger international financial crises (Question 13, 2012), and promoting an unfair and unstable international economic order (Question 31, 2004; Question 13, 2012; Question 14, 2013).

Similarly, American protectionism is depicted as unfairly targeting Chinese businesses, including those in clean energy development (Questions 15, 2012). A 2013 question, for example, asked students about the acquisition of the Four Wind Power Project in the United States that was later prohibited by an executive order from the Obama administration as a threat to national security (Question 14, 2013).[12] The question emphasized the unfair playing field facing Chinese enterprises and that the United States regularly tips the scales of the international economy, which triggers economic instability. At the same time, these negative images of the U.S. are often put into sharp contrast with China, which is portrayed as cooperating globally, establishing friendly relations with other countries and "promoting mutual economic prosperity" (Question 5, 1987; Question 9, 1990; Question 39, 2005; Question 32, 2004; Question 19, 2015; Question 18, 2017). Thus, while the U.S. is irresponsibly provoking crises, China is promoting cooperation.

UNDERMINING CAPITALISM

Another way the politics subject-test undermines alternatives is by asking students to discuss the exploitative nature of capitalism. Over the seven decades, students have had to enumerate the downsides of capitalism, such as linking it to imperialism (Question 11, 1952; Question 4, 1956; Question 23, 1985; Question 39, 1986; Question 30, 1987), colonialism and the slave trade (Question 39, 2009), and show how capitalism provokes economic crises, instability, and unemployment (Question 4, 1980; Question 10, 1984; Question 40, 1987). Students are expected to demonstrate the basic contradictions within a capitalist society and discuss how these contradictions will lead to capitalism's inevitable demise (Question 2, 1962; Question 22, 1983).

On the examination, capitalists are associated with "greed" or having a "mercenary nature" and capitalism is denounced for its exploitation of workers and ethnic minorities as well as for making it "impossible for working people to enjoy equal footing with the bourgeoisie" (Answer key, Question 7, 1953; Question 1, 1977; Question 3, 1982; Question 19, 1982; Question 22, 1983; Question 21, 1985; Question 9, 1986; Question 32, 1986; Question 11, 1989; Question 10, 1994). Some questions make an emotional appeal in their condemnation of capitalist societies, as in the following example of a dialogue between a miner's child and her mother.

'The weather is cold, why don't we light our furnace?' – 'We do not have the money to buy coal because your father lost his job. – 'Why did he lose his job?' – 'Because too much coal was produced.'

What principle of political economics does this dialogue present:

A. The decrease of purchasing power of workers in capitalist countries
B. The capitalist economic crisis is a crisis of absolute overproduction
C. The capitalist economic crisis is a crisis of relative overproduction
D. The anarchic state of capitalist social production

(Question 13, 1986)

The expected answer is C and tests students' knowledge of the consequences of overproduction and the consequences for working families in capitalist countries.

Interestingly, the anti-capitalist rhetoric continued throughout Opening and Reform, even when China was welcoming foreign capitalists and recruiting Chinese entrepreneurs into the communist party. Of course, the examination questions never describe China as embracing capitalism, but rather as building "Socialism with Chinese Characteristics" (Question 1, 1983; Question 41, 1987; Question 19, 1988; Question 18, 1991; Question 39, 1993; Question 1, 1994; Question 35, 1995; Question 31, 1996; Question 8, 1997). Moreover, students are tested on the superiority of Chinese socialism over capitalism. One question asked test takers to respond to a statement by Deng Xiaoping: "Which one is good: a socialist system or a capitalist system? Of course, a socialist system is good" (Question 23, 1984). Here, part of the expected answer notes that while China may be less developed than some capitalist countries, it is not because socialism is weak. Rather, "with the development of the socialist construction, the superiority of the socialist system will surely be more and more fully shown" (Answer key, Question 23, 1984). Thus, the lesson for Chinese students is that it is only a matter of time until Chinese socialism surpasses capitalism in the West.

UNDERMINING CAPITALIST DEMOCRACY

Gaokao questions also go to considerable lengths to foster skepticism of different political systems. Liberal democracies are referred to as "capitalist democracy" and questions ask students about the failures of democratic institutions. In the mid-1990s, students had to identify the shortcomings of democratic capitalism and its contradictions. One question asked about the "contradiction within democratic capitalist countries between equality-in-form and inequality-in-fact" (Question 10, 1995). The contradiction is that democratic rights are restricted by private ownership in capitalist democracies, and therefore, democracies are highly unequal political systems. At the same time, the exam generally overlooks the advent of private ownership in China.

Examination questions additionally point to the weaknesses of democratic elections and the two-party system in the United States. The goal here is to identify the hypocrisies of democratic systems and to demonstrate how they are inferior to communist party rule. Questions stress the elite nature of Western democracy, such as a political system used to coordinate the interests of the bourgeoisie and "create illusions of democracy that deceive the people" (Question 43, 1991; Question 15, 1990). The general lesson is that "capitalist democracy is always going to be a democracy enjoyed by the minority, the bourgeoisie, and the wealthy" (Question 7, 1997).

In undermining elections, questions tend to focus on the outsized role of money, such as suggesting candidates in Japan participate in "money elections" to buy their seats, or that "capitalist democracy is enjoyed by the wealthy few" (Question 32, 1990). Democracy in the United States is described as being in the "hands of the monopoly bourgeoisie" and that Congress is packed with millionaires to remind students that American democracy is the rule of the few over the many (Question 9, 1997). The following question provides a particularly cynical view of the role of money in U.S. elections:

> Some Western commentators sarcastically pointed out that during the 2004 United States presidential election, the competition between Bush and Kerry was not about the guiding principles of government, but rather about money. Whoever raised more money had better odds to win. In light of this, the conclusion that we propose is that:
>
> A. U.S. democracy possesses the nature of a superclass
> B. In the U.S., political parties have lost their meaning with regards to politics
> C. In the U.S., money is the mother's milk of politics
> D. In the U.S., as long as you have money you can become president
> (Question 32, 2006)

While all of the answers seem plausible considering how Western democracy is portrayed, the expected answer is C – that money drives American politics. This suggests students are taught that in democracies, like the U.S., political authority is purchased.

American elections are further undermined by showing the unchecked influence of the media. The following example questions the competitive nature of American elections by referencing a political rumor that Republican presidential candidate, George H.W. Bush, was having an extramarital affair.[13] The question notes that this affair was not reported in the American media, in contrast to earlier coverage of an affair by presumed Democratic nominee, Gary Hart.

> On October 19th, 1988, right before the United States presidential election, news reached Wall Street in New York; the next day, the *Washington Post* was going to publish a report exposing personal secrets of the presidential candidates. If published, the result of the presidential election would have been completely changed. In the end, all the major bourgeois media outlets (including the *Washington Post*) kept this candidate's private life a secret and said nothing about it. Meanwhile, they broadcast details of the private life of the other candidate instead of imposing a news blackout. This indicates that:
>
> A. The President of the United States is elected
> B. The press of the United States is not free
> C. The United States presidential election is manipulated by the bourgeoisie
> D. American democracy is merely a formalistic democracy to the bourgeoisie
> (Question 7, 1992)

The expected answer is C – U.S. elections are manipulated by the bourgeoisie. The answer key explains that choice D is incorrect and a distraction because it confuses the form and essence of democracy – that is, democracy in the United States is capitalist democracy, not only in form but also (and more so) in essence. It also notes that the level of difficulty of the question is "hard" and "requires the capability of possessing and utilizing Marxist views, standpoints, and methods to judge right from wrong, and requires having some basic common sense" (Answer key, Question 7, 1992).

Of course, these questions are designed so that the expected answers require students to express the superiority of the Chinese system – that is, "it represents the fundamental interests of the working class and the broad masses of the people," that the "CCP is the ruling party," and all the democratic parties "accept the leadership of the CCP," and are friendly with and actively cooperate with the CCP (Answer key, Question 43, 1991; Question 35, 2007). China's socialist democracy surpasses capitalist democracy because it is enjoyed by the majority of the people, is extensive and authentic, and "the people are the masters of the state" (Question 11, 1994; Question 36, 1997). The contrast for Chinese students should be evident: Chinese-style democracy is superior.

The Xi Jinping Effect

The rise of Xi Jinping has had small but significant shifts on the politics subject-test. The most conspicuous is his presence on the examination, including direct mentions of Xi and the personalization of his leadership style. While other Chinese leaders are also referenced over the years – most notably Mao Zedong – the inclusion of Party leaders by name is less common in the post-Mao era. Xi's predecessor, Hu Jintao, only appears in five questions in the decade he was in power. Indeed, the norm has been that the Party plays the starring role on the examination – that is, it is the Party advancing China, not any specific leader.

Under Xi Jinping there is growing evidence that this norm is changing. Figure 2.1 shows the percentage of questions that mention a specific Chinese leader or the Party by decade. Here, we can observe that Xi is the second most frequent leader to appear on the examination following Mao. We also see that since coming to power, Xi is mentioned in more questions than Mao and is also closing the gap with the Party.

However, it is not only that Xi Jinping appears in examination questions; it is also the context in which he is mentioned that is important. Xi is distinguished with various titles to signify his importance, such as General Secretary (Question 22, 2013), Comrade (Questions 15 and 16, 2017), President (Question 17, 2016; Question 18, 2020), and even Chairman (Question 20, 2014), a term that has generally been reserved for Mao. We also find many of the same attributes used to describe the CCP are applied to Xi. Many questions, for instance, portray Xi as a strong and capable leader. He is humble and driven, guiding Chinese youth, serving the people, and building a strong China. A 2013 question describes Xi meeting with model worker representatives (Question 22, 2013) to signify his respect for labor and working people. The questions also show him meeting with teachers of ideological and political education. Here, Xi is encouraging teachers to "plant the seeds

58 Karrie J. Koesel

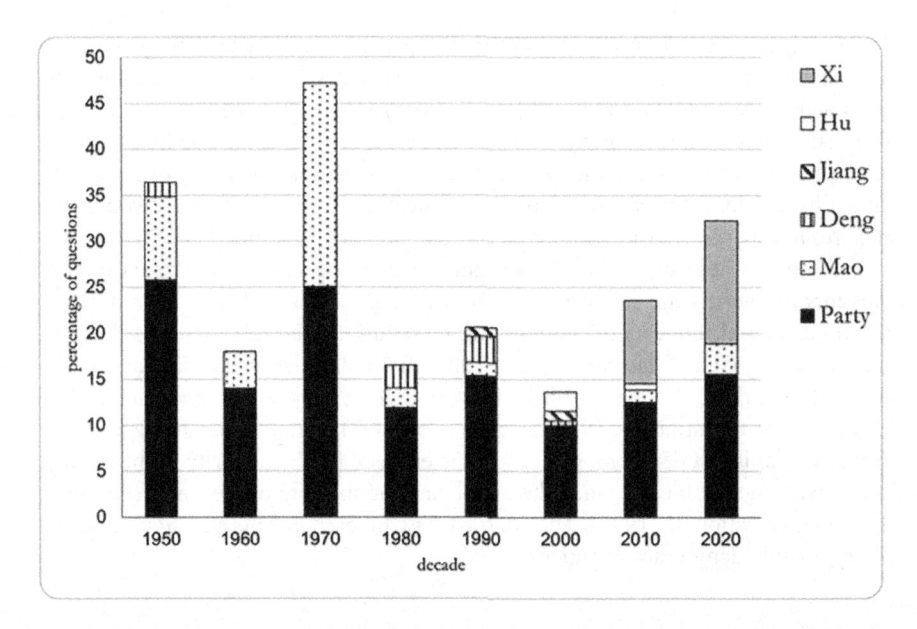

Figure 2.1 Chinese Leaders and Party Mention by Decade, 1951–2022
Source: Author

of truth, kindness and beauty in the hearts of students" because "correct values are important guides for young students to take a good life path" (Question 22, 2020). In another example, Xi is promoting the innovation of ideological and political work at colleges and universities to ensure these ideals take hold (Question 23, 2017). Xi's connection to youth is further evident in a question where he calls for a "spirit of labor among students" to develop a nation of "socialist builders and successors" (Question 26, 2022).

Xi is also depicted as a strong and confident leader guiding the Party. In one question, he calls on the Party to adhere to "the spirit of nailing." According to Xi, "We [the Party] must have the spirit of nailing. Sometimes, we cannot drive nails with only one hit. We must hammer again and again until the work is done. It is fruitful to do our work consistently" (Question 12, 2019). This construction metaphor reinforces the image of a driven Xi building a strong China, but also a leader firmly in charge of the Party.

Xi Jinping's steadfast determination is further developed in questions that focus on him as a problem-solver. Students, for instance, must explain how Xi's strategy of poverty alleviation will be manifested through "common prosperity" (Answer key, Question 15, 2017). Xi is credited with minimizing the impact of the COVID-19 epidemic (Question 11, 2021) as well as advancing Chinese scientific and democratic decision-making to "enhance China's soft power" (Question 20, 2016). Interestingly, Xi's leadership is portrayed as having global resonance. He is associated with China's peaceful rise and global influence. In one question, Xi says that China has risen and is a "peaceful, amiable, and civilized nation" that will bring the "world opportunities, rather than threats, peace rather than war, and progress rather than regression" (Question 20, 2014). Similarly, students need to explain why the Belt and Road Initiative advanced under Xi is adding "new positive energy to world peace and development" and helping "developing countries achieve regional economic integration" (Question 26, 2016; Question 18, 2020). The message is that Xi is an accomplished leader at home and respected abroad.

Another salient shift on the exam is the emphasis of Xi as "core" to the communist party. In 2017, two questions include the phrase, "*with Comrade Xi Jinping at its core*" to signify his position within the Party (Questions 15 and 16, 2017, *emphasis added*). As the core of the Party, students must demonstrate fluency with Xi's signature policies and developing ideology, such as knowledge of "Socialist Core Values," the "Chinese Dream," "Common Prosperity," and "Xi Jinping Thought on Socialism with Chinese Characteristics for a New Era" (Question 23, 2014; Question 20, 2014; Question 38, 2016; Question 21, 2018). Students are expected to know that Xi Jinping Thought is advancing Chinese socialism and solving problems that previous leaders (and their ideologies) have been unable to solve (Answer key, Question 21, 2018).

The prominence of Xi on the Gaokao raises a related question: How is the constitutional change that made it possible for Xi to remain as China's top leader addressed? The short answer is democracy. The exam asks students to explain "How amending the constitution illustrated our country's socialist democratic politics?" (Question 39, 2018) To answer this prompt, students are given a long passage about the amendment process that depicts it as deliberative and democratic. The process is outlined in several key steps, such as the Politburo establishing a working group to study the issue; the Central Committee soliciting opinions on amending the constitution and receiving 2,639 opinions. These opinions were then forwarded to relevant departments and to "people outside of the Party" for deliberation. Next, the Central Committee drafted a proposal for constitutional amendments and solicited opinions from within the Party, while Xi "presided over a symposium for people outside of the Party, to listen to opinions and suggestions." After all of these steps, the deliberate process concludes with the "National People's Congress voting to pass the constitutional amendment" (Question 39, 2018).

In summary, the constitutional change is described as not only transparent and democratic, but also the will of the Chinese people. The Central Committee solicited public opinion, and Xi actively listened to the suggestions of non-Party members. The answer key reinforces this point and notes that the Party "widely gathered wisdom from the people to form a consensus on amending the constitution, which reflect the organic unity of the Party's proposition and the will of the people" (Answer key, Question 39, 2018). Thus, the Gaokao signals that it is the will of the people that Xi remains China's top leader indefinitely.

Conclusion

The purpose of this chapter has been to examine how the Chinese authorities attempt to promote political allegiance among their youth. It used the Gaokao politics subject-test as a window into how political legitimacy is articulated and maintained over time. I argued that the Chinese leadership takes political education extremely seriously and uses it to politically orient young people (and future elite) favorably toward the Party. The analysis demonstrated that examination questions present an accountable and responsive Party – a communist party that is confident and capable, serving the people, and tackling even the most formidable obstacles. This pro-Party narrative is bolstered by a second narrative to orient students away from political and ideological competitors, especially the West, and particularly the United States. Questions shine a spotlight on Western imperialism and aggression, the exploitative nature of capitalism, and the hypocrisy of American elections. Here, the goal is to erode any support for alternatives to communist party rule.

There are several implications to this dual narrative. One is that it reveals what the Party fears and sees as potential threats to its legitimacy. Another is that offers new insight into how generations of young people are being taught to think about the rest of the world, especially the United States. A third implication is that it shows the complexity of political legitimacy in contemporary China. It is not enough to simply prop up and idealize the communist party; this must be balanced with the weakening of support for political and economic alternatives. In a context where China is asserting greater global influence and established democracies are facing erosion and a weakening of institutions, understanding how political legitimacy is constructed and undermined is essential.

The chapter also provided insight into general trends of political education in China. Gaokao questions have become less ideologically dogmatic and CCP accomplishments are less sensational. Western imperialism and aggression have shifted to Western protectionism, whereas capitalist democracy is seen as less responsive and representative than socialist democracy. These shifts are not by accident but by design, and they align with broader trends in Chinese thought work. Xi Jinping has argued that for contemporary propaganda to be persuasive, it must not look like propaganda but should "let the target of the propaganda march in the direction that you hoped, believing that it is the path he has chosen himself" (China Copyright and Media 2013). This is precisely the trajectory of political education reflected on the Gaokao. It is more nuanced, sophisticated, and worldly in building support for communist party rule.

The analysis also revealed important shifts in thought work under Xi Jinping. Most notable is the personification of Xi on the exam. Xi is not only depicted as a strong and determined leader, guiding China domestically and globally, but also is situated at the core of the communist party. These shifts are subtle, but nevertheless significant. They indicate that Xi Jinping is not simply depending on earlier strategies of political education to build support for communist party rule among a globally minded youth but is using political education to safeguard his position at the helm of the communist party and preempt potential challenges.

Up until now the chapter has focused on how the party-state uses political education to socialize youth, but we should not ignore the broader issue of how the lessons of political education are being received by Chinese students and whether they are successfully orienting youth toward the party-state and away from the

West. This is a tricky question to answer because political education does not operate in a vacuum and students are incentivized to reproduce "standard answers" on the Gaokao to increase access to higher education. Indeed, Martin Whyte has shown that the goals of thought reform often go unrealized as youth participate in political rituals but do not necessarily believe in them (Whyte 1974, 231). Along these lines, it is also not difficult to imagine that some Gaokao questions may also have unintended consequences. For instance, the undermining narrative designed to discredit Western political and economic systems may also encourage students to reflect more critically about the Chinese system. Questions critical of U.S. millionaires in Congress and not reflecting the American population or rumors of extramarital affairs and corruption could also be leveled at communist party leaders. Similarly, the focus on high unemployment in capitalist countries may also resonate with Chinese youth struggling to find jobs. In 2022, 19.9 percent of urban youth (16–24 years old) were unemployed (Huang et al. 2023).

Conclusively answering whether political education is cultivating regime stakeholders is beyond the scope of this chapter, but research on Chinese youth provides some answers. Research has shown that Chinese college students tend to dislike their political education classes. One survey found that "only 2.2 percent rated these courses highly, and another 15.8 percent said they were comparatively good, for a total of 18 percent" (Rosen 2010, 170–171). Another survey revealed that only 4 percent of students liked the mandatory courses "very much" and 17.6 percent "liked them somewhat" (Chen 2011, 26). If these results are any indication of how well political education is cultivating loyalty, it would seem that the Chinese government still has a long way to go.

Other studies have investigated whether political education is influencing perceptions of other countries and political systems. Here, the results are mixed. Wu (2012) finds that perceptions of Japan do not map with how the country is presented in school curriculum, and Chinese youth tend to resist anti-Japanese messaging embedded in political and ideological education. Similarly, Chen (2011, 25) reports that the majority of Chinese students like the U.S. political system (56.2%), including values of democracy and freedom, multiparty competition, and checks and balances on political power. These figures are all the more striking considering the same survey reports less than 30 percent of students have favorable opinions of the Chinese political system (Chen 2011, 26). In contrast, Cantoni et al. (2017) find that curriculum changes in political education are promoting more favorable attitudes toward the party-state, including trust in Chinese political institutions, governance, and socialist democracy.

If the effects of political education are uneven, why does the party-state continue to invest so heavily in it? One reason is that it may be difficult to dismantle. To eliminate political education from the national curriculum, which has been a core component since before the communist party came to power, may call into question China's socialist experiment and the legitimacy of the political project. This is too risky, especially considering what might fill this void and the implications for social stability. Another explanation is that all states use education to build support for the nation and the regime and China is no exception to this generalization.

China's response has been not to lessen political education, but to reimagine the curriculum and expand it in other arenas, such as media, film, and music (Cantoni et al. 2017; Repnikova 2017). It is also likely that the party-state is fully aware of the disconnect between political education and how youth perceive the Party and its competitors. Cultivating uncritical acceptance of the CCP is challenging, especially in an increasingly globalized and interconnected world. It is possible that the Chinese authorities are content with the younger generations being able to reproduce the Party's worldview – at least on the Gaokao – in hopes that most will comply with it, and some may even learn to share it.

Notes

1 This chapter draws from a larger book project, *Learning to Be Loyal: Political Education in Authoritarian Regimes*, which is a comparative study of political education in China and Russia.
2 "Deng Xiaoping Speech to the Martial Law Troops on June 9, 1989," translated and reprinted in the *New York Times*, June 30, 1989, section A, page 6.
3 On political education in the late Qing and Republican eras, see, especially, Zarrow (2015), Law (2011), and Culp (2007).
4 Generally speaking, political education is required in primary school and junior high, during two of the three years of high school, during the first two years of college, and the first year of graduate school. In schools for religious training, students are required to devote at least 30 percent of their studies to political education (Order No. 16, Measures for the Administration of Religious School, article 39, 2021).
5 The Gaokao was first offered as an experimental exam in 1951 and nationwide in 1952. The examination was suspended during the Cultural Revolution (1966–1976) when universities were closed and top leaders saw "the entrance exam as the 'flaw' in the 'revolution' of the cultural and educational spheres" (Zheng 2010 [1997], 17). Since 1977, this high-stakes examination has been offered annually; however, China's examination culture did not begin with the Gaokao. As early as the Sui Dynasty (581–618 CE), the imperial service examination (科举) was used to select capable elites for the civil service and served as a stabilizer for imperial rule (see, especially, Elman 2000, 2013; Feng 1995; Miyazaki 1976 [1963]; Yu and Suen 2005).
6 The Gaokao is currently offered each June, but before 2003 was taken in July. All students test in mathematics, Chinese, and English, but those seeking to major in the humanities (文科) take different subject-tests than those pursuing the sciences (理科). Currently, the humanities track tests only one of the three sciences covered on the exam (biology, chemistry, and physics) and the science track does not test in politics.
7 See, for example, "2013 Xin ke biao gaokao dagang [2013 New Standard General Guideline for the college entrance examination in humanities]" Zhongguo Jiaoyu Zaixian [China Education Online] 2013, available at: https://gaokao.eol.cn/gkdg/gedi/201303/t20130301_909724.shtml.
8 The caveat is that students may reproduce the "expected" answer to receive maximum points but not necessarily subscribe to the political message.
9 There is more than one official Gaokao, and some regions customize their exams to better align with local curriculum standards, which has led to the proliferation of examinations over time. In 2004, for example, 10 different versions of the Gaokao were offered nationwide and this increased to 16 in 2016 (Zhang 2016). In recent years, there has been an effort to limit the number of different exams. Chinese authorities still monitor the examinations and special attention is given to the politics subject-test to ensure that the political knowledge is standardized and reflects the core interests of the party-state.

10 Specifically, the national exams from 1951–1957, 1959–1965 and 1977–2022. Since the 1950s, the Gaokao has gone through various reforms and renaming. I use the politics subject-test of the National Unified Exam (全国统一考试) from 1951–1999. During this time, the exam was referred to by different names (全国高等学校招生政治试题, 全国高等学校招生政治常识试题, and 普通高等学校招生全国统一考试). In the 2000s, China experienced curricular reforms and the development of multiple Gaokaos; therefore, I use the New National Curriculum Examination (全国新课程卷) from 2000–2003 and the National Exam I (全国卷一) from 2004–2021. In 2022, National Exam I was renamed again (全国乙卷).

11 The politics subject-test assesses understanding of core themes of political education, such as philosophy, economics, political institutions, governance, law, culture, and current events. These themes are identified using political education textbooks, various outlines for the NCEE distributed by the Ministry of Education, and the *China Education Yearbook 1949–1981* (1984).

12 See, for example, "Order Signed by the President regarding the Acquisition of Four U.S. Wind Farm Project Companies by Ralls Corporation," The White House, Office of the Press Secretary, September 28, 2012, at: https://obamawhitehouse.archives.gov/the-press-office/2012/09/28/order-signed-president-regarding-acquisition-four-us-wind-farm-project-c.

13 Eleanor Randolph, "Bush Rumor Created Dilemma for Media," *The Washington Post*, 1988. www.washingtonpost.com/archive/politics/1988/10/22/bush-rumor-created-dilemma-for-media/c3cd7118-00ae-457d-9986-e12ccf820eea/.

References

Action Plan for Patriotic Education. 2006 [1994]. "Aiguozhuyi jianyu shishi gangyao." Reprinted in *Chinese Education and Society* 39(2) (March/April): 7–18.

Baldwin, Clare, and Nicole Li. 2015. "China's Third-Ranked Leader Says Pay More Attention to HK Youth." *Reuters*. March 5. www.reuters.com/article/china-parliament-hongkong/chinas-third-ranked-leader-says-to-pay-more-attention-to-hk-youth-idINKBN0M10F120150305.

Cantoni, Davide, Yuyu Chen, David Y. Yang, Noam Yuchtman, and Y. Jane Zhang. 2017. "Curriculum and Ideology." *Journal of Political Economy* 125(2): 338–392.

Chen, Shengluo. 2011. "Survey Study on Chinese University Students' Perceptions of the Political Systems of China and the United States." *Chinese Education and Society* 44(2–3) (March–April/May–June): 13–57.

China Copyright and Media. 2013. "Xi Jinping's 19 August Speech Revealed (Translation)." *China Copyright and Media*. November 12. https://chinacopyrightandmedia.wordpress.com/2013/11/12/xi-jinpings-19-august-speech-revealed-translation/.

China Education Yearbook Editorial Board, eds. 1984. "Zhongguo renmin zhengzhi xieshang huiyi gongtong gangling" [Common Framework for Chinese People's Political Negotiations]. In *Zhongguo jiaoyu nianjian 1949–1981* [China Education Yearbook 1949–1981]. Beijing: People's Education Press.

Culp, Robert J. 2007. *Articulating Citizenship: Civic Education and Student Politics in Southeastern China, 1912–1940*. Cambridge: Harvard East Asian Monographs.

Doyon, Jerome, and Konstantinos Tsimonis. 2022. "Apathy Is Not Enough: Changing Modes of Student Management in Post-Mao China." *Europe-Asia Studies* 74(7): 1123–1145.

Easton, David. 1965. *A System Analysis of Political Life*. New York: Wiley.

Easton, David, and Jack Dennis. 1969. *Children in the Political System: Origins of Political Legitimacy*. New York: McGraw-Hill.

Easton, David, and Robert Hess. 1962. "The Child's Political World." *Midwest Journal of Political Science* (6): 229–246.

Education Bureau. 2021. "Curriculum Framework of National Security Education in Hong Kong, the Government of Hong Kong Special Administrative Region of the People's

Republic of China." May. www.edb.gov.hk/attachment/en/curriculum-development/kla/pshe/national-security-education/nse_framework_en.pdf.

Elman, Benjamin A. 2000. *A Cultural History of Civil Examination in Late Imperial China*. Berkeley: University of California Press.

Elman, Benjamin A. 2013. *Civil Examinations and Meritocracy in Late Imperial China*. Cambridge: Harvard University Press.

Fairbrother, Gregory. P. 2003. *Toward Critical Patriotism: Student Resistance to Political Education in Hong Kong and China*. Hong Kong: Hong Kong University Press.

Feng, Yuan. 1995. "From the Imperial Examination to the National College Entrance Examination: The Dynamic of Political Centralism in China's Educational Enterprise." *The Journal of Contemporary China*: 28–56.

Hayhoe, Ruth. 1992. "Moral-Political Education and Modernization." In *Education and Modernization: The Chinese Experience*. Oxford: Pergamon Press, 211–238.

Hayhoe, Ruth. 1993. "Political Texts in Chinese Universities before and after Tiananmen." *Pacific Affairs* 66(1): 21–43.

Houn, Franklin W. 1961. *To Change a Nation: Propaganda and Indoctrination in Communist China*. New York: The Free Press.

Howlett, Zachary M. 2021. *Meritocracy and Its Discontents: Anxiety and the National College Entrance Exam in China*. Ithaca: Cornell University Press.

Huang, Haifeng. 2018. "The Pathology of Hard Propaganda." *The Journal of Politics* 80(3): 1034–1038.

Huang, Huizhao, Han Wenrong, Hu Xueyan, and Kelly Wang. 2023. "Solving China's Soaring Youth Unemployment." *Caixin*. March 16. https://asia.nikkei.com/Spotlight/Caixin/Solving-China-s-soaring-youth-unemployment.

Huang, Shiqui. 1992. "Restoration of National Unified College Entrance Examination in the People's Republic of China." *Examinational Comparative and International Studies* (January): 33–60.

Implementation Outline of Patriotic Education in the New Era. 2019. "Issued by the State Council of the Central Committee of the Communist Party of China." November 12.

Law, Wing-Wah. 2011. *Citizenship and Citizenship Education in a Global Age: Politics, Politics and Practices in China*. New York: Peter Lang.

Li, Ping, Minghua Zhong, Bin Lin, and Hongjuan Zhang. 2004. "Deyu as Moral Education in Modern China: Ideological Functions and Transformations." *Journal of Moral Education* 33(4): 449–464.

Li, Tian, Chao Huang, Yue Wu, and Ena Zhao. 2022. "Big Political Education Class: A Major Event in the Heart of the General Secretary." *Zhongqing zaixian: People's Daily*. May 22. http://news.cyol.com/gb/articles/2022-05/22/content_gP4b3slne.html.

Liu, Chuyu, and Xiao Ma. 2018. "Popular Threats and Nationalist Propaganda: Political Logic of China' Patriotic Campaign." *Security Studies* 27(4): 633–664.

Luo, Jiali, and Frederick C. Wendel. 1999. "Preparing for College: Senior High School Education in China." *NAASP Bulletin* (October): 57–86.

Merelman, R. Magaret. 1986. "Revitalizing Political Socialization." In *Political Psychology: Contemporary Problems and Issues*, ed. M. Herman. San Francisco: Jossey-Bass, 279–319.

Ministry of Education of the PRC. 2018. "The Ministry of Education Issued the Basic Requirements for Teaching Theoretical Courses on Ideology and Politics in the New Era." *moe.gov.cn*. April 13. www.moe.gov.cn/srcsite/A13/moe_772/201804/t20180424_334099.html.

Miyazaki, Ichisada. 1976 [1963]. *China's Examination Hell: The Civil Service Examinations of Imperial China*. Translated by Conrad Schirokauer. New Haven and London: Yale University Press.

Morris, Paul, and Edward Vickers. 2015. "Schooling, Politics and the Construction of Identity in Hong Kong: The 2012 'Moral and National Education' Crisis in Historical Context." *Comparative Education* 51(3): 305–326.

"Order No. 16, Measures for the Administration of Religious School [in Chinese]." 2021. Issued by SARA. *Chinese Government Web.* www.gov.cn/gongbao/content/2021/content_5623053.htm.

Paglayan, Agustina S. 2022. "The Historical Political Economy of Education." In *The Oxford Handbook of Historical Political Economy*, eds. Jeffery A. Jenkins, and Jared Rubin. Online edn, Oxford Academic, August 18. Oxford and New York: Oxford University Press. https://doi.org/10.1093/oxfordhb/9780197618608.013.45.

Reinoso, Peitong, and Karrie J. Koesel. forthcoming. "Church & State in Contemporary China: Securing Christianity." *Politics and Religion.*

Repnikova, Maria. 2017. "Thought Work Contested: Ideology and Journalism Education in China." *China Quarterly* 230(June): 399–419.

Rosen, Stanley. 1983. "Education and Political Socialization." In *Education and Social Change in the People's Republic of China*, ed. John N. Hawkins. New York, NY: Praeger, 97–133.

Rosen, Stanley. 2010. "Chinese Youth and State-Society Relations." In *Chinese Politics: State, Society and the Market*, eds. Stanley Rosen and Peter Hays Gries. New York: Routledge, 160–178.

State Education Commission. 2006 [1995]. "Notice on the Formal Promulgation of the 'Outline on Secondary School Moral Education' [Guojia jiaowei guanyu zhengshi banfa zhongxue deyu dagang de tongzhi]." February 27, 1995, reprinted in *Chinese Education and Society* 39(2): 21–36.

Truex, Rory. 2020. *The Party Is Me.* Unpublished Manuscript.

UNESCO Institute for Statistics. 2009. *Education Database.* http://data.uis.unesco.org/.

Vickers, Edward. 2009. "Selling 'Socialism with Chinese Characteristics' 'Thought and Politics' and the Legitimization of China's Development Strategy." *International Journal of Educational Development* 29: 523–531.

Vickers, Edward, and Paul Morris. 2022. "Accelerating Hong Kong's Reeducation: 'Mainlandisation', Securitization and the 2020 National Security Law." *Comparative Education* 58(2): 187–205.

Wang, Ming-Xiao, Tao Zhang, Miao-Rong Xie, Bin Zhang, and Ming-Qiu Jia. 2011. "Analysis of National Coal-Mining Accident Data in China, 2001–2008." *Public Health Reports* 126(2): 270–275.

Wang, Zheng. 2008. "National Humiliation, History Education, and the Politics of Historical Memory: Patriotic Education Campaign in China." *International Studies Quarterly* 52: 783–806.

Whyte, Martin King. 1974. *Small Groups and Political Rituals in China.* Berkeley: University of California Press.

Wu, Zeying Zena. 2012. "The Effects of Patriotic Education on Chinese Youths' Perceptions of Japan." Master's thesis. Lingnan University, Hong Kong. https://commons.ln.edu.hk/pol_etd/10/.

Xi, Jinping. 2014. "Xi Jinping's Speech at a Symposium in the Ethnic Primary School in Haidian District, Beijing." *People's Daily.* 30 May. http://cpc.people.com.cn/n/2014/0531/c64094-25088947.html.

Xinhua. 2008. "Li Changchun Attended the Work Conference on Strengthening and Improving Ideological and Political Theory Courses in Colleges and Universities" [李长春出席加强改进高校思想政治理论课工作会议]. July 9. www.gov.cn/ldhd/2008-07/09/content_1040644.htm.

Xinhua. 2010. "Various Regions Improve Ideological and Political Theory Courses in Colleges and Universities to Make Theories Closer to College Students" [各地改进高校思想政治理论课让理论更贴近大学生]. May 24. www.gov.cn/jrzg/2010-05/24/content_1612497.htm.

Xinhua. 2019. "Xi Stresses Ideological and Political Education in Schools." March 18. www.xinhuanet.com/english/2019-03/18/c_137905379.htm.

Xinhua. 2020. "Xi Jinping: Ideological and Political Courses Are the Key Courses to Implement the Fundamental Task of Lideshuren" [习近平：思政课是落实立德树人根本任务的关键课程]. August 31. www.xinhuanet.com/politics/2020-08/31/c_1126434567.htm.

Yan, Xiaojun. 2014. "Engineering Stability: Authoritarian Political Control over University Students in Post-Deng China." *The China Quarterly* 218: 493–513.

Ye, Biao. 2013. "Gaokao mingti gaige zhe" [College Entrance Exam Reformers]. *Southern Weekly*. June 6. www.infzm.com/content/91228.

Yurchak, Alexei. 2005. *Everything Was Forever, Until It Was No More: The Last Soviet Generation*. Princeton: Princeton University Press.

Zarrow, Peter. 2015. *Educating China: Knowledge, Society, and Textbooks in a Modernizing World, 1902–1937*. New York: Cambridge University Press.

Zeng, Jinghan. 2016. *The Chinese Communist Party's Capacity to Rule: Ideology, Legitimacy and Party Cohesion*. New York: Palgrave Macmillan.

Zhang, Yu. 2016. *National College Entrance Exam in China: Perspectives on Education Quality and Equity*. Singapore: Springer.

Zhao, Suisheng. 1998. "A State-Led Nationalism: The Patriotic Education Campaign in Post-Tiananmen China. *Communist and Post-Communist Studies* 31(3): 287–302.

Zheng, Ruoling. 2010 [1997]. "'Ju Guo Da Kao' de heli xing - Gaokao de shehui jichu gongneng yu yingxiang zhi fenxi [On the Rationality of the College Entrance Examination: Analysis of Its Social Foundations, Functions, and Influences] *Journal of Higher Education* 28(6) (2007): 33–37, translated in *Chinese Education and Society* 43(4): 11–21.

3 The Private Economy Under Party-State Capitalism

Margaret M. Pearson, Meg Rithmire, and Kellee S. Tsai

Since the initiation of "reform and opening" in the late 1970s, China's private sector has flourished, outperforming state-owned enterprises on multiple indicators. Indeed, the private sector has expanded well beyond the rather limited and weakly protected goals that early reform leaders envisioned: to raise incomes and employment in the rural sector, bolster flagging productivity, and fill gaps in weak, consumer-oriented industries (Naughton 2008). Having proved its worth, the private sector gained some legal protection in China's Constitution (2004) and developed into an important component of "market socialism with Chinese characteristics." Operating in parallel to the massive state-owned sector, private enterprises have been the primary source of productivity and employment gains in China since 1978 (Huang 2008; Kroeber 2016: 104). The contributions of private firms to the Chinese economy are often expressed in the shorthand phrase, "50/60/70/80/90," conveying that small and medium enterprises generate over 50 percent of the country's tax revenues, over 60 percent of GDP, over 70 percent of technological innovation, over 80 percent of urban employment, and over 90 percent of new jobs and firms (People's Republic of China State Council 2018a). Although Xi Jinping repeated this saying at a private entrepreneurs' symposium in a supportive spirit, within his first decade in office, the private sector's contribution to China's GDP declined by over 15 percent, going from 75 percent in 2012 to 60 percent in 2019 (Verma 2022). Meanwhile, state-owned enterprises (SOEs) became larger, more indebted, and less profitable (Lardy 2019). The Chinese Communist Party (CCP) also extended its reach into the economy through a variety of mechanisms. What accounts for these shifts in China's political economy? How have different segments of the private sector been impacted?

This chapter starts by reviewing the economic context that Xi encountered upon his assumption of power. Next, it delineates the ways in which China has evolved from a familiar form of state capitalism into a more politicized variant that we call "party-state capitalism" (Pearson et al. 2021). The main manifestations of this include the elevation of economic affairs into the realm of national security; rise of mixed-ownership enterprises; and enhanced party-state influence in firms through purchases of equity stakes. In combination, these practices have blurred the boundaries between private and state firms and triggered backlash from Western countries against Chinese firms operating abroad.

The Context for Prioritizing Risk Management

When Xi came into power in 2012, several trends seemed to pose an acute threat to the CCP's legitimacy and regime durability. The global financial crisis in 2008 already called into question the sustainability of China's export-oriented model as global demand plummeted and other countries offered lower wages for manufacturing. Corruption also seemed out of control. The newly appointed Xi thus declared that China had entered a "new normal" era of more modest growth and launched a vigorous anti-corruption campaign to take down venal cadres at all levels of government. At the Third Plenum of the 18th Party Congress in 2013, over 300 reform measures were announced, leading some observers to anticipate deeper liberalization. These early Xi-era expectations were not unwarranted. The Third Plenum's core document, "Decision on Major Issues Concerning Comprehensively Deepening Reforms," specified that markets would play a "decisive role" (*juedingxing zuoyong* 决定性作用) in allocating resources in the economy, an elevation from markets playing a "fundamental role" (*jichuxing zuoyong* 基础性作用) in prior policy communiqués. Private and mixed-owned enterprises were affirmed as "important" components of China's socialist market economy. Restrictions on sectors open to foreign direct investment and competition would be relaxed. Private entrepreneurs would be permitted to establish small and medium-sized financial institutions.

Yet the same Decision also emphasized that state-owned enterprises (SOEs) would remain the core of China's economy as "the dominant form of ownership." And more tellingly, a new Central National Security Commission was established to manage a wide range of perceived threats to domestic security and social stability. Unrest in Tibet and Xinjiang in 2008 and 2009, respectively, were proximate triggers for the establishment of this centralized security council. But several other structural challenges loomed as well, including inequality, industrial overcapacity, and local government debt. External events compounded the Xi administration's sense of insecurity, including the Arab Spring uprisings and Edward Snowden's revelations that the National Security Agency had hacked the Chinese telecommunications giant, Huawei. Taken together, these domestic and external developments contributed to the party-state's threat mentality and prioritization of a risk management strategy over the developmental, growth-seeking approach of the first three decades of China's reform era (1978–2008).

Scholars have long observed that PRC policy, including economic policy, tends to vacillate between phases of relaxation (*fang*) and tightening (*shou*), a hallmark of Mao Zedong that extended into the reform era (Baum 1996; Pye 1995). For the private sector, the "fang-shou" (放收) cycle leads us to expect periodic shifts in policy between liberalization and decentralization on the one hand, and constriction and (re)centralization on the other. Yet under Xi, we sense a hardening, a greater persistence of "shou" resulting from this threat mentality and institutional changes in the reach of the party-state into non-state firms in ways that might prove difficult to relax.

From State Capitalism to Party-State Capitalism

By the late 2000s, China's political economy had coalesced around a set of features associated with contemporary state capitalism (Naughton and Tsai 2015). Under state capitalism, the economy has a tiered structure, such that critical sectors are state-owned, aspirational strategic sectors benefit from targeted industrial policy, and the rest of the economy is fully marketized (Pearson 2005). At the apex of the economy, SOEs under the State-owned Asset Supervision and Administration Commission (SASAC) dominate strategic sectors such as finance, telecommunications, petroleum, shipping, and defense. Such firms are also large. State- and mixed-owned enterprises account for 130 of the Fortune 500 Global largest companies (Huang and Véron 2022). Meanwhile, China's four sovereign wealth funds (SWFs) rank among the top ten largest funds in the world. Although established to manage the country's vast foreign exchange reserves, the SWFs have been deployed to recapitalize domestic state-owned commercial banks in preparation for their initial public offerings (IPOs). State ownership at the "commanding heights" of the economy, coupled with directing state assets and industrial policy to promote national priorities, are core components of state capitalism. Yet the state neither owns nor plans the entire economy as under state socialism. Instead, especially since China's accession to the World Trade Organization (WTO) in 2001, most of the economy is open to market competition and foreign investment – and Chinese firms have a significant presence in global supply chains. By 2008, China had overtaken the US and Germany as the world's largest exporter (UNCTAD 2021).

Within this state capitalist context, private firms are active in all industries except for those monopolized by SOEs. Subject to market competition and fluctuations, private enterprises hold a dominant position in manufacturing, exports, retail (including e-commerce), and services. China's private sector is thus vast and segmented – encompassing conglomerates with diverse holdings, publicly-listed tech giants, property developers, and over 42 million micro, small, and medium enterprises (MSMEs) that contribute to 50/60/70/80/90 percent of China's key economic indicators (Chen and Shou 2019). The relative impact of China's transition from state capitalism to party-state capitalism is similarly differentiated. For example, the growth of party branches and expectations of political fealty have affected large private firms and multinationals operating in China more directly than MSMEs. Technology and data-intensive industrial sectors have also been subject to greater political and regulatory scrutiny than traditional labor-intensive manufacturing segments of the private economy.

Among China's largest firms, a core feature of party-state capitalism is the blurring of lines between state and private enterprises due to mixed-ownership reforms and financialization of the economy. The inefficiency of the state-owned sector has long vexed China's leaders and was a major impetus for the legitimation and massive expansion of the private sector. In the mid-1990s, the creation of SASAC intended to foster both efficiency in large SOEs and state control of these important industries. Yet as the goal of SOE efficiency remained elusive, government leaders sought other avenues. One important avenue was through "mixed ownership" reforms (*hunhe qiye gaige*, 混合企业改革). Originally proposed in 1999 (Decision 1999), the party has actively promoted "mixed ownership" since 2013, one year into Xi's tenure. The Fourteenth Five-Year Plan guidance released in 2020 further reiterated the goal of moving toward mixed ownership in a wide variety of sectors. While the precise parameters of mixed ownership have not been defined clearly or consistently (Naughton 2019, 179), the system is roughly defined as "cross holding by, and mutual fusion between, state-owned capital, collective capital, and non-public [private] capital" (Decision 2014). By allowing private capital to acquire minority stakes in SOEs, such partial privatization may make state capital more efficient. Mixed ownership also allows SOEs and state funds to take ownership shares in private enterprises. Investments of capital between state and private firms has been made easier by greater financialization of the economy, i.e., the greater role played by liquid capital investments, including through venture capital and state-owned capital investment companies. The impact of these reforms in terms of ownership statistics has been substantial. In March 2020, SASAC announced that 41.6 percent of SOE group holding companies and 62.7 percent of their subsidiaries had achieved "mixed ownership" by adding private shareholders (ASPI 2020).

Investments of minority shares by private capital into SOEs at first glance implies the dilution of state ownership and amplification of the private sector, as state ownership in MOEs has declined and private ownership increased. Yet the party-state can retain control absent majority ownership by either controlling interests in a legal person entity that itself controls an MOE, or by agreement that the state shareholder retains control via "golden" (overweighted) voting shares (Meyer and Wu 2014). This arrangement was highlighted in early 2023 when Beijing announced it was taking "golden shares" in two major technology platform companies, Alibaba and Tencent (Lockett and Leng 2023). The government's hand also can be strengthened when there are many private owners, each with a minority stake (Chiu 2019). This separation of ownership from managerial control blurs the boundaries between the state and private sectors, and marks a sharp departure from the previously longstanding idea that ownership was the main lever of control (Milhaupt and Zheng 2016).

Concurrent with the emergence of party-state capitalism, five main developments in the private sector during the Xi era distinguish it from the preceding decades of reform. First, certain private sector conglomerates were judged to constitute systemic risks and therefore found themselves targets of the regime's ire. Second, although private tech firms led China's digital transformation in a relatively lax regulatory environment, some of the largest tech firms were subject to a crackdown toward the end of Xi's second term. Meanwhile, societal problems such as corruption and inequality triggered ideological backlash against certain segments of the private sector in the name of "common prosperity." Third, the rise of the platform economy and internet finance created new opportunities for MSMEs. Fourth, the Covid-19 pandemic presented an unexpected shock to the economy. Finally, advanced industrial democracies introduced bans on Chinese products involving sensitive technology.

Risk Management of Private Sector Conglomerates

Xi Jinping inherited a political economy in 2012 that was home to many large non-state conglomerates. Sizable, diversified business groups and conglomerates are present in many developing economies, and scholars generally see these corporate forms as solutions to problems of institutional underdevelopment and debate their effect on overall economies (Leff 1978; Khanna and Yafeh 2007). As China's economy grew, particularly in sectors like finance and real estate, private sector firms also expanded in scale, and their connections to the state became more centralized (Wang 2016). Many of these large firms, such as the telecom giant Huawei or leading tech firms like Alibaba, had ties to the state and were regarded as national champions. Yet, especially under Xi Jinping, many large non-state firms came to be seen as undisciplined sources of social risk, and therefore became targets of the state's regulatory and coercive apparatus.

Measuring the size of Chinese non-state firms is difficult due to the idiosyncrasies of corporate organization. Because many of the largest companies are not listed, their financial data is unavailable. Many others are organized in ways that intend to obfuscate, with sprawling webs of related companies for which determining asset sizes and relationships is anything but straightforward (Rithmire and Chen 2021). In the aggregate, the share of the total revenue of Chinese Fortune 500 firms essentially doubled from less than 10 percent in 2010 to nearly 20 percent in 2020 (Huang and Véron 2022). The size of large firms has also increased in terms of revenues and corporate structure. Firms like Evergrande, Dalian Wanda, Fosun, HNA, and Anbang grew to comprise hundreds and even thousands of subsidiaries.

Over the course of the early years of Xi's tenure, several trends emerged that led the party-state to fix its sights on the behavior of large conglomerates. First, the anti-corruption campaign ensnared high- and low-level public officials with ties to large firms. Second, the debt burdens of many of these firms ballooned, often while they expanded rapidly overseas. Many of the most indebted firms, including Evergrande, were among those who had most expanded overseas and into what regulators would eventually call "irrational investments," meaning ones in leisure or real estate sectors rather than strategic sectors consistent with the state's strategies like infrastructure development or technology acquisitions (Rithmire 2022).

When stock markets in Shenzhen and Shanghai suffered a crisis in 2015–2016 and the RMB experienced a rapid devaluation when it floated in 2015, officials started to worry about financial risks in political terms. After initially welcoming a correction to the overheated stock market, regulatory authorities then signaled intolerance for an "overly rapid correction" and injected trillions of RMB into the market to arrest the slide in prices. In addition to this and other technocratic actions, Beijing began to crackdown on various participants in Chinese equity markets, arresting journalists, fining firms for participating in margin lending, and, eventually, targeting financial sector regulators for collusion with firms. For example, Xiang Junbo (项俊波), chair of the China Insurance Regulatory Commission since 2011, was expelled from the party in 2017 and accused of "colluding with financial predators" who "hunted" Xiang and other officials in the financial sector.

Xiang was connected with Anbang, a large insurance firm that was nationalized in 2018 amid accusations of illegal financing of overseas acquisitions and fraud in its domestic sales of insurance products (Yang and Han 2017).

In the aftermath of the equity market crisis, the regime sought to address financial risks. Xi and others began to speak of "grey rhinos" (*hui xiniu* 灰犀牛), meaning threats that pose systemic risk to the country's economic stability. Four large firms in particular – HNA, Dalian Wanda, Fosun, and Anbang – were large investors overseas, and came under official investigation in 2017 over their international expansions. Two of those firms, HNA and Anbang, were nationalized and dismantled over the next several years, and the other two began a process of unwinding their debt and international positions. Executives at HNA and Anbang were charged with financial crimes, and Fosun's flamboyant founder, Guo Guangcheng, was detained several times between 2015 and 2016, although never arrested or charged.

While some portrayals of the Xi era characterize the private sector as suffering as the "state" has advanced its economic power (Lardy 2019; Schubert and Herberer 2020), the fate of even these large conglomerates shows variation in how private firms have fared, as well as important limits on state power (Hou 2022). For firms like Evergrande or China Minsheng Investment Group (CMIG), the latter a private firm founded in 2013 at the request of the state to become "China's JP Morgan," financial overextension became a burden of the state. CMIG, because of mismanagement and self-dealing that may have resulted from a feeling of impunity with the state's blessing, entered state receivership in 2019, after only a few years of failed operations.

Evergrande's trajectory, both its expansion and troubles, underscore the "reciprocal dependence" (Culpepper 2015) between large private firms and the state. Evergrande grew out of the regime's particular configuration of economic institutions, namely the dependence of local governments on land sales and the eagerness of households to see their wealth grow through real estate investment (Rithmire 2017). As Evergrande became large in scope, it diversified into other sectors, invested abroad, and accessed domestic and international debt markets. But when the economy slowed during the pandemic and the real estate sector hit predictable troubles, Evergrande's problems became the CCP's to solve. The regime cannot let Evergrande and firms like it founder in markets because their fates are tied with the critical priorities of social and economic stability. China's version of party-centric "state capitalism," like financial capitalism in the West, nurtures firms that become "too big to fail."

It is easy to see the CCP's cascading crackdowns on various sectors – large conglomerates, large tech, tutoring, and so forth – as purely politically or ideologically motivated. But such a perspective is incomplete, as it overlooks the party-state's fixation with risk and resulting securitization of the economy. Responses to economic distortions and inequality also motivate Xi's administration. While these explanations are not mutually exclusive, viewing the private sector as the CCP's hapless victim elides its diversity and sources of power to constrain state behavior and generate problems for the regime.

Managing Perceived Threats to Stability and "Common Prosperity"

Following the 19th Party Congress in November 2017 and especially after 2020, the Xi administration adopted a number of policy positions that seemed to direct political attention, most of it negative, at individual sectors. Taken together, the various "crackdowns," some of which took the form of strict new regulations as others were more campaign-style, seemed to presage a more politicized environment for private sector activity. While popular accounts of Xi's "crackdown on everything" (Kuo 2021) emphasize ideology (Rudd 2022), we suggest that it is the regime's focus on risk management that underlies its apparent turn on many elements of the private sector.

As discussed earlier in the cases of large, indebted private firms, the financial instability of 2015–2016 gave the regime impetus to address financial risks. In addition to going after individual firms, the administration also initiated efforts to control risks in "shadow banking," or activities that expand credit but do not appear on the balance sheet of Chinese banks (Hachem 2018). Although the flow of credit to the private sector has grown significantly larger over time (from 125 percent of GDP in 2002 to 164 percent in 2018, according to data from the World Bank and the BIS), tight bank regulations restrict the formal supply of credit, and therefore many private firms continue to rely on shadow banking or informal finance (Collier 2017; Tsai 2017). The crackdown on shadow banking intended to limit risks in ballooning corporate debt, but also had the effect of slowing capital expansion to the private sector just as the CCP was attempting massive economic upgrading and innovation-driven growth. Perhaps ironically, the private sector's need for capital was one of the rationales given for the expansion of state investment in non-state firms (Xiao 2019).

The campaign to "sweep away black and evil" (*saoheichu'e* 扫黑除恶), or "*saohei*," began in early 2018 to target "gangs and evil forces," unmistakably close to Xi's erstwhile rival, Bo Xilai's, campaign in Chongqing in 2009–2010. While most of the propaganda associated with the campaign has emphasized organized crime and even violent crime as the targeted behavior, the campaign has extended to private sector entrepreneurs for nonviolent crimes such as illegal finance and the formation of "protective umbrellas" among business actors and officials to shield themselves from scrutiny (Hillman 2021). Practically, the campaign has underscored the liminality of private sector economic activity. Many "economic crimes," such as taking out illegal loans and colluding with local officials to access resources, were pragmatic compromises that entrepreneurs had to make to do business in China's inhospitable formal institutional environment.

In the year leading up to the 20th Party Congress and Xi's assumption of a third term in office, the administration became more proactive in reining in large firms and sectors that appeared problematic, whether for political, social, or financial reasons. Most notably, at least to international audiences, was the November 2020 suspension of Ant Financial's IPO. While commentators flocked to focus on the audacious personality and views of Jack Ma, the company's head, the stated reason for the suspension was the company's violation of financial regulations, for which it was later fined a historic $1 billion and forced to restructure. Critically, the company was governed and organized as a technology firm rather than a financial holding company, the latter deemed more appropriate for a firm holding more than $180 bn in assets under management. Next, the CCP targeted overseas listings of large Chinese firms with access to vast quantities of data on Chinese citizens, forcing the behemoth ride-hailing firm Didi (China's Uber) to delist from the New York Stock Exchange.

Other regulatory changes targeted entire sectors rather than individual firms. The tutoring and educational services industry, for example, was decimated following the sudden issuance of new regulations in July 2021. The so-called "Double Reduction" policy abruptly banned for-profit tutoring on school curriculum studies in grades one through nine, advertising for after-school tutoring, public offerings of shares in tutoring firms, and foreign capital investment in the sector. Further, the regulations prohibited private tutors from giving classes online or in unregistered venues (such as residential buildings, coffee shops, and so forth) (Ministry of Education 2021). The sector was essentially regulated away: within three months of the policy, two-thirds of tutoring centers in Beijing had closed. Giants like New Oriental and TAL announced they would pivot business approaches, the former using the talent of its pool of English teachers to sell agricultural products on e-commerce platforms.

The attack on the sector was viewed through the lens of "common prosperity" (共同富裕), Xi's slogan signaling that social equality concerns should drive economic policy-making and the efforts of firms. Indeed, the massive expense of resources on extracurricular tutoring has been a source of anxiety and ballast for China's hypercompetitive education ecosystem, privileging families with greater means and exacerbating the unwillingness of most families to have more than one child. The latter problem was felt with increasing acuteness as demographic trends showed a falling birthrate, compounding population and macroeconomic imbalances (Gietel-Basten 2022).

The private tutoring sector had also been a favorite of capital markets in the years preceding the crackdown, attracting significant investment and featuring rapid and highly profitable IPOs. Yet it was also plagued with scandals involving unqualified companies, uncertified teachers, and problematic collusion between K-12 teachers and for-profit companies (Zhang 2019). The 2021 regulations, in fact, followed a 2018 regulation that set out credentialing and permit requirements, required that classes end by 8:30 pm, and limited the ability of firms to charge fees for more than a three-month period (People's Republic of China State Council 2018b). These trends underscore that Xi's "crackdown on everything" was not merely an impulsive turn against the private sector writ large, but rather a culmination of attempts at regulating several complex and rapidly growing sectors that had important social impacts and seemed impervious to earlier government efforts at regulation.

Micro, Small, and Medium Enterprises During the Xi Era

While large private conglomerates and certain sectors deemed to be inconsistent with the goals of common prosperity were subject to disciplinary action and regulation by the party-state, MSMEs, the "50/60/70/80/90" backbone of China's private sector, have experienced a different economic and policy context from their high-profile counterparts. Starting in the early 2010s, the digital revolution transformed the terrain for China's private sector through the creation of new markets and financing opportunities. While petty trade and retail sales traditionally relied on face-to-face interactions, the advent of e-commerce and financial technology ("fintech") for digital payments enabled a new generation of entrepreneurs to establish and expand their businesses in a virtual space that reduced the need for travel, while developing commercial networks in an increasingly de-territorialized manner. Even local officials in traditionally less market-oriented regions became more supportive of private entrepreneurs operating in the new platform economy.

More specifically, Alibaba's Taobao (China's eBay) created a virtual marketplace for small-scale vendors to sell their products to consumers throughout the country. As selling on Taobao significantly reduced the transaction costs of attending trade fairs and renting public-facing retail space, rural household producers increasingly shifted to producing exclusively for online shoppers – to the point that new private categories of political economy emerged, called "Taobao Villages," "Taobao Towns," and even "Taobao Counties." Being designated a Taobao village requires being located in a rural area, annual village sales of at least 10 million yuan, and either 100 households or 10 percent of local households selling on Taobao. Alibaba launched the new model in 2009 with three Taobao villages. Five years later, there were 212, and by 2021, there were 7,023 registered Taobao villages (Zuo 2021). Most of such villages were initially concentrated in southeastern provinces, but in recent years they have grown more rapidly in central and western China.

The expansion of e-commerce coincided with the take-off in internet finance and fintech more broadly. During 2004–05, Alibaba and Tencent introduced their own third-party electronic payment systems (Alipay and Tenpay/WeChat Pay) that support online commercial transactions. Shortly thereafter, China's first peer-to-peer (P2P) online lending platforms in 2006–07 (CreditEase.com and Ppdai.com) and crowdfunding sites (DreamMore) were established. In contrast to Alipay and WeChat Pay, which enable businesses and individuals with bank accounts to send funds to one another, P2P lending platforms bypass the formal financial system by brokering online loans between businesses in need of funding and ordinary lenders and investors. P2P platforms appeal to both supply and demand in China's financially repressed environment. On the supply side, ordinary savers seeking higher returns than those provided by low deposit rates in banks welcome investment opportunities offering lucrative returns in a relatively short period of time. Meanwhile, small business owners seek start-up and working capital to expand their operations, but typically lack the collateral and credit history to access bank loans. In the early 2010s, P2P platforms proliferated in a lax regulatory environment. By mid-2016, the ratio of new P2P loans to bank loans peaked at 40 percent; the number of P2P platforms reached nearly 5,000 in 2017; and by May 2018, the value of outstanding P2P loans exceeded $200 billion (Duan 2020). The rapid rise of P2P lending not only helped alleviate the credit constraints of SMEs, but also boosted economic indicators such as urban employment, GDP growth, and tax revenues between 2014 and 2019 (Naysary and Daud 2021).

As with earlier forms of informal finance, however, the emergence of destabilizing risks from poorly managed and fraudulent P2P platforms led to waves of collapses, protests by investors who lost their life savings, regulatory crackdowns, and outright banning of P2P lending. The short-lived Ezubao platform (June 2014-December 2015) was the largest P2P collapse in China, as it managed to mobilize and lose 50 billion yuan (US$7.6 billion) from approximately 900,000 investors (Xin 2016). Ezubao and many other P2P platforms were in retrospect clearly Ponzi pyramid schemes promising unrealistically high returns. Meanwhile, other P2Ps closed down due to inept management, lack of regulatory oversight, and loss of local governmental support. In October 2020, Beijing cited financial risk as the official reason for abruptly suspending Ant Group's (Alipay and Ant Financial) expected $34.5 billion IPO. Ant subsequently complied with regulatory requests to separate Alipay from other financial services (Huabei – consumer credit, Jiebei – microlending, Yu E Bao – wealth management, Sesame Credit – credit scoring). Over two years after the thwarted IPO, in early 2023 the China Banking and Insurance Regulatory Commission authorized Ant's consumer finance unit (Huabei and Jiebei) to raise $1.5 billion in a restructured arrangement that made an entity owned by the Hangzhou city government the second-largest owner, leaving Ant holding a 50 percent share (Chen 2023). Such a resolution is characteristic of party-state capitalism. Rather than full nationalization, Ant's consumer unit became an MOE with partial ownership and oversight by a local government.

The Shock of Covid-19

The outbreak of Covid-19 levied an immediately harsh toll on China's GDP, which declined by 6.8 percent year-on-year during the first quarter of 2020 (Hale et al. 2020). It was the first time that the Chinese economy had contracted in four decades. The impact was more severe on private industrial enterprises than state-controlled ones in terms of value added, revenue growth, fixed asset investment, and exports (Huang and Lardy 2020). As in other countries, the pandemic disproportionately affected MSMEs in China, and microenterprises suffered the most from the sudden drop in demand in service sectors involving in-person contact such as tourism, catering, and hospitality. In manufacturing, lockdowns disrupted supply chains, constrained the supply of labor, and increased the price of inputs. Limited access to credit compounded these economic pressures. The 2017 restrictions on bank lending to microfinance intermediaries, coupled with the banning of P2P platforms in 2019, drastically curtailed non-banking sources of credit to MSMEs. The result was crushing for small businesses. As shown in Figure 3.1, within the first 11 months of 2020, 4.37 million micro and small enterprises had shut down ("deregistered") and the number of new business registrations plunged from 6.13 million in 2020 to 1.32 million in 2021 (Ji 2021). By the third year of the pandemic (2022) the situation remained dire; an AliResearch survey found that over 76 percent of MSMEs experienced a decline in sales revenues and a quarter of respondents with fewer than ten employees had gone out of business (Li 2022, 2).

Despite these hardships, those MSMEs engaged in e-commerce, including food delivery, were more likely to be resilient during the pandemic, as quarantined

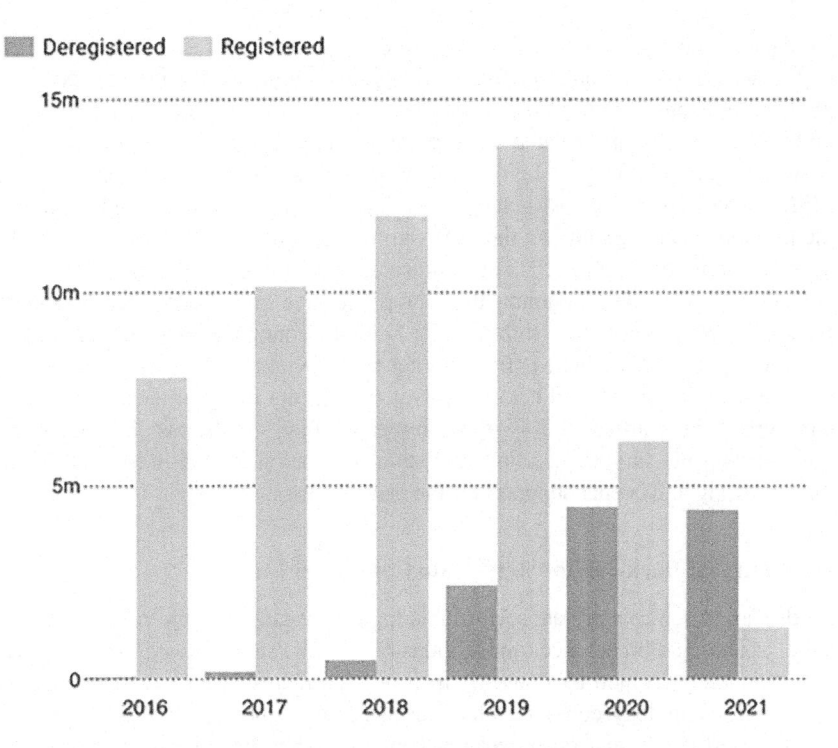

Figure 3.1 Registration and Deregistration of Small and Microenterprises, 2016–2021
Source: Ji (2021).

consumers shopped from their homes. The National Bureau of Statistics reports that between 2020 and 2021 China's online commercial transactions grew by 11.3 percent, with 13.09 trillion RMB in online sales (Ma 2022). By 2022, China had the largest e-commerce penetration rate in the world, with 46.3 percent of all retail sales occurring online (Coppola 2022). While the pandemic likely accelerated the shift of consumption from brick-and-mortar stores and restaurants to the platform economy, it also enhanced demand for online educational services and entertainment. Perhaps ironically, some of the targets of China's tech crackdown – online tutoring, gaming, and celebrity influencers – had flourished with the Covid-related lockdowns, school closures, and lengthy quarantining. In short, the combination of draconian pandemic policies with regulatory reactions to undesired social effects in the name of common prosperity had a devastating effect on China's private economy.

Societal frustration with the party-state's "dynamic zero-covid" policy reached a breaking point in November 2022, when at least 10 people died in a fire in Xinjiang due to lockdown measures. Protests spontaneously erupted in dozens of cities, both domestically and abroad – and the government abruptly lifted all pandemic control restrictions shortly thereafter. Following the unexpected outburst of societal discontent, and in light of rather dismal economic predictions about economic performance, the annual Central Economic Work Conference in December 2022 articulated several measures for economic recovery, including support for the private sector and platform economy. With both domestic and foreign (investor) audiences in mind, policymakers in Beijing flagged the importance of protecting private property rights, ensuring equal treatment of both the state and private sectors, increasing credit to MSMEs, and providing assistance to the struggling property sector. In contrast to the previous year's document, there was no mention of "common prosperity." The agenda-setting meeting for 2023 also indicated that China would join key economic and trade agreements, including the Comprehensive and Progressive Agreement for the Trans-Pacific Partnership and the Digital Economy Partnership Agreement (DEPA) to help SMEs benefit from digital trade (Xinhua 2022). If realized, these commitments would indeed help the private sector, but many of these policy goals have already been articulated – without implementation – in the past. It remains to be seen whether the similarities to a "*fang*-style" relaxation are followed through with longer-lasting and deeper supports for the private sector.

International Backlash to Party-State Capitalism

As discussed, China's private sector includes a wide range of enterprises, large and small, spanning a broad spectrum of industries. While small private firms were disproportionately harmed by domestic measures to address the Covid-19 pandemic, large high-technology companies have been deeply impacted by international tensions with the U.S. and other wealthy countries. They have been impacted by or faced serious challenge from backlash (Pearson et al. 2022). Indeed, contrary to expectations that economic interdependence promotes peace between countries, the activities of Chinese firms have become the locus of conflict between China and OECD countries, especially the United States. The emergence of party-state capitalism in response to perceived domestic and external threats has generated insecurity among countries with deep economic ties to China, causing these countries in turn to adopt measures to constrain Chinese firms. In recent years – and amplified under Xi Jinping – Beijing has expanded party-state authority in firms through changes in corporate governance and state-led financial instruments, and through laws that restrict the autonomy of Chinese companies on national security grounds. The Chinese government has further expanded efforts to enforce political loyalty by domestic and multinational firms to PRC political goals. In combination, these moves have increasingly blurred the distinction between state and private capital in China. This has resulted in a sharp backlash overseas. Prominent examples are U.S. government efforts to ban installation of Huawei equipment and sales of advanced semiconductor chips and equipment to Chinese-related firms, and to ban the Chinese-owned social media platform TikTok. More generally, the U.S. and other governments have intensified investment reviews, enacted policies to exclude Chinese firms from strategic sectors, imposed export controls on sensitive technology (e.g., semiconductors), and created new international institutions with allies to address perceived threats from Chinese actors. Under the justification of national security, these moves have stricken a sometimes-deadly blow to Chinese firms operating in sensitive areas.

Conclusion

The private sector remains an important source of growth and dynamism for the Chinese economy. Nevertheless, although private businesses have faced many discriminatory policies and operational obstacles throughout the reform era, the prioritization of political goals over economic growth under party-state capitalism and during Xi Jinping's tenure is redefining both the incentives and challenges for private entrepreneurs and the governmental actors that interact with them. A certain degree of mutual dependence and even cooperation in government-business relations continues in industrial sectors identified as critical for China's future. As indicated in the *Made in China 2025* industrial policy issued in 2015, these include aerospace and aeronautical equipment, biotech, new-energy vehicles, semiconductors, smart manufacturing, and so forth. However, businesses operating in industries that have experienced regulatory crackdowns have a greater sense of uncertainty. Compared with the 1990s and 2000s, the climate for private entrepreneurship and innovation has been tempered by various political campaigns, including Beijing's "dynamic zero covid" policy that lasted nearly three years from early 2020 to late 2022.

At the same time, another major policy shift under Xi, "dual circulation" (*guoneiguoji shuangxunhuan* 国内国际双循环), holds potential for supporting the private sector. The dual circulation policy, introduced in 2020, conceptually segments China's economy into a domestic consumption-driven economy ("internal circulation") and an economy that remains open to external trade and investment ("external circulation") (Xinhua 2020). Much commentary has focused on the ways in which the policy seeks to reduce China's reliance on external and therefore volatile sources of technology and growth. While external markets and inputs would remain important, policy should now amplify domestic consumption as a major driver of growth (García-Herrero 2021). Yet a concomitant goal of internal circulation is to guide China's economy away from fixed asset investment that favors SOEs and toward domestic consumption that, at least in theory, should favor private enterprises and the service sector. While the boost to the private sector from this policy is not yet clear, it is hoped to be a source of growth as China's economy recovers from the Covid-19 pandemic in a context where key international markets have become increasingly wary of Chinese firms.

References

Asia Society Policy Institute and Rhodium Group (ASPI). 2020 (Summer). "State-Owned Enterprise." *China Dashboard* 29. https://chinadashboard.gist.asiasociety.org/summer-2020.

Baum, Richard. 1996. *Burying Mao: Chinese Politics in the Age of Deng Xiaoping*. Princeton, NJ: Princeton University Press.

Chen, Guangjin, and Dan Shou, eds. 2019. *Zhongguo siying qiye fazhan baogao* [Report on the Development of Private Enterprises in China]. Vol. 7. Beijing: Chinese Academy of Social Sciences Publishing House.

Chen, Lulu Yilun. 2023. "Jack Ma's Ant Group Wins Approval for $1.5 Billion Capital Plan." *Bloomberg*. January 4.

Chiu, Dominic. 2019. "CSR 2019: Challenges to SOE Mixed Ownership Reform in China – A Case Study." *SAIS China Studies Review*. https://saiscsr.org/2019/10/30/csr-2019-challenges-to-soe-mixed-ownership-reform-in-china-a-case-study/.

Collier, Andrew. 2017. *Shadow Banking and the Rise of Capitalism in China*. London: Palgrave Macmillan.

Coppola, Daniela. 2022. "Countries with the Highest Share of Retail Sales Taking Place Online 2022." *Statistica.com*. October 11. www.statista.com/statistics/1042763/worldwide-share-online-retail-penetration-by-country/.

Culpepper, Pepper. 2015. "Structural Power and Political Science in the Post-Crisis Era." *Business & Politics* 17: 391–409.

"Decision of the Central Committee of the Communist Party of China on Some Major Issues Concerning Comprehensively Deepening the Reform." (English translation), January 16, 2014. www.china.org.cn/china/third_plenary_session/2014/01/16/content_31212602.htm.

"Decision of the Central Committee of the Communist Party of China on Major Issues Concerning the Reform and Development of State-Owned Enterprises." (English translation), September 22, 1999. www.lawinfochina.com/display.aspx?lib=law&id=991&CGid.

Duan, Jinhui. 2020. "5,000 P2P Companies Have Returned to Zero in Three Years: What Happened to Those Who Left?" *STCN*. December 1. Available in Chinese. https://news.stcn.com/sd/202012/t20201201_2583380.html.

García-Herrero, Alicia. 2021. "What Is Behind China's Dual Circulation Strategy." *China Leadership Monitor* (Fall) (69). Available at: SSRN. https://ssrn.com/abstract=3927117.

Gietel-Basten, Stuart. 2022. "Demographic and Social Anxieties: The Second Demographic Transition in Asia." *China Population and Development Studies* 6(3): 338–349.

Hachem, Kinda. 2018. "Shadow Banking in China." *Annual Review of Economics* 10(1): 287–308.

Hale, Thomas, Xinning Liu, and Yuan Yang. 2020. "China's Economy Shrinks for First Time in Four Decades." *Financial Times*. April 17. www.ft.com/content/8f941520-67ad-471a-815a-d6ba649d22ed.

Hillman, Ben. 2021. "Law, Order and Social Control in Xi's China." *Issues and Studies* 72(2) (June).

Hou, Yue. 2022. "The Evolving Relationship between the Party and the Private Sector in the Xi Era." In *The Party Leads All: The Evolving Role of the Chinese Communist Party*, eds. Jacques deLisle and Guobin Yang. Washington, DC: Brookings Institution Press, 211–236.

Huang, Tianlei, and Nicholas R. Lardy. 2020. "Bias against Private Sector Slows China's Recovery from COVID-19." *PIIE China Economic Watch*. April 28. www.piie.com/blogs/china-economic-watch/bias-against-private-sector-slows-chinas-recovery-covid-19.

Huang, Tianlei, and Nicolas Véron. 2022. "China's Top Ranked Corporations Are Not as Opaque as They May Seem." *PIIE*. July 18. www.piie.com/blogs/realtime-economic-issues-watch/chinas-top-ranked-corporations-are-not-opaque-they-may-seem.

Huang, Yasheng. 2008. *Capitalism with Chinese Characteristics: Entrepreneurship and the Chinese State*. New York: Cambridge University Press.

Ji, Siqi. 2021. "China's Smallest Firms Failing at Historic Pace as 4.37 Million Close Up Shop and Registrations Plummet." *South China Morning Post*. December 30. www.scmp.com/economy/china-economy/article/3161554/chinas-smallest-firms-failing-historic-pace-437-million-close.

Khanna, Tarun, and Yishay Yafeh. 2007. "Business Groups in Emerging Markets: Paragons or Parasites?" *Journal of Economic Literature* 45(2): 331–372.

Kroeber, Arthur R. 2016. *China's Economy: What Everyone Needs to Know*. New York: Oxford University Press.

Kuo, Lily. 2021. "Xi Jinping's Crackdown on Everything Is Remaking Chinese Society." *Washington Post*. November 16. www.washingtonpost.com/world/asia_pacific/china-crackdown-tech-celebrities-xi/2021/09/09/b4c2409c-0c66-11ec-a7c8-61bb7b3bf628_story.html.

Lardy, Nicholas. 2019. *The State Strikes Back: The End of Economic Reform in China?* Washington, DC: Peterson Institute for International Economics.

Leff, Nathaniel. 1978. "Industrial Organization and Entrepreneurship in the Developing Countries: The Economic Groups." *Economic Development and Cultural Change* 26(4): 661–675.

Li, Gan. 2022. *Challenges, Responses, and Transformation of MSMEs in the Post-Pandemic Era*. Research for MSME Day 2022. Alibaba.com x AliResearch.

Lockett, Hudson, and Cheng Leng. 2023. "China Tech Stocks Stage $70bn Recovery Rally." *Financial Times*. January 27. www.ft.com/content/65e60815-c5a0-4c4a-bcec-4af0f76462de?segmentId=114a04fe-353d-37db-f705-204c9a0a157b.

Ma, Yihan. 2022. "Online Shopping Market Gross Merchandise Volume in China, 2015–2021." *Statistica.com*. October 7. www.statista.com/statistics/278555/china-online-shopping-gross-merchandise-volume/.

Meyer, Marshall W., and Changqi Wu. 2014. "Making Ownership Matter: Prospects for China's Mixed Ownership Economy." In *Paulson Policy Memorandum*. Chicago: Paulson Institute. https://macropolo.org/wp-content/uploads/2017/05/PPM_Making-Ownership-Matter_Meyer-and-Wu_English_R.pdf.

Milhaupt, Curtis J., and Wentong Zheng. 2016. "Why Mixed-Ownership Reforms Cannot Fix China's State Sector." *Paulson Policy Memorandum* 5(11). www.paulsoninstitute.org/wp-content/uploads/2016/01/PPM_SOE-Ownership_Milhaupt-and-Zheng_English.pdf.

Ministry of Education. 2021. "Opinions on Further Reducing the Burden of Homework and Off-Campus Training for Compulsory Education Students" (关于进一步减轻义务教育阶段学生作业负担和校外培训负担的意见). July 21. www.moe.gov.cn/jyb_xxgk/moe_1777/moe_1778/202107/t20210724_546576.html.

Naughton, Barry. 2008. "A Political Economy of China's Economic Transition." In *China's Great Transformation*, eds. Loren Brandt and Thomas G. Rawski. New York: Cambridge University Press, 91–135.

Naughton, Barry. 2019. "Financialisation of the State Sector in China." In *China's Economic Modernization and Structural Changes: Essays in Honour of John Wong*, eds. Yongnian Zheng and Sarah Y. Tong. Singapore: World Scientific, 167–185.

Naughton, Barry, and Kellee S. Tsai. 2015. "State Capitalism and the Chinese Economic Miracle." In *State Capitalism, Institutional Adaptation, and the Chinese Miracle*, eds. Barry Naughton and Kellee S. Tsai. New York: Cambridge University Press, 1–24.

Naysary, Babak, and Siti Nurbaayah Daud. 2021. "Peer to Peer Lending Industry in China and Its Implication on Economic Indicators: Testing the Mediating Impact of SMEs Performance." *International Journal of Financial Research* 12(2): 106–114.

Pearson, Margaret. 2005. "The Business of Governing Business in China: Institutions and Norms of the Emerging Regulatory State." *World Politics* 57(2): 296–322.

Pearson, Margaret, Meg Rithmire, and Kellee S. Tsai. 2021. "Party-State Capitalism in China." *Current History* 120(827) (September): 207–213.

Pearson, Margaret, Meg Rithmire, and Kellee S. Tsai. 2022. "China's Party-State Capitalism and International Backlash: From Interdependence to Insecurity." *International Security* 47(2): 135–176.

People's Republic of China State Council. 2018a. "Liu He Presided over the First Meeting of the State Council Leading Group for Promoting the Development of Small and Medium-Sized Enterprises." August 20. www.gov.cn/guowuyuan/2018-08/20/content_5315204.htm.

People's Republic of China State Council. 2018b. "Office of the State Council's Opinions on Regulating the Development of After-School Tutoring Centers" (国务院办公厅关于规范校外培训机构发胀的意见). August 22. www.gov.cn/zhengce/content/2018-08/22/content_5315668.htm.

Pye, Lucian W. 1995. "Chinese Politics in the Late Deng Era." *The China Quarterly* 142: 573–583.

Rithmire, Meg. 2017. "Land Institutions and Chinese Political Economy: Institutional Complementarities and Macroeconomic Management." *Politics & Society* 45(1): 123–153.

Rithmire, Meg. 2022. "Going Out or Opting Out? Capital, Political Vulnerability, and the State in China's Outward Investment." *Comparative Politics* 54(3): 477–499.

Rithmire, Meg, and Hao Chen. 2021. "The Emergence of Mafia-Like Business Systems in China." *China Quarterly* 248(1) (December): 1037–1058.

Rudd, Kevin. 2022. "The World According to Xi Jinping: What China's Ideologue in Chief Really Believes." *Foreign Affairs* 101(8).

Schubert, Gunter, and Thomas Herberer. 2020. "State-Business Relations under Xi Jinping." In *Chinese Politics and Foreign Policy under Xi Jinping*, eds. Arthur S. Ding and Jagannath P. Panda. London: Routledge, Ch. 5.

Tsai, Kellee S. 2017. "When Shadow Banking Can Be Productive: Financing Small and Medium Enterprises in China." *Journal of Development Studies* 53(12): 2005–2028.

UNCTAD. 2021. "China: The Rise of a Trade Titan." *UNCTAD*. April 27. https://unctad.org/news/china-rise-trade-titan.

Verma, Raj. 2022. "Increasing Centralisation in China: A Bane for Economic Growth." *Asian Affairs* (September): 1–21.

Wang, Yuhua. 2016. "Beyond Local Protectionism: State-Business Relations in the Last Two Decades." *China Quarterly* 226: 319–341.

Xiao, Gang. 2019. "Manage the Pace and Intensity of Risk Management and Promote the Healthy Development of the Asset Management Industry – Report for the 2019 China Wealth Management 50 Forum." *Xinhua News*. August 20. www.xinhuanet.com/money/2019-08/20/c_1124896522.htm.

Xin, Zhou. 2016. "China's HK$59 Billion Online Ponzi Scheme: Who Started It, How Did It Happen and Now What?" *South China Morning Post*. February 1. www.scmp.com/news/china/money-wealth/article/1908096/chinas-hk59-billion-online-ponzi-scheme-who-started-it-how.

Xinhua. 2020. "Xi Jinping Chairs the Meeting of Standing Committee of the Political Bureau of the CPC Central Committee." *Xinhua Net*. May 14. www.xinhuanet.com/politics/leaders/2020-05/14/c_1125986000.htm (accessed January 3, 2023).

Xinhua. 2022. "Update: China Holds Central Economic Work Conference to Plan for 2023." *Xinhua Net*. December 17. https://english.news.cn/20221217/134fd89613434a8c9459c9da3ddc3a2a/c.html (accessed January 7, 2023).

Yang, Qiaolong, and Han Wei. 2017. "Special: What to Watch for at the End of Xiang Junbo's Five Years at the Insurance Regulatory Commission" (特稿：项俊波保监会五年落幕有看点). *Caixin*. April 10.

Zhang, Wei. 2019. "Regulating Private Tutoring in China: Uniform Policies, Diverse Responses." *ECNU Review of Education* 2(1). https://journals.sagepub.com/doi/full/10.1177/2096531119840868.

Zuo, Chenming. 2021. "The List of Taobao Villages in 2021 Has Been Released, and the Number of Taobao Villages Across the Country Has Exceeded 7,000." *AliResearch*. October 12. Available in Chinese. www.aliresearch.com/ch/information/informationdetails?articleCode=256317657652006912&type=%E6%96%B0%E9%97%BB#:~:text=2021%E5%B9%B4%EF%BC%8C%E5%85%A8%E5%9B%BD28%E4%B8%AA,%E5%85%B7%E6%9C%89%E8%BE%83%E5%A4%A7%E6%BD%9C%E5%8A%9B%E7%A9%BA%E9%97%B4%E3%80%82.

4 Xi Jinping's Partnership with Technology Companies and Social Media Platforms

Daniela Stockmann and Ting Luo

Contrary to conventional wisdom, even Xi Jinping, who is often depicted in the media and pundit world as having centralized control over nearly every dimension of Chinese governance, still must rely on powerful technology corporations to carry out his will in the increasingly important Internet sector. This suggests a model of political control significantly more nuanced than most observers realize.

In this chapter, we argue that Xi Jinping does not rule the Internet and more specifically social media via a tight command-and-control structure, which implies that he is the ultimate decision-maker and companies simply implement his policy decisions. Instead, we argue – and demonstrate based on empirical evidence – that China's governance of the Internet is best understood as a corporate management model, whereby the Chinese state engages in a partnership with technology companies. Xi Jinping assumes a leadership role enforced by state instruments of control and cooptation strategies. At the same time, the state remains dependent on companies due to their platform power, expertise, and knowledge. As we will show, the foundation for this relationship was laid well before the Xi Jinping years.

We start to lay out this argument by critically assessing the claim that China's tightened control over the Internet is associated with Xi Jinping as General Secretary of the Chinese Communist Party (CCP). As is widely known, the Chinese state has separated its domestic information flows from the World Wide Web via the Great Firewall of China. Within the Chinese Internet, the state plays a crucial role in passing directives to technology companies that are then in charge of blocking, deleting, and filtering content online. Under Xi Jinping many observers have noted the tightened screws that his leadership has exerted over traditional media as well as the Internet. By the time Xi was re-appointed at the 20th Party Congress in 2022, Freedom House had noted an increase in Internet control by 6 points since his original appointment in 2013. Since these changes have coincided with a strengthening of his leadership within the party to him as a person (Shirk 2018), many observers have attributed tightened Internet control to Xi Jinping as a ruler. Here we critically examine this claim.

In order to understand exactly what difference Xi Jinping has made, we need to take a closer look at the changes in the relationship between technology companies and state institutions over time. Here we systematically compare Internet governance under the leadership of Hu Jintao and Xi Jinping. To lay the foundation for our inquiry, we first present needed information about the composition of Chinese Internet users based on nationally representative survey data. Since our chapter concentrates on content control, we focus on use of the Internet to share and obtain information about politics. These data allow us to assess which technology companies had the largest reach in terms of political information flows under the two consecutive leaderships. We then systematically investigate Hu and Xi's Internet Governance Strategies. As we will show, even under the more tightly controlled rule of Xi Jinping, Chinese state authorities were dependent on key corporate actors. In contrast to conventional wisdom, the Chinese state under Xi Jinping has entered a partnership with technology companies in order to exert control over political information online. While Xi's personal influence is noticeable with respect to his vision for the Chinese Internet, the foundation for the state's partnership with technology companies was laid before his rule. Under Xi's rule the partnership evolved to concentrate on the so-called tech giants. To support Xi's vision, government-directed investment was distributed in a more structured manner and on an unprecedented scale. A selected group of technology companies, including Tencent, Baidu, Alibaba, and Sina, received preferential treatment for funding, licensing, and support to expand business abroad. Even after China's crackdown on these companies, dependency remains. Without these companies Xi's vision cannot be achieved, making him resemble less a dictator than a corporate manager.

Political Information Flows

As is widely known, China has the largest number of Internet users in the world with growing numbers. As shown in Figure 4.1, the percentage of Internet users has grown exponentially between 2000 and 2021, according to official data from the China Network Information Center (CNNIC). These data are widely used by scholars and journalists to describe Chinese Internet users. In 2018 we conducted the nationally representative China Internet Survey (CIS). The CIS relied on GPS random sampling to interview Chinese permanent residents aged 18 to 65 years face-to-face in mainland China. These survey data allow us to draw representative conclusions about Internet users and non-Internet users in mainland China. In contrast to common wisdom, the CIS (indicated in a gray bar) shows that Internet use has been significantly underestimated. In 2018, CNNIC estimated that 56% of the Chinese population were Internet users, while the CIS 2018 estimated that 73% of the Chinese population used the Internet in 2018.[1]

While it is well known that WeChat has become the most popular platform in China, it had already covered *all* users by 2018. 99% of Internet users self-reported using WeChat, an instant messenger with Facebook-like features. QQ was China's second most used platform and yet had a far lower percentage of users, at 64%. Livestreaming platforms, despite being relatively new, quickly rose to the third place in terms of popularity with 52% of Internet users in 2018. About half of Internet users used Baidu Wiki and the YouTube-like platform Youku. The once-popular Twitter-like platform Weibo had gone through a noticeable decline (Xu and Benney 2018). The CIS also confirms this decline, estimating 21% of Internet users used the platform. Platforms built around interest groups, Tieba and Douban, had

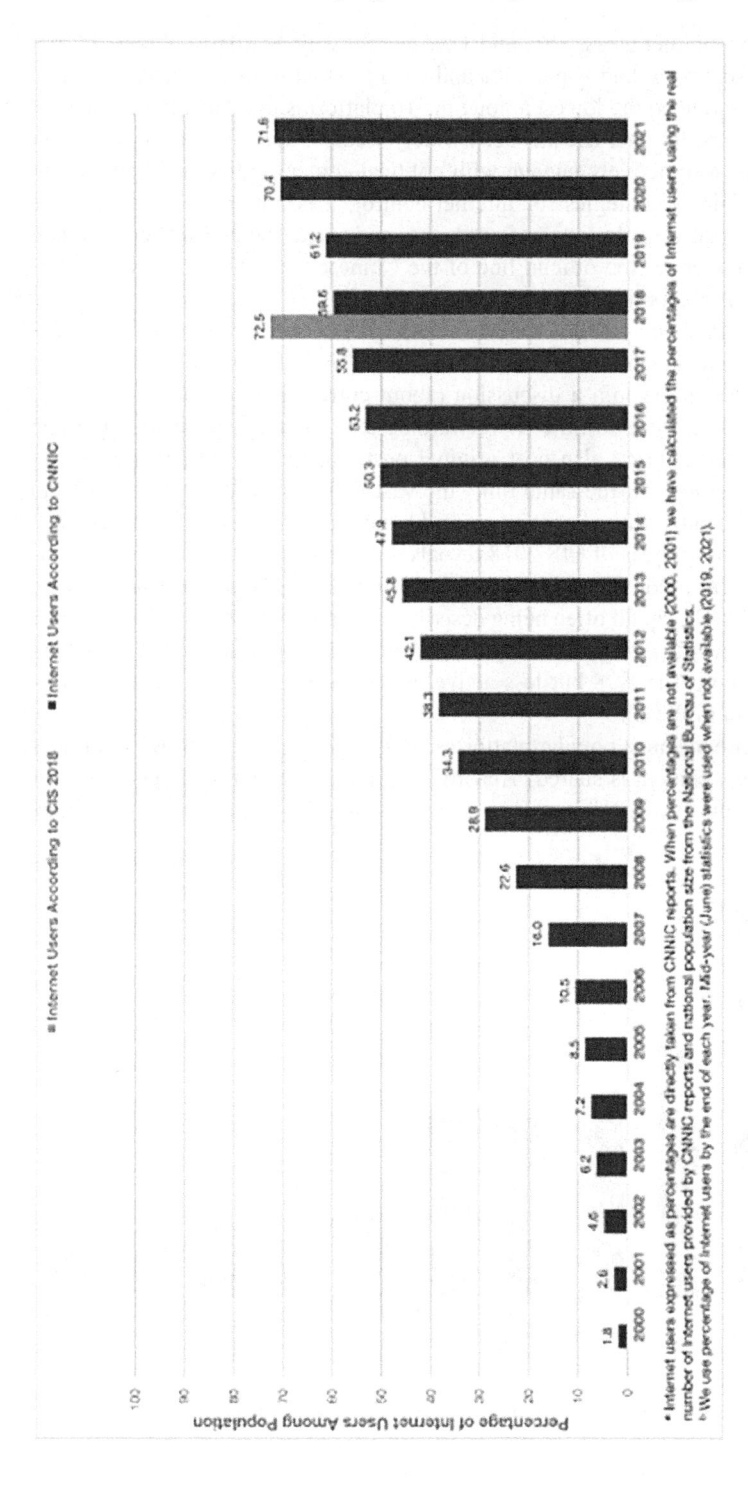

Figure 4.1 Percentage of Internet Users in China, 2000–2021

Sources: CNNIC 2002; Stockmann and Luo 2018 (conducted by the authors)

relatively few internet users, 15% and 12% respectively. Similarly, Zhihu, a Q&A forum, and Sina blog, had about 14% and 13% Internet users respectively. These four platforms ranked the lowest among the 10 platforms in terms of popularity.

While general Internet use has been widely studied, much less is known about Internet users who actively engage with political content online in China. Yet to understand China's strategies for Internet control, it is important to identify the most popular platforms in terms of producing and spreading political content that potentially challenges the official line of the Chinese Communist Party and thus may destabilize the political system.

Despite China being famous for censorship, a significant proportion of Chinese Internet users engage in online political discussion. According to CIS 2018, about 15% of Internet users join a discussion (about current political affairs or social "hot" issues) from time to time by forwarding and commenting, while only one percent of Internet users also post original posts (about current political affairs or social hot issues). At the same time, the vast majority of Internet users (84%) actively "lurk" into political content created largely by this small minority online.

Our in-depth analysis of CIS 2018 reveals that the minority producers of political content were predominantly located in Shanghai, Hebei, and Henan. Despite Beijing as China's capital often being described as a highly political place, our data revealed that people living in Beijing, at least in 2018, were quite active producers of political content (17%), but less active in comparison to other places (Stockmann and Luo In Press).

So, what are the most popular platforms, and which companies provide services where political content is shared? According to the CIS, the most important technology company as of 2018 was Tencent, with about 73% of producers of political

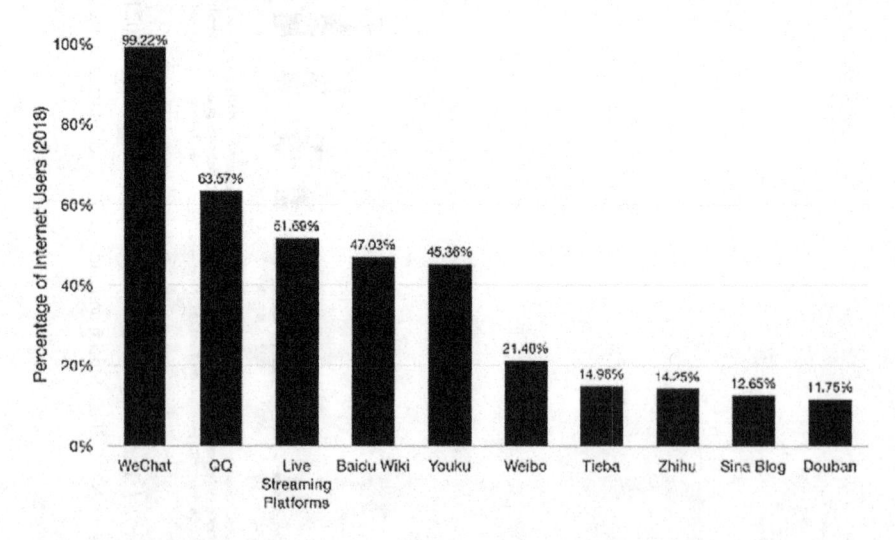

Figure 4.2 Percentage of Internet Users Using Social Media Platforms
Sources: China Internet Survey 2018 (conducted by the authors)

information posting, forwarding, and commenting on politics on WeChat, and 25% on QQ. All other platforms, including Sina Weibo and Baidu Tieba, were used by less than 12% (Stockmann and Luo In Press). Clearly, during the Xi years, Tencent had developed into the most important technology company in terms of operating the two main platforms generating political information flows. However, Sina and to a lesser extent Baidu also remained important players.

These patterns significantly differ from the years prior to Xi's appointment, where Internet users largely relied on websites, BBS chat forums, blogs, and QQ for obtaining and producing political information (Stockmann 2015). During China's early stages of Internet development more organizations (not all of them companies) operated platforms and not one player, like Tencent, had developed a monopoly. With the emergence of WeChat shortly before Xi Jinping took office, political content moved from publicly visible platforms (blogs, Weibo, and websites) toward WeChat, which keeps information private. This shift in web3.0 technology also increased the ability of governmental control over what interests, issues, and values were publicly visible (Creemers 2017). As we will see, this shift in technology coincides with different approaches toward managing political content online between Hu and Xi.

Internet Governance Strategies Under Hu Jintao

Internet governance has been broadly defined at the World Summit on the Information Society in 2001 as the principles, norms, rules, decision-making procedures, and programs that shape the evolution and utilization of the Internet (Kurbalija 2010). Our focus here is on what Benkler (2006) referred to as the content layer comprising content shared and exchanged within the network and data about users. As explained earlier, content control in China, as in other regions of the world, is largely implemented by companies who have accepted their role as "proxy censors" (Hintz 2016), whereby they invest training, staff, and funding into implementing government requests. To compare the Chinese government's strategy toward Internet governance systematically over time, we first explain the broader vision of the state for the Internet, followed by an examination of the toolbox in the hands of the state and companies to shape content control.

Hu Jintao's Vision of the Internet

Under the leadership of Hu Jintao, the central government clearly recognized that the Internet was simultaneously "vital and dangerous" (MacKinnon 2011, 37). According to the 2010 government white paper (State Council 2010), the Internet could promote economic growth to ensure long-term global economic competitiveness but also satisfy societal needs for information, provide convenient and cheaper access to commercial services and products, and improve government services. At the same time, the government emphasized the need to ensure information security crucial to national security. This led to a bifurcated strategy toward managing online information flows.

On the one hand, the government promoted online participatory space by loosening control and encouraging citizen participation. The Internet could provide citizens with convenient access to government information and services while also allowing the government to receive feedback on government policies and goals from citizens, hence increasing the government's organizational efficiency (Ding 2009; Kluver 2005; MacKinnon 2011; Noesselt 2014). New ways of bottom-up reporting by citizen journalists on issues like corruption were deemed helpful in controlling local officials (Cairns 2017). Both Hu Jintao and Wen Jiabao publicly emphasized the importance of collecting online public opinion on government policies and goals and helping the government initiate and modify policies and address social problems (Lin 2006). So-called "public opinion supervision" (*yulun jiandu* 舆论监督) provided opportunities for citizens to speak their minds. Such expressions of online public opinion were thought to strengthen the CCP's legitimacy in the eyes of China's population (Kluver 2005) and to avoid large-scale uprisings (Qiang 2011).

On the other hand, the government expanded its focus on censorship to a more sophisticated strategy of public opinion guidance (*yulun yindao* 舆论引导). Censorship tied into Hu's narratives of "building a harmonious society" envisioned an orderly political and social environment with regained morale, which was necessary to counter social divide, discontent, and tensions (Wang et al. 2016). In 2007, at a Politburo study meeting, Hu stressed that to strengthen the administration and development of the country's Internet culture, the party must maintain a dominant position on online public opinion and continue to improve its skills in guiding public opinion online. The party must also advocate civilized online space and purify the Internet environment (Xinhua News Agency 2007). On strengthening public opinion guidance, paid web commentators, now known as the fifty-cent party, were an innovation under the Hu leadership to actively channel and shape online public discussion in the direction favorable to the government (Bandurski 2008). Similarly, official online media, such as Xinhuanet and People's Net, as the mouthpieces of the party were expected to lead and guide online public opinion, as Hu had emphasized in his visit to *People's Daily* in 2008 (Li 2008). On purifying the Internet environment, the government built an extensive system for Internet surveillance and censorship, which included configuration of Internet gateway infrastructure (Boas 2006), a sophisticated system of Internet filtering (Zittrain and Edelman 2003), Internet policing (Brady 2007), and regulation of Internet service providers (MacKinnon 2009).

Hu's shift toward tightening public opinion guidance became evident after the Arab Spring and Wenzhou train collision in 2011 (Cairns 2017). To our knowledge, this shift was based on a consensus emerging amongst the CCP leadership instead of being pushed by individual leaders. Toward the end of the Hu leadership, the Beijing Municipal government was already initiating real-name registration rules for microblog service providers in December 2011 (Global Times 2012). This was the starting point of a series of legal provisions which were passed mostly under the Xi leadership but rooted at the end of the Hu administration.

Institutional Structure

Built after the Soviet model, the Chinese state comprises territorial divisions at the center, province, city, county, and township. It is composed of numerous government and Communist Party units (commissions, ministries, bureaus, and departments) at the national level, which replicate themselves in a vertical chain through lower levels of government. In many policy areas this vertical structure increases conflict and fragmentation between administrative levels, but Internet policy tends to involve fewer administrative levels, which allows the center to delegate oversight to fewer lower-level governments and intervene expediently when needed. This is the result of the location of tech companies in Beijing, Shanghai, Guangdong, but almost none in other provinces (Cairns 2017). As a result, policy directives are issued on the central government level and mostly at the provincial level, with major policy decisions being provided centrally. Overall, the central government plays the most important role compared to lower-level governments with respect to Internet governance.

At the same time, responsibilities and decision making tend to be scattered around several authorities on the same horizontal levels, even at the central level (Luo and Lv 2021). This fragmented horizontal structure reduced the ability of the central government under the leadership of Hu Jintao to enforce control. To complicate the bifurcated strategy toward managing online participatory spaces, party units prioritized censorship and public opinion guidance, while state units prioritized the vital role of the Internet in economic and social development (Luo and Lv 2021; Zheng 2008). These objectives quite often led to conflicting decisions and policies about the Internet (Lee and Lio 2016), further weakening the ability of the central government to exercise control under Hu.

During this time, the government approached the Internet similar to traditional media, thus putting authorities with a portfolio on controlling content of traditional media in charge of online information flows (Luo and Lv 2021). At the same time, the Internet had developed as part of the telecommunications bureaucratic structure rather than the propaganda apparatus, which led to greater fragmentation compared to governance of traditional media. The Ministry of Information Industry (MII), created in 1998 through a merger of the Ministry of Posts and Telecommunications and the Ministry of Electronic Industry, was put in charge of regulating the technological and industrial structures of the Internet as well as licensing of Internet service providers (ISPs). Conflict between the MII and the State Administration for Radio, Film, and Television (SARFT) over licensing of Internet and TV services led to the foundation of a new regulatory institution as coordinator, the State Council Information Management Commission (SCIMC) (*guowuyuan xinxihua guanli weiyuanhui* 国务院信息化管理委员会). A major institution involved in the monitoring of Internet news and Bulletin Board Services (BBS) constituted the Internet Information Management Bureau, which was added to the State Council Information Office (SCIO) in 2000. This institution was also put in charge of directing party-state propaganda on the Internet, whereby the Propaganda Department provided guidance (Brady 2007; Zhao 2008). However, in addition to these, other party and state agencies, from the Ministry of Culture to the Ministry of Public Security and the Chinese military, had some jurisdiction over the Internet. To overcome this fragmentation and coordinate better, the State Leadership Group of Informatization (*guojia xinxihua lingdao xiaozu* 国家信息化领导小组), traditionally led by the premier and composed of major Politburo members and heads of commissions, ministries, party departments, and government agencies responsible for the communication and information industry, provided the highest and broadest oversight over the further development of the Internet.

The difficulty involved in controlling online discussion and silencing criticisms in the aftermath of the Wenzhou train crash in 2011 made the government realize its strategy and institutional structure was incapable of controlling the "harmful" social and political potential of the Internet. Large-scale reforms were introduced in 2011, but most were enforced under Xi. The SCIO became the State Internet Information Office in 2011 and was given broader authority under Xi when it became the Cyberspace Administration of China (CAC) in 2014.

Despite coordination efforts and large-scale reforms toward the end of the leadership of Hu Jintao, fragmentation remained a dominant feature of Internet governance under Hu. Internet governance was as a result adequately reactive to emergency events on priority topics, but inadequately proactive in the sense that it lacked the capability to uphold censorship on a daily basis and to complement censorship with effective positive propaganda (Cairns 2017).

State Instruments

To enforce directives the government used a carrot-and-stick approach toward governing online content: on the one hand, the state could use licensing, directives by the state, and laws and regulations to enforce its demands for censorship and surveillance. On the other hand, the state offered rewards in the form of investment, absence of regulation, and protection from foreign competition. Those laid the foundation for Xi's approach, which focused on building a comprehensive legal regulatory framework combined with fostering a discourse among users on how to behave in a regime-desired way (see e.g., Creemers 2017; Economy 2018).

Since the emergence of the Chinese Internet, all technology companies have to comply with state censorship demands in order to keep their business licenses (MacKinnon 2009). The same requirement for *licensing* also applies to foreign technology companies offering services in China. The most notable example is Google, which ran a censored version of its search engine to the Chinese market from 2006 until it left China in 2010 (Cao 2022; MacKinnon 2009).

Censorship is imposed via *directives by the state* issued electronically to technology companies. Based on new directives and rules developed over time, technology companies develop lists of sensitive words or phrases and determine what content to ban (MacKinnon 2009; Qiang 2011). Sensitive content is taken down by a combination of automated content moderation tools and human coders (Bandurski 2008; Qiang 2011). Almost every large technology company has a department dedicated to carrying out "content moderation" (MacKinnon 2011). By handing over content moderation to providers the government outsources censorship to private entities, encouraging self-censorship (Liang and Lu 2010; Qiang 2011).

Laws and regulations also support content control. The Ministry of Industry and Information Technology (MIIT) required all non-commercial websites in 2005 to register with the MIIT at the expense of a financial penalty (Jiang 2010). Since December 2009, all applicants for Internet domain names ending in "cn" were required to submit proof of a government-issued ID and a photo, which effectively undermined anonymous domain-name registration (MacKinnon 2011). To purge online rumors/fake news and curtail raging public discourse and criticisms in response to the Wenzhou train collision, the Beijing Municipal Government issued real-name registration rules for microblog service providers in December 2011 (Jiang 2016). These laid the foundation for a more comprehensive regulatory framework that was passed under Xi (see e.g., Creemers 2017; Liebman 2014).

In addition, the state also coopted companies into compliance. The first means of cooptation includes rewards when companies act in favorable ways. Tech start-ups rely on outside investments and space to innovate in early stages of growth. In China, lack of investment is a problem that has plagued Internet development from its early stage (Hong 2017; Jia 2018; Zhou 1997). *Government-directed investment* became an essential external source of funding to ensure their existence and growth, which in return ensured loyalty toward the state (Cairns 2016). The state also gave technology companies space to experiment and innovate before enacting regulations to control them (Woetzel et al. 2017). For example, the first online payment service was launched by Taobao (Alibaba's e-commerce app) as early as 2003, while the state acquiesced to the service and only enacted related regulations in 2010 (Lv and Luo 2018). The *absence of regulations* provided space for innovation during the Hu years.

In addition, the state also offered Internet companies *protection from foreign competition* in return for favorable behavior.[2] Google struggled with market entry when it had to comply with state directives, while domestic companies were given favorable treatment as long as they were compliant with censorship directives (Cairns 2016). Thus, domestic technology companies tend to have a competitive advantage over foreign companies.

Company Instruments

While the rapid growth of the Internet industry only took off during the leadership of Xi Jinping, the growth of China's technology giants had started under Hu. Technology companies have contributed to the growing Internet economy in China. As of 2010, China's Internet-related expenditures stood at 3.3% of its GDP, catching up with Canada (3.0), Germany (3.2), and the United States (3.8), according to a report by McKinsey Global Institute (2014).

During this time, technology companies built a growing user base that increased their ability to offer convenient access to needed services and information for citizens. For example, in 2002, the beginning of Hu's term, roughly 10.3% of Internet users used the Internet to do online shopping or e-commerce activities; toward the end of Hu's term in 2012, this figure had risen to 39% of Internet users (China Internet Network Information Center (CNNIC) 2002, 2012). By 2012, online consumers numbered 210 million – 5 times more than in 2002 (46 million) (China Internet Network Information Center (CNNIC) 2002, 2012). These data illustrate that technology companies were in the process of building *platform power*. As more users started to rely on free and convenient access to services and information provided by technology companies, a certain degree of dependency of both citizens and governments on those platforms was created. On the side of the state, this dependency is visible in politicians' fear of losing public support if citizens are deprived of the conveniences offered by these companies in their everyday lives (Culpepper and Thelen 2020).

In addition, technology companies have needed *expertise and knowledge* to design effective mechanisms for control and surveillance (see, for example, MacKinnon 2009). Through offering free and convenient services and information, technology companies have the capacity to reach, surveil, and manipulate citizens in real time. Moreover, because of their reliance on customer satisfaction in their business models (Sieker 2021), these companies also develop the capability to collect and analyze customer feedback and provide customer-oriented solutions. These skills and capabilities make technology companies an important asset to governments. Increasing platform power and expertise and knowledge on the side of technology companies laid the foundation for even greater dependency of the state during the Xi years.

Governance Strategies Under Xi Jinping

Xi's Vision of the Internet

"We have put forward the Chinese Dream of the great rejuvenation of the Chinese nation and proposed promoting national rejuvenation through a Chinese path to modernization," states Xi Jinping in his report to the 20th Party Congress (Xi 2022). Xi Jinping envisions the Internet as the core of realizing the *China dream* (*Zhongguo meng* 中国梦). The China dream, brought up by Xi in November 2012 as the ideological underpinning of his leadership, stands for the "great rejuvenation of the Chinese nation." It involves achieving the "two 100s": building a moderately prosperous society by the 100th anniversary of the founding of the CCP in 2021 and building a modern and strong socialist country (*shehuizhuyi xiandaihua qiangguo* 社会主义现代化强国) by the 100th anniversary of the founding of the People's Republic of China in 2049. (QSTHEORY.CN 2021). Narratives in the China dream are often tied to the historical narrative of national humiliation. According to this national humiliation discourse, China did not undertake the industrial revolution and thus fell backward, which ultimately led to invasion and humiliation by Western nations and Japan. Xi views the information revolution, in which the Internet takes a central role, as a new window of opportunity for China to overtake developed countries, especially the US (Tuo 2015).

The leadership's attitude toward the role of the Internet in promoting economic growth and facilitating governance can be dated back to the Jiang era. The leadership under Jiang already showed a clear preference to utilize information technology to promote economic growth, which led to heavy state investment in the sector and reform in the governance structure of the information and communications technology (Zheng 2008). Hu Jintao continued this legacy and offered carrots and sticks to technology companies, laying a solid foundation for the rise of tech giants under Xi. Xi's innovation was built on longstanding techno-nationalism and regarded the Internet "as the underlying infrastructure to be harnessed to further strengthen national power and social governance and as a sector that would allow for profit accumulation and economic growth" (Jia 2021, 98). With this new vision of the Internet, Xi announced China's Cyber Power strategy in 2012, which was then expanded into China's Cyber Super-Power strategy in 2018 (Xinhua News Agency 2022).

Toward these ends, he introduced the Internet + plan, a comprehensive plan to digitize the economy and society by building new information technology solutions for a wide range of policy areas (Wübbeke et al. 2016). The ultimate goal is to integrate the Internet + plan with "Made in China 2025" – a sector-specific plan to transform China's industry digitally in order to make China into a manufacturing superpower (State Council 2015). According to this plan, China aims to substitute foreign with "home-made" technology, speed up China's technological catch-up, and leapfrog technological development stages.

As part of these overall strategic goals, the leadership's attitude toward the role of the Internet has changed substantially under Xi. Under Hu, the leadership's attitude toward the public discourse element of the Internet was ambivalent (Cairns 2017; Creemers 2015; Taylor 2022). The ambivalence in how to deal with public discourse on social media was a symptom of the political stasis that characterized the second half of the Hu administration (Miller 2015). This ambivalence is partially a result of the choice of the Hu administration to receive genuine policy feedback and concerns from the citizens via new communication technology (Cairns 2016). According to Cairns' interviews with officials (2016), the Hu administration was often perceived as 10 years of chaos and weakness in controlling online public discourse. This widespread view foreshadowed Xi's 90-degree shift in Internet governance.

Xi's approach has been characterized as proactive, centralized, and top-down (Cairns 2017; Creemers 2017; Taylor 2022). As shown next, Xi centralized control and leadership over online content, transcending interdepartmental bargaining, interests, and boundaries and creating direct links to the central leadership, especially to Xi himself (Creemers 2015).

Institutional Structure

Under Xi, the institutional fragmentation described earlier was addressed by establishing the Central Leading Group for Cybersecurity and Informatization (CLGCL) chaired by Xi in 2014, a high-level Party group overseeing Internet policy, and simultaneously diminishing the power of central-level propaganda officials, particularly the CPD. The CLGCL along with its functional office – the Cyberspace Administration of China (CAC) – were the key institutions through which Xi achieved centralization of administration and regulation. The CAC enjoys a broad range of authority in areas related to cyberspace, including online content, e-commerce, e-finance, cybersecurity, online fraud, and crime, which were previously mandates of various departments, bureaus, and ministries at the central level (Cairns 2017; Luo and Lv 2021). To overcome unclear administrative boundaries between different agencies, technical bodies like CNNIC, which is responsible for domain registry, were made directly responsible to the CAC (Creemers 2017). In addition, the CAC also took over law enforcement related to the Internet from the Ministry of Public Security (Luo and Lv 2021). The CAC, under the leadership of the CLGCL chaired by Xi, thus became the undisputed head in charge of cyberspace administration with a clear mandate, authority, and legal enforcement power, and the single most important and powerful institution within the Internet regulation realm at the central level.

Despite the CAC's undisputed authority in cyberspace administration, its responsibility and routine work prioritized the regulation of online content, especially regarding sensitive content deemed harmful to the regime and to party rule (Creemers 2017; Luo and Lv 2021). This is also in line with Xi's purpose to create a centralized and integrated institutional framework for propaganda and public opinion work in China's cyberspace (Creemers 2017). On controlling and monitoring sensitive content and public opinion management, the CAC has been strict and swift in response. The State Internet Information Office, absorbed into the CAC, launched two campaigns in 2013, targeting online rumors and web media (Creemers 2017).[3] The CAC has also ensured enforcement where regulations had previously only been implemented laxly. For example, in 2016, the CAC ordered Sina, Souhu, 163.com, and ifeng, a few famous commercial media sites, to shut down their popular news programs online for publishing independently gathered unverified news reports (Huang and Piao 2016), which violated a regulation promulgated in 2005 by the State Council Information Office and the Ministry of Information Industry (Fu 2016).

Even though the CAC has the power to initiate and lead coordination on Internet regulation, tensions between the CAC and ministries and bureaus remain (Creemers 2017). Particularly in gray areas that do not obviously link to stability, the CAC does not have final authority, and existing departmental tensions and competition make ministries and bureaus less likely to cooperate. For example, issues such as regulating online fake medical advertisements, the selling of counterfeit products on online e-commerce platforms, the conflict between the party units' prioritization of political stability and the state units' prioritization of Internet-driven development persisted, and the CAC has neither the intention to enforce nor the capacity to coordinate governmental actions (Luo and Lv 2021). In this regard, Xi's recentralization did not end the fragmentation of Internet regulation completely; instead, the recentralization concentrated on strengthening enforcement of propaganda and public opinion work.[4]

State Instruments

As outlined earlier, new regulations had already been passed under Hu, but in light of a more centralized institutional structure, laws were more strictly enforced under Xi. As discussed, the real-name registration rules for microblog service providers by the Beijing Municipal government were promulgated in December 2011, toward the end of the Hu administration. This was enforced under Xi. The deadline for compliance with the rule was set to March 16, 2012, following the principle of "front stage voluntary, backstage real name" (Jiang 2016). Users of microblogs could use pseudo-usernames, but they were expected to register their real identities with the microblog service providers. Unregistered users could continue to view microblogs, but could no longer post, comment, or forward any information (Sohu 2017). Such rules aimed to end online anonymity and made it easier to identify and prosecute sources of unwanted content (Creemers 2015). To further *strengthen enforcement*, financial penalties were imposed on technology companies for non-compliance. In September 2017, the CAC imposed heavy fines on Tencent, Baidu, and Weibo for failure to prevent users from spreading illegal content and for hosting fake news, pornography, and other harmful content (Vella 2017).

In addition to strengthening enforcement of existing regulations, Xi also built a *comprehensive legal and regulatory framework* to govern online content. In response to heightened online criticism, especially after the Wenzhou train collision, the State Internet Information Office launched an anti-rumors campaign targeting web media in 2013. In August 2013, a broad crackdown on opinion leaders – so-called "Big Vs" – on Weibo was initiated shortly after Xi took office, and influential opinion leaders on Weibo were detained or arrested by government authorities (China File 2014). One month later, new rules promulgated by the Supreme People's Court imposed defamation charges on citizens whose online rumor posts had reached 5000 or more views or been retweeted 500 times or more (Supreme People's Court 2013). These measures explicitly targeted the online public platforms, most notably Weibo, and aimed to silence dissent online.

With these measures targeting public online environments, users inevitably shifted political discussion from a more public environment like Weibo to a more private one, such as WeChat (Qin et al. 2017). In response to this shift, the CAC promulgated new rules on instant messaging services in August 2014, known as "Ten Articles on WeChat" (*Weixin Shitiao* 微信十条) (He and Yimo 2016). In addition to real-name registration, the new rules also required that all applications for a public account need to be examined and verified, encouraged government organizations to register a WeChat public account, and only specific licensed bodies were permitted to publish and disseminate current social and political affairs-related information and news.

In addition to these new rules to guide content regulation, Xi Jinping also enacted policies that went beyond public opinion guidance to include data governance, which is at the core of platform power explained earlier. The Cyber Security Law enacted in July 2017 requires companies to store personal information and other "important data" within the PRC (Economy 2018; Shi-Kupfer and Ohlberg 2019). Cross-border sharing of data and access to critical infrastructure by technological companies had to be reviewed by government authorities and faced restrictions. This reduced the autonomy of domestic technology companies over user data when offering services outside of the Chinese Firewall.

Another noticeable example constitutes a Civil Code and Personal Information Protection Law enacted in 2021, aimed at the protection of user privacy. This law can be seen as a response to heightened concern among users to privacy breaches by tech companies that started as early as 2012 (Yuan et al. 2013), but may also have been encouraged by the passing of the General Data Protection Regulation (GDPR) by the European Union in 2018 and similar privacy regulations in many other countries since. China's new privacy law prohibits companies from disclosing personal information without customer permission and requires them to limit the amount of information they collect. However, unlike the GDPR, China's law does not restrict government or ruling party access to personal information under matters of personal security (Horsley 2021). Again, this new law decreases technology companies' autonomy while increasing the ability of the government to take advantage of platform power.

In addition to tightened sticks, technology companies were also offered *greater rewards* that were distributed in a more structured manner. Building on government-directed investment under Hu, the CAC and the Ministry of Finance established the China Internet Investment Fund in 2017 in order to support China's Cyber Super-Power strategy with 100 billion RMB (36kr 2022). According to its website (www.ciifund.cn/), as of 2022, it has invested in dozens of Chinese technology companies in Internet infrastructure and platforms, network security, network information services, artificial intelligence, big data, cloud computing, and e-governance and services.

When distributing investment, Xi Jinping selected specific technology companies to receive *preferential treatment for funding, licensing, and support to expand business abroad*. In 2017, the Ministry of Science and Technology selected four technology companies to co-develop a state-owned artificial intelligence open-innovation platform: Baidu for self-driving cars, Alibaba for smart cities, Tencent for medical imaging, and iFlyTek for voice recognition (Xinhua News Agency 2017). Among those Baidu, Alibaba, and Tencent (BAT) were allowed to be listed on foreign stock markets and to acquire foreign capital (Pan 2017; Shi-Kupfer and Ohlberg 2019). In building the social credit system, the government gave eight technology companies temporary licenses in 2015 to begin pilots for a commercial social credit system for six months.[5] Even after the six-month temporary license expired, these companies were still allowed to continue their pilot projects. Telecommunications companies like ZTE, Huawei, Datang, and Great Dragon have all received funding from the government and other benefits, such as preferential procurement (Fan and Gao 2016; Shi-Kupfer and Ohlberg 2019).

Overall, Xi Jinping streamlined the instruments in the state's toolbox for governing online information flows. Building on the carrots and sticks approach developed under Hu, Xi centralized the institutional framework to partially overcome fragmentation, which greatly strengthened enforcement. Xi Jinping also developed a comprehensive legal and regulatory framework that reduced the autonomy of technology companies and increased the reach of the state into platform power. Finally, financial rewards were provided to technology companies at an unprecedented scale, with a number of handpicked winners to receive a greater share compared to others.

Company Instruments

Simultaneously with these changes in Internet governance, China's digital economy took off under the Xi administration. Since about 2016, Chinese Internet companies are no longer dismissed as copycats of Google, Twitter, and Amazon. China's vibrant startup scene in Beijing, Shanghai, Shenzhen, Hangzhou, and second-tier cities broke boundaries with their own innovations built for smartphones, such as mobile wallet, mobile shopping in groups, mobile video streaming with live commentary, and bike sharing. New innovations like TikTok and WeChat were adopted outside of China, while US- and EU-based companies, including Facebook, Google, Twitter, Wikipedia, and Dropbox, do not operate inside the Great Chinese Firewall (Fannin 2019).

During this time, technology companies increased in importance for China's economic development. As the digital economy grew from 15% of GDP in 2008 to 33% in 2017 (Zhang and Chen 2019), technology companies became an important source of employment. In the e-commerce sector, Alibaba's platform has created over 30 million jobs over the past decade, and in the sharing economy section, the Didi taxi platform (China's Uber) had 13 million drivers (Zhang and Chen 2019). Among technology companies, Baidu, Alibaba, and Tencent (BAT) became especially important as a driver of digital innovation. In 2016, BAT provided 42% of all venture capital investment in supporting the development of the digital sector in China, far more than Facebook, Amazon, Netflix, and Google in the US, which contributed 5% in the same year (Woetzel et al. 2017). BAT funded one in five top Chinese startups, and another 30% received funding from BAT firms (Woetzel et al. 2017). In other words, technology companies' investment decisions and profit-driven activities played a crucial role in economic growth and employment in China. As a result, the importance of technology companies for China's economy, especially the BAT, grew during this period.

While *platform power* started to emerge under Hu, it really took off under Xi. BAT linked online and offline services and expanded into various areas, such as health, e-commerce, social interactions, etc., offering a one-stop shop for users (Jia and Kenney 2016; Lv and Luo 2018; Woetzel et al. 2017). An entire platform ecosystem was created, incorporating almost all aspects of daily lives. Greater dependence on online services provided by the tech giants became a bargaining chip for technology companies since politicians fear losing public support if citizens are deprived of convenient, easy, and cheap access to information and services offered by technology companies (Culpepper and Thelen 2020).

These dynamics are illustrated in the development of Yu'e Bao, funded by Alibaba's Ant Financial Group as a money market fund. Assets rose from CNY185 billion in the final quarter of 2013 to CNY1689 billion at their peak in the first quarter of 2018 (Fitch Ratings 2021). It was the world's largest money market fund at its peak. People relied on Yu'e Bao to manage their spare money. As of September 2021, Yu'e Bao had more than 50 million investors. In light of the size of assets and number of investors, Xi's government attempted to impose restrictions gradually to ensure financial market stability. Since 2017, daily contribution caps and subscription limits have been imposed in order to limit the size of assets and the number of investors. Partly because of these restrictions, Yu'e Bao's size decreased by more than 55% from its peak in 2018 (Yue and Jia 2022).

Finally, technology companies were heavily involved in supporting the government based on their *knowledge, resources, and expertise*. This is visible when analyzing procurement information regarding contracts that were given to Baidu, Alibaba, Tencent, or Sina because they were the only companies that qualified in providing the service needed (single-source procurement). Between August 2011 and January 2022, 371 single-source government procurement contracts were signed with Baidu, Sina, Tencent, and Alibaba. Among these 371 notices, 66% (244) were related to public opinion surveillance and guidance, as well as big data analysis to achieve goals by various government units.[6] For example, the Propaganda Department of the CCP at Fuzhou city, the capital city of Fujian Province, had published several notices to promote the beautiful scenery and life, the image of hardworking people, and to praise the achievements of the CCP in Fuzhou. All these contracts were outsourced to WeChat, Weibo, and the Tencent news app. Other contracts involving big data analysis by Tencent highlighted the company's location-based services and its massive amount of fine-grained real-time data. For example, the Department of Transportation of Guangdong Province put up a single-source procurement notice to purchase Tencent's big data analysis in assisting transport arrangement during the Chinese spring festival in 2017. The Department of Transportation would provide basic information on public transportation, while Tencent would contribute accurate real-time customer locations, large user base, relational data connecting locations to local services, and accurate cloud computing and analysis power. This expertise would allow for surveillance of real-time traffic flows, identification and provision of early warnings of public emergencies to citizens, and provide information for decision-making to the department. Such strategic collaboration with Tencent was mentioned as part of the Internet + plan in public transportation. These examples illustrate that technology companies – especially BAT and Sina – have the knowledge, expertise, and resources to implement the goals and policies of various levels of government.

Conclusion: A Partnership Between Companies and the State

Most studies on Chinese content control are based on an implicit assumption that companies operating platforms simply implement state directives for censorship and surveillance. This analysis clearly shows that this assumption is mistaken. Chinese technology companies have emerged as powerful players with strong instruments due to their importance in the digital economy and platform power, as well as expertise, resources, and knowledge. The foundations for this toolbox on the side of technology companies were laid during the Hu Jintao years, but the more dominant role of tech giants Tencent, Baidu, and Alibaba only emerged under Xi Jinping.

While it is true that Xi Jinping centralized a fragmented institutional structure which enabled greater enforcement of content control, he also followed in the footsteps of his predecessor in creating a comprehensive legal and regulatory framework, which clearly went beyond content control in line with his ambitious visions for the digital economy to push China to become a superpower. Although state control clearly increased under Xi Jinping, co-optation strategies were perhaps even more significant. At an unprecedented scale, government-directed investment was distributed in a more structured manner. A selected group of technology companies, including Tencent, Baidu, Alibaba, and Sina, received preferential treatment for funding, licensing, and support to expand business abroad.

Clearly, Xi Jinping as a leader made a difference, but many developments had already started during the later years of Hu Jintao's leadership. Most importantly, it would be wrong to assume that Xi Jinping alone is the mastermind exerting coercive control over companies that lack influence and simply execute orders of the great leader. To the contrary, neither China's success in building an innovative tech industry nor tightened censorship and surveillance can be explained without considering the power of China's tech giants. While the Chinese state's partnership with big tech was rooted in the Hu years, it fully evolved into a mutually beneficial relationship under Xi Jinping. From this perspective, the mysterious disappearance of Jack Ma and the crackdown on the tech giants since 2018 should be seen as an effort to reassert the state's leadership over increasingly powerful commercial actors.

Notes

1 The CIS measured Internet use based on self-reports as well as use of smartphones. Both measures lead to identical estimates. CNNIC is unclear about its measurement. Sampling populations differ but are *larger* for CNNIC, which can thus not explain higher estimates of CIS.
2 Blocking alone is insufficient to explain the success of QQ, Weibo, and Youku, however (Pan 2017; Taneja and Wu 2014).
3 The State Internet Information Office (SIIO) was previously established within the State Council Information Office (SCIO) with the responsibility of coordinating online content regulation. Later, it became independent from the SCIO with independent staff and absorbed into the CAC in 2014.
4 Xi's government also centralized media governance by merging the press regulator – General Administration of Press and Publications – and audiovisual media regulator – the State Administration of Press, Publications, Radio, Film and Television – into the State Administration of Press, Publications, Radio, Film and Television. Right after the merge, the new institution issued a notice that banned journalists from submitting stories based on online information and obligated them to only open Weibo accounts when permitted (Creemers 2017).
5 The social credit system evaluates a person's trustworthiness based on surveillance and encourages compliance by giving ratings that can determine access to loans, jobs, and travel. "Renmin Yinhang Yinfa 'Guanyu Zuo Hao Geren Zhengxin Yewu Zhunbei Gongzuo de Tongzhi'" (People's Bank of China Issued a Notice on the Preparation of Personal Credit Business), available at www.gov.cn/xinwen/2015-01/05/content_2800381.htm, accessed December 14, 2020.
6 Procurement data provided by ChinaFile. This dataset consists of 76,000 procurement notices that central and local government offices posted for goods and services. Some notices also include supplemental documents that elaborate on the basic terms of the notice.

References

36kr. 2022. "Zhong Wang Tou: Ba Fuwu Wangluo Qiangguo Jianshe Zuowei Touzi Shouyao Renwu" (中网投：把服务网络强国建设作为投资首要任务) [China Internet Investment: Serving the Construction of a Strong Network Country as the Primary Task of Investment]. *36kr*. https://36kr.com/p/2031012542147845 (accessed December 19, 2022).

Bandurski, David. 2008. "China's Guerilla War for the Web." *Far Eastern Economic Review* 171(6): 41.

Benkler, Y. 2006. *The Wealth of Networks: How Social Production Transforms Markets and Freedom*. 9/23/07 ed. New Haven, CT: Yale University Press.

Boas, Taylor C. 2006. "Weaving the Authoritarian Web: The Control of Internet Use in Nondemocratic Regimes." In *How Revolutionary Was the Digital Revolution? National Responses, Market Transitions, and Global Technology*, eds. John Zysman and Abraham Newman. Stanford, CA: Stanford Business Books, 361–378.

Brady, Anne-Marie. 2007. *Marketing Dictatorship: Propaganda and Thought Work in Contemporary China*. Lanham, MD: Rowman & Littlefield Publishers, Inc.

Cairns, Christopher Marty. 2016. "Fragmented Authoritarianism? Reforms to China's Internet Censorship System under Xi Jinping." In Philadelphia, Pennsylvania, USA.

Cairns, Christopher Marty. 2017. "China's Weibo Experiment: Social Media (Non-) Censorship and Autocratic Responsiveness." *Cornell University*. https://ecommons.cornell.edu/handle/1813/51558 (accessed October 22, 2022).

Cao, Sissi. 2022. "Google Shuts down One of Its Last Remaining Services in China as Big Tech Exits the Country." *Observer*. https://observer.com/2022/10/alphabet-shut-google-translate-china-big-tech/ (accessed November 19, 2022).

China File. 2014. "Closing Time? China's Social Media Crackdown Has Hit Weibo Hard." *China File*. www.chinafile.com/reporting-opinion/media/closing-time-chinas-social-media-crackdown-has-hit-weibo-hard (accessed December 19, 2022).

CNNIC (China Internet Network Information Center). 2002. *The 10th Statistical Report on Internet Development in China*. China Internet Network Information Center. www.cnnic.cn/NMediaFile/old_attach/P020120612484921379852.pdf (accessed November 22, 2022).

CNNIC (China Internet Network Information Center). 2012. *The 30th Statistical Report on Internet Development in China*. China Internet Network Information Center. www.cnnic.cn/NMediaFile/old_attach/P020120723477451202474.pdf (accessed November 22, 2022).

Creemers, Rogier. 2015. "The Pivot in Chinese Cybergovernance." *China Perspectives* 2015(4): 5–13.

Creemers, Rogier. 2017. "Cyber China: Upgrading Propaganda, Public Opinion Work and Social Management for the Twenty-First Century." *Journal of Contemporary China* 26(103): 85–100.

Culpepper, Pepper D., and Kathleen Thelen. 2020. "Are We All Amazon Primed? Consumers and the Politics of Platform Power." *Comparative Political Studies* 53(2): 288–318.

Ding, Sheng. 2009. "Informing the Masses and Heeding Public Opinion: China's New Internet-Related Policy Initiatives to Deal with Its Governance Crisis." *Journal of Information Technology & Politics* 6(1): 31–42.

Economy, Elizabeth C. 2018. *The Third Revolution: Xi Jinping and the New Chinese State*. Oxford: Oxford University Press.

Fan, Peilei, and Xudong Gao. 2016. "Catching Up and Developing Innovation Capabilities in China's Telecommunication Equipment Industry." In *China as an Innovation Nation*, eds. Yu Zhou, William Lazonick, and Yifei Sun. Oxford: Oxford University Press, 215–239.

Fannin, Rebecca A. 2019. *Tech Titans of China: How China's Tech Sector Is Challenging the World by Innovating Faster, Working Harder, & Going Global*. Boston, MA; London: Nicholas Brealey Publishing, an imprint of John Murray Press.

Fitch Ratings. 2021. "Regulatory Cap on Yu'e Bao May Affect Other Chinese Funds." *Fitch Ratings*. www.fitchratings.com/research/fund-asset-managers/regulatory-cap-on-yu-e-bao-may-affect-other-chinese-funds-25-04-2021 (accessed December 19, 2022).

Fu, Caide. 2016. "Zhongguo Duo Jia Menhu Wangzhan Yuanchuang Xinwen Lanmu Zao Guan Ting" (中国多家门户网站原创新闻栏目遭关停) (Original News Columns of Several Chinese Portals Shut Down). *New York Times*. https://cn.nytimes.com/china/20160726/china-media-sina-sohu-netease-phoenix/ (accessed December 19, 2022).

Global Times. 2012. "Weibo Launches Real-Name Registration." *Global Times*. www.globaltimes.cn/content/700489.shtml (accessed December 19, 2022).

He, Xiaojin, and Wang Yimo. 2016. "'Weixin Shitiao' Zhe Yi Nian" ("微信十条" 这一年) ['Ten Articles on WeChat' This Year]. *Cyberspace Administration of China*. www.cac.gov.cn/2016-01/01/c_1117646261.htm#:~:text=%E9%A1%BE%E5%90%8D%E6%8
0%9D%E4%B9%89%EF%BC%8C%E2%80%9C%E5%BE%AE%E4%BF%A1%E
5%8D%81%E6%9D%A1%E2%80%9D%E6%9C%89,%E5%BC%80%E8%AE%B
E%E5%85%AC%E4%BC%97%E8%B4%A6%E5%8F%B7%EF%BC%8C%E6%9C%
8D%E5%8A%A1%E7%A4%BE%E4%BC%9A%E3%80%82 (accessed December 19, 2022).

Hintz, Arne. 2016. "Restricting Digital Sites of Dissent: Commercial Social Media and Free Expression." *Critical Discourse Studies* 13(3): 325–340.

Hong, Yu. 2017. *Networking China: The Digital Transformation of the Chinese Economy | Illinois Scholarship Online | Oxford Academic*. Urbana, IL: University of Illinois Press. https://academic.oup.com/illinois-scholarship-online/book/17241 (accessed November 22, 2022).

Horsley, Jamie P. 2021. "How Will China's Privacy Law Apply to the Chinese State?" *Brookings*. www.brookings.edu/articles/how-will-chinas-privacy-law-apply-to-the-chinese-state/ (accessed December 19, 2022).

Huang, Angwei, and Piao Vanessa. 2016. "Wang xin Ban: Shejiao Meiti Xiao Xi Buneng Zhijie Kan Fa" (网信办：社交媒体消息不能直接刊发) [Cyberspace Administration of China: Social Media Messages Cannot Be Published Directly]. *New York Times*. https://cn.nytimes.com/china/20160706/china-internet-social-media/ (accessed December 19, 2022).

Jia, Kai, and Martin Kenney. 2016. "Mobile Internet Business Models in China: Vertical Hierarchies, Horizontal Conglomerates, or Business Groups." BRIE Working Paper 2016–6. Working Paper: Berkeley Roundtable on the International Economy. https://brie.berkeley.edu/sites/default/files/working-paper-2016-6.jiakenney.pdf.

Jia, Lianrui. 2018. "Going Public and Going Global: Chinese Internet Companies and Global Finance Networks." *Westminster Papers in Communication and Culture* 13(1). www.westminsterpapers.org/article/id/256/ (accessed August 10, 2022).

Jia, Lianrui. 2021. "Building China's Tech Superpower: State, Domestic Champions and Foreign Capital." In *Power and Authority in Internet Governance*. Abingdon, UK: Routledge.

Jiang, Min. 2010. "Authoritarian Deliberation on Chinese Internet." *Electronic Journal of Communication* 20(3 & 4).

Jiang, Min. 2016. "Managing the Micro-Self: The Governmentality of Real Name Registration Policy in Chinese Microblogosphere." *Information, Communication & Society* 19(2): 203–220.

Kluver, Randolph. 2005. "US and Chinese Policy Expectations of the Internet." *China Information* 19.

Kurbalija, Jovan. 2010. *An Introduction to Internet Governance*. Msida, Malta: Diplo Foundation. www.diplomacy.edu/sites/default/files/AnIntroductiontoIG_7th%20edition.pdf.

Lee, Ming-Hsuan, and Mon-Chi Lio. 2016. "The Impact of Information and Communication Technology on Public Governance and Corruption in China." *Information Development* 32(2): 127–141.

Li, Baosheng. 2008. "Hu Jintao: Ba Tigao Ao Lun Yindao Nengli Fang Zai Tuchu Weizhi" (胡锦涛：把提高奥伦引导能力放在突出位置) [Hu Jintao: Putting the Improvement of the Ability to Guide the Olympic Theory in a Prominent Position]. *Beijing Review*. www.beijingreview.com.cn/news/txt/2008-06/21/content_128615.htm (accessed December 19, 2022).

Liang, Bin, and Hong Lu. 2010. "Internet Development, Censorship, and Cyber Crimes in China." *Journal of Contemporary Criminal Justice* 26(1): 103–120.

Liebman, Benjamin L. 2014. "Legal Reform: China's Law-Stability Paradox." *Daedalus* 143(2): 96–109.

Lin, Shuanchuan. 2006. "Zhongyang Lingdao Gaodu Zhongshi Wangluo Yulun Wangluo Minyi Hui Ru Zhongnanhai" (中央领导高度重视网络舆论 网络民意汇入中南海) [Central Leaders Attach Great Importance to Online Public Opinion, and Online Public Flows into Zhongnanhai]." *Central People's Government of the People's Republic of China.* www.gov.cn/jrzg/2006-04/10/content_249975.htm (accessed December 19, 2022).

Luo, Ting, and Aofei Lv. 2021. "'Nine Dragons Run the Water': Fragmented Internet Governance in China." In *Power and Authority in Internet Governance*, eds. Blayne Haggart, Natasha Tusikov, and Jan Aart Scholte. Abingdon, UK: Routledge.

Lv, Aofei, and Ting Luo. 2018. "Asymmetrical Power between Internet Giants and Users in China." *International Journal of Communication* 12: 3877–3895.

MacKinnon, Rebecca. 2009. "China's Censorship 2.0: How Companies Censor Bloggers." *First Monday.* https://journals.uic.edu/ojs/index.php/fm/article/view/2378 (accessed January 19, 2022).

MacKinnon, Rebecca. 2011. "Liberation Technology: China's 'Networked Authoritarianism'." *Journal of Democracy* 22(2): 32–46.

McKinsey Global Institute. 2014. *China's Digital Transformation: The Internet's Impact on Productivity and Growth.* www.mckinsey.com/~/media/mckinsey/industries/technology%20media%20and%20telecommunications/high%20tech/our%20insights/chinas%20digital%20transformation/mgi%20china%20digital%20full%20report.pdf (accessed November 22, 2022).

Miller, Alice. 2015. "The Trouble with Factions." *China Leadership Monitor* (46).

Noesselt, Nele. 2014. "Microblogs and the Adaptation of the Chinese Party-State's Governance Strategy." *Governance* 27(3): 449–468.

Pan, Jennifer. 2017. "How Market Dynamics of Domestic and Foreign Social Media Firms Shape Strategies of Internet Censorship." *Problems of Post-Communism* 64(3–4): 167–188.

Qiang, Xiao. 2011. "Liberation Technology: The Battle for the Chinese Internet." *Journal of Democracy* 22(2): 47–61.

Qin, Bei, David Strömberg, and Yanhui Wu. 2017. "Why Does China Allow Freer Social Media? Protests versus Surveillance and Propaganda." *Journal of Economic Perspectives* 31(1): 117–140.

QSTHEORY.CN. 2021. "Shixian Zhonghua Minzu Weida Fuxing Zhongguo Meng de Guanjian Yibu" (实现中华民族伟大复兴中国梦的关键一步) [A Key Step in Realizing the Chinese Dream of the Great Rejuvenation of the Chinese Nation]. *QSTHEORY.CN.* www.qstheory.cn/zhuanqu/2021-07/22/c_1127683059.htm (accessed December 19, 2022).

Shi-Kupfer, Kristin, and Mareike Ohlberg. 2019. "China's Digital Rise: Challenges for Europe." *Mercator Institute for China Studies (MERICS).* https://merics.org/sites/default/files/2020-06/MPOC_No.7_ChinasDigitalRise_web_final_2.pdf (accessed December 5, 2022).

Shirk, Susan L. 2018. "The Return to Personalistic Rule." *Journal of Democracy* 29(2): 22–36.

Sieker, Felix. 2021. "Disruption or Continuation? The Role of Platforms in Transforming Work." PhD thesis. The Hertie School, Berlin.

Sohu. 2017. "Zhuyi! Wei Shiming Yonghu Jin Qi Wufa Fa Wei Bo Ye Wufa Pinglun!" (注意！未实名用户今起无法发微博也无法评论！) [Notice! Users without Real Names Cannot Post on Weibo or Comment from Now On!]. *SOHU.com.* www.sohu.com/a/192372296_480095 (accessed December 19, 2022).

State Council. 2010. "Zhongguo Hulianwang Zhuangkuang Baipishu" [China's Internet Development White Paper]. *Central People's Government of the People's Republic of China.* www.gov.cn/zhengce/2010-06/08/content_2615774.htm (accessed July 13, 2010)

State Council. 2015. "Guowuyuan Guanyu Yinfa 'Zhongguo Zhihao 2025' de Tongzhi" (国务院关于印发《中国制造2025》的通知) [Notice of the State Council Regarding the Issuance of 'Made in China 2025']. *Central People's Government of the People's Republic of China.* www.gov.cn/zhengce/content/2015-05/19/content_9784.htm (accessed December 19, 2022).

Stockmann, Daniela. 2015. "The Chinese Internet Audience: Who Seeks Political Information Online?" In *Urban Mobilization and New Media in Contemporary China*, eds. Hanspeter Kriesi, Daniel Kübler, and Lisheng Dong. London: Ashgate, 19–32.

Stockmann, Daniela, and Ting Luo. 2018. "China Internet Survey." Unpublished.

Stockmann, Daniela, and Ting Luo. In Press. *Governing Digital China*. New York: Cambridge University Press.

Supreme People's Court. 2013. "Guanyu Banli Liyong Xinxi Wangluo Shishi Feibang Deng Xingshi Anjian Shiyong Falü Ruogan Wenti de Jieshi" (《关于办理利用信息网络实施诽谤等刑事案件适用法律若干问题的解释》的理解与适用) [Interpretation Concerning Some Questions of Applicable Law When Handling Uses of Information Networks to Commit Defamation and Other Such Criminal Cases]. www.court.gov.cn/shenpan-xiangqing-5913.html.

Taneja, Harsh, and Angela Xiao Wu. 2014. "Does the Great Firewall Really Isolate the Chinese? Integrating Access Blockage with Cultural Factors to Explain Web User Behavior." *The Information Society* 30(5): 297–309.

Taylor, Monique. 2022. *China's Digital Authoritarianism: A Governance Perspective*. Cham: Palgrave Macmillan.

Tuo, Jiang. 2015. "Hulianwang Shi Zhongguo Meng de Zhongda Jiyu" (互联网是中国梦的重大机遇) [The Internet Is a Great Opportunity for the Chinese Dream]. *China Daily*. http://china.chinadaily.com.cn/2015-11/01/content_22337740.htm (accessed December 19, 2022).

Vella, Heidi. 2017. "Chinese Social Media Hit with Massive Fines for Spreading Porn and Fake News." *Tech Wire Asia*. https://techwireasia.com/2017/09/chinese-social-media-hit-massive-fines-spreading-porn-fake-news/ (accessed December 19, 2022).

Wang, Xuan, Kasper Juffermans, and Caixia Du. 2016. "Harmony as Language Policy in China: An Internet Perspective." *Language Policy* 15(3): 299–321.

Woetzel, Jonathan, et al. 2017. "China's Digital Economy: A Leading Global Force." www.mckinsey.com/featured-insights/china/chinas-digital-economy-a-leading-global-force (accessed August 7, 2022).

Wübbeke, Jost, et al. 2016. "Made in China 2025." *Mercator Institute for China Studies (MERICS)*. https://merics.org/en/report/made-china-2025 (accessed November 29, 2022).

Xi, Jinping. 2022. *Report to the 20th National Congress of the Communist Party of China*. www.fmprc.gov.cn/eng/zxxx_662805/202210/t20221025_10791908.html (accessed January 31, 2023).

Xinhua News Agency. 2007. "Hu Jintao: Yi Chuangxin de Jingshen Wangluo Wenhua Jianshe He Guanli" (胡锦涛：以创新的精神加强网络文化建设和管理) [Hu Jintao: Strengthen the Construction and Management of Internet Culture with an Innovative Spirit]. *Central People's Government of the People's Republic of China*. www.gov.cn/test/2007-10/10/content_773145.htm (accessed December 19, 2022).

Xinhua News Agency. 2017. "Keji Bu Zhaokai Xin Yidai Rengong Zhineng Fazhan Guihua Ji Zhongda Keji Xiangmu Qidong Hui" (科技部召开新一代人工智能发展规划暨重大科技项目启动会) [The Ministry of Science and Technology Held a New Generation of Artificial Intelligence Development Plan and a Major Science and Technology Project Launch Meeting]. *Cyberspace Administration of China*. www.cac.gov.cn/2017-11/16/c_1121964697.htm.

Xinhua News Agency. 2022. "Cong Wangluo Daguo Xiang Wangluo Qiangguo Kuobu Maijin – 'Zhongguo Zhe Shi Nian' Xilie Zhuti Xinwen Fabu Hui Jujiao Xin Shidai Wangluo Qiangguo Jianshe Chengjiu" (从网络大国向网络强国阔步迈进 – "中国这十年"系列主题新闻发布会聚焦新时代网络强国建设成就) [Striding Forward From a Network Power to a Network Power – 'China's Decade' Series of Themed Press Conferences Focus on the Achievements of Building a Network Power in the New Era]. *Central People's Government of the People's Republic of China*. www.gov.cn/xinwen/2022-08/20/content_5706135.htm (accessed December 19, 2022).

Xu, Jian, and Jonathan Benney. 2018. "The Decline of Sina Weibo: A Technological, Political and Market Analysis." In *Chinese Social Media: Social, Cultural and Political Implications*, eds. Mike Kent, Katie Ellis, and Jian Xu. Abingdon, UK: Routledge, 221–235.

Yuan, Elaine J., Miao Feng, and James A. Danowski. 2013. "'Privacy' in Semantic Networks on Chinese Social Media: The Case of Sina Weibo." *Journal of Communication* 63(6): 1011–1031.

Yue, Quan, and Denise Jia. 2022. "China Curbs Money Market Funds, among Them Ant's Yu'e Bao." *Nikkei Asia*. https://asia.nikkei.com/Spotlight/Caixin/China-curbs-money-market-funds-among-them-Ant-s-Yu-e-Bao (accessed December 19, 2022).

Zhao, Yuezhi. 2008. *Communication in China: Political Economy, Power, and Conflict*. Lanham, MD: Rowman & Littlefield Publishers.

Zhang, Longmei, and Sally Chen. 2019. *China's Digital Economy: Opportunities and Risks*. Washington, DC: International Monetary Fund.

Zheng, Yongnian. 2008. *Technological Empowerment: The Internet, State, and Society in China*. Stanford, CA: Stanford University Press.

Zhou, He. 1997. "A History of Telecommunications in China: Development and Policy Implications." In *Telecommunications and Development in China*, ed. Paul S. N. Lee. Cresskill, NJ: Hampton Press, 55–87.

Zittrain, Jonathan, and Benjamin Edelman. 2003. "Internet Filtering in China." *Internet Computing, IEEE* 7: 70–77.

5 Technology Policy Under Xi Jinping, 2012–2022

Douglas B. Fuller and Ricardo L. Kotz

Introduction

Technology is a fundamental input of economic growth as it engenders productivity gains across different sectors, as the People's Republic of China has long recognized. Even prior to the Cultural Revolution, China endorsed the Four Modernizations of agriculture, industry, science and technology (S&T), and defense, only to shelve them once the Cultural Revolution got underway (MacFarquhar and Schoenhals 2006, 380). At the Fourth National People's Congress in 1975, the Four Modernizations were reaffirmed, and in 1991 the government moved S&T from the third priority to the first (Fewsmith 2001, 47). Ever since, China has emphasized technological development as necessary in order to attain economic development.

This chapter will evaluate the continuities and changes as well as successes and failures of China's technology policy, defined here as policies aiming to promote a country catching up to and even attaining pole position at the global technology frontier under Xi Jinping's leadership.

From the 1980s, the Chinese state took an active role in promoting technological research and diffusion. The Key Technologies R&D Program started in 1982 with the aim to help the technical needs of agriculture and industry, although it has evolved into a program supporting university-industry cooperation. The 863 Program targeting cutting-edge technology started in 1986 and initially was not focused on commercialization of technology at all. Thus, in 1988, the Torch Program was established with the objective of commercializing R&D.

While some recent scholarship has dismissed or downplayed the efforts of regional and local governments in technology policy (Naughton 2021), going back to the 1990s there were already serious efforts to diffuse international technology to local industry in sectors such as automobiles (Thun 2006) and information technology (Segal 2003), with varying degrees of success. Moreover, as other scholars have pointed out, provincial governments can be key to how central government policies, including technology policies, are implemented at the local level (Jaros 2019).

Nevertheless, scholars such as Naughton (2021) and Tan (2021) are correct that the Chinese state's ambitions as expressed in funding size and goals grew explosively from 2006 onward. Of course, this growth is not surprising given the larger size of the economy, the narrower gap between China's technological level and the global technological frontier in many industrial sectors, and the long-held techno-nationalist ambitions of many in China's governing elite, expressed in many report series connected to the state bureaucracies involved in technology policy, such as the Ministry of Science and Technology's (MOST) 调研报告 (*Diaoyan Baogao*) and the State Council's Development Research Centre's 调查研究报告 (*Diaocha Yanjiu Baogao*. To put it another way, indigenous innovation (自主创新) has been given rhetorical prominence over the last 15 years but long before this rhetorical change, techno-nationalist aims have been a stated goal in policy discussions and, albeit unevenly, in implementation as the techno-nationalist goals from Beijing have often conflicted with the incentives of local officials for more globalist industrialization (Fuller 2016, Ch. 2).

The policy that signaled China's increasing policy ambitions to the world was the Medium-and-Long-term Plan (MLP) for Science and Technology (2006–2020). While rolling out the MLP, the Chinese government emphasized the term *indigenous innovation*, underlining a commitment to bolstering the technological capabilities of domestic firms, including increased production of their own intangible assets, such as intellectual property (IP). The MLP document proposed 16 megaprojects in strategic sectors ranging from electronics, wireless communication, oil and gas, and water sanitation and pollution, among others. The remaining goals included improving basic research, greater investments in science and technology, and improving human resources; it outlined 68 priority sectors, 27 frontier sectors, and 18 basic research areas. It included three main goals: R&D at 2.5 percent of GDP, reducing dependence on foreign technology to 30 percent, and productivity gains representing 60 percent of total growth until 2020 (Chen and Naughton 2016).

A subsequent key pre-Xi policy was the Strategic Emerging Industries (SEI) initiative first announced in November 2009 (launched in 2010). As with many Chinese S&T policies, subsequent policies have often absorbed and subsumed previously announced policies' projects. For example, the 16 mega-projects (重大专项) of the MLP heavily overlapped with the seven broad sectors of the subsequent SEI initiative, with the exception of clean energy vehicles as a new priority under the SEI initiative, except the three unknown classified sectors of the MLP (Li 2009; Springut et al. 2011).

Xi's technology policy can be understood as a continuation as well as an amplification of China's technology policies preceding him under the Hu-Wen administration. Xi has continued to promote policies designed to propel China to the technological frontier in a number of critical sectors. Made in China 2025 (MIC 2025) and the Internet-Plus Plan in 2015, along with the overarching Innovation-Driven Development Strategy (IDDS) framework in 2016 and following supplemental plans, all have targeted sectors viewed as critical for China's security and technological development. Xi has also continued past administrations' favoritism toward SOEs in technology policymaking (Huang 2003, 2008; Fuller 2016).

At the same time, Xi's technology policies represent an amplification of past policies from several vantage points. First, the depth and breadth of the industrial targets have grown. For example, the IDDS expresses the vision that new critical technologies, such as artificial intelligence (AI), are emerging, and that China could jump ahead of developed countries by focusing its own industrial capacity on leapfrogging to the global technology frontier in these technologies. Second, concomitant with the growing ambitions of China's technology policy, the Chinese state has made larger financial commitments to back up these ambitions (Naughton 2021). For example, even as GDP has risen under Xi's leadership, R&D as a share of GDP has grown faster from just under 2 percent in 2012 to 2.55 percent in 2022.[1] Finally, Xi has not just continued the positive policy bias toward the state sector but doubled down on it by going as far as attacking some of China's most successful tech entrepreneurs, such as Jack Ma (马云).

This chapter proceeds as follows. The next section discusses the successes and failures of China's technology policy during the first two decades of the 21st century and evaluates how Xi's broader policies have attempted to resolve but ultimately exacerbated many of the institutional constraints undermining the Chinese state's technological efforts. The third section focuses in detail on the largest technological policy effort under Xi, the MIC 2025 policy. The conclusion examines how China's tensions with the United States and other advanced economies potentially will further constrict the scope of China's technological development.

Innovation Successes Amidst Persistent Problems in China's Technology Policy, 2000–2022

Strengthening the Foundation of Science and Technology: Education

Any account of China's technology policy and technological development must acknowledge the large quantitative improvements in the number and percentage of Chinese students receiving tertiary education and the large increase in scientific output from China. Gross enrollment in tertiary education has gone from 8 percent in 2000 to 64 percent in 2021.[2] While there are damning critiques of the quality of Chinese education at tertiary levels and below (Zhao 2014; Abrami et al. 2014), the overall output of graduates, particularly in science and engineering (Simon and Cao 2009), is very impressive, notwithstanding the very serious ongoing problem of the left behind, nutritionally and educationally neglected children in the countryside (Rozelle and Hell 2020).

Increasing Output: Publications, Patents, and Production

The increasingly educated population combined with large investments in the university system (Simon and Cao 2009) have unsurprisingly led to an explosive increase in academic publications from China. By 2018–2022, China accounted for 23.4 percent of the scientific papers, more than any other country.[3] Here again, however, there is a debate about the quality of this quantitative explosion. In 2019, China published 8,422 articles in the top 1 percent category of most cited papers in the world, against 7,959 from the US and 6,074 in the European Union out of 20,413 such publications[4] (Wagner et al. 2022; Wagner 2023). Yet, the difference in the number of highly cited papers between the US and China was not statistically significant and the totals included academic articles outside of the natural sciences and engineering. For example, Chinese scholars had a statistically significant larger share of highly cited papers in Business and Finance than American scholars.[5] Looking across a range of disciplines (Wagner et al. 2022) found in A.I., the number of most-cited papers from China were double those of the US. The researchers also found that Chinese papers touched upon a wide variety of disciplines and often produced interesting interdisciplinary work, thus suggesting that China is indeed an innovator and not just an imitator. Counterbalancing this impressive output, China still has the largest problem with fraudulent and plagiarized scientific papers. Using Web of Science data from 1978–2017, a scholar at Fudan University found that China has almost three times as many retractions controlling for global share of publications (8.2 percent of publications compared to 24.2 percent of retractions) (Tang 2019). In health science publications, China accounted for half of all fraudulent papers from 2015–2018 (Palla et al. 2020).

Similarly, China has seen an explosion of patenting, first with patents granted by China's State Intellectual Property Office (and consequently appearing in WIPO statistics) and then in Triadic (EU, Japan, and American granted) patents, which are generally regarded as higher-quality patents. However, much of this surge can be explained by the progressively larger inducements the state has offered to pursue patenting (Fuller 2016; Li 2012). The signal to patent abroad was explicit in the National Patent Development Strategy (2011–2020) which called for doubling foreign patents. It is thus not surprising that with the increasing inducements to patent abroad as well as at home, the quality of China's foreign patents began to decline using the rigorous metric of time-limited forward citations.[6] The decline in quality of China's US patents began in 2005 and by 2014 were the lowest of the patenting countries/regions collected by Jefferson and Jiang (2021). Even worse, in an industry featuring both high international patenting activity and a high level of policy commitment by the Chinese state, semiconductors, China's foreign patent quality has declined considerably (Jiang et al. 2020).

Finally, during the last two decades, China has become the largest exporter and largest industrial economy in the world. As part of its rapid industrialization, China has displaced a significant portion of advanced economies' production of goods, including in product areas normally seen as high technology: smartphones, flat-panel displays, light emitting diodes (LEDs), solar panels, and telecommunications equipment (OECD 2021). One of the benefits, especially early in the process of industrialization, of financial repression – defined as "keeping interest rates lower than would otherwise prevail"[7] – is it encourages heavy investment in industry that propels the type of big push industrialization experienced by successful industrializers in the past (Klein and Pettis 2020; Pettis 2013).

While one could attribute this export performance, particularly in sectors the Chinese state seeks to promote, to China's technology policy, there are other factors involved that contradict a technology policy-led upgrading narrative. First, there are legitimate concerns that China is pursuing beggar-thy-neighbor mercantilism. Chinese exports are fueled by direct state subsidies (OECD 2021) and

China's still undervalued currency (Klein and Pettis 2020), so they are more the outcome of mercantilist manipulation of relative costs than upgrading local capabilities. Of course, when the value of these products is disaggregated by country of origin, Chinese value capture is often much lower than headline trade statistics suggest (Fuller 2016), even if Chinese value is incrementally growing (Xing 2020). Moreover, the successful industrial firms are very often precisely those not favored by the state. The state often chooses the wrong, frequently state-owned, firms to support and through profligate support curses these firms with soft budget constraints that sap rather than bolster their capabilities (Fuller 2016). Also, the state often has been so pro-SOE as to stifle the intra-industry competitiveness conducive to upgrading (Brandt and Thun 2016, 2021). The upgrading and the bulk of the productivity gains made by China from 1998–2008 resided precisely in the efforts made through encouraging private entrepreneurship as well as through foreign direct investments. Two-thirds of the productivity gains in that period came from new entrants, most of them private enterprises (Brandt and Thun 2021). For all the Chinese state's technology policy efforts, in 2018, four decades after the start of reforms, only one large firm, Huawei, often targeted for state support had become the major international tech giant the Chinese envisioned, and Huawei's relationship with the Chinese state featured more contestation and less of an obedient patron state-client firm relationship typical of firms in China's 国家队 (national team; *guojiadui*) (Fuller 2019b).

One area where one could argue technology policy succeeded was in creating market demand in new product areas. Through state procurement and other supportive measures, China created large-scale demand in various clean energy products (Nahm 2021). Doing so brought China's large-scale economies in manufacturing to these new products and drove down costs globally.

The State's Reaction to Continuing Constraints on Technological Development

The concerns about China's technological shortcomings began to loom larger for China's leaders as it became apparent that growth in output for 25 years had not done much to close the knowledge gap with the international technology frontier. Thus, in January 2006 President Hu Jintao announced one of China's main goals would be indigenous innovation at the National Conference on Science and Technology (Gammeltoft and von Zedwitz 2021). According to Chen and Naughton (2016), 2006 was the beginning of the revival of industrial policy, after the increasing marketization of the previous decades, with the adoption of the Medium and Long-Term Program of Science and Technology (MLP). The program was quickly expanded in the aftermath of the global economic crisis of 2008, resulting in the new Strategic Emerging Industry initiative (SEI). Both Naughton (2021) and Tan (2021) agree that 2006 was a turning point to more activist state policy, although Naughton goes too far in downplaying the substantial state industrial and technology policies, often in part delegated to regional governments, before that time (Segal 2003; Thun 2006; Harwit 2008).[8]

These same concerns about China's technological backwardness remained after the leadership transition from Hu to Xi occurred in 2012–2013, as demonstrated by the flurry of new policies that followed the consolidation of Xi's leadership. The launch of the MLP and SEI had still not been sufficient to make China into an innovation power. The general trend of relying upon state agency and the idea of leapfrogging in specific strategic sectors thus intensified in 2015. In that year the SEI was reformulated, and the State Council launched Made in China 2025 and the Internet Plus, two programs that would be tied to the general framework of the Innovation-Driven Development Strategy (IDDS) launched in 2016. The IDDS expressed the vision that a new technological frontier is being developed in some industries and that China could jump ahead of developed countries by focusing on its own industrial capacity and domestic technologies.

The official policies after 2015 include goals for specific sectors, such as increasing data processing capacity and big data, developing capabilities in artificial intelligence, 5G telecommunications, green energy, and driverless vehicles, among others. The idea is that the triangulation between communication technologies, artificial intelligence, and data capacity can come together to foster innovations that can impact society across a wide variety of dimensions, such as industrial production, transportation, health, energy, and the military.

Made in China 2025 aimed at increasing the Chinese domestic content in technology sectors to 40 percent by 2020 and to 70 percent by 2025. Its policy instruments included funding for R&D coming from state agencies and reduced taxation for tech companies, especially directed to manufacturing firms in the areas of digitization and sustainability. The encompassing policy also aims at raising the number of mergers and acquisitions, thus trying to obtain technology by buying foreign firms in different sectors (Zenglein and Holzmann 2019). The plan already had the goal of improving the country's self-reliance with a focus on indigenous innovation, a concept which was later reinforced in the 14th Five Year Plan for 2021–2025.

As demonstrated by China's 14th Five Year Plan for 2021–2025 (National People's Congress of the People's Republic of China 2021), the country now wants to focus on the qualitative dimension of development, aiming at producing technological capabilities in core sectors, including artificial intelligence (AI), electric vehicles, and semiconductors, among others. The 14th Five Year Plan set goals such as increasing spending in R&D by more than 7 percent annually and raising the funding of basic science by 10.6 percent annually. The main objective is to transform China into a technological great power fully adapted to the Fourth Industrial Revolution. Furthermore, the plan also emphasized the transition to a low-carbon economy and the idea of elevating China's regional and global leadership profile (National People's Congress 2021).

The cumulative lessons drawn by the Hu and Xi administrations as revealed by their policies are that China should commit more resources to domestic technological development and at the same time reduce foreign technological dependency. Even the rhetorical turn toward focusing on the qualitative dimension of innovation in the 14th FYP is still backed up by hard targets for spending. However, the Chinese leadership does not seem to be able or willing to confront other institutional constraints that have been making China's technology policies less effective than they could be. We now turn to those.

Institutional Constraints on China's Technology Policies

There are four institutional continuities that have constrained the effectiveness of China's technology policy for decades. First, there is the pro-SOE bias of credit allocation and policy. Second, there are the information asymmetries that come from the scale of China geographically, demographically, and bureaucratically. Third, there is the failure to use exports as an informational and disciplinary tool. Connected to the latter is the fourth problem of the incentives provided to local governments.

In terms of the first constraint, the Chinese financial system has been a state-dominated banking system since the beginning of reforms. There has also been bias in bank lending favoring SOEs for the entire period and consequently, this nexus between the state banks and SOEs has created a very inefficient misallocation of credit that is a drag on the entire economy (Pettis 2013; Walter 2022), as well as hampering technology policy efficacy to the extent that SOEs are the favored targets of such policies (Brandt and Thun 2016; Fuller 2016). A number of scholars have argued that the bias toward the state sector has gotten worse since 2005/2006 as state firms used their various advantages in terms of cheap credit and other hidden or formal subsidies and policy favoritism to encroach on private enterprise, the *guojin mintui* (国金民退; state advanced and private sector retreats) phenomenon (Naughton 2021; Tan 2021; Walter 2022). While some trace the blame for the industrial and technology policy ambitions to the MLP, where they were first articulated (Naughton 2021; Tan 2021), Xi's policies did not correct this pro-SOE bias. Instead, his technology policies have actively encouraged even more *guojin mintui* in areas designated as strategic to the state (Fuller 2019a). On top of this, Xi's government has in recent years launched policies to severely constrict the power of China's technology giants through coerced gifts of "golden shares" that bestow upon the state a wide range of powers over these heretofore non-state-owned tech giants and onerous regulation of their businesses. At the time of writing, the heavy-handedness of the technology regulations may be beginning to lighten but the direction of policy in terms of more state control remains.[9]

Turning to the second constraint, there has long been recognition of how difficult it is to implement a coherent nationwide policy in China due to its large population and demographic size, as well as fragmented authority divided between regional and central government ministries, the so-called *tiaotiao kuaikuai* (条条块块) issue (Schurmann 1968; Lieberthal and Lampton 1992). While some have celebrated this semi-chaotic policymaking as policy experimentation (Heilmann 2011), more and more evidence is accumulating that turbo-charging the funding of technology policy in this fragmented system has only led to greater misallocation and waste (Walter 2022). Xi's policies have only thrown oil on this fire. Of course, this problem of waste is also deeply tied to the incentives of those running the *kuai*, the regional and local areas, which will be discussed as the fourth constraint.

The third constraint is the failure to follow the Northeast Asian states in using exports as a key information input to guide policy. China's policies have not been as effective in picking winners as the Northeast Asian success stories of Japan,

Korea, and Taiwan because those economies used export success as the metric to award firms (Haggard 2004), whereas China has not (Fuller 2016). This is not to say that China should have been as export-oriented as a share of GDP as these other economies. Instead, China simply has not made use of the information export performance provides to guide the allocation of policy benefits to firms. The Chinese state has heavily relied on direct procurement or "markets" in which the state had a heavy hand in determining outcomes. The signals sent from these sales serve to tell the state little about the performance of the targets of policies and firms, and more about the connections of these firms to the state (Fuller 2016, 2019b). Xi's emphasis on import substitution as a solution for technological dependence has only made information-rich exports less useful as policymaking metrics.

Finally, the fourth constraint is the incentive structure for local officials. Local governments have been given a variety of hard targets, including investment targets, by which to judge their performance. They have also been strapped for revenue vis-à-vis the expenditures required of them since the 1994 fiscal reforms. Whether local officials are motivated by careerist motivations of hitting their hard targets (Bulman 2016) or revenue-maximization (Su et al. 2020), their motivations do not push them to focus on upgrading firms or industrial ecosystems under their jurisdiction. Undertaking such upgrading also takes too long given that tenures for the top leaders of each level of local government are short (approximately less than three years) so local leaders end up myopically focusing on investment, whether for careerist or revenue-maximization reasons, to the detriment of sustainable upgrading (Fuller 2016). Moving away from hard targets has never been successfully completed despite various plans to do so. Meanwhile, the vast overinvestment in real estate development due to the revenue such investment created for local governments has left China overleveraged and yet still reluctant to pop this real estate bubble because of its immense size. Such moves to make local governments more efficient have too many political downsides, so at best the state will try to pursue only very gradual movement away from this investment-heavy growth model (Levitz 2023).

Made in China 2025 (MIC 2025)

Whereas the Innovation-Driven Development Strategy (Central Committee of the Communist Party of China and the PRC State Council 2016) is a protocol of intentions, outlining a generalist strategic vision for the priorities to be followed by the country in terms of innovation, aiming at the 2030- and 2050-time horizons, the MIC 2025 defines key economic sectors and has specific goals to be attained in 2020 and 2025, so has more clearly defined plans that require implementation. Thus, this section specifically analyzes the MIC 2025 initiative as China's main technology policy developed and implemented under Xi Jinping.

As previously stated, MIC 2025 is a continuum among China's industrial policies aiming at building national champions that are globally competitive in key strategic sectors. The idea is that by indigenizing China's R&D and innovation efforts, the country will be better positioned in global value chains, reducing its dependence on foreign technologies and ultimately conquering global markets in different industries.

The sectors included in the initiative are: 1) next-generation information technology; 2) high-end numerical control machinery and robotics; 3) aerospace and aviation equipment; 4) marine engineering equipment and high-tech ship manufacturing; 5) advanced rail equipment; 6) energy-saving and new-energy vehicles; 7) electrical equipment; 8) agricultural machinery; 9) new materials; 10) biomedicine and high-performance medical devices (State Council of the People's Republic of China 2015). Table 5.1 summarizes examples of goals for different products in eight of these sectors.

Specific tasks and priorities cited in the official documents include raising the investment directed toward science and technology (S&T), strengthening innovative design capabilities in manufacturing, and improving the intellectual property system in the country with special emphasis on sustainable and digital technologies. Establishing IP standards to foster R&D and new smart manufacturing products is also cited as a priority. Other goals include the production and use of robotics, big data, and the internet of things (IoT) in order to apply these technologies to industrial processes. Finally, MIC 2025 emphasizes improving military-civil fusion, envisioned as a bi-directional flow of knowledge and innovation between civilian and military technological sectors, and IDDS 2016 reiterates this goal.

Other priorities include strengthening brand building for China's manufacturing firms, a point often overlooked in previous governmental plans. In addition to that, the focus on green technologies is also a strategic move, seeing that its relevance will likely only grow in the next decades. Improving sustainability standards is fundamental for accessing developed markets and their consumers in addition to being important for the environment.

On the topic of green manufacturing, there is emphasis on improving the product lifecycle and fostering the circular economy, improving waste management

Table 5.1 Domestic Market Share Goal for Products Made by Chinese Firms (%)

Examples of goods	Goal for 2020	Goal for 2025
Mobile phone semiconductors	35	40
Industrial robots	50	70
New-energy vehicles	70	80
Renewable energy equipment	Not specified	80
High-capacity aircraft	10	20
High-tech ship parts and components	40–60	50–80
High-performance medical devices	60	80
High-capacity tractors and harvesters	30	60

Sources: Elaborated by the authors based on data extracted from State Council of the People's Republic of China (2015), Center for Security and Emerging Technology (2020)

and use of resources, and developing smart grids. Other broad measures include improving the energy mix of the country by seeking to reduce dependence on coal and sources that are high in carbon dioxide emissions while also increasing energy efficiency.

Within the MIC 2025, different provinces have launched their respective plans and funds, focusing on specific economic sectors to contribute to the general initiative. Examples include Guangdong Province's 2015 plan for the development of smart manufacturing, Anhui Province's 2015 plan for the development of advanced pharmaceutical and image scanning equipment and Hainan's similar 2016 plan for the pharmaceutical industry, among others (US Chamber of Commerce 2017).

There are many different intersecting plans which interact with one another within the broader umbrella of MIC 2025, and the same can be said of the funding mechanisms for the initiative. Examples of central and provincial government funds destined to contribute to this are the central government's Advanced Manufacturing Industry Investment Fund (US$ 3 billion), the National Emerging Industries Investment Guiding Fund (US$ 6 billion), the Special Constructive Funds (which covers MIC 2025 and Internet Plus and other initiatives) estimated at US$ 270 billion, the Shaanxi MIC 2025 Fund (US$ 117 billion), the Gansu MIC fund (US$ 37 billion), the MIC 2025 Strategic Cooperation Agreement between China Development Bank and the Ministry of Industry and Information Technology (MIIT) amounting to US$ 45 billion (US Chamber of Commerce 2017). And the central government's Integrated Circuits Investment Fund (Tranche 1: ~US$ 20 billion; Tranche 2: ~US$30 billion[10]; Tranche 3: ~US$143 billion, possibly rescinded[11]).

Due to the strategic importance of different sectors comprised by MIC 2025, we will focus on analyzing the following industries, which not only have high potential to generate economic growth, innovation, and positive externalities, but that could be important for the consolidation of China's power and influence in the global economy: 1) semiconductors; 2) electric vehicles (EVs); and 3) artificial intelligence. Moreover, they represent three different outcomes thus far for Xi's technology policy in three areas heavily promoted by the Chinese state. China has failed to close the gap with the international technology frontier in semiconductors. Despite the enormous hype some interested parties have generated for China's AI push (Lee 2018), China's AI development, while more promising than semiconductors, also has faced many challenges even before the Biden administration tightened export controls, so it is at best a case of mixed success. EVs, on the other hand, represent the best case for Chinese policy success (International Energy Association 2022).

Next-Generation Information Technology Components: Semiconductors

In the area of next-generation information technology, the semiconductors sector looms large as one of the country's major vulnerabilities and sources of external dependence. The MIC 2025 set the goal of achieving 70 percent self-sufficiency in semiconductors by 2030. In fact, the semiconductors sector has a whole section for it in a second document, called the Roadmap of Major Technical Domains for Made in China 2025 (State Council of the People's Republic of China 2015). Semiconductors are important inputs in many industrial goods such as mobile phones, computers, and cars, and in advanced technologies such as advanced military, robotics, artificial intelligence, and cutting-edge manufacturing. Hence, there are strategic reasons as well as economic ones to promote this sector. The Roadmap generally follows 2014's National IC Industry Development Promotion Outline (Fuller, 2019a). Growth until 2020 was set at 20 percent for the industry, and the major industry segments (fabrication, design, and packaging) were supposed to reach the international technology frontier by 2030 as reiterated in MIC 2025 and the Roadmap.

In terms of sheer industrial production objectives, the push in ICs seems to be falling short. As of the end of 2021, China produces 21 percent of the approximately US$ 185 billion dollars it consumes in semiconductors (IC Insights 2022), so it still is not doing much to solve its dependency on imports. Chinese firms are well positioned in the assembly and testing (lower value-added activities) nodes of the semiconductors value chain, while they still lag a bit behind in design capabilities, and far behind in fabrication, electronic design automation (EDA) software needed to design chips, and capital equipment (Fuller 2021). In terms of fabrication, there has been progress in quantitative terms, but not to the point of reaching the official policy goal of producing 70 percent of China's consumption, and even less so in terms of reaching the current international technology frontier represented by TSMC and Samsung. Moreover, this failure to catch up was true prior to the Trump and Biden export controls kicking in (Fuller 2019a).

Even more of a failure were the institutions designed to spur this industrial development. The state created a National IC Fund to guide investments in this industry alongside other investors which had strong, sometimes direct links, to the state. Armed with an enormous amount of money, the National IC Fund mainly engaged in taking over non-state firms, including ones listed overseas, before these overseas activities brought a backlash of investment scrutiny in the US, Europe, Japan, and Taiwan. At the same time, Tsinghua Unigroup, a conglomerate linked to Tsinghua University and, prior to the IC Megaproject's launch in 2014, one that had nothing to do with the IC industry, became the foremost national vehicle for this industry, especially in fabrication. Rather than creating more competition and entrepreneurship, this funding led to state encroachment on formerly promising firms such as SMIC (Fuller 2019a). Moreover, the signal from the central government that the purse strings were open has led to a deluge of funding for unsustainable fabrication investments, inadvertently putting the cart of building chip factories ahead of the horse of training enough engineers to run these factories. Wuhan Hongjin, a US$18.5 billion chip project, collapsed in 2020. Tsinghua Unigroup got into serious debt trouble in 2021 and subsequently the central government ordered other cities, such as Chongqing, to shut down some of their planned factories as the waste became too obvious to hide from the central government. By 2022, the central government had launched a sweeping rectification program, arresting Zhao Weiguo, who led Tsinghua Unigroup into the chip industry, Xiao Yaqing, MIIT's minister, and many of the top leaders of the National IC Fund.

And yet, it is still unclear whether the central government has fundamentally changed its approach. The firms that the state approved to take over the bulk of

Tsinghua Unigroup's chip-related assets, JAC and Wise Road, are not scrappy entrepreneurial funds disrupting China's industry. JAC is majority-owned by China's sovereign wealth fund but also partially owned by the mysterious controlling owner of Wise Road, Li Bin. Before getting into legal trouble, Tsinghua Unigroup's Zhao Weiguo on WeChat Moments had already hinted at Li being related to an unnamed senior Chinese leader. Other industry insiders believe this to be the case given how Li has been able to operate very closely with state entities and yet has kept a substantial shareholding in these state entities for himself.

Electric Vehicles (EVs)

The key driver to China's successful promotion of electric vehicles has been subsidies for purchasing EVs (given to the auto manufacturers for each car sold) that the state first put into place in 2009. Although they were supposed to be phased out several times, including this year, there is again discussion about extending them.[12] Over time, the subsidies have been adjusted due in large part to widespread fraud on the part of auto manufacturers selling cars to themselves and running state certification tests with larger batteries than were used in the cars sold on the market in order to qualify for larger subsidies (subsidies were related to battery size). Tax rebates for EVs have also played a role and will loom larger as China eventually gets rid of the subsidies. The government also introduced a credit system in 2018. Automakers received credits for each EV sold with the aim to force automakers to sell more EVs as a percentage of total cars sold.

The cost of building this industry has been substantial for the government. From 2009–2019, the total cost was just under 100 billion USD. Almost half the total were the EV purchase subsidies. As subsidies have been ratcheted down, the state has increased R&D spending. For both 2018 and 2019, each year's R&D spending was almost six times the spending on R&D for the 2009–2017 period. While many have hailed the government's investment in the infrastructure of EVs, it has not been costly relative to the other types of expenditure. Four of the top ten recipients of subsidies in China are automotive manufacturers and most of those subsidies are for EVs: SAIC, BYD, Great Wall, and JAC. Contemporary Amperex Technology Co. Limited (CATL) was the eleventh-largest recipient, and two other automakers were in the top20.

The goal for 2020 was for new energy and electric vehicles to account for 70 percent of the domestic market. Moreover, China aimed to produce two firms ranking in the top 10 players worldwide. Electric batteries, motors, and other components should have reached an international level of quality and represent 80 percent of China's market. By 2025, Chinese EV firms should represent 80 percent of the domestic market and two homegrown companies should be in the ranks of the 10 leading firms with 10 percent of their total sales (State Council of the People's Republic of China 2015; Center for Security and Emerging Technology 2020).

The electric vehicles industry presents an interesting example of China's growing proficiency in the production of electric batteries (ion-lithium batteries), with CATL being the most well-known success case. Founded in 2011, the company has advanced quickly in global markets and in 2021, it accounted for more than 32 percent of the global market share of ion-lithium batteries, making it the biggest producer in the world (Sanderson 2022).

China's domination of lithium batteries for EVs has also been a direct product of government policy. The government operated a "whitelist" of approved domestic battery manufacturers that were the only producers that EV manufacturers could use if they wished to receive the government subsidies for EVs. This policy led directly to the rise of CATL and helped BYD transition from phone batteries to auto batteries. With Guoxuan, these three are the second-, fifth-, and ninth-largest EV battery makers in the world. From 2014–2017, CATL's sales increased at a compound annual growth rate of 263 percent.

By 2019, local firms, including JVs, already dominated China's EV market with 85 percent market share.[13] As of now SAIC, Geely, and BYD have had a certain degree of success in their internationalization strategy, especially exporting to European markets. Other firms like BAIC and Chery continue to be suppliers mainly to the domestic market. There are also smaller brands, such as Nio Inc. and Xpeng, which are trying to expand internationally. In fact, SAIC-GM-Wuling (a joint venture with General Motors) and BYD ranked third and fourth in the largest sales of EVs in 2021, with market shares of 10.5 percent and 9.1 percent respectively, which means China has reached the goal of producing two major international players in the sector (Kane 2022).

In 2021, China accounted for more than half of the world's global sales of EVs. However, the structure of the EV market in China is still fragmented with more than 200 firms producing parts, components, and the other steps in the EV value chain. Trends suggest that there will be growing competition in the domestic market between the established firms, SAIC-GM-Wuling, BYD, Geely, and newcomers such as Nio and Xpeng (Daxue Consulting 2022). Sanderson (2022) points out that state funding and subsidies that have been directed to the industry since 2009 have contributed to the rise of new firms in this sector.

While the building of large-scale battery makers has been successful, subsidies have encouraged the entry of firms into the EV market and allowed too many of them to continue to survive. There were 119 producers of EVs in 2020. With a market of approximately 1.5 million EVs, each producer on average was producing 12,600 vehicles, far below the necessary scale economies.

The other issue is that the quality of Chinese EVs still lags. They generally only export to developing countries. While BYD sells more units than Tesla, Chinese EV firms generally sell to the low and middle tiers of auto buyers. The Chinese makers comprise 80 percent of the domestic market, which at 3.3 million cars sold in 2021 comprised 53 percent of global sales in units. However, the top tier is dominated by the foreign firms, such as Tesla, which now has its largest plant in China.

Artificial Intelligence

Artificial intelligence has three main areas: algorithms, machine learning, and computing. China has been very active in pushing AI development, particularly due to recognition of its importance for military applications. The first uptick in state-sponsored AI policies was in 2012–2014, when the Ministry of Science and Technology released the Special Plan of the Development of Intelligent Manufacturing Science and Technology for the 12th FYP. From 2015–2017, China put forth a slew of policies, including MIC 2025, 2015 Guiding Opinions on Actively Promoting the "Internet Plus" Action, 2015 Action Outline for Promoting the Development of Big Data, the 13th FYP, and the 2017 New-Generation Artificial Intelligence Development Plan.

Many, including AI technologist and entrepreneur Kai-fu Lee (2018), have touted China's advantage in AI because of the enormous amount of data available to Chinese AI companies due to China's large population and very weak privacy regulations. This "data as oil of the 21st century" argument posits that the country with the most data will "win" the AI race by crunching more data to achieve better machine learning and faster algorithm development. Others have questioned this assertion from two vantage points. First, China's data is quite fragmented and more trapped in private, proprietary data pools than many recognize (Ahmed 2019). Second, bulk data might not be as useful as smaller pools of quality data (think oil pumped out of the ground versus refined oil), and there may be more sophisticated learning techniques less reliant on data quantity than the current state of machine learning that relies on brute force processing of large quantities of data.

In some areas, China has succeeded spectacularly. Primarily due to machine learning drawing on these large pools of data, China has made large advances in language processing and recognition and visual recognition (including facial recognition, which was too controversial for the US to pursue vigorously given privacy considerations). These are reflected in the successes of Chinese firms, such as iFlytek in speech recognition and Megvii and SenseTime in facial recognition.

These successes are also seen in the tremendous surge of patents and AI research coming out of China. China has more AI citations than the US and more patent applications in AI's hottest sub-field, deep learning. However, the US still had more patents granted overall in 2021 and Japan beat out China for second place. Also, centers like the Stanford Institute for Human-Centered Artificial Intelligence, when tabulating AI patent counts, include all WIPO patents rather than simply using Triadic (EU, US, Japan patent offices) patents where the patents tend to be of higher quality. WIPO includes patents granted by China's patent office, which tend to be seen as relatively low-quality patents. Similarly, many view citations from conference papers as more leading-edge than citations from published journal articles due to the long lag in publication, and the US still leads China in conference paper citations. Furthermore, China has put out more AI journal articles for the last 12 years. China's acceleration has been impressive, with AI journal publications nearly tripling from 2017 to 2021, whereas American AI publications have only increased by approximately 60 percent.[14]

There are some weaknesses that remain in China's AI advancement. China has not done as well at algorithm development and developing top-tier talent. According to Tsinghua University, China had less than 20 percent of the top-tier AI scientists of the US as of 2018. China's effort has been almost entirely funded by the government and pursued through the government and state universities. In contrast, American investors have invested more than twice the money Chinese investors, including the state, have into AI commercial enterprises. Three times the number of AI-related firms have been founded in the US than in China from 2013–2021, despite the state largesse that has poured money into venture capital to support state goals in China.

Another bottleneck for China's AI development has been the processors running the supercomputers that crunch the large quantities of data. China is still very dependent on two American firms, AMD and Nvidia, for the processors. The US government has recently announced that it will not allow AMD and Nvidia to sell certain advanced chips to China for just this reason. There are no good alternatives in China, and other broad measures to control the export of advanced semiconductor technologies to China that are about to be enacted will make China's development of these even more unlikely. Counterbalancing this grim news, there are reports that Chinese AI firms have managed to circumvent American export controls by renting processing power from third-party cloud-based vendors.[15]

The domestic politics of AI have also become trickier in China. Baidu, Alibaba, and Tencent (the so-called BAT firms) sit on an enormous amount of data. They have also driven much of China's internet innovation, so they are the most likely corporate vehicles to drive AI innovation in China. However, it is still an open question whether the state, with its demands for golden shares and concomitant greater corporate control over these firms, will allow the BAT firms and other entrepreneurial firms to have enough freedom to innovate.

In the meantime, the US is searching for other ways to compete that undermine China's advantage in the "oil" of information. Different ways of AI learning beyond statistical machine learning are being introduced that negate large quantities of data. Supervised learning techniques or model-based learning approaches are among the promising new routes to address this potential weak point for the US.

Conclusion

Xi's ambitious pursuit of technology policies without reforming the institutions and practices through which such policies are pursued sets distinct limits on China's prospects for technology policy success. Moreover, the sustained industrial and technology policies of Xi and his predecessors that have resulted in forcing economic adjustment on China's trade partners (OECD 2021) have elicited foreign backlash that further narrows the scope for success. While Trump's unilateral moves to decouple posed threats to specific Chinese firms such as Huawei, the Biden administration's policy combining multilateral rhetoric with what were initially simply expanded unilateral measures (announced October 7, 2022) poses a much greater threat to China's ambitions in semiconductor and AI technologies, arguably the two most critical sector-spanning technologies for the near- to medium-term. The recent agreements by the Netherlands and Japan[16] to follow American controls on semiconductor manufacturing equipment for semi-mature manufacturing nodes demonstrate that nods to multilateralism can pay dividends.[17] If the broad and deep controls on semiconductor manufacturing equipment were effectively enforced, China would not be able to build advanced nodes at commercial efficiency and scale for at least a decade, if not longer.

The controls on AI chips are shaping up to restrict advances there as well. While there were concerns that the new restrictions announced in 2022 would present loopholes, such as dividing one chip into two separate chips in order to fall below the various technical performance limits set by the Department of Commerce's Bureau of Industry and Security (BIS), BIS has already signaled that it will revise the technical metrics as necessary; the main advanced foundry for AI chips, Taiwan's TSMC, and the Taiwanese government have also announced that they will not cooperate with Chinese firms trying to navigate these loopholes. With these restrictions in place, China's hurdles in the computing aspect of AI look formidable. Even if China manages to get some controlled chips from the likes of Nvidia and AMD via gray channels, the scale of its efforts will be constrained.

Notes

1. National Bureau of Statistics data at: http://english.www.gov.cn/archive/statistics/202301/23/content_WS63ce3db8c6d0a757729e5fe5.html#:~:text=After%20deducting%20price%20factors%2C%20China's,points%20from%20the%20previous%20year
2. World Bank data at https://data.worldbank.org/indicator/SE.TER.ENRR?locations=CN
3. www.theguardian.com/world/2022/aug/11/china-overtakes-the-us-in-scientific-research-output
4. As some publications have authors from multiple countries and regions, the subtotals for each country/region when combined are greater than the total number of top 1 percent most cited articles.
5. As a published author in journals within the Business and Finance category of SSCI, one of the authors of this chapter can vouch for the utter lack of any contribution to advancing the natural sciences and engineering of such journals.
6. The time-limited forward citations metric is often referred to as a "citation lag" metric and means that one only counts the forward citations (citations of the relevant patent made by subsequent patents) within a given time interval, e.g., three years, as used in the Jefferson and Jiang chapter.
7. Carmen Reinhart (2012) cited in Pettis (2013).
8. Naughton (2021, 13) clearly states his view of a great divergence pre- and post-2006: "As is described in Chapter 3, beginning in 2006, China promulgated a series of policies and programs that represented the launch of its modern industrial policies." Fuller, Harwit, Segal, Thun, and many others provide evidence for many significant state industrial policies prior to 2006.
9. See this recent discussion at Digicha: https://digichina.stanford.edu/work/is-chinas-tech-crackdown-or-rectification-over/.
10. Estimates from Ramani and Arcuri, "China EDA Deep Dive Part 2 – Structurally Challenged, Primed for a 'Big Bang' Moment," UBS, July 15, 2020.
11. www.reuters.com/technology/china-plans-over-143-bln-push-boost-domestic-chips-compete-with-us-sources-2022-12-13/.
12. Provincial governments have stepped in to make up for the shortfall in central government subsidies (www.bloomberg.com/news/articles/2023-03-07/china-s-provinces-offer-ev-sweeteners-as-national-subsidies-fade#xj4y7vzkg).

13 McKinsey "Winning the Chinese BEV Market," May 4, 2021.
14 This publication data is all from the Stanford Institute for Human-Centered Artificial Intelligence.
15 www.ft.com/content/9706c917-6440-4fa9-b588-b18fbc1503b9.
16 Japan may be backing away from any commitments to American-style export controls in semiconductors, see https://techwireasia.com/2023/03/japan-remains-in-a-state-of-limbo-after-the-dutch-join-the-us-in-restricting-chip-exports-to-china/.
17 Or, alternatively, faced with the reality that China won't be able to build chip factories for even semi-mature nodes without American equipment anyway, the Netherlands and Japan acquiesced to keeping allied amity without sacrificing any plausible future sales. See https://chinatechtales.wordpress.com/2022/11/06/as-the-fog-lifts-reflections-on-the-chip-wars-impact-after-one-month-chip-fabrication/.

References

Abrami, Regina M., William C. Kirby, and Franklin W. McFarlan. 2014. *Can China Lead?: Reaching the Limits of Power and Growth*. Boston, MA: Harvard Business School Press.
Ahmed, Shazeda. 2019. "The Messy Truth about Social Credit," *Logic* (7), May 1.
Atradius Group. 2022. *Industry Trends in Information and Communication Technology (ICT): Focus on Sector Business Performance and Credit Risk*. Amsterdam: Atradius N.V. Publisher.
Brandt, Loren, and Eric Thun. 2016. "Constructing a Ladder for Growth: Policy, Markets, and Industrial Upgrading in China." *World Development* 80(C): 78–95.
Brandt, Loren, and Eric Thun. 2021. "The Great Dialectic: The State Versus Market in China." In *The Oxford Handbook of China Innovation*, eds. Xiaolan Fu, Bruce Mckern, and Jin Chen. Oxford: Oxford University Press, 135–156.
Bulman, David. 2016. *Incentivized Development in China: Leaders, Governance, and Growth in China's Counties*. Cambridge: Cambridge University Press.
Center for Security and Emerging Technology. 2020. *Roadmap of Major Technical Domains for Made in China 2025*. Translation made by the Georgetown University of the original document: The State Strategic Advisory Committee. 2015. *Roadmap of Major Technical Domains for Made in China 2025*. Beijing: The People's Republic of China. Chinese Academy of Engineering Press. https://cset.georgetown.edu/wp-ontent/uploads/t0181_Made_in_China_roadmap_EN.pdf.
Central Committee of the Communist Party of China and the PRC State Council. 2016. *Outline of the National Innovation-Driven Development Strategy*. Beijing: The People's Republic of China & Xinhua News Agency Press.
Chen, Ling, and Barry Naughton. 2016. "An Institutionalized Policy-Making Mechanism: China's Return to Techno-Industrial Policy." *Research Policy* 45(2): 2138–2152.
China National Bureau of Statistics. 2023. "China's spending on R&D hits 3 trillion yuan in 2022". *Xinhua News Agency*. January 23. http://english.www.gov.cn/archive/statistics/202301/23/content_WS63ce3db8c6d0a757729e5fe5.html#:~:text=After%20deducting%20price%20factors%2C%20China's,points%20from%20the%20previous%20year.
Daxue Consulting. 2022. "China's EV Market, the Rise of a Global Leader." Available at: China's EV Market: The Rise of a Global Leader. daxueconsulting.com.
Fewsmith, Joseph. 2001. *China Since Tiananmen: The Politics of Transition*. Cambridge: Cambridge University Press.
Fuller, Douglas B. 2016. *Paper Tigers, Hidden Dragons: Firms and the Political Economy of China's Economic Development*. Oxford: Oxford University Press.
Fuller, Douglas B. 2019a. "Growth, Upgrading, and Limited Catch-Up in China's Semiconductor Industry." In *Policy, Regulation and Innovation in China's Electricity and Telecom*

Industries. eds. Loren Brandt and Thomas G. Rawski. Cambridge: Cambridge University Press, Chapter 7, 262–303.

Fuller, Douglas B. 2019b. "Searching for China's Technological Champions: What Past Structural Flaws and Policy Failures Tell Us about the Likelihood of Success for Current Policies." East Asian Institute Working Paper.

Fuller, Douglas B. 2021. "China's Counter-strategy to American Export Controls in Integrated Circuits." *China Leadership Monitor*, March, No. 67.

Gammeltoft, Peter, and Max von Zedwitz. 2021. "The Political Economy of China's R&D Internationalization: Policy-led Innovation and Changes in China's Growth Model." In *Innovation from Emerging Markets: From Copycats to Leaders*, eds. Fernanda Cahen, Lourdes Casanova, and Anne Miroux. Cambridge: Cambridge University Press. 185–221.

Haggard, Stephan. 2004. "Institutions and Growth in East Asia." *Studies in Comparative International Development* 138(4): 53–81.

Harwit, Eric. 2008. *China's Telecommunications Revolution*. Oxford: Oxford University Press.

Heilmann, Sebastian. 2011. "Policymaking through Experimentation: The Formation of a Distinctive Policy Process." In *Mao's Invisible Hand: The Political Foundations of Adaptive Governance in China*. eds. Sebastian Heilmann and Elizabeth Perry. Cambridge, MA: Harvard University Asia Center, 62–101.

Huang, Yasheng. 2003. *Selling China: Foreign Direct Investment during the Reform Era*. New York: Cambridge University Press.

Huang, Yasheng. 2008. *Capitalism with Chinese Characteristics: Entrepreneurship and the State*. Cambridge: Cambridge University Press.

IC Insights. 2022. "Research Bulletin on China-Based Semiconductors." Available at: bulletin0517.icinsights.com.

International Energy Association. 2022. *Global EV Outlook 2022: Securing Supplies for an Electric Future*. Paris, France: IEA Publications.

Jaros, Kyle A. 2019. *China's Urban Champions: The Politics of Spatial Development*. Princeton: Princeton University Press.

Jefferson, Gary, and Renai Jiang. 2021. "China's Science and Technology Progress through the Lens of Patenting." In *The Oxford Handbook of China Innovation*, eds. Fu Xiaolan, Bruce Mckern, and Jin Chen. New York: Oxford University Press, 90–112.

Jiang, Renai, Haoyue Shi, and Gary H. Jefferson. 2020. "Measuring China's International Technology Catching up." *Journal of Contemporary China* 29(124): 519–534.

Kane, Mark. 2022. "Global Sales of Electric Vehicles Q1-Q4 2021." *Inside EVs*. https://insideevs.com/news/564800/world-top-oem-sales-2021/.

Klein, Matthew, and Michael Pettis. 2020. *Trade Wars are Class Wars: How Rising Inequality Distorts the Global Economy and Threatens International Peace*. New Haven, CT: Yale University Press.

Lee, Kai-Fu. 2018. *AI Superpowers*. Boston: Houghton Mifflin Harcourt.

Levitz, Eric. 2023. "China's Economic Model Is in Crisis (and Xi Knows It)." *New York Magazine*, January 24.

Li, Liu. 2009. "Research Priorities and Priority-Setting in China." In *Vinnova Analysis Report 2009–21*. Stockholm: Vinnova.

Li, Xibao. 2012. "Behind the Recent Surge of Chinese Patenting: An Institutional View." *Research Policy* 41(1): 236–249.

Lieberthal, Kenneth, and David M. Lampton. 1992. *Bureaucracy, Politics and Decision Making in Post-Mao China*. Berkeley, CA: University of California Press.

MacFarquhar, Roderick, and Michael Schoenhals. 2006. *Mao's Last Revolution*. Cambridge, MA: Belknap Press.

Nahm, Jonas. 2021. "Testimony before the U.S.-China Economic and Security Review Commission Hearing on "China's Energy Plans and Practices." March 17. www.uscc.gov/sites/default/files/2022-03/Jonas_Nahm_Testimony.pdf.

National People's Congress of the People's Republic of China. 2021. *Outline of the People's Republic of China 14th Five-Year Plan for National Economic and Social Development and Long-Range Objectives for 2035*. Beijing: The People's Republic of China & Xinhua News Agency Press.

Naughton, Barry. 2021. *The Rise of China's Industrial Policy from 1978–2020*. Mexico: Universidad Autónoma de Mexico, Centro de Estudios sobre China.

OECD. 2021. "Measuring Distortions in International Markets: Below Market Finance." *OECD Trade Policy Paper n. 247*. France: Paris. OECD Trade and Agriculture Directorate.

Palla, Ishfaq A., Mangkhollen Singson, and Suseela Thiyagarajan. 2020. "A Comparative Analysis of Retracted Papers in Health Sciences from China and India" *Accountability in Research Review* 27(7): 401–416.

Pettis, Michael. 2013. *Avoiding the Fall: China's Economic Restructuring*. Washington, DC: Arnegie Endowment for International Peace.

Reinhart, Carmen. 2012. "The Return of Financial Repression." *Financial Stability Review* 16: 37–48.

Rozelle, Scott, and Natalie Hell. 2020. *Invisible China: How the Urban-Rural Divide Threatens China's Rise*. Chicago, IL: The University of Chicago Press.

Sanderson, Henry. 2022. *Volt Rush: The Winners and Losers in the Race to Go Green*. London: Oneworld Publications.

Schurmann, Franz. 1968. *Ideology and Organization in Communist China*. Berkeley, CA: University of California Press.

Segal, Adam. 2003. *Digital Dragon: High-Technology Enterprises in China*. Ithaca, NY: Cornell University Press.

Simon, Denis F., and Cong Cao. 2009. *China's Emerging Technological Edge: Assessing the Role of High-End Talent*. Cambridge: Cambridge University Press.

Springut, Micah, Stephen Schlaikjer, and David Chen. 2011. "China's Program for Science and Technology Modernization: Implications for American Competitiveness." Prepared for the US – China Economic and Security Review Commission.

State Council of the People's Republic of China. 2015. *Notice of the State Council on the Publication of "Made in China 2025"*. Beijing: The People's Republic of China. State Council Publisher. www.gov.cn/zhengce/content/2015-05/19/content_9784.htm.

Su, Fubin, Ran Tao, and Dali Yang. 2020. "Rethinking the Institutional Foundations of China's Growth." In *The Oxford Handbook on the Politics of Development*, eds. Carol Lancaster and Nicholas van de Walle. Oxford: Oxford University Press, Chapter 29, 626–651.

Tan, Yeling. 2021. *Disaggregating China, Inc.: State Strategies in the Liberal Economic Order*. Ithaca, NY: Cornell University Press.

Tang, Li. 2019. "Five Ways China Must Cultivate Research Integrity." *Nature* 575: 589–591.

Thun, Eric. 2006. *Changing Lanes in China: Foreign Direct Investment, Local Governments, and Auto Sector Development*. New York: Cambridge University Press.

US Chamber of Commerce. 2017. *Made in China 2025: Global Ambitions Built on Local Protections*. Washington, DC: US Chamber of Commerce Editor. www.uschamber.com/international/made-china-2025-global-ambitions-built-local-protections-0.

Wagner, Caroline. 2023. "China now publishes more high-quality science than any other nation – should the US be worried?" *The Conversation*. January 10. https://theconversation.com/china-now-publishes-more-high-quality-science-than-any-other-nation-should-the-us-be-worried-192080.

Wagner, Caroline, Lin Zhang, and Loet Leydesdorff. 2022. "A discussion of measuring the top-1% most-highly cited publications: Quality and impact of Chinese papers". *Scientometrics* 127: 1825–1839.

Walter, Carl. 2022. *The Red Dream: The Chinese Communist Party and the Financial Deterioration of China.* Hoboken, NJ: John Wiley and Sons, Ltd.

Xing, Yuqing. 2020. "How the iPhone Widens the US Trade Deficit with China: The Case of the iPhone X." *Frontier Economics in China* 15(4).

Zenglein, Max, and Anna Holzmann. 2019. *Evolving Made in China 2025 China's Industrial Policy in the Quest for Global Tech Leadership.* Berlin: Mercator Institute for China Studies Press.

Zhao, Y. (2014). *Who's Afraid of the Big Bad Dragon: Why China Has the Best (and the Worst) Education System in the World.* San Francisco: Jossey-Bass.

6 Chinese Urban Poverty

Negligence or Disdain?[1]

Dorothy J. Solinger

Two glaring misperceptions plague public views about current and recent Chinese destitution: one about its abolition and the other about its measurement. These two misconceptions, both of which come from announcements in 2021, appear often in Chinese media and especially in Party chief Xi Jinping's statements. These are first, about the country having abolished poverty, and second, about Xi's campaign for "common prosperity." The mistaken viewpoints conceal the double disregard in which the *urban* poor subsist, placed as they are outside the system [*tizhi yiwai* 体制 以外, or the framework under which the dominant components of the population are treated].

The neglect of the city-situated poverty-stricken is a function of its members being caught between municipal localities' and local leaders' lofty aspirations paired with their prevalent shortage of funds on one hand, and Xi and the central government's Dream of Modernization, speedy economic growth, technical superiority, and world prominence (Solinger 2022)[2] on the other. Together these two forces squeeze the city impoverished into a box of exclusion (Ye Xiangqun 2013, 72; Du and Wang 2017, 26; He and Liu 2015, 86; Gallagher 2020, 191–193; Xie 2022).

Misunderstandings

Poverty Gone?

The most blatant misunderstanding is that when Xi Jinping hailed the elimination of extreme poverty as[3] a "complete victory" in February 2021,[4] the fulfillment of a cardinal aim of his regime, he was totally ignoring the uncounted millions of poor in the cities. He did, however, go on to admit that he was referring just to the rural areas where, and only where, his campaign to wipe out penury had been promoted. Xi alleged that the country had invested nearly 1.6 trillion yuan in poverty alleviation in the eight years since his accession to power which, again, went just to agrarian regions, thereby managing to "lift" more than 10 million poor people from indigence annually over these years (Li 2022). He also announced that "all 98.99 million poor rural population have been taken out of poverty [what he and The World Bank both claimed to be over 770 million people] and 832 poverty-stricken counties as well as 128,000 villages removed from the poverty list" (thefluxmedia 2021).

DOI: 10.4324/9781003257943-7

Of note is a contrast with the words of former Party General Secretary Hu Jintao who, on the eve of relinquishing his post at the 2012 Eighteenth Party Congress, had pronounced explicitly that, "By 2020 *urban and* rural residents' average income will double as compared with that in 2010," thereby indicating his concern for the livelihood level of citizens living in *both* urban and rural locales (Tang 2012, 213) [emphasis added].

Even if extreme rural poverty was truly eradicated, a Nanjing University scholar wrote in 2018 that "After rural *absolute* poverty has been completely eliminated, an even larger scale, more complex *relative* poverty[5] mass will become conspicuous [emphasis added]." Those in that cluster are mostly scattered throughout cities compared to the closely concentrated rural *absolute* poor, their surrounding environment having a higher economic level, with more complete infrastructure. They often appear as individuals, making them less visible as well as more difficult to administer. All this was that scholar's explanation for the omission of city folk (Wang 2018, 61).[6]

A number of studies have found that *urban* poverty, unlike rural indigence, has only been increasing in the years since Xi took command. As one explained, "The poor are getting poorer, very difficult to raise their ability to earn a living, they lack power to throw off poverty" (Li 2012, 280; Du and Wang 2017, 27; Wei and Wang 2013, 9; Mo 2022). Underlining this judgment, the 2022 National Statistical Yearbook shows that from 2015 to 2021 the per capita disposable income of the lowest-income urban households declined from 18.7 percent of that of the highest-income quintile to just 16 percent in 2021.[7]

Measurement

The second misconception is that the rural poverty line is a national one. In fact, unlike in the countryside for which there is a definite uniform nationwide "poverty line," there is, to the contrary, no such *urban* standardized demarcation to designate who is poor (Li and Sun 2015, 78). Instead, each city, and sometimes each district within a city, determines its own lowest minimum livelihood norm (the *dibao* 低保 – the short name for the Minimum Livelihood Guarantee [*zuidi shenghuo baozhang*, 最低生活保障] launched nationally in 1999, which supplies the minimal amount of funds that local assessors deem necessary for survival in a given city or district to families whose average income falls short of the norm). City administrators assign the standard principally on the basis of that locality's funds and the costs of living in that place, the final figure the result of wrangles among local bureaucracies.

There are also great regional disparities in levels of poverty, with the west and central part of China having the most indigence and the east having the least (Li and Sun 2015, 79; Du and Wang 2017, 26). Absence of a unified benchmark makes it "difficult to accurately estimate the national situation, and hard to set a national, unified policy to fight urban poverty," noted several researchers at the Chinese Academy of Social Sciences (CASS) (Wang et al. 2016, 32). Not only this, but researchers' use of different methods to calculate poverty rates lead to significant discrepancies, while various urban bureaucracies each have their own reckonings, including labor/social security, statistics, the trade union, and civil affairs. For instance, as of the middle of Xi's first decade in power, statistics departments were taking as the poor population the five percent of the urban populace with the lowest incomes, while municipal civil affairs bureaus simply viewed the number of *dibao* recipients in their jurisdictions as the count of the poverty-stricken (Li 2012, 280–281; Solinger 2022, 94–97; Wang et al. 2021, 40; Wang et al. 2016, 33–35).

But using the total of recipients of the urban *dibao* across the country at a given time as the total of poor people in cities is a flawed means of computing. This is because the extent of the *dibao* itself is politically determined and can be adjusted up or down on the basis of local policy contrivances that fail to correspond to the true numbers of the impoverished (Li 2018, 92). As an example, when Xi came to power in 2013, the actual number of the poor came to more than twice the total of those getting the *dibao*, amounting to 7.5 to 8.7 percent of the urban population, according to data from collaborative research between the National Bureau of Statistics (NBS), the Ministry of Civil Affairs, and some local agencies (Li and Sun 2015, 78, 79; Tang and Cao 2015, 113; Wei and Wang 2013, 9).[8] But three years later, the same bureau announced the rate of urban poverty as around 10 to 15 percent, when a mere 1.88 percent of the urban populace was being granted the *dibao* (Wang 2019, 80).

Another study estimated the urban poor population at about 44 million (or around six percent of the city populace) as of the middle of the decade, not including those whose income was on the poverty line but who remained abjectly poor, such as farmers who had lost their land, recent college graduates, or people who, because of serious illness or natural disasters, had met sudden impoverishment (Tang and Cao 2015, 113).[9] In sum, despite the wide-ranging disparities (perhaps the result of varying methods of calculation), there is a consensus that, as two economists reported, "Because funds for the urban *dibao* are limited and the norm is low, the population living in poverty in cities must be far beyond those who enjoy the *dibao*" (Li and Sun, *op. cit.*, 78).

Wang, Wei, and Su, publishing in 2016, hold that since 2010 (when the number of *dibao* beneficiaries began to slip), the *dibao* norm had fallen below 40 percent of low-income urban households' average disposable income (Wang et al. 2016, 35). But by the end of the decade, the CASS social bluebook reported that, "After 2011, the urban *dibao* norm generally accounted for just 18 percent of the average urban per capita disposable income" (Li 2018, 94). Other researchers calculated that in 2005 the *dibao* norm represented 17.8 percent of average urban *income*, but fell to 2015's 16.9 percent, even as the norm's percent of average urban *expenditure* went from 2005's 23.6 percent up to 2015's 24.6 percent (Du and Wang 2017, 28). The apparently climbing consumption must have been possible only because of poor people's borrowing money, which they are compelled to do for such critical matters as seeing doctors, for schooling, for normal daily spending, and for housing.[10]

Yet one more piece, published in 2021, notes that using 40 percent of urban residents' median income for a poverty line would likely result in a "relative" poverty line of 12,000 yuan/year, yielding a total of around 70 million indigent people, and a poverty rate of nine percent. But at the time of that article's publication, there were just 9.4 million urbanites being granted the *dibao*! Besides, these authors assess that "whether income or consumption is used to measure absolute urban poverty, the urban poor population amounts to 12 to 20 percent of urban dwellers, including migrants" (Wang et al. 2021, 40, 44). And these figures do not take note of the indigent whose income may be temporarily above the *dibao* line, but whose situation is nonetheless precarious and dire. A final point, often raised by academics in the past few years, is that although urban *income* poverty may account for about half the hardships of the poor, actual impoverishment is multidimensional, so that inferior education, health, and livelihood conditions also play a major role in the circumstances besetting the lower-incomed (Yu 2019, 26–28; Han and Fan 2016, 49).[11]

One positive statistic on the government's treatment of the urban poor: from the time that *tekun renyuan jiuzhu* [特困人员救助, assistance for people in especially difficult situations][12] began in 2014 up through 2017, the numbers served climbed from 68,000 up to 254,000 (Li 2018, 86). This increase likely was at least in part a result of former *dibao* and *sanwu* beneficiaries being shifted to the *tekun* category (more on this later). Nonetheless, the plight of the urban poor, and the picture of poverty in the city, would seem to have worsened under Xi; indeed, inattention mixed with unconcern appear to be the mark of his rule.

I go on to explore the causes behind this situation and survey the groups who make up the impoverished, along with the conditions under which they scrape by. I then mention some policies pertinent to the poor publicized during Xi's period in power, measures that were apparently not seriously implemented.[13] I conclude by pointing to the grim future for the Chinese urban impoverished under Xi.

Causes of Urban Penury

The two chief drivers of the straits in the cities both derive from policies decreed by the state itself and linked to the label "economic reform." The first of these was the dramatic dismantling of tens of thousands of money-losing or obsolete factories once filled with underskilled, "over-aged" (beyond the age of 35), and poorly educated workers, perhaps some 60 million of whom were sacked almost in one fell swoop (Wang 2001, 24; Wang 2004, 53).[14] Certainly millions among them were thrust into destitution suddenly, losing not just their income but also their benefits, which had been attached to their work units (Solinger 2022). As a research team wrote in 2017:

> The scale of urban poverty is still very large, and possibly will expand because the continuing deepening of state-owned enterprise reform will lead to new layoffs and the "new-style" urbanization project [of 2014] will make more rural-*hukou* [户口, household registration] holders enter the cities.
> (Zhang et al. 2017, 74)

Accordingly, the second source of new and abrupt insolvency in cities was the surging entry of often hard-up farmers from the countryside, some by choice and some as a result of their land having been appropriated, after which they were mandatorily relocated into municipalities. Surely many of these incoming masses managed to find at least a scant livelihood in town, however onerously acquired, and had contrived to better their lot in life by leaving the farms. But the upshot of these moves was to immediately produce an unwieldly and unprepared throng of new low-income urban residents (Solinger 1999).

Additional factors have been the inadequate social security system, the demolition of old urban houses, high living costs in the municipalities, and the lack of benefits for employees in non-public enterprises, plus highly competitive labor markets that those (especially migrants and laid-off workers) with so-called low *suzhi* [素质, quality, usually implying a low level of education], low social position, and few social resources or contacts find it formidable to break into (Pang 2014, 90). Such persons' only options are to take on odd, irregular jobs or to work in low-end manufacturing or physical labor (construction, transport, packaging), for which jobs are unstable, wages low, and welfare lacking (Li and Sun 2015, 80; Tang and Cao 2015, 115–116).

There is also the matter of inflation, which puts a decent style of living far out of reach for those without means (Feng and Chen 2019, 103; Du and Wang 2017, 23, 27). While wages for migrant factory labor did rise until the latter part of the '10s when the economy began to slow down, real wages failed to keep pace with the salary increases and improved standards of living enjoyed by people bearing an urban *hukou* (Unger and Siu 2019, 771). Furthermore, given their scarcity of funds, poor people are ill-prepared to handle an unexpected illness, accident, or disaster.

Groups and Investment

Rural migrants began surging into the cities in the mid-1980s and immediately confronted discrimination, a labor market marked by only the low-grade, poorly paying, benefit-lacking, physically exhausting work open to them (Solinger 1999). But for the most part, it was not until formerly lifetime-secure workers were ejected from their factory positions in the late 1990s and early 2000s (Yang and Huang 2003, 226–234; Zhang 2002; Lu 2002, Sun 2002; Cook 2002; Hussain 2002; Solinger 2022) that researchers took note of the millions of "new urban poor" pouring into the streets, whether in protest about their job loss or in desperate efforts to earn the wherewithal to survive.[15]

A paper from 2021 determined that the poor in the cities fell into three categories, according to the years when each became prominent: before 1992, it was the "old urban poor," mainly consisting of the *sanwu*[16]; from 1992 to "now" [2021], the "new urban poor," mainly laid-off staff and workers, migrant workers, and those at-work with low wages or owed wages; and "emergent groups": the relative poor and the multi-dimensionally poor (Wang et al. 2021, 44). Variously, three scholars considering the *dibao* grantees as "the urban poor" report that as of 2002 laid-off and unemployed workers amounted to 44 percent of *dibao* recipients, while by 2009 and 2015 the proportions of disabled, old, and those with "flexible employment" were continuously increasing (Wang et al. 2016, 35; Bai et al. 2013, 122).[17] Others, writing in 2017 and 2019, divided the new urban poor into three other groups: those lacking an opportunity to work [who would principally be the laid-off workers, continuing to suffer from indigence], those in "relative poverty,"[18] and the traditional *sanwu*, adding that the main group was still those without a chance to work. Of these, the absolute majority are the unemployed and laid-off, whose plight was brought about by reform of state enterprises, this analysis averred (Zhang et al. 2017, 74; Feng and Chen 2019, 102–103; Du and Wang 2017, 23, 26).

In 2014, a "Temporary Method of Social Assistance"[19] went into effect to serve sudden, urgent, short-term difficulties of basic livelihood, presumably a less expensive program for the government. Two years later, the Ministry of Civil Affairs began to enter some of the *sanwu* and *dibao* subjects into the category of the most abjectly poor [the *tekun*]. Thence, the Ministry's statistical yearbook no longer separately listed data on the *sanwu* (Li 2018, 85–86). This could have been a means of cutting back on the numbers of those getting the *dibao*, whose allowances were longer-term and larger (*Ibid.*, 86).

Giving weight to this surmise, before *tekun* became a separate assistance item, urban *sanwu* had generally been covered by the urban *dibao* and had received the full amount of the *dibao* allowance. Perhaps cutting laid-off workers from the *dibao* and filling the *dibao* ranks with more old, disabled, and diseased was one more way to save money, as people with these attributes might be viewed as justifiably offered fewer funds.

And yet one more sign of reduced generosity under Xi was a reduction in financial investment in the temporary assistance system in the middle of the decade: though 5.7 billion yuan had been allocated to it by the state in 2014, a figure which rose to 13.1 billion in 2016, in 2017 the amount dropped to 10.7 billion (Li 2018, 87). Probably relatedly, investment in the urban *dibao* declined as a percent of total government expenditure yearly from 2014, whereas it had been increasing in the years before that (*Ibid.*, 80; Solinger 2022, 29, Table 2.1).[20] It seems likely that shifting people off the *dibao* rolls,[21] inventing new, cheaper forms of welfare for the poor, and cutting back on investment were all of a piece.

Besides, a "rise in the ranks of the poor" was noted in an article from 2015, with the biggest change being an uptick in unemployed college graduates (Cui et al. 2015, 34). The CASS 2016 social bluebook described the "population in difficulty" as being "still large scale," but in these writers' views, "most" were said to be the sick, the elderly, the disabled, and the unemployed (Cui et al. 2015, 34). Indeed, the disabled among the *dibaohu* [低保户, recipients of the *dibao*] had risen from 2010's 7.82 percent to 2014's 8.6 percent and the elderly went from 14.6 to 16.8 percent, while the registered unemployed dropped from 21.3 down to 16.6 percent in those years (Jiang and Wang 2015, 138, 139). Since the researchers here refer to percentages among the *dibao* recipients, one could reasonably speculate that these segments of the population had by then become the chief targets of the *dibao*, rather than necessarily representing the actual proportions of the city population who were poorest.

The Farmers and the Fired

Farmers

A 2015 journal article attested that more and more peasants are becoming "urban people." The majority of them, however, once ensconced in the city, simply fall into the stratum of the urban poor (Cui et al. 2015, 35). As one scholar wrote in

2018, well into Xi Jinping's time in office, "Peasant workers have become the new main body of the urban poor, but the management of their poverty is the blind spot in China's present urban system to oppose poverty" (He 2018, 107). A much-heralded announcement appeared in 2014 of an initiative aimed at encouraging farmers to enter towns and cities and acquire registration there, the "National New-type Urbanization Plan (2014–2020),"[22] termed by *hukou* (户口) expert Kam Wing Chan as "the most ambitious hukou reform program since its inception in 1958."

Regardless, Chan nonetheless judged in mid-2021 that by the time of the 2020 Census (when those living away from their place of household registration amounted to over a quarter of the total Chinese population at 26.6 percent) (Chan 2021, 2), there was an even greater gap in social services provision between urbanites with city *hukou* registration and city dwellers lacking that certification, as compared with what had existed in 2013. Any upgrading in benefits that might have been occasioned by that 2014 program has mostly been disbursed in small and medium cities, which unfortunately are unequipped to offer much in this regard, or else by means of a strict "points system" that favors just the wealthy and the well-educated. Chan also asserted that in the major metropolises the children of migrants have recently met with greater difficulties in obtaining education than in the years before. "*Hukou* reform has basically stalled" and "even arguably regressed," he concluded (Chan 2021, 2).

Of the 133-plus million rural workers living in cities and towns as of 2021, 68 percent were married, and the average age of the group was nearly 37, both of which figures had mounted over the years. Only 17 percent had an education above senior middle school. But it appears that their average income in 2020 was 4,072 yuan per month (calculated from Guojia tongjiju 2022, 3), whereas the average urban disposable income for 2020 was 3,653 yuan monthly (Jia 2022, 26). On this basis, one must wonder if the average employed migrant in cities ought to be counted among the urban poor.[23] Nearly half (48 percent) were involved in either manufacturing or construction work, with another 24 percent in service work or commercial activities, all jobs calling for low skills (Guojia tongjiju 2022). These are the very trades that have seen major cutbacks in employment between 2014 and 2019.[24] And of course, millions more jobs disappeared during Covid.

Regrettably, official reports fail to indicate how much time people actually spend working even if "employed." But a writer in Xi's early term did note that they "mainly depend on short-term jobs and are often unemployed or semi-employed" (Pang 2014, 90). That this situation only persisted seems likely, as a 2017 study that sampled nearly 10,000 families in difficulty reported that a mere 21 percent had found stable employment, 17 percent were doing "flexible labor," and 25 percent were *getihu* [个体户, self-employed]. The same work uncovered that 45 percent of the migrant sample was living in inferior housing, and that, while five percent of those with urban *hukou* were getting price subsidies from the government, none of the migrants were (Jiang et al. 2017, 238, 244, 251). Only 10.5 percent of their children attended privately-operated schools that had been granted state subsidies (Guojia tongjiju 2022, 4).

And according to a 2016 survey, in cities nearly half the migrants (45 percent) still had no access to social insurance, while about half were laboring without a formal labor contract, as research done a year later noted (Gallagher 2020, 187, 197).

The 2017 investigation of 10,000 families showed that while 24 percent of urban poor people were getting some medical assistance, just 11 percent of migrants were receiving such assistance; for educational help, the figures were, respectively, 15 and six percent, and for housing, eight and three percent (Jiang et al. 2017, 251; Jiang and Wang 2015, 141; Jiang et al. 2018, 245).[25]

Without an urban *hukou*, temporary residents in some megacities must wait some seven years to apply for it, and even then may be able to acquire it only if they have been awarded sufficient points or made a significant investment into a local company (Chan and O'Brien 2019). An academic commentator wrote in 2012, at the time of Xi's rise to power, that the offspring of these people cannot have the necessary conditions for upward mobility (Duan 2012, 55). This assessment is only underlined and rendered graphic in the subsequent poignant work on these hapless youths published later in his incumbency by Terry Woronov and Minhua Ling (Woronov 2016; Ling 2019). Sadly, these descriptions and assessments indicate that there has been little improvement over more than two decades in the circumstances of peasants coming to cities to live and work (Solinger 1999). This lack of substantial change suggests that Xi's regime did not attempt to deal with this issue.

The Fired

The other numerous, now long-outstanding group among the urban poor are the laid-off workers and staff [*xiagang zhigong*, 下岗 职工] who originally were the primary takers of the *dibao*. After Xi became Party leader, the overall number of recipients of the *dibao* dissipated steadily and drastically, going from a total of 22.8 million in 2011, the year before he acceded to power, to 7.247 million in 2021 (Solinger 2022, 47, Table 2.7).

Various reasons have been officially offered for this decline. These explanations include that people's incomes had increased – a claim challenged by a number of scholars; owing to tighter inspection of the financial situation of recipients and applicants,[26] leading to the uncovering of malpractices (or what were judged to be irregularities) and then to removing those who had mistakenly been granted the allowance; because some localities boast (possibly untruthfully) that they have reduced poverty; or due to former recipients having received their pensions and so no longer being eligible (Wang et al. 2021, 43; Li 2018, 90).[27] Cai Fang reported in early 2022 that of the total pension funds issued to urban residents with formal pensions supplied by the government, just 5.9 percent went to the urban-rural residents' pension fund (a contributory scheme), the most likely source of pension funding for both laid-off workers and migrants (Cai 2022).

Another indicator of the drop in significance that Xi's regime accorded the city poor in recent years has to do with a relative decline in the *dibao* norm. This norm is effectively the standard each city sets as its poverty line, and poor people with per-person incomes below that line in a city should be entitled to the *dibao*. From 2008 to 2016, the average level of this norm across cities nationwide was about 205 yuan per month, and it did rise by the year 2016 to 494.6 yuan; that is, it more than doubled. But critically, the percent of the urban population covered by the *dibao* over that time span fell from 3.74 percent of the city populace in 2008 down to just 1.88 percent in 2016. Even the numbers of those counted as "relatively poor," though declining, continued to represent as much as 10 percent of the population (Wang 2019, 80–81).[28] Moreover, Yu Tao, writing in 2019, reported that by the end of the 2010s the average *dibao* norm had been dropping continuously as a percentage of average disposable urban income (Yu 2019, 28). It would appear that laid-off workers were being given short shrift, perhaps because as measly as the *dibao* funds were, costs were being cut by several means, as noted earlier.

Besides all this, the *dibao* from the start has been plagued with a multitude of flaws. First, its norm is judged to be set too low and the scope of its coverage far too narrow in the view of many in China who study the subject, rendering this so-called program of "social assistance" hard to rely upon to guarantee even a basic livelihood. As Ye Xiangqun wrote at the time of Xi's accession to Party chiefdom, "After the *dibao* families get the *dibao*, they still face education, medical, housing, etc. difficulties; they urgently need fuller social relief" (Ye 2013, 73).

But as of 2016, Wang Kai states, the condition of the urban poor had not improved (Wang 2019, 81). By the close of Xi's second term, an article in the 2019 CASS social bluebook documented the ongoing need for the poor to borrow money (Jiang et al. 2018, 246–247).[29] In a volume to be published in 2023, Qin Gao cited a 2017 study that concluded: "The participants were dissatisfied and confused about the [*dibao*]'s program's participation requirements; plus its investigator learned that the employment assistance purportedly provided by a 2014 governmental program had been unable to help them leave welfare and become self-sufficient" (Gao 2023, 124; Solinger 2022, Chapters 3 and 5). These calculations and appraisals of what are probably still the two most numerous groups among the urban poor (if not among the *dibao* targets) would appear to indicate that there was no alleviation of urban poverty during the reign of Xi Jinping to date, but instead, exacerbation of it.

Living Conditions of the Urban Poor

The Chinese urban poor are clearly trapped in an unending cycle of destitution that positions their offspring to relive and replay the circumstances of their parents. Both ongoing poverty from which there is no egress – neither by their own efforts nor from sincere succor coming from the state – and the intellectual and economic limitations that poverty engenders render the "*pin er dai*" [贫二代, second generation of poor] stuck in place. For the low family income severely restricts these youths' living standard, causing them to acquire what is only substandard education and training, thereby limiting their access to social resources and contacts that might ameliorate their situation. These factors lead them, when grown, to replicate the status and mode of existence in which they themselves had been raised.

Indeed, just one-eighth of youngsters raised in low-income households were receiving an education higher than middle vocational schools when Xi came in, while nearly a fifth of those in better-off families were. By late in the decade, a joint study conducted by research centers at the Ministry of Civil Affairs and Beijing University found that among families in special difficulty, the same circumstances persisted: at that time some 80 to 90 percent were educated just to the level of junior high or below. Once lacking in schooling, there is no way that such students can fare creditably in today's intense market competition, where high skills and technological sophistication are critical (Deng and Gao 2012, 9; Duan 2012, 53–55).[30] Du and Wang laid out the situation in mid-decade: they hold low-paying jobs [if any]; have no cash to buy social insurance; can't afford a good education, so have no hope of attaining upward mobility. As researchers noted, "Because of high housing costs and inflation, poor masses are gradually isolated in dirty, chaotic, inferior marginal districts in cities . . . they have no way to catch up with the march of urban development" (Du and Wang 2017, 27; Tang and Cao 2015, 115).

To guide the poor in managing their lives, the welfare system overall has not been of much assistance and was not upgraded to any noticeable extent during the first Xi decade. Multiple scholars support this determination. Four years into Xi's term, three researchers asserted that, "The various items in our entire social relief investment come to less than one percent of our financial expenditure and this has been falling in recent years" (Zhang et al. 2017, 74). That same year, Du and Wang pronounced that, in light of the "daily increasing urban poor population, the social security and relief system is very narrow in scope" (Du and Wang 2017, 27).

This comment is fortified by economist Andrew Collier's research published in late 2022 which recorded that, "Since 2016 [up through 2019], Xi has reduced expenditures on social services as a percentage of gross domestic product from 8.5 to 7.6 percent" (Collier 2022). These findings justify the remarks of Jiang, Huang, and Tian in the 2019 CASS bluebook that, "Our social security still does not realize full coverage of all of society; some members of society participate in a level that is still rather low" (Jiang et al. 2018, 251). Kam Wing Chan reported in late 2021 that the numbers of migrants who lack social benefits coverage has risen steadily since 1980 (Chan 2021, 2).

Besides, what assistance there is, as several commentators have noted, is generally applied after the fact, with development, prevention, and long-term sustainable livelihood provision ignored (Li and Sun 2015, 81; Du and Wang 2017, 28). As a sign of the lack of attention to this issue, in 2012, Deng and Gao criticized the government's form of relief of the poor as being a kind of "blood transfusion" instead of fostering ability and engendering long-term improvement in the skills of the poor, which ideally might avert the occurrence of indigence at best, or at least enable them to throw off poverty permanently (Deng and Gao 2012, 9). But even nearly a decade later, Ma and Feng still characterized "our policy" as having an "emergency and lagging-behind nature." This meant that officialdom's approach remained rising to the occasion only after problems had already emerged (Ma and Feng 2020, 72).[31]

Policy

At both the Third Plenum of the 18th Party Congress in November 2013 and again at the 19th Party Congress in 2017, the leadership made declarations on behalf of the poor. In his 2013 speech, Xi called for increasing the incomes of low-income groups; in 2017 he urged the formation of a social security system that covered the whole population, both rural and urban dwellers, as well as for the improvement of the people's livelihood (Hofman 2022, 115; Jiang et al. 2018, 239). Pronouncements and policies were not totally ungenerous when it came to the urban poor. The problem is that implementation often fell short of promise, if the reckonings of the scholars cited here are largely accurate.

Another sign of lack of fulfillment of commitments is that several of the directives enunciated had to be repeated within a few years, an indication that they had not yet been observed. For instance, in 2007, the State Council issued an opinion on solving the housing difficulties of low-income households, and renovation did take place, but just in a few cities between 2008 and 2012 (Wei and Wang 2013, 11). And in 2013, an urban housing security project was announced (Li and Sun 2015, 80). But in the 13th Five Year Plan of 2017, still more mention was made of a plan to promote better housing (Wang et al. 2021, 44), while in 2019 there was a new opinion on developing public rental housing (Ma and Feng 2020, 72).

Then again, in 2012, migrant rural-to-urban children were decreed eligible to take the exam for higher education [the *gaokao*, 高考] in their city of residence (Li and Sun 2015, 81). But in 2019, the National Development and Reform Commission again decreed that migrant students in public schools were permitted to take the *gaokao* in cities (Wang et al. 2021, 41; Gao 2023, 124). That the same policy was enunciated within seven years is a likely sign that the initial order had not been executed.

One more instance is that in 2018, the Ministry of Civil Affairs joined with the Ministry of Finance in demanding that temporary relief work be strengthened and improved (Ma and Feng 2020, 72). But employment assistance plans had supposedly been mounted in 2012, and once again in 2014 (Wang et al. 2021; Gao 2023, 124). Perhaps all this is best summed up by Wang, Feng, and Luo's article of 2021 thusly: "Though the government has mounted a series of urban poverty guarantee and relief measures (the *dibao*, job promotion), [the term] 'urban poverty' has still not entered into the official discourse system" (Wang et al. 2021, 44).

Concluding Thoughts

There has never been an open official explanation put forth for why rural poverty and its reduction attracted such state concern and attention while urban indigence was slighted, largely overlooked, perhaps discounted or even dismissed. True, in August 2021 Xi Jinping did advance a slogan, "common prosperity," the achievement of which was celebrated as a central regime goal for some months (Nikkei 2022; Hofman 2022; Bradsher 2022; Whyte 2022, 26). Had it been taken seriously, it is likely that poor people in cities would have seen some redress. But its execution seems to have faltered (Xie 2022).

It makes sense to point to the persistent blight of the Covid virus and its shock to the economy as one explanation for that program's nonfulfillment. Also, the pandemic broke out against the backdrop of an ongoing and radical slackening of the pace of the Chinese economy – a situation that had begun to manifest as early as 2012, even before Xi took over the reins (by 2015 there had been a slide from 2011's 9.5 percent in annual growth down to 6.9 percent) (Wang et al. 2021, 34; Lyu 2016, 31). Indeed, already in 2014 Xi had come up with a justification for a changed orientation in economic matters with his "New Normal" announcement (He and Liu 2015, 85).

But more plausibly, given Xi's constant refrain about modernization, talent, and development, and his shift from plenty for the masses to nurturing an expanding middle class (Hofman 2022, 115), one can look to his most recent statement, his October 18, 2022 Report to the 20th Party Congress, to fathom the focus of his vision. There he spoke of "cultivating a large workforce of high-quality talent" being "of critical importance to the long-term development of China and the Chinese nation"; and again, "No effort should be spared," he admonished, "and no rigid boundaries drawn in the endeavor to bring together the best and brightest from all fields for the cause of the Party and the people" (Xi 2022). Surely the urban poor can have no role in this vision.

Notes

1 I extend my gratitude to Haotian Chen for locating articles for me in Chinese academic journals; I also thank Thomas Bernstein, Kam Wing Chan, Jane Duckett, and Martin Whyte for helpful comments on the initial draft.
2 Although I have written a book on rural migrants coming into cities (Solinger 1999) and one on the poor in cities who have urban household registration (Solinger 2022), this chapter uses almost entirely sources I have not used before.
3 Scholars of poverty define "absolute poverty" as "income or consumption level of an individual or family falls below an established poverty line" (Gao 2023, 116). Wang (2019, 80) considers the "*dibao* (低保)" masses to be the "absolute poor."
4 www.bbc.com/news/world-asia-china-56194622.
5 "Relative poverty" has been defined by a Chinese scholar as "having an income level inferior to the overall level in a society or group." Internationally, it is often measured as being a monthly income that is 50 to 60 percent of a place's average middle-class income (Feng and Chen 2019, 102).
6 Since researchers use differing methods to measure relative poverty in China, its extent has been said to amount to anywhere from 1.8 to 37.1 percent of the urban population (Wang et al. 2021, 40).
7 Tables 6–7 in the 2022 National Statistical Yearbook, p. 172, at https://urldefense.com/v3/__https://data.oversea.cnki.net/chn/download/excel?filecode=N2022110021-000101__;!!CzAuKJ42GuquVTTmVmPViYEvSg!Ldt3hnj12UijRUQyLPtcK-rqjTnvji-OeeZlGZ_6eq4QIfJ_4QLUItsn-hZRwyImu8hjwdvY1RZNu7Q$; He and Liu, 2015, 85 state that according to official statistics, in 2011 that ratio was a bit better, at 1:20.
8 Wei and Wang (2013, 9) write that the Chinese Social Sciences bluebook for 2011 also reported that the number of urban poor was more than twice the figure for *dibao* recipients.
9 This is not incompatible with Cui et al. (2015, 34), who claim that the absolute poor in cities had gone from 2000's 10 million to more than 50 million in 10 years.
10 As of 2017, the very poorest urban families [*tekun jiating* 特困家庭] were on average in debt to the amount of 26,330 yuan. 76 percent of their debts were for seeing doctors, 32 percent for children's schooling, 26 percent for daily expenses and 22 percent for shelter (Jiang et al. 2018, 246–247).

11 Han and Fan also list resource poverty, systemic poverty, cultural poverty, and operational poverty.
12 This was created as a merger of the former "three withouts" [*sanwu*, 三无] population – those in cities without the ability to work, any source of livelihood, or a legal supporter – with a similar rural program, the *wubao* [五保, five protections], for the countryside.
13 There is a vast literature on the failure of localities to carry out central policies. I have published on this with regard to urban poverty (Solinger and Jiang 2016).
14 Wang Depei refers to "numbers as high as sixty million" in 2001. Wang Shaoguang states that from 1995 to 2002 the number of state-sector employees had declined by 40.98 million people, a decrease of 36.4 percent, and the numbers working in urban collectives had gone down by 20.25 million, a drop of 64.3 percent. Together this was a decline of 61.23 million people, or 42.5 percent.
15 According to the NSB, "The number of workers employed in the state-owned sector fell from 113 million to 67 million, a decline of 40 percent over the five years 1996 to 2001"; NSB, *China Statistical Yearbook* (Beijing: China Statistics Press, 2002), both cited in Park and Giles (2003, 1).
16 See n. 10.
17 According to Bai, Qiao, and Xu, as early as January 2010, the city of Beijing began specially supporting the old and the disabled, before the rest of the country moved to this emphasis, apparently.
18 See n. 3; Solinger, *Poverty*.
19 In May 2014 the State Council passed the Social Assistance Temporary Law, making this new form of aid one of eight kinds of assistance (Zhang et al. 2017, 74).
20 By 2021 the *dibao* was serving less than 30 percent of the number of recipients it had assisted in 2009.
21 *Ibid.*, 47, Table 2.7.
22 www.gov.cn/zhengce/2014-03/16/content2640075.htm.
23 Calculating from Guojia, 2022, 3, in 2020 nearly half of the migrants (48 percent) were employed in manufacturing and construction, in both of which trades the average monthly income was relatively high (4,096 yuan per month for manufacturing, employing 27.3 percent of migrants; 4,699 yuan monthly for construction work, where 18.3 percent of them worked). These figures show that over 45 percent of employed migrants were earning above migrants' average monthly wage. But 51.5 percent were working in the tertiary sector, where the average wage was lower, at 3,387 yuan per month, clearly below the average urban disposable income.
24 The NBS announced that, "Nearly 17 million jobs in industry and construction were lost since 2014" (Magnus 2020).
25 Jiang and Wang state that in 2014 attending high school took up 22 percent of a poor family's income. Jiang, Huang, and Tian reported on a study showing that in 2017 medical expenses accounted for 39 percent of the consumption costs of families in difficulty.
26 In 2014, the state began to implement a strategy it termed "accurately support poverty," following which both the *dibao* population and the extent of its coverage began to fall (Lyu and Wang 2017, 68). But the actual total of poor people continued to be greater than the numbers of *dibao* beneficiaries (Li 2018, 92).
27 Wang, Feng, and Luo, *op. cit.*, 43; Li Zhengang, *op. cit.* 90. I have examined and disputed the claim about pension receipt (Solinger, *Poverty,* Chapter 10).
28 See notes 5 and 6 for "relative poverty."
29 See n. 8s.
30 Deng Guoying and Gao Bonan, "Woguo chengshihua jingchengzhong chengshi pinkun wentide shizheng yanjiu – jiyu Chengdushide diaocha" [Research on urban poverty during the period of rapid urbanization in China: based on the case study of Chengdu], *Chengshi fazhan yanjiu* [Urban development studies], 21, 9 (2012), 9; Duan, *op. cit.*, 53–55.
31 This is an issue in policy execution in many realms of policy in China.

References

Bai, Rui, Qiao Dong-ping, and Xu Yuebin. 2013. "Chengshi pinkun laonianrende zhengce zhichi – ji yu Beijingshi Xichengqu de anlie yanjiu" [Policy Support for Poor Elderly in Cities – Based on Beijing's Xicheng District's Case Research]. *Beijing shehui kexue [Beijing Social Science]* 2: 120–126.
Bradsher, Keith. 2022. "As China's Party Congress Begins, the Economic Impact is Considered." *New York Times*. October 10, B2.
Cai, Fang. 2022. "Zhuzhu pochu eryuan jiegoude chuanghuqi" [Grasp the Period of a Window in Eliminating the Dual Structure]. January 17. www.aisixiang.com/data/131017.html.
Chan, Alexsia T., and Kevin J. O'Brien. 2019. "Phantom Service: Deflecting Migrant Workers in China." *The China Journal* 8, January: 103–122.
Chan, Kam Wing. 2021. "Internal Migration in China: Integrating Migration with Urbanization Policies and Hukou Reform." *Knomad Policy Note 16*, November.
Collier, Andrew. 2022. "The Politics of Covid in China." *GlobalSource Partners*. December 7. GlobalSource Partners | The politics of Covid in China.
Cook, Sarah. 2002. "From Rice Bowl to Safety Net: Insecurity and Social Protection during China's Transition." *Development Policy Review* 20(5): 615–635.
Cui, Xuegang, Wang Chengxin, Wang Xueqin, and Wang Botao. "Xinxing chengzhenhua beijingxia woguo chengshi pinkun wenti ji duice" [Under the Background of New Style Urbanization Our Country's Urban Poor Problem and Measures to Deal With it]. *Hongguan jingji guanli [Macroeconomic Management]* 7(2015): 34–36, 39.
Deng, Guoying, and Gao Bonan. 2012. "Woguo chengshihua jingchengzhong chengshi pinkun wentide shizheng yanjiu – jiyu Chengdushide diaocha" [Research on Urban Poverty During the Period of Rapid Urbanization in China: Based on the Case Study of Chengdu]. *Chengshi fazhan yanjiu [Urban Development Studies]* 21(9): 8–11, 16.
Du, Weigong, and Wang Jing. 2017. "Zhuanxingqi de Hezhongguo chengshi pinkun wenti ji zhili" [The Urban Poverty Problem During the Period of China's Social Transition and its Governance Policy]. *Dangdai jingji guanli [Contemporary Economic Management]* 39(6): 23–30.
Duan, Huidan. 2012. "Woguo chengshi pinkun daiji chuandi wenti fenxi – jiyu shehui liudong lilun shijiao" [Analysis of My Country's Urban Poverty Generational Transmission Problem – Based on the Angle of the Theory of Social Mobility]. *Shanghai qingnian guanli ganbu xueyuan xuebao [Shanghai Youth Management Cadres' Institute Journal]* 4: 53–56.
Feng, Danmeng, and Chen Jie. 2019. "2020 nian hou woguo chengshi pinkun yu zhilide xiangguan wenti" [Problems of Urban Poverty and Governance in China After 2020]. *Chengshi fazhan yanjiu [Urban Development Studies]* 26(11): 102–107.
Gallagher, Mary E. 2020. "Can China Achieve Inclusive Urbanization?" In *Fateful Decisions: Choices that will Shape China's Future*, eds. Thomas Fingar and Jean C. Oi, Stanford: Stanford University Press, 180–199.
Gao, Qin. 2023. "Urban Poverty in China: Has Dibao Been an Effective Policy Response?" In *China Urbanizing: Impacts and Transitions*, eds. Weiping Wu and Qin Gao. Philadelphia: University of Pennsylvania Preds, 115–130.
Guojia tongjiju [National Statistical Bureau]. 2022. "2021 nian nongmin gong jiance diaocha baogao" [Report of an Investigation Monitoring Rural Migrant Workers in 2021]. April 29. www.stats.gov.cn/tjsj/zxfb/202204/t20220429_1830126.html.
Guojia tongjiju [National Statistical Bureau]. "National Statistical Yearbook 2022." https://urldefense.com/v3/__https://data.oversea.cnki.net/chn/download/excel?filecode=N2022110021-000101__;!!CzAuKJ42GuquVTTmVmPViYEvSg!Ldt3hnj12UijRUQyLPtcK-rqjTnvjiOeeZlGZ_6eq4QIfJ_4QLUItsn-hZRwyImu8hjwdvY1RZNu7Q$.
Han, Yingying, and Shimin Fan. 2016. "Jiegouhua lilun shijiaoxia chengshi pinkunde zhipin yindu ji xuoyong jili" [Urban Poverty's Elements That Lead to Poverty and its Function Mechanism from Angle of Structuration Theory]. *Qiusuo [Exploration]* 7: 49–54.

He, Qingsheng, and Ye Liu. 2015. "Lun woguo chengshi pinkun zhilide xianshi kunjing yu lujing xueze" [On My Country's Urban Poverty Governance's Implementation Predicament and the Selection of a Path]. *Xuexi yu zhijian [Study and Practice]* 12: 89–94.

He, Shui. 2018. "Nongmingong chengshi pinkun celiang zhibiao tixi goujian-jiyu duoweidude tansuo" [Construction of a Measurement Index System for Urban Poverty of Migrant Workers – Based on Multi-Dimensional Perspective]. *Tansuo yu zhengming [Exploration and Contention]* 8: 107–112.

Hofman, Bert. 2022. "Common Prosperity." In *CPC Futures: The New Era of Socialism with Chinese Characteristics*, eds. Frank N. Pieke and Bert Hofman. Singapore: NUS Press, 113–120.

Hussain, Athar et al. 2002. "Urban Poverty in the PRC." (Asian Development Bank Project No. TAR: PRC 33448).

Jia, Degang. 2022. "2021 nian Zhongguo chengxiang jumin shouru he xiaofei baogao" [Income and Consumption Report of Urban and Rural Residents in China]. In *2022 nian Zhongguo shehui xingshi fenxi yu yuce* [2022 analysis and forecast of Chinese social situation], eds. Li Peilin, Chen Guangjin, and Wang Chunguang. Beijing: shehui kexue wenxuan chubanshe [Social Sciences Academic Press], 24–43.

Jiang, Zhiqiang, Wang Jing, and Tian Feng. 2017. "Zhongguo chengxiang kunnan qunti zhuangkuang diaocha baogao" [Investigation Report on the Situation of China's Urban and Rural Masses in Difficulty]. In *2018 nian Zhongguo shehui xingshi fenxi yu yuce* [2018 Analysis and Forecast of Chinese Social Situation], eds. Li Peilin, Chen Guangjin, and Zhang Yi. Beijing: shehui kexue wenxuan chubanshe [Social Sciences Academic Press], 234–254.

Jiang, Zhiqiang, and Wang Weijin. 2015. "Zhongguo chengxiang kunnan cunqunti zhuangkuang diaocha baogao" [Difficult Population Report of Urban and Rural Areas of China]. In *2016 nian Zhongguo shehui xingshi fenxi yu yuce* [2016 Analysis and Forecast of Chinese Social Situation], eds. Li Peilin, Chen Guangjin, and Zhang Yi. Beijing: shehui kexue wenxuan chubanshe [Social Sciences Academic Press], 136–151.

Jiang, Zhiqiang, Huang Yongliang, and Tian Feng. 2018. "Zhongguo chengxiang kunnan jiating zhuangkuang diaocha baogao" [Investigation Report on Chinese Urban and Rural Difficult Families' Situation]. In *2019 nian Zhongguo shehui xingshi fenxi yu yuce* [2019 Analysis and Forecast of Chinese Social Situation], eds. Li Peilin, Chen Guangjin, and Zhang Yi. Beijing: shehui kexue wenxuan chubanshe [Social Sciences Academic Press], 239–263.

Li, Li. 2012. "Chengshi pinkun wenti fenxi ji fanpinkunde duice yanjiu" [Research on the Issue of Urban Poverty and Measures to Counter Poverty]. *Cai zhi [Intelligence]* 20: 280–281.

Li, Shanshan, and Jiuwen Sun. 2015. "Zhongguo chengshi pinkun kongjian fenyi yufanpinkun zhengce tixi yanjiu" [Research on Chinese Urban Poverty Spatial Differentiation and the Policy System to Counter Poverty]. *Xiandai jingji tansuo [Modern Economic Research]* 1: 78–82.

Li, Yuan. 2022. "Migrant Workers Tale of Inequality Grips China, Then is Erased." *New York Times*. January 31.

Li, Zhengang. 2018. "2018 nian chengxiang shehui jiuzhu fazhan zhuangkuang fenxi baogao" [Analysis Report on the Situation in the Development of Urban and Rural Social Assistance in 2018]. In *2019 nian Zhongguo shehui xingshi fenxi yu yuce* [2019 Analysis and Forecast of Chinese Social Situation], eds. Li Peilin, Chen Guangjin, and Zhang Yi. Beijing: shehui kexue wenxuan chubanshe [Social Sciences Academic Press], 77–100.

Ling, Minhua. 2019. *The Inconvenient Generation: Migrant Youth Coming of Age on Shanghai's Edge*. Stanford, CA: Stanford University Press.

Lu, Xueyi. 2002. *Dangdai Zhongguo shehui jieceng yanjiu baogao* [A Research Report on China's Current Social Structure]. Beijing: shehui kexue wenxuan chubanshe.

Lyu, Qingzhe. 2016. "2016 nian Zhongguo chengxiang jumin shouru he xiaofei baogao" [2016 Income and Consumption Situation of Urban and Rural Residents in China], In *2017 nian Zhongguo shehui xingshi fenxi yu yuce* [2017 Analysis and Forecast of Chinese Social Situation], eds. Li Peilin, Chen Guangjin, and Zhang Yi. Beijing: shehui kexue wenxuan chubanshe [Social Sciences Academic Press], 23–35.

Lyu, Xuejing, and Yongmei Wang. 2017. "2017 nian Zhongguo shehui baozhang shiye gaige fazhan baogao" [Report on the Development of the Reform of China's Social Security], In *2018 nian Zhongguo shehui xingshi fenxi yu yuce* [2018 analysis and forecast of Chinese social situation], eds. Li Peilin, Chen Guangjin, and Zhang Yi. Beijing: shehui kexue wenxuan chubanshe [Social Sciences Academic Press]: 62–81.

Ma, Xiaojuan, and Feng Yuting. 2020. "Gaige kaifang yilai Zhongguo chengshi pinkun zhili zhengce tanxi" [Investigation and Analysis of China's Urban Poverty Governance Policy Since Reform and Opening]. *Sheke zongheng [Social Sciences Review]* 35(4): 70–74.

Magnus, George. 2020. "Opinion: Beijing's Delicate Balancing Act Relies on Job Creation." *Financial Times*. January 2.

Mo, Zhexun. 2022. "Is East Asia Becoming Plutocratic? Income and Wealth Inequalities in Mainland China, Hong Kong and Taiwan (1981–2021)." *World Inequality Lab Issue Brief*. November 11.

Nikkei. 2022. November 4. https://asia.nikkei.com/Politics/China-s-party-congress/Transcript-President-Xi-Jinping-s-report-to-China-s-2022-party-congress.

Pang, Kai. 2014. "Shehui ziben shijiaoxia woguo chengshi pinkun wenti zhili yanjiu" [Research on Our Country's Urban Poverty Issues' Governance from the Viewpoint of Social Capital]. *Kaifa yanjiu [Research on Development]* 4: 89–93.

Park, Albert Park, and John Giles. 2003. "How has Economic Restructuring Affected China's Urban Workers?" October (ms.).

Solinger, Dorothy J. 1999. *Contesting Citizenship in Urban China*. Berkeley and Los Angeles, CA: University of California Press.

Solinger, Dorothy J. (with Ting Jiang). 2016. "When Central Orders and Promotion Criteria Conflict: Recent Urban Decisions on the Dibao." *Modern China* 42(6): 571–606.

Solinger, Dorothy J. 2022. *Poverty and Pacification*. Lanham, MD: Rowman & Littlefield.

Sun, Liping. 2002. "90 niandai zhongqi yilai Zhongguo shehui jiegou yanbiande xin qushi" [New Trends in the Evolution of Chinese Social Structure Since the Mid-1990s]. *Dangdai zhongguo yanjiu [Modern China Studies]* 9(3): 5–28.

Tang, Jun. 2012. "2012 Zhongguo xin xing shehui jiuzhu tixi jiben jiancheng" [China's New-Style Social Assistance System is Basically Established]. In *2013 nian Zhongguo shehui xingshi fenxi yu yuce* [2013 Analysis and Forecast of Chinese Social Situation], eds. Lu Xueyi, Li Peilin, and Chen Guangjin. Beijing: shehui kexue wenxuan chubanshe [Social Sciences Academic Press], 213–225.

Tang, Liping, and Junjun Cao. 2015. "Chengshihua beijingxia woguo chengshi pinkun wenti yanjiu" [Research on Our Country's Urb Poverty Question Under the Background of Urbanization]. *Gansu Lilunxuekan [Gansu Theory Research]* 5: 113–117.

thefluxmedia. 2021. "98.99 Million People Out of Destitution in China (thefluxmedia.com; Lifting 800 Million People Out of Poverty – New Report Looks at Lessons from China's Experience (worldbank.org) (CGTN, Feb. 25)".

Unger, Jon, and Kaxton Siu. 2019. "Chinese Migrant Factory Workers Across Four Decades: Shifts in Work Conditions, Urbanization, and Family Strategies." *Labor History* 60(6): 765–778.

Wang, Depei. 2001. "San min yu erci gaige" [Three Types of People and the Second Reform]. *Gaige neican [Reform Internal Reference]* 7: 2–26.

Wang, Hongxin, Feng Yu, and Luo Qian. 2021. "Zhongguo chengshi pinkun: huigu yu zhanwang [China's Urban Poverty: Review and Prospects]." *Shehui zhili [Social Governance]* 3: 32–46.

Wang, Kai. 2018. "Zhongguo chengshi pinkun xianxiangde shizheng yanjiu" [An Empirical Investigation of China's Urban Poverty]. *Chongqing shehuixue yanjiu [Chongqing Sociology Research]* 11: 61–76.

Wang, Kai. 2019. "Yi xiangdui pinkun lai kan chengshi pinkun: linian bianxi yu Zhongguo shizheng" [Use Relative Poverty to Consider Urban Poverty: Concept Differentiation and China's Empirical Evidence]. *Beijing shehui kexue [Beijing Social Science]* 7: 74–83.

Wang, Ning, Wei Houkai, and Su Hongjian. 2016. "Dui xin shiqi Zhongguo chengshi pinkun biaojun de sikao" [Reflections on China's Urban Poverty Norm in the New Period]. *Jianghuai luntan [Jianghuai Forum]* 4: 32–39.

Wang, Shaoguang. 2004. "Shunying minxin de bianhua: zong caizheng zijiu liuxiang kan zhongguo zhengfu zhengce tiaozheng" [A Change that Conforms with Popular Sentiments: From the Flows of Financial Funds Observe the Chinese Government's Policy Adjustments]. *Zhanlue yu Guanli [Strategy and Management]* 2: 51–60.

Wei, Houkai, and Ning Wang. 2013. "Canyu fanpinkun: Zhongguo chengshi pinkun zhilide fangxiang" [Participate in the Attack Urban Poverty: The Direction of Chinese Urban Poverty Governance]. *Jianghuai luntan [Jiangsu Anhui Forum]* 5: 9–17.

Whyte, Martin King. 2022. "Xi Jinping Confronts Inequality: Bold Leadership or Modest Steps?" Unpublished ms. December 26.

Woronov, T. E. 2016. *Class Work: Vocational Schools and China's Urban Youth*. Stanford, CA: Stanford University Press.

Xie, Stella Yifan. 2022. "Xi Jinping's 'Common Prosperity' was Everywhere, but China Backed Off." *Wall Street Journal*. April 3.

Yang, Yong, and Huang Yanfen. 2003. "Zhongguo jumin shouru fenpei xin geju" [The New Pattern in Income Distribution Among Chinese Urbanites]. In *Shehui lanpishu: 2003 nian: Zhongguo shehui xingshi fenxi yu yuce* [Social Blue Book: 2003 Analysis and Predictions of China's Social Situation], eds. Ru Xin, Lu Xueyi, and Li Peilin, Beijing: shehui kexue wenxuan chubanshe [Social Science Documents Company], 226–234.

Ye, Xiangqun. 2013. "Woguo chengshi pinkun wenti yu zuidi shenghuo baozhang zhidu" [Our Urban Poverty Issue and the Dibao System]. *Jingji yanjiu kaocha [Economic Research Investigation]* 43: 70–75.

Yu, Tao. 2019. "Zhongguo chengshi fupinde duowei cedu ji zhili [The Measurement and Governance of the Multidimensionality of Chinese Urban Poverty]." *Hebei jingmao daxue xuebao [Journal of Hebei University of Economics and Business]* 40(3): 23–30.

Zhang, Wanli. 2002. "Twenty Years of Research on Stratified Social Structure in Contemporary China." *Social Sciences in China* 23(1 Spring): 48–58.

Zhang, Xichun, Fan Shi-min, and Han Ying-ying. 2017. "Wo guo chengshi pinkun zhili pingjia ji chuangxin lujing yanjiu" [Research on the Evaluation and Innovation of Governance of Our Country's Urban]. *Huanan ligong daxue xuebao (shehui kexueban) [Journal of South China University of Technology (Social Science Edition)]* 2: 69–77.

7 How to Think Xi Jinping Thought

Jean Christopher Mittelstaedt and Patricia M. Thornton

The Western media is thoroughly exorcised about the "cult of Xi." In the run-up to the Twentieth Party Congress, Cai Xia, a former professor at the Central Party School, charged that Xi Jinping demands "a degree of loyalty and admiration for the leader not seen since Mao" due to an inferiority complex that stems from his comparatively modest educational attainment. "Thin-skinned, stubborn and dictatorial," Cai redounded: "his hubris and paranoia threaten China's future" and generated countless humanitarian disasters (Cai 2021). The *Financial Times*' Gideon Rachman fulminated that, whereas the model of "reform and openness" put in place by Deng Xiaoping rejected the cult of personality in favor of an injunction to "seek truth from facts," the Party's more recent decision to incorporate Xi Jinping's "thought" into its Charter and abolish term limits for the post of General Secretary will only make China's governance structure more fragile. Widespread obeisance to the person of the leader, Rachman argues, is "intrinsically humiliating" for educated Chinese citizens and officials, who are forced to study and parrot back pet phrases from Xi's works in public discourse. "The Xi cult means that insincerity and fear are now baked into the Chinese system ... Xi is now a danger to his country" (Rachman 2021). The inclusion of Xi's thought into the national curriculum via textbooks for primary school students prompted one Weibo user to observe that in Xi's China, "brainwashing starts in childhood" (Agence France-Presse 2021), a comment that was widely reported in Western media, as was the inclusion of two Xi Jinping quotes on the annual college entrance exam in 2023 (Cai 2023).

The narcissistic self-aggrandizement of individual leaders and a perceived need to bolster flagging popular legitimacy are frequently cited as the main drivers of so-called "cults of personality" in state socialist systems. In 1956, Khrushchev insisted that the Stalinist personality cult had "acquired such [a] monstrous size chiefly because Stalin himself, using all conceivable methods, supported the glorification of his own person" (Khrushchev 1956). Likewise, one best-selling biography of Mao Zedong proposed that "Every step in the construction of his cult was choreographed by Mao himself," an effort that began in Yan'an during the early 1940s (Chang and Halliday 2005, 327). Others reject psychology-based assessments and view cults instead as a tool upon which many autocrats rely in extending their hold on power. In his recent survey of eight infamous dictators, Dikötter (2019, xi–xii) observes that, among the tools they used to neutralize their rivals, "the cult of personality was the most efficient," because it turned "everyone into a liar ... making it more difficult to find accomplices and organise a coup." Huang Haifeng (Huang 2018a, 1034) finds that although crude and heavy-handed propaganda like that associated with personality cults frequently backfires by worsening popular views of leaders, they signal a regime's ability to "command great resources and organizational capacity to impose such unpersuasive messages on society and thus deter dissent." Still others invoke Max Weber's concept of "charismatic authority" to argue that in poorly integrated nondemocracies, staged public displays of loyalty to a single despotic leader can help compensate for the general lack of patriotism among the ruled, a suppressed sense of community, or an unreliable or absent rule of law system (Brandenburger 2005, 249–250).

Yet such explanations don't square particularly well with the Chinese case. Although the much-hyped publication of Xi Jinping's *The Governance of China* has been compared to Mao's 1964 "little red book," as Alice Miller points out, the 2014 volume does not purport to convey or encapsulate Xi's "unique ideological genius." Instead, by contrast, *The Governance of China* emphasizes "the *collective* authority of its contents" (Miller 2017, 2, emphasis added), making it a relatively poor example of a vanity project. Perhaps surprisingly, Xi Jinping Thought on Socialism with Chinese Characteristics for a New Era, the official name for Xi's eponymous school of thought, has not been characterized either in official documents or media as the actual creation of Xi Jinping himself. To the contrary, the established formulation characterizes Xi's thought as "the crystallisation of the Party's collective wisdom" (党的决议是党的集体智慧的结晶), which "embodies the interests of the party and the opinions of the overwhelming majority of Party members" (体现了党的利益和绝大多数党员的意见). Furthermore, as the publisher's note in the second volume of Xi Jinping's *The Governance of China* points out, it is in fact "the Communist Party of China, with Xi Jinping as its main representative, that created Xi Jinping Thought on Socialism with Chinese Characteristics for a New Era," acknowledging that although Xi is its "principal founder," he is by no means its only one (Editorial Team 2017, ii).

Nor does it appear that the mass practices most commonly associated with Xi's "personality cult" are being relied upon to prop up a tottering regime that is in imminent danger of losing popular support. To the contrary: a 2020 Harvard Kennedy School report on Chinese public opinion based on over 31,000 face-to-face interviews and eight waves of surveys found that since 2003, overall citizen satisfaction with the Party-state has steadily increased across virtually every sector of government performance, with members of marginalized groups in poorer inland regions comparatively more likely to report increases in satisfaction over time (Cunningham et al. 2020). Likewise, the World Values Survey also recorded high levels of popular support that have continued to rise over the course of Xi's tenure in power: 94.6 percent of surveyed Chinese citizens expressed 'a great deal' or 'quite a lot' of confidence in the central government in 2018, up from 84.6 percent in 2013 (Tsang and Cheung 2022, 230). More recent smaller-scale online polls of urban residents conducted by the China Data Lab at the University of California, San Diego indicate that public trust in the central government has remained over

90 percent, weakening only slightly between July 2021 and March 2022, despite COVID-19 lockdowns and worsening economic conditions (Lin 2022).

In this chapter, we offer an alternative reading of the role of the promotion of Xi Jinping Thought on Socialism with Chinese Characteristics for a New Era (hereafter, Xi Jinping Thought) at the grassroots of contemporary Chinese society. Focusing on the simultaneous construction and management of "New Era Civilized Practice Centers" (新时代文明实践中心) and "Integrated Media Centers" (融媒体中心) – a project introduced in 2018 to propagate and disseminate Xi Jinping Thought at the county level and below – we argue that the mass practices associated with Xi's so-called "personality cult" are better understood as forms of infrastructural state building (Mann 2008), and as public-facing collective spaces designed to encourage the civic performance of exemplary authoritarian citizenship (Distelhorst and Fu 2019). This "new era" *civilized* citizenship is a product both of the "state-enlisted voluntarism" (Yang et al. 2022) mobilized by the practice centers, and the well-recorded public performances of gratitude by the local recipients of services (Sorace 2020, 2021) circulated by the county-level media centers.

New Era Civilized Practice Centers are tasked with *actualizing* the "core content" of Xi Jinping Thought by mobilizing volunteers to meet the needs of local residents; these are then selectively recorded, framed, and recirculated through the county-level Integrated Media Centers as celebrated examples of Xi Jinping Thought. Drawing on an original data set of 2,991 collated local news items generated by a private WeChat account detailing the work of "New Era Civilization Practice Centers" between July 2018 and April 2021, we demonstrate how these networks of civilizational practice and circuits of civility are engineered and refashioned by the so-called "Two Centers" as exemplary manifestations of Xi Jinping Thought.

However, more to the point, we argue that an exclusive focus on Xi's "personality cult" elides the more lasting institutional impact of these efforts, which has been to extend and transform the Party-state's role at the social grassroots. Instead of the "personality cult" serving as an exercise in *despotic* power imposed on social forces from above, we argue that the "Two Centers" extend the Party-state's *infrastructural* power, defined by Mann as "the capacity of the state to actually penetrate civil society and implement its actions" (2008, 355) through significant institutional realignments at the grassroots. As Yang (2017, 1946) notes, in contemporary usage, the Chinese term "wenming" can be translated as both "civilization" and as "civility." "Wenming" discourses in contemporary China thus operate both ideologically as *civilizational* discourses of legitimating "the governance and administration of society," and as strategic technologies to manage *civility* on social media and in digital spaces. The "Two Centers" aim to do both: the New Era Civilized Practice Center system – which includes "centers" (中心) at the county level, institutes (所) at the township level, and stations (站) in the villages – work to organize the *civilizational* practice of Xi Jinping Thought in ordering society, and, through the network of county-level Integrated Media Centers, generate the "positive energy" (正能量) of exemplars of *civility* on social media (Wei 2022). Discursively, the "Two Centers" thus legitimate new granular practices of social governance and generate pro-Party content beneath the umbrella of Xi Jinping Thought; institutionally, they also facilitate the "platformization" (平台化) of Party and state offices at the county level and below, giving them a greater operational reach and visibility than their limited human and capital resources might otherwise permit. As such, although independent reports on the impact of disseminating the content of Xi Jinping Thought as a propaganda tool have found the success of the Practice Centers difficult to assess, organizationally speaking, the "Two Centers" digital platforms have succeeded in providing new and efficient ways for local and sub-local governments to connect, scale, intermediate, and mobilize (Ansell and Miura 2020, 262–263), thereby contributing to public administration and governance in tangible ways. Without denying their propagandistic role, we propose that a more fruitful way to understand some of the practices associated with leadership cults is as exercises in infrastructural state-building.

"Civilized" State-Building, Xi Jinping-Style

Although the PRC's founding in 1949 saw the establishment of culture halls and stations as nodes for literacy education, propaganda, and various cultural activities supported by the Ministry of Culture and the Propaganda Department, the onset of "reform and opening" in 1978 plunged the existing remnants of Mao-era cultural infrastructure into crisis. Rapid economic development left scarce resources, personnel, and space for the support of cultural and ideological activities at the social grassroots. Notwithstanding this lack of resources, Deng Xiaoping called upon local governments to propagate socialist spiritual civilization as early as October 1979 (Dynon 2008, 86), which was envisioned as a form of mass culture that accepts market forces but "resolutely rejects all the ugly and decadent things of capitalism" (摒弃资本主义的一切丑恶腐朽的东西) (CCP Central Committee 1986). This mission took on a more distinctly nationalist tone in the wake of the 1989 Tiananmen Square demonstrations, particularly after the introduction of the nationwide patriotic education campaign. By 1997, Jiang Zemin had established a Spiritual Civilization Steering Committee under the Office of the Party Central Committee (中央精神文明建设指导委员会) to oversee a network of provincial-, district-, and work unit-level Spiritual Civilization Offices that coordinated a framework of locally administered compacts (公约) promoting civility and "civilized" behavior. This project was gradually absorbed into Hu Jintao's socialist or civilized "harmonious society" (和谐社会) (Dynon 2008, 99–100) alongside a comprehensive restructuring of cultural infrastructure beginning in 2005, and the introduction of the "public cultural service system" (Guanyu jinyibu 2005). This initiative rebranded grassroots cultural stations as "comprehensive township cultural stations," which hypothetically provided a hub for a wide array of both *civilizational* services and *civilizing* activities, although they were plagued by integration and coordination issues through the end of the Hu Jintao era (Guanyu quanmian 2013).

In July 2018 with Xi Jinping serving as chair, the "Central Leading Small Group for Comprehensively Deepening Reform" (全面深化改革领导小组) sought to address the lack of integration and coordination in the grassroots cultural services system. The commission's "Guiding Opinion on Establishing New Era Civilized Practice Center Pilots" (中央全面深化改革委员会关于建设新时代文明实践中心试点工作的指导意见) called for the creation of 50 experimental centers at the county-level and below in thirteen provinces to deepen the propagation of Xi Jinping Thought. The pilots, which were initially spread over 12 provincial-level jurisdictions, were engineered to "gather and guide" the masses (凝聚、引导群众), "mobilize all forces," "integrate all resources," (调动各方力量) and "use China's socialist ideology and morality to firmly occupy the countryside's ideological and cultural position" (用中国特色社会主义文化、社会主义思想道德牢牢占领基层宣传思想文化阵地). The Centers bridge "the last mile" (最后一公里) in "propagating, educating, caring for, and serving the masses" (宣传群众、教育群众、关心群众、服务群众), as well as to "promote Xi Jinping Thought on Socialism with Chinese Characteristics for a New Era to be more deeply embedded in the hearts of the people" (推动习近平新时代中国特色社会主义思想深入人心) (CLSGCDR 2018).

In October 2019, following a review of the successes and shortcomings of initial experiments, the number of official pilots was expanded to 500; and the following year, a "Guiding Handbook" for the pilots was released, streamlining best practices and distilling model experiences for further refining local implementation (CCOFB 2020). In November 2020, the Party's Fifth Plenum went so far as to designate the Centers as a key prong in the realization of the Fourteenth Five-Year Plan's long-term goal to "improve the civilizational level of society" by 2035 (CCP Central Committee 2020).

The 2018 *Guiding Opinion* designated three levels of Civilized Practice Centers. County-level "Centers" (中心) command and coordinate (指挥协调) projects, staff members, times, and locations. "Institutes" (所) operate at the township or *xiang* level, and "stations" (站) at the village (村) level are designed to respond to the "demands of the masses" (群众需求), providing an "efficient linkage" (有效对接) between the "local reality" (本地实际) and the New Era Civilized Practice network resources. Some localities carried the activity to an even lower administrative level: New Era Civilized Practice "Points" (点) are even more granular, operating in work units or housing compounds (单元) (CCOFB 2020, 155). Notwithstanding significant regional variation, data from 31 of the 50 original pilots shows that the median number of people served per Center, Institute, or Station was 2,604 people – dovetailing with the 19th Party Congress's aim of "moving the center of gravity of social governance even further down to the grassroots" (推动社会治理重心向基层下移) (Xi 2017).

On paper, this has resulted in an unprecedented level of Party-state penetration, particularly in rural areas. Thus, Shaanxi's Yangchuan, with a population of only 170,100, constructed a whopping 387 Civilized Practice Centers, one for every 440 people (Yan'an Ribao 2019). Oddly, the difference between heavily populated and less populated areas is negligible: Shandong's Pingdu boasted the third-lowest number of people served per Center (765) (Qingdao Wenmingwang 2020), whereas Hainan's Meilan District, with half the population, succeeded in penetrating far less successfully, with each center serving a median of 11,635 (Haikouwang 2019).

There are also wide regional disparities in "comprehensive high-density coverage" among the pilot areas; however, of the 31 pilots for which there is data, 26 jurisdictions managed to create sufficient numbers of Centers, Institutes, and Stations that, at least in theory, distributed coverage to fewer than 5,000 residents per Center.

Centers, Institutes, Stations, and Points both speak in the "Party's voice" (党的声音) and act as the "nerve tips" (神经末梢) of the Party's propaganda apparatus, ensuring that "Xi Jinping Thought" can "fly into the homes of ordinary people" (飞入寻常百姓家) (CCOFB 2020, 165, 25). The aim is to achieve omnipresence, creating "comprehensive high density coverage without blind spots or dead ends" (高密度、无盲区、无死角的全覆盖) (Kong 2020). As such, they "realize the positive interaction between state governance under the Party's leadership, social regulation, and the residents' self-governance" (实现党领导下的政府治理和社会调节、居民自治良性互动) (Hainan Haikou Jingshan District 2019).

However, these broad institutional arrangements serve as the backdrop against which the work of putting Xi Jinping Thought into lived practice takes place. The "co-creation" of Xi Jinping Thought arises in the interactions between the Centers, the volunteers that they mobilize, and local residents. The pilot Centers were originally tasked with improving service provision by building new integrated "service platforms" (服务平台) across five key areas: theory dissemination (chiefly Xi Jinping Thought), education, culture, popularizing technology usage, and health and fitness. Pilot locations were further encouraged to innovate by tailoring these platforms to meet local needs (CLSGCDR 2018). The pilot in Zhejiang's Cixi Municipality, for example, developed an additional three "platforms" tailored to local conditions: one to address the health and medical needs of elderly residents; one dedicated to meeting the personal safety and legal service needs of migrant workers; and another to assist the public-facing Party-state and approved civic organizations with developing user-friendly websites to make them more accessible to local residents (Sixiang zhengzhi gongzuo yanjiu 2019). Two years after the pilots were launched, the 2020 *Guiding Handbook* proposed a "8+N" set-up in which volunteer teams established by county-level government departments (县域某一行业部门) cover the five areas stipulated in the original pilot plan as well as legal services, sanitation and environmental protection, and charitable assistance for the poor; the "N" represents any number of ad-hoc services (beyond the stated eight) that may be provided in response to the needs of the community at any time (CCOFB 2020, 103–104).

Community needs are envisioned as falling into one of three general categories: "livelihood problems" (民生领域的问题) experienced by individuals or families facing various hardships; problems of "mass interest" (群众利益) that impact groups of residents within a county, township, village, or urban community; and unforeseen "big issues" like regional conflicts, "public health emergencies" (突发公共卫生事件), or natural disasters. Beyond these broad categories, pilot Centers were advised to mobilize volunteer teams capable of providing a full range of services to meet community needs; they were also tasked with developing dedicated databases of local resources, including talents, places (such as shopping malls, public squares, bus stations, and others), and projects (CCOFB 2020, 53, 127).

However, simply carrying out tasks and staging events in a system in which "nobody is willing or able to do mass work" (破解群众工作没人做、不愿做、不会做) (CCOFB 2020, 14) means little if the activities are not linked to grander narratives. Civilized Practice Centers leverage volunteers and "Integrated Media Centers" to resolve both issues – the focus of the next two sections.

Volunteering to Construct Xi Jinping Thought

At least as early as August 2016, Xi Jinping emphasized the importance of "volunteer service" (志愿服务) in "cultivating and practicing socialist core values" (培育和践行社会主义核心价值观), and "satisfying people's growing spiritual and cultural needs" (满足人民群众日益增长的精神文化需求) (Gongchandangyuan wang 2016). In recent years, the number of volunteers has exploded in China, from 94.48 million (6.9 percent of the population) in 2015 to more than 209.59 million volunteers (14.9 percent), more than doubling in only four years (Huizeren 2020).

The New Era Civilized Practice Centers allow the Party to brand its involvement and control over this sector, with teams of volunteers identified as the "main force" (主体力量) of their operations (CLSGCDR 2018). One Central Propaganda Ministry and the Central Spiritual Civilization Office joint implementation plan aimed to register 13 percent of the population to participate in "New Era Civilized Practice volunteering services," creating a "radiation" (辐射) effect in which a core of volunteers establish a local norm that other residents follow such that "all citizens volunteer, the entire region volunteers, everyone becomes a volunteer, volunteering everywhere" (全民志愿、全域志愿，人人做志愿者，处处做志愿者) (CPMCSCO 2019, 106), "enlisting everyone as a participant in civilized practice" (让人人成为文明实践参与者) (Gao 2020). The goal is comprehensive coverage (全覆盖) such that "wherever the masses gather, so must civilized practice extend and cover" (群众聚集在哪里，文明实践就延伸覆盖到哪里) (Yanji Municipal CCP Propaganda Department 2019).

The Practice Center pilots chiefly mobilize volunteers from two sources: employees of Party and government agencies, state-owned enterprises and institutions, and current employees of government departments, schools, and Party schools; and from the ranks of local professionals, retirees, college and university students, and entrepreneurs (CLSGCDR 2018). Specifically, county-level government departments (县域某一行业部门) in most pilot areas drafted their volunteer teams from the ranks of their own employees. In the counties hosting the pilots, 80 percent of Party members were required to contribute 20 volunteering hours per year, or just under two hours per month.

However, due to their mandate to inspire "civilized practice" in society at large, the Centers also made it painfully easy for ordinary residents to become volunteers. In Fuzhou's Jin'an District, the "Lei Feng Volunteer Service Recruitment Station" is located just inside the entrance to the exhibition hall of the local Civilized Practice Center, allowing potential volunteers to scan a QR code and register immediately (Gao 2020). Ad-hoc groups are often assembled for special events by the Centers, with a variety of actors recruited for short-term or specific project-based volunteer activities. For example, in Jiangsu's Hai'an Municipality, youth volunteers frequently engage in a variety of patriotic "red culture" events and performances (Gao 2021). Similarly, in Fuzhou, "junior volunteers" (小小志愿者) from middle and primary schools participated in a "civilized queuing day" (文明排队日) (Zhongguo wenming wang 2021), which aimed to reorient local practice by incentivizing residents to queue peaceably. Volunteering events were also integrated with festivals and local culture.

Most registered Center volunteers are organized into specialized teams. Jiangsu's Practice Centers reportedly boasted 16,450 "civilized practice volunteer teams" in 27 pilot counties in 2019 (Wang 2019); Shandong's Rongcheng County organized its 155,000 volunteers into over 1,300 teams that conducted more than 2,000 activities per month (You et al. 2020). Fujian province, for example, has 1.25 million "Civilized Practice volunteers" (文明实践志愿者) organized into 15,000 teams, allocated to its 646 Institutes and 7,324 Stations (Gao 2020). In Shandong's Xiangzhou Village, each Civilized Practice station boasted five volunteer teams with no fewer than five members per team. Each team conducts at least one event per month, with events planned well in advance (Shandong Zucheng 2020). In Qufu, registered volunteers were required to do at least two hours of volunteering work per month (Zhao 2020).

Volunteer teams are often organized with a particular specialization in mind. For example, Zhejiang's Nanhu District developed five categories of teams, each devoted to a particular category of service activities – "red," "people's benefit," "culture," "customs," and "happiness" – with 36 teams in total. Of these, six are directly supervised by the Party, with the rest managed either by mass organizations like the local CCP Youth League, Worker's Union, or Women's Federation, or by local state bureaus. Teams pursuing the "people's benefit" include those working on the popularization of legal services led by the justice bureau, healthcare workers mobilized by the district health bureau and local Red Cross, and taxation assistance teams supported by the local tax bureau (xsdwmsjzx 2019). Jiafa Township in Anhui's Tongling County boasts nine different volunteer teams, including a "Leading Pioneer" team, "Theory Publicity" team, a "Civilized and Courteous" team, and a "Civilized Countryside" team, among others. Each team is led by a village cadre responsible for a grassroots Party organization, and the teams receive direct support from functional local government bureaus (Xu 2020). The *Guiding Handbook* suggested that pilot counties develop "Party member parenting" (党员爸妈) programs in which teachers, cadres, work unit employees, and entrepreneurs volunteered to be linked with district children, organizing meals and activities with them (CPMCSCO 2019, 119). In other cases, employees of local legal bureaus were instructed to register and launch legal popularization, mediation, or volunteer legal consultation services; after enlisting, employees of electric companies were encouraged to establish "mobile business halls" to assist in the discovery of hidden dangers, make small repairs, and providing other services (CPMCSCO 2019, 160).

New Civilized Practice Centers link volunteers with the needs of the masses using a "demand-side" (需求侧) model of questionnaires, home visits, and feedback forms to determine what kinds of events and volunteering services are required (CPMCSCO 2019, 153). Ideally, over time, this list becomes more refined and reflective of local circumstances. Civilized Practice Centers are to establish a "mass demands" database (群众需求库), a "volunteer services database" (志愿服务项目库) and a "talent pool" (人才库) to allow specialized volunteers to develop projects flexibly according to "time, place, and situation" (Zhong 2020). Residents "order" volunteering services from the local lists, generally through either apps or downloaded extensions (小程序) on WeChat, via WeChat public accounts or local platforms set up within *Xuexi Qiangguo* 学习强国 (CPMCSCO 2019, 62).

In theory, the local New Era Civilized Practice Center compiles residents' requests and distributes them downstream to lower-level Institutes and Stations, which dispatch teams to provide the services. Upon completion, the masses then rate and assess the services delivered, generally all within the same online system or platform. In Anhui's Hefei, the platform developed by the Chaohu City New Era Civilized Practice Center involves six steps (see Figure 7.1).

Huicheng District in Guangdong's Huizhou Municipality developed a customized WeChat mini-program in 2020 that allows users to order volunteer services, view a roster of ongoing "Civilized Practice" events and activities, provide feedback on services received, and redeem points collected from their own volunteering activities in exchange for goods. The mini-program's rolling news feed publicizes New Era Civilized Practice Center information and keeps a running tally of the numbers of registered volunteers, volunteer teams, and activities sponsored by the local Center. One resident committee Party cadre boasted that the mini-program is "very convenient," allowing residents to access Center-organized services – like "free health checks" – without leaving their residential compounds (Huizhou Wenmingwang 2021).

Ideally, people can reach out to volunteers for *any* issue; the *Guiding Handbook* instructs the pilot Center volunteer teams to operate on a model of "you call, and I respond" (CPMCSCO 2019, 116). For example, in Inner Mongolia's Guyang County, Party member volunteers registered with the local Center clean windows, visit lonely elderly people, and "scientifically" dispose of rodents. The Center also established volunteer teams to assist residents with day-to-day tasks, like "helping in the kitchen," "hairstyling," "doing the marketing," "home repairs," "mediation services," "mobile phone help," "butchering pigs," and "talking" to people

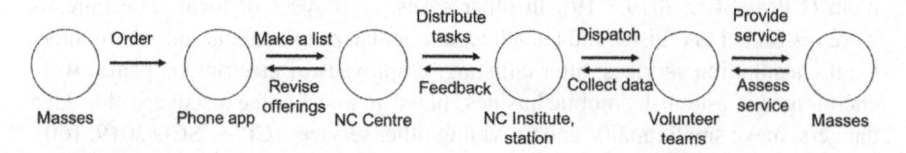

Figure 7.1 Chaohu City Mass-Volunteer Integration

Source: CCOFB 2020, 127

– offering an informal version of one-on-one counseling (Renminwang 2020). In Fujian's Xiamen, Haicang New Civilized Practice Center volunteers "create civilized traffic" (打造文明交通); set up "caring heart service stations" (爱心服务站) to provide outdoor workers with free drinking water, temporary rest, and mobile phone charging facilities; and carry out "environmental protection" volunteer work to remove unsightly trash from nearby Caijianwei Mountain, an important recreational and tourist spot in the district (Lin 2020).

At the same time, however, the Center volunteers conjoin their service to "ideological and political work" (思想政治工作): every act of volunteering must be infused with "ideological content" (思想内涵) such that the act of volunteering takes the study and propagation of Xi Jinping Thought as its core (CPMCSCO 2019, 51, 116). For example, while imparting farming advice to residents in need, volunteers are to expound on Xi Jinping's "important discussions" (重要论述) on the "three agricultural problems" (三农), the "strategy to rejuvenate the countryside," to extol the virtues of the Party's "innovative scientific theories," and agricultural policies beneficial to farmers (CPMCSCO 2019, 114). According to the *Guiding Handbook*, while "caring for and serving the masses," volunteers are always to "educate and guide" them as well (CPMCSCO 2019, 117) by sharing "famous quotes" that shed light on the relationship between the "Party's scientific theory" and "the people's good life" (人民美好生活) during their work with residents in need (CPMCSCO 2019, 27, 114). Volunteers are advised to use the simple and direct "language of the masses" (群众的语言), and preferably local dialects, whenever possible. Storytelling is to be both educative and inductive, starting from concrete examples drawn from the lives of ordinary local people, before building broader and more theoretical conclusions. Volunteers are encouraged to supplement these narratives with simple comparisons and/or photos, such that the people will "feel the care of the Party, narrowing the relationship between the Party and the masses, and further consolidating the ruling foundation of the Party" (CPMCSCO 2019, 37).

Registered volunteers meet regularly to share and refine their methods. Volunteer training events staged at the New Civilized Practice Center in Ningxia's Yuanzhou begin with the singing of patriotic songs, a recitation of the "Volunteer's Oath" (志愿宣誓), and a reading of "golden quotations" (金句) from the *Xuexi Qiangguo* website. This "civilized practice workflow" (文明实践工作流程), they claim, enhances the "sense of ritual" for the participants, elevates Center events, and strengthens the political and ideological dimensions of volunteers' grassroots work (Wu 2019).

In building and maintaining New Era Civilized Practice Centers, local Party officials clearly rely heavily on online resources and digital platforms – like Weibo, WeChat, and Xuexi Qiangguo – to pool requests for services, coordinate activities, and collate feedback from their events. Due to this interdependence of online and offline resources, the construction and development of the New Era Civilized Practice Center system was tied to the simultaneous construction of county-level "Integrated Media Centers," which proved critical in enabling the pooling of information and resources at the grassroots.

The "Civilizing" Role of the Integrated Media Centers

At the National Propaganda Work Meeting in August 2018, one month after the New Civilized Practice Centers pilot program was launched, Xi called for the creation of county-level Integrated Media Centers that would work alongside and support them in "better guiding and serving the masses" (Xi 2018). Within weeks, speaking in Inner Mongolia, Propaganda Minister Huang Keming underscored the import of the two projects in strengthening grassroots political and ideological work and building "spiritual socialist civilization." Huang further called for the appointment of "red literary and artistic hussars" (红色文艺轻骑兵) at the grassroots, the enhanced delivery of popular cultural and artistic events at the county level and below, and the improvement of political and ideological work to deepen popular understanding of the need for national unity and progress (Huang 2018b).

County-level Integrated Media Centers are designed to strengthen the Party's control over local media in response to three challenges: the shift in media production from the collective (traditional Party-state dominated media) to fragmented (self-media 自媒体 content posted to digital platforms like WeChat and Weibo; the shift from a predominantly fixed rural to a more mobile urban society; and the shift in user access devices from television and radio to smartphones (Cao 2019). Collectively, these three shifts required a new level of media integration and supervision capable of pushing a more unified message that is also more responsive to local and individual needs. Hence, while the Practice Centers have their own "media officers" (新闻官) (Wang 2020), the Integrated Media Centers are designed to serve as digital platforms amplifying the Practice Centers' messages and link grassroots ideological work to broader, central narratives. "Two Centers" collaborate, with each "borrowing from, and promoting each other" (互相借力，互相促进), alighting on "the wings of the Internet" (互联网的翅膀) (Cao 2019). Thus, although Practice Centers report to the local Propaganda Department (区委宣传部) and the District Party Standing Committee (区委常委), in some cases the "Two Centers" share office space (合署办公), as is the case in Jilin's Panshi Municipality and Shaanxi's Feng County.

Integrated Media Centers accumulate examples of Civilized Practice volunteer team activities on their news client platforms, edited to accommodate user preferences for "skimming" (浅阅读) and "browsing" (轻阅读), and then disseminate them, aiming to generate "positive energy" (正能量) in digital spaces. The media centers also use livestreaming broadcasts to promote Practice Center events, including "online Party classes," "online tourism" (网上旅游) of patriotic sites, and lectures and events (CCOFB 2020, 169). Hubei's Hefeng County relies on QQ and WeChat groups that combine members from both of the Two Centers: Civilized Practice Center volunteers share their activities, where it is picked up by Integrated Media Center employees, who then integrate these events into daily news reporting and publicize them on different media channels (Hefeng 2020). Inner Mongolia's Guyang County likens this process to a "service loop," in which the Integrated Media Center pools information about people's "needs" (了解需求) and guides the masses to "order" (点单) services; Practice Center volunteers "take orders" (接单) and resolve practical problems (解决实际问题).

The "platformization" (平台化) function of the Integrated Media Centers is fundamental to their design: two months after the Central Leading Group for Comprehensively Deepening Reform approved the pilot program, the State Administration of Radio, Film and Television released guidelines detailing technical specifications for both provincial and county-level Integrated Media Centers that would utilize cloud computing, big data, and other technologies specifically facilitated by China's development of 5G networks (Zhong and Zhu 2020). Shandong's Qihe County Integrated Media Center created a unified platform conjoining the local TV station, local radio station, the Qihe County newspaper, local government websites, multiple WeChat and Weibo public accounts, as well as Toutiao and Douyin. The resulting "Qihe Information Clearinghouse" platform was celebrated as a model of 3 (traditional media), plus 9 (new media), plus N, allegedly demonstrating that in the platformization of local government, "there is no limit to integration" (Sun and Li 2019). Jiangxi's Gongqingcheng established the "3+1+1" work model in August 2018, integrating three grassroots public cultural service centers, one Civilized Practice Center, and one Integrated Media Center. To accomplish this, the media center combined twelve different media sources, including television, the official Weibo, and public WeChat accounts, into one integrated platform interface that uses TV, computer, mobile phone, and touchscreens to reach users. With this level of media and public service integration, Gongqingcheng claims that it can "smoothly" promote "civilizational practices" using a targeted approach. Rather than "flooding" (大水漫灌) and overwhelming viewers, Gongqingcheng promotes its platform integration as a method of "precise drip irrigation" (精准滴灌) that "caters" (配餐) to the needs and viewing habits of local users. To attract viewers to the site, residents select and watch a "movie of the week" on Mondays, free of charge. In the process, they are also exposed to other propaganda resources like the "cloud lecture hall" (livestreaming educational material and Party propaganda), "farmhouse bookstore" (online library), and other service platforms. Specialized and trained "rural" lecturers offer taped lectures on a variety of topics for "on demand" viewing by local residents, as well as an ongoing serialized "Story of Gongqingcheng." A total of 400 local events were accessible through the Gongqingcheng Integrated Media Center platform in 2019. In addition, national-level resources feature prominently: rural residents are encouraged to access *Xuexi Qiangguo*'s "classic sentences" three times a day through the media center platform to realize "full coverage for the masses and Party members" (Liang 2019).

Similarly, in Xiamen's Haicang, Civilized Practice Centers and Integrated Media Center are integrated "seamlessly" (无缝对接) through "one system, one app, one service team" (一系统、一App、一服务) to "maximize information aggregation, serve the people, walk the online mass line, sing the Party's good voice, and let the new culture enter thousands of households" (合信息、服务民众，走好网络群众路线，唱响党的好声音，让新文化走进千家万户) (Lin 2020).

Given the fact that Integrated Media Centers only exist at the county level, they rely on Practice Center volunteers to generate "vivid, lively and grounded" (鲜活, 生动, 接地气) information and "newsworthy material" (多值得宣传的新闻素材) to circulate on their platforms (CCOFB 2020, 179). According to the *Guiding*

Handbook, the goal is to create a virtuous cycle: Integrated Media Centers "excavate news clues, typical cases and touching stories" (挖掘丰富的新闻线索鲜活的典型案例和感人的暖心故事) which provide "fresh nutrition" (鲜活营养) for local audiences, drive up the numbers of users, and fuel further expansion (CCOFB 2020, 180). The media centers do not merely push Practice Center content – rather, the media centers have emerged as service hubs as well, and two integral parts of a single integrated whole. For example, a volunteer service team working in Jinshan Town learned that a forthcoming harvest of locally produced watermelons had no buyers and reported that fact to the Guyang County Integrated Media Center. The media center then put out a call across its media platforms; 20 days later, more than 60 catties of Jinshan watermelons had been sold (Renminwang 2020).

Both institutions were named as key prongs for carrying out grassroots work in the 2019 "Implementation Outline for Citizen Moral Construction in the New Era" (CCP-CCSC 2019) and the Party's 2021 "Propaganda Work Regulations," which called upon Party and state workers at all levels to strengthen their construction (CCPCC 2021). In 2022, both were also specifically highlighted as "effective platform innovations for carrying out the construction of rural spiritual civilization" in the all-important Party Central Committee and State Council Central Document No. 1, which outlines the key tasks for rural revitalization in the upcoming year (CCPCCSC 2022).

Assessing Impact

Two years after the first pilots were rolled out, Hezhong Zeyi, a Beijing-based GONGO (government-organized NGO), conducted a full-scale review of 48 of the original 50 pilot Centers. While positive in tone, the Hezhong Zeyi report was sobering in its assessment of the state of Center operations. It flagged the fact that the pilots had in fact suffered from an overall lack of resources, both human and financial, and that most had failed to elicit broader public participation. Two years after they began operation, more than half (54.9 percent) of the Centers had three or fewer staff members in total, with 77.08 percent reporting that the problem of insufficient staff had proved to be their main hurdle in the first two years of operation. Well over 90 percent of the work done, volunteer or otherwise, was conducted by Propaganda Department personnel; most of the Centers admitted that the participation of social forces had been "low," and that the overwhelming majority of volunteers mobilized were in-service Party members. With respect to projects completed, the pilot Centers reported that by 2020, Center volunteers had spent far more time ensuring local compliance with "zero-COVID" policies than on "strengthening grassroots ideological and political work." All those surveyed agreed, however, that the teams had "contributed to the construction of local spiritual civilization" (Hezhong Zeyi 2020).

Financial resources also proved problematic for the pilots, with already-strapped county fiscal year budgets providing most of the funding (58.33 percent) for most of the sites, supplemented by Propaganda Department funds (41.67 per cent). Just over 54 percent of the pilots received some specially earmarked pilot subsidies from the central government, but only 12.5 percent of them had managed to attract the much-hoped-for local corporate donations. Thirty percent of the pilots agreed that their operations had been "less than ideal" (Hezhong Zeyi 2020). Nonetheless, in November 2021, Propaganda Minister Huang Keming hailed the "fruitful results and accumulated rich experience" of the "Two Centers" pilots and called for the process of constructing of New Civilized Practice Centers to not only continue, but to expand (Huang 2021).

But to what extent have the New Civilized Practice and Integrated Media Centers – as understaffed and poorly resourced as they appear to be – succeeded in ensuring that Xi Jinping Thought "enters the hearts and minds" (入脑入心) of ordinary local residents? Here we wish to propose that, instead of interpreting the pilot program of constructing the "Two Centers" as a manifestation of Xi's reputed "personality cult," we consider their effectiveness in terms of extending the Party-state's infrastructural power at the county level. Authoritarian regimes are challenged to collect accurate information on citizen needs and preferences in the absence of recognizable democratic mechanisms. In the Chinese case in particular, this process has historically been further complicated by the fact that local officials are incentivized to conceal or thwart upward reporting of grassroots grievances and local mishaps (Wallace 2016; Gao 2016). Fragmentation among multiple agencies across jurisdictions has led to bureaucratic "stove-piping" and official intransigence (Mertha 2009).

However, a key focus of the "Two Centers" pilots has been on the construction of digital platforms, which has significantly enhanced their scalability and effectiveness at the local and grassroots levels despite the challenges of minimal staffing and insufficient funds, allowing their scant resources to have a much greater impact than their budgets and human resources might suggest. As Ansell and Miura have pointed out, "platformization" affords local and sub-local governments new means for connecting with a variety of different actors, "engaging citizens and stakeholders in powerful new ways;" crowdsourcing platforms – like those of the Civilized Practice Centers – represent highly efficient tools for aggregating distributed citizen inputs; the rapid scaling-up of volunteer efforts to address shifting resident needs, as occurred during the recent COVID lockdowns; they also serve as "force multipliers" enabling communities to mobilize underutilized resources and, arguably, to distribute them more efficiently according to need (Ansell and Miura 2020, 262–263). By leveraging digital technology, the "Two Centers'" platforms demonstrated a capacity to streamline the process of matching the needs of local residents with available resources and volunteers, while also ensuring the efficient deployment of services to those in need. The adoption of digital platforms by the "Two Centers" thus generated a multiplier effect in the pilot communities that enabled a more scalable, flexible, and efficient deployment of services at the local and grassroots levels, thus enhancing the infrastructural power of the Party-state. The utilization of online questionnaires, push notifications, and feedback forms allowed for the efficient collection of information on local needs and preferences. This data-driven approach allows them to tailor their services more precisely to the specific requirements of the local communities they serve. The use of apps, WeChat extensions and applets, and other digital tools streamlined and simplified the process of requesting and providing feedback on volunteer services. This user-friendly approach at least potentially encourages participation from local residents and promoted additional accountability and transparency that reduced risks to the Party-state, while at the same time boosting popular perceptions of official responsiveness, even in locales in which not all requests were met. The incorporation of feedback into the system allowed the Centers to update and refine their offerings and improve the quality of their services. This increased connectivity ensures that resources and services can be distributed more efficiently and rapidly, maximizing the impact of the Centers' efforts at the local level.

In conclusion, although the "Two Center" pilots may have failed as yet in achieving their more ambitious aims with respect to increasing the power and popular appeal of Xi Jinping Thought at the social grassroots, the platformization of local and sub-local government offices and services arguably created a multiplier effect that enhances their scalability and effectiveness at the social grassroots, at least partially offsetting the limitations they face in terms of staff and resources. By leveraging digital technology and platform governance, the Centers can better respond to the needs of the masses, allocate resources more efficiently, and improve the overall quality of their services, thereby expanding the infrastructural power of the Party-state at the county level.

References

Agence France-Presse. 2021. "China's Children Start First Day Schooled in 'Xi Jinping Thought.'" *The Guardian*. September 1. https://archive.ph/alkxc.

Ansell, Christopher, and Satoshi Miura. 2020. "Can the Power of Platforms be Harnessed for Governance?" *Public Administration* 98: 261–276.

Brandenburger, David. 2005. "Stalin as Symbol: A Case Study of the Personality Cult and Its Construction." In *Stalin: A New History*, eds. Sarah Davies and James R. Harris. Cambridge: Cambridge University Press, 249–270.

Cai, Vanessa. 2023. "China's Gaokao Exam Tests Grasp of Xi Jinping Thought, so Students Can 'Understand the Power of Truth'." *South China Morning Post*. June 11. https://archive.ph/nRlte.

Cai, Xia. 2021. "The Weakness of Xi Jinping: How Hubris and Paranoia Threaten China's Future." *Foreign Affairs* 101: 5. https://archive.ph/d9OsU.

Cao Feng [曹峰]. 2019. "Building County-Level Integrated Media Centers and New Era Civilized Practice Centers" [建好县级融媒体中心和新时代文明实践中心]. *Red Flag* [红旗文稿]. December. https://archive.ph/dzsKv.

CCP Central Committee. 1986. "Resolution of the CCP Central Committee on the Guidelines for the Construction of Socialist Spiritual Civilization" [中共中央关于社会主义精神文明建设指导方针的决议]. September 28. https://archive.ph/2Vyua.

CCP Central Committee. 2020. "CCP Central Committee's Suggestions for Formulating the 14th Five-Year Plan for National Economic and Social Development, with Long-Term Goals for 2035" [中共中央关于制定国民经济和社会发展第十四个五年规划和二〇三五年远景目标的建议]. October 29. https://archive.ph/xFbxe.

CCP Central Committee. 2021. "Propaganda Work Regulations" [中国共产党宣传工作条例]. November 10. https://archive.ph/qNNEv.

CCP Central Committee and State Council (CCPCCSC). 2019. "Implementation Outline for Citizen Moral Construction in the New Era" [新时代公民道德建设实施纲要]. October 27. https://archive.ph/XdwK.

CCP Central Committee and State Council (CCPCCSC). 2022. "Opinion on Comprehensively Promoting Key Rural Revitalization Work" [关于做好2022年全面推进乡村振兴重点工作的意见]. January 4. https://archive.ph/6cC1E.

Central Civilization Office First Bureau (CCOFB) [中央文明办一局]. 2020. *Guidebook for Building New Age Civilized Practice Centers* [建设新时代文明实践中心指导手册]. Beijing: Wenming chubanshe.

Central Leading Small Group for Comprehensively Deepening Reform (CLSGCDR) [全面深化改革领导小组]. 2018. "Guiding Opinion on the Pilot Work of Building a Civilized Practice Center in the New Era" [关于建设新时代文明实践中心试点工作的指导意见]. July 6. https://archive.ph/H2age and https://archive.ph/kjUBx.

Central Propaganda Ministry and Central Spiritual Civilization Office (CPMCSCO) [中共中央宣传部中央文明办]. 2019. "Implementation Plan for Constructing New Era Civilization Practice Volunteer Service Mechanisms" [关于新时代文明实践志愿服务机制建设的实施方案]. https://archive.ph/txFqa.

Chang, Jung, and Jon Halliday. 2005. *Mao: The Unknown Story*. New York: Alfred A. Knopf.

Cunningham, Edward, Tony Saich, and Jessie Turiel. 2020. "Understanding CCP Resilience: Surveying Chinese Public Opinion Through Time." *Ash Center for Democratic Governance and Innovation*.

Dikötter, Frank. 2019. *How to Be a Dictator: The Cult of Personality in the Twentieth Century*. New York: Bloomsbury.

Distelhorst, Greg, and Diana Fu. 2019. "Performing Authoritarian Citizenship: Public Transcripts in China." *Perspectives on Politics* 17(1): 106–121.

Dynon, Nicholas. 2008. "'Four Civilizations' and the Evolution of post-Mao Chinese Socialist Ideology." *The China Journal* 60 (July), 83–109.

Editorial Team [本书编辑组]. 2017. "Publisher's Note" [出版说明]. *The Governance of China* [习近平谈治国理政] 2: i–ii.

Gao Feng. 2021. "Hai'an: Cultural Self-Confidence Leads Civilized Practice, 'Hai'an Exemplar' is Praised" [海安：文化自信引领文明实践，"海安样本"获点赞]. April 14. https://archive.ph/KpUNe.

Gao Jianjin. 2020. "Fujian: Making Everyone a Participant in Civilized Practice" [福建：让人人成为文明实践参与者]. *Guangming Daily [光明日报]*. April 12. https://archive.ph/izA6o.

Gao, Jie. 2016. "Bypass the Lying Mouths: How Does the CCP Tackle Information Distortion at Local Levels?" *The China Quarterly* 228: 950–969.

Gongchandangyuan wang [共产党员网]. 2016. "Xi Jinping Presided Over the Twenty-Seventh Meeting of the Central Leading Group for Comprehensively Deepening Reform, Emphasizing Strengthening the Foundation, Emphasizing Integration and Improving the Mechanism, Strict Supervision, According to the Timetable and Roadmap for Advancing Reform" [习近平主持召开中央全面深化改革领导小组第二十七次会议强调 强化基础注重集成完善机制严格督察 按照时间表路线图推进改革]. August 30. https://archive.ph/YXgI4.

"Guanyu jinyibu jiaqiang nongcun wenhua jianshe de yijian" 关于进一步加强农村文化建设的意见 [Opinions on Further Strengthening the Construction of Rural Culture] 2005, Nov. 7. https://archive.ph/2UE3e.

"Guanyu quanmian shenhua gaige ruogan zhongda wenti de jueding" 关于全面深化改革若干重大问题的决定 [Decision on Several Major Issues of Comprehensively Deepening Reform]. 2013. November 15. https://archive.is/defCN.

Haikouwang. 2019. "Haikou Meilan New Era Civilized Practice Center Holds Fundraising Event to Support the Needy and Disabled" [海口美兰新时代文明实践中心举行募捐活动 资助困难残疾人士]. *Sina.com*. May 19. https://archive.ph/s2Uai.

Hainan Haikou Jingshan District. 2019. "Relying on 'Fengqiao Experience' to Enhance the Endogenous Power of the Civilized Practice Center in the New Era" [依靠"枫桥经验"提升新时代文明实践中心的内生动力]. December 25. https://archive.ph/xRWnQ.

Hefeng [鹤峰]. 2020. "'Three Interconnections'" Realize the Integrated Development of 'Two Centers'" [三个互通"实现"两个中心"融合发展]. *Yangtze Cloud Client [长江云客户端]*. June 9. https://archive.ph/su7yd.

Hezhong, Zeyi [和众泽益]. 2020. "Research Report on the Work of Building New Era Civilized Practice Centers" [新时代文明实践中心建设工作成效调研报告]. https://archive.ph/of5Ku.

Huang, Haifeng. 2018a. "The Pathology of Hard Propaganda." *The Journal of Politics* 80(3): 1034–1038.

Huang, Keming [黄坤明]. 2018b. "Better Meeting the New Expectations of the People's Spiritual and Cultural Lives" [更好满足人民精神文化生活新期待]. *People's Daily [人民日报]*. August 29. https://archive.ph/pJmo0.

Huang, Keming [黄坤明]. 2021. [黄坤明在拓展新时代文明实践中心建设工作电视电话会议上强调总结试点经验 把握时代要求全面深化拓展新时代文明实践中心建设]. *Xinhuanet*. November 23. https://archive.ph/qJpH4.

Huizeren [惠泽人]. 2020. "2020 China Volunteer Service Annual Development Report" [中国志愿服务年度发展报告]. September 29. https://archive.ph/0X09K.

Huizhou Wenmingwang [惠州文明网]. 2021. "Dispatches Sent on the 5th [of Every Month]! Launching Guangdong Huizhou City Huicheng District's New Civilized Practice Center 'Themed Activity Day'" [逢5出发"！广东惠州惠城区新时代文明实践"主题活动日"启动]. March 10. https://archive.ph/tQMVL.

Khrushchev, Nikita. 1956. "Speech to the 20th Congress of the CPSU." February 24–25. https://archive.ph/DZ03.

Kong, Linglei. 2020. "'Hometown Rainbow' Blasts Civilization Wind – Documenting Qinghai's Huzhu Tu Autonomous County's Creation of a National Civilized City" [彩虹故乡"劲吹文明风 – 青海省互助土族自治县创建全国文明城市纪实]. September 10. https://archive.ph/43rx4.

Liang Chuyan [梁楚烟]. 2019. "Jiangxi's Gongqingcheng Builds a '3+1+1' New Era Civilized Practice Work Model" [江西共青城构建"3+1+1"新时代文明实践工作模式]. *Xinhua Wang [新华网]*. August 19. https://archive.ph/DzLZW.

Lin Cen [林岑]. 2020. "Haicang: Benefiting the People and Watering the Hearts of the People, the Practice of Civilization in the New Era 'Blossoms Everywhere'" [海沧：惠民实事润民心 新时代文明实践"遍地开花]. *Xiamen Civilization Network [厦门文明网]*. November 9. https://archive.ph/XGCQa.

Lin, Liza. 2022. "What Do Chinese People Think of Xi Jinping? It's Very Hard to Tell." *Wall Street Journal*. October 13. https://archive.ph/Z0w1J.

Mann, Michael. 2008. "Infrastructural Power Revisited." *Studies in Comparative International Development* 43: 355–365.

Mertha, Andrew C. 2009. "Fragmented Authoritarianism 2.0: Political Pluralization in the Chinese Policy Process." *The China Quarterly* 200: 995–1012.

Miller, Alice L. 2017. "What Would Deng Do?" *China Leadership Monitor* 54(2). www.hoover.org/sites/default/files/research/docs/clm52am.pdf.

Qingdao Wenmingwang [青岛文明网]. 2020. "Qingdao's Pingdu City Highlights 'Five Modernizations' and Integrates Resources to Make the Flower of New Era Civilization Bloom Brilliantly" [青岛平度市突出"五化"整合资源 让新时代文明之花绚丽绽放]. November 12. https://archive.ph/XQmeM.

Rachman, Gideon. 2021. "The Xi Personality Cult is a Danger to China." *Financial Times*. September 13. https://archive.ph/e3zoc.

Renminwang [人民网]. 2020. "Inner Mongolia's Guyang County: Deeply Integrating the 'Two Centers' to Create a New Path of Civilized Practice" [内蒙古固阳县："两个中心"深度融合 打造文明实践新路径]. May 12. https://archive.ph/8IfyM.

Shandong Zucheng [山东诸城]. 2020. "Let the Practice of Civilization 'Walk the Streets and Alleys' to Every 'Nerve Ending'" [山东诸城：让文明实践"走街串巷"到每一个"神经末梢"]. December 1. https://archive.ph/f3KkC.

Sixiang zhengzhi gongzuo yanjiu [思想政治工作研究]. 2019. "Explore the 'Cixi Path' for the Construction of a New Era Civilization Practice Center" ["探索新时代文明实践中心建设 '慈溪路径'"]. January 9. https://archive.ph/8x0h3.

Sorace, Christian. 2020. "Gratitude: The Ideology of Sovereignty in Crisis." *Made in China* 5(2): 166–169.

Sorace, Christian. 2021. "The Chinese Communist Party's Nervous System: Affective Governance from Mao to Xi." *The China Quarterly* 248(S1): 29–51. https://doi.org/10.1017/S0305741021000680.

Sun Maotong [孙茂同], and Li Xiaonan [李晓楠]. 2019. "Guiding Self-Media to Promote Social Justice and Conveying the New Voice of New Era Civilized Practice – A Beneficial Exploration of Building an Integrated Media Center in Shandong's Qihe County" [引导自媒体弘扬社会正气 传递新时代文明实践新声 — 山东省齐河县推进融媒体中心建设的有益探索]. *Media [传媒]*. August 15: 77–79.

Tsang, Steve, and Olivia Cheung. 2022. "Has Xi Jinping Made China's Political System More Resilient and Enduring?" *Third World Quarterly* 43(1): 225–243.

Wallace, Jeremy. 2016. "Juking the Stats? Authoritarian Information Problems in China." *British Journal of Political Science* 46(1): 11–29.

Wang, Mingrun. 2020. "Look at them! Shunde New Civilized Practice Center 'News Officers' Have Arrived!" [看，认真的他们！顺德新时代文明实践"新闻官"来了]. *Guangzhou Daily [广州日报]*. July 30.

Wang, Xiaoying [王晓映]. 2019. "The 'Jiangsu Exploration' of the Construction of Civilization Practice Center in the New Era: The Guidance and Cohesion of the Masses" [新时代文明实践中心建设的"江苏探索"： 在服务群众中引导和凝聚群众]. May 28. https://archive.ph/qexWC.

Wei, Qing [韦青]. 2022. "Expand the Construction of New Era Civilized Practice Centers and Build a Solid Foundation for Grassroots Propaganda, Ideological and Cultural Work" [拓展新时代文明实践中心建设 筑牢基层宣传思想文化工作基石]. *Struggle [奋斗]*. July 12. https://archive.ph/SBZo8.

Wu, Diansheng. 2019. "Yuanzhou's Exploration of Civilized Practice in the New Era" [新时代文明实践的原州探索]. *People's Daily Online Ningxia Channel [人民网-宁夏频道]*. November 5. https://archive.ph/vckLL.

Xi, Jinping [习近平]. 2017. "Winning a Decisive Victory in Building a Moderately Prosperous Society in an All-Round Way and the Great Victory of Socialism with Chinese Characteristics in the New Era – Xi Jinping's Report at the Nineteenth National Congress of the Communist Party of China" [决胜全面建成小康社会 夺取新时代中国特色社会主义伟大胜利 – 在中国共产党第十九次全国代表大会上的报告]. October 27. https://archive.ph/RDwMb.

Xi, Jinping. 2018. "Xi Jinping Attends the National Propaganda and Ideological Work Conference and Delivers an Important Speech" [习近平出席全国宣传思想工作会议并发表重要讲话]. August 22. https://archive.ph/iL7K8.

Xsdwmsjzx. 2019. "Zhejiang: Implementation Plan for the Construction of a New Era Civilization Practice Center in Nanhu District" [浙江： 南湖区新时代文明实践中心建设工作实施方案]. May 16. https://archive.ph/tH5Tx.

Xu, Lailong [许来龙]. 2020. "Nanling County: Civilized Practice Sticking Close to People's Hearts and Their Aspirations are Blooming" [南陵县： 文明实践贴民心 志愿之花朵朵]. August 3. https://archive.ph/1lRC9.

Yan'an, Ribao [延安日报]. 2019. "Where the Masses are, the Civilized Practice will Extend – A Snapshot of the Pilot Work of the Yanchuan County Civilized Practice Center in the New Era Pilot" [群众在哪里，文明实践就延伸到哪里 – 延川县新时代文明实践中心试点工作掠影]. *Phoenix News [凤凰新闻]*. January 7. https://archive.ph/VHvhc.

Yang, Fan, Shizong Wang, and Zhihan Zhang. 2022. "State-enlisted Voluntarism in China: The Role of Public Security Volunteers in Social Stability Maintenance." *The China Quarterly* 249(March): 47–67.

Yang, Guobin. 2017. "Demobilizing the Emotions of Online Activism in China: A Civilizing Process." *International Journal of Communication* 11: 1945–1965.

Yanji Municipal CCP Propaganda Department [中共延吉市委宣传部]. 2019. "The 'Yanji Model' of Doing Mass Work Well" [做好群众工作的"延吉模式"]. *Research on Ideological and Political Work [思想政治工作研究]*. October 15. https://archive.ph/htgQf.

You, Yi [游仪] et al. 2020. "Dedication, Friendship, Mutual Help and Progress – Documenting in Depth the Development of Volunteering Via the New Era of Civilized Practice Center" [奉献友爱互助进步 – 各地新时代文明实践中心深入开展志愿服务纪实]. *People's Daily [人民日报]*. August 8. https://archive.ph/si8su.

Zhao, Qiuli [赵秋丽]. 2020. "Shandong's Qufu: The New Era Civilization Practice Station is Really Lively" [山东曲阜：新时代文明实践站真热闹]. *Guangming Daily [光明日报]*. July 28. https://archive.ph/0csx6.

Zhong, Qinglan [钟清兰]. 2020. "Bringing Forward a New Style and Singing New Music! Ganzhou Vigorously Promotes New Era Civilized Practice" [弘扬新风尚 唱响新乐章！赣州大力推进新时代文明实践工作]. *Ganzhou Propaganda [赣州宣传]*. November 24. https://archive.ph/H3mfW.

Zhong, Ying [钟瑛], and Zhu Yue [朱雪]. 2020. "The Role and Function of County-Level Integrated Media Platforms in Improving the Modernization of Grassroots Governance" [县级融媒体平台化对提升基层治理现代化的作用和路径]. *Dongyue Tribune [东岳论丛]*. April: 73–79.

Zhongguo, Wenming Wang [中国文明网]. 2021. "Fuzhou: Volunteer Service Enters the Subway to Build a Landscape of 'Mobile Civilization'" [福州：志愿服务进地铁 共筑"流动文明"风景线]. 19 April. https://archive.ph/1W9fc.

8 The 20th Party Congress

Toward Personalistic Autarky?

Joseph Fewsmith

The much-anticipated 20th Party Congress of the Chinese Communist Party (CCP) took place in Beijing from October 16–22, 2022. It was anticipated because the issue that caught people's attention was whether or not Xi Jinping (习近平), frequently described as the most powerful Chinese leader since Mao Zedong (毛泽东), would secure a third term as general secretary of the Chinese Communist Party (CCP). When the congress was over and Xi was victorious, the press widely reported that he had won an "unprecedented" third term. In some sense this was correct. Jiang Zemin (江泽民) had served two terms (plus the final three years of Zhao Ziyang's (赵紫阳) term and continued with two additional years as chairman of the Central Military Commission (CMC) after stepping down as general secretary), and Hu Jintao (胡锦涛) had served just two terms (without retaining his position as head of the CMC). But the implication that Xi Jinping had broken with an increasingly institutionalized system was simply wrong.

What was unusual was not that Xi had secured a third term, but that Jiang Zemin and Hu Jintao had served only two terms each. They had done so not because of institutionalization but because Deng Xiaoping (邓小平) had mandated that Hu would replace Jiang at the Fifteenth Party Congress in 2007, and Hu did not have the political strength to continue past the Eighteenth Party Congress in 2012 (Fewsmith 2022, 80–81). It would have been more accurate to have said that Xi was reverting to the tradition of staying in power as long as a leader was physically and politically able to. Contrary to the widespread belief that the CCP was institutionalizing, party tradition revolved around a single leader rising to the top and staying there, promoting allies to important positions, particularly those that might be considered "critical," such as Organization, Propaganda, State Security, Public Security, and most important, the military. As we will see, Xi has reinforced this tradition and extended it in a form of strong-man rule not seen since the days of Deng Xiaoping.

As we look back on the eras of Jiang Zemin and Hu Jintao, we see a China that appeared to be institutionalizing politically, integrating with the world economically, and developing a degree of pluralism and perhaps civil society domestically. Despite the growth of nationalism and "New Left" thinking, there seemed to be something of a convergence between China and the "West." Although corruption and the loss of ideology were serious issues, there seemed to be no reason why the

DOI: 10.4324/9781003257943-9

further development of law and the expansion of civil society could not lead China toward a stable "soft authoritarian" form of government, much as Taiwan had been in the 1970s and early 1980s. It had been a long march from the totalitarian days of Mao's China, but there seemed to be no turning back. But no Leninist system has undergone "peaceful evolution"; all had either maintained their Leninist systems or collapsed. China had reached an inflection point.

The same trends that raised hopes in much of the world raised fears in Xi Jinping. Shortly after being named general secretary of the Chinese Communist Party (CCP) in November 2012, Xi went to Guangdong and famously said that the Communist Party of the Soviet Union (CPSU) had collapsed because it had lost its "ideals and confidence." Just as important, when it was collapsing, "nobody was a real man; nobody came out to resist" (Buckley 2013). Xi was obsessed with the collapse of the CPSU and was determined to prevent the CCP from suffering the same fate. Xi's concerns were not unreasonable. Corruption was serious and had become part of the way the CCP operated. Belief in socialism, however defined, was waning, and "mass incidents" were happening at an alarming rate. It was not unreasonable to think that the CCP might collapse. This was a "political platform" that one could run on. The ambition of Bo Xilai (薄熙来), the party secretary of Chongqing who seemed to be challenging Xi, and the corruption of Ling Jihua (令计划), head of the General Office and close aide to Hu Jintao, exemplified the challenge the party faced. Xi believed he could "save" the party.

Judging by Xi Jinping's report to the 20th Party Congress, he remains obsessed with the party and believes that his predecessors had presided over frightening developments. Under his predecessors, Xi reported, there had been "a slide toward weak, hollow, and watered-down party leadership . . ." And "despite repeated warnings," "pointless formalities, bureaucratism, hedonism, and extravagance [had] persisted in some localities and departments." The economy, he said, quoting without attribution former premier Wen Jiabao (温家宝), was "unbalanced, uncoordinated, and unsustainable." And ideologically there had been "misguided patterns of thinking," including "historical nihilism" – ways of thinking that challenged official narratives of party history.

No doubt there were many ways to tackle such issues. Outside observers no doubt would have encouraged greater attention to building stronger legal institutions, strengthening intra-party democracy, and paying greater attention to civil society. But such measures, Xi no doubt concluded, would have weakened the Leninist features of the CCP that Xi saw as essential to the preservation of the party. Drawing on the lessons he learned from his father, Xi chose to tighten party discipline, strengthen ideology, crack down on opposition forces, enhance surveillance, and build a stronger military. This was, of course, trying to apply a 1950s model to a twenty-first century China. Being a princeling apparently came with notable baggage.

Xi's attack on trends that he saw as corrosive of party rule followed three main paths. The best known is his campaign against corruption. Since corruption was nearly universal, it was a convenient tool for ridding himself of political opponents as well as tightening party control in general. Bo Xilai (薄熙来), the son of party "immortal" Bo Yibo (波一波), was ousted by Xi's predecessor, Hu Jintao, but as a Politburo Standing Committee (PBSC) member, Xi no doubt had a voice in how to deal with Bo. Zhou Yongkang (周永康), the powerful but retired head of the Political and Legal Affairs Commission, became one of Xi's first targets after taking office.

The prosecution of Zhou, followed by those of People's Liberation Army (PLA) vice chairmen Xu Caihou (徐才厚) and Guo Boxiong (郭伯雄) were unusual because all were retired and Zhou was a former member of the PBSC. The CCP has not normally prosecuted retired officials and it had not punished a member of the PBSC in the reform era. As the saying went, punishment does not rise to the Standing Committee level (刑不上常). Breaking this norm let everyone in the party know that he or she was vulnerable. That vulnerability was highlighted by Xi in November 2014 at a meeting on political work in the PLA in Gutian. The 420 officers attending would have all been well aware of the importance of the original Gutian conference held in December 1929, when Mao had made clear that the party would command the military (Mulvenon 2015). A new era of strong man rule was shaping up.

The campaign against corruption would continue and expand, ensnaring 26 officials at or above the ministerial level along with 129 officials at the vice-ministerial level over the course of Xi's first term (Fewsmith 2022, 143).

Although Xi's efforts to gain control over the military were originally pitched as part of his campaign against corruption, it should be viewed as a separate part of his effort to consolidate power. When Jiang Zemin left his post as general secretary in 2002, he had retained his job as chairman of the CMC, suggesting that the military post is the more important of the two positions. At the same time, he was able to appoint two protégés, Xu Caihou and Guo Boxiong, as the vice chairs of the CMC. These appointments meant that the incoming general secretary, Hu Jintao, would never gain effective control over the military. Even when Jiang gave up his position as head of the CMC, Xu Caihou and Guo Boxiong continued to run the military.

From the perspective of a Leninist party, the lack of direct, personal control over the military is dangerous. Xu Caihou and Guo Boxiong retired in 2017, but their influence ran deep in the PLA. Since Xu had risen to head of the General Political Department in 2012, he had screened the promotions of some 83 officers promoted to the rank of general. So, corruption was not the only issue. As Xu Qiliang (许其亮), the senior vice chairman of the CMC under Xi Jinping, explained in 2019, Xu and Guo had "misused their power" to form a "faction and pursue their private interests." Such actions "hollowed out and weakened the Central Military Commission chairman responsibility system, creating great danger for the party's absolute leadership over the military and causing great losses to military construction." To correct this problem, the 19th Party Congress specifically wrote "the Central Military Commission implements the chairmanship responsibility system" into the party constitution. Xu Qiliang's explanation that control over the military was at stake is more convincing than simply accusing Xu and Guo of corruption, though that was no doubt true as well.

The third prong in Xi's effort to discipline the party and crack down on civil society started when *Southern Weekend*, the reform-minded newspaper, prepared a New Year's editorial entitled "China's Dream Is the Dream of Constitutional Government." Before the paper hit the streets, however, the editorial was rewritten by the Guangdong provincial propaganda department. More seriously, the incident resulted in the party issuing "Document No. 9," which outlined seven topics that should not be discussed in the media. Number one was "Western constitutional government" (Bandurski). Xi followed this up by visiting *People's Daily*, Xinhua, and CCTV to remind them that it was necessary to "put politics in the first place." Finally, in July 2015, China's police carried out a sweeping crackdown on "rights" lawyers (维权律师) – some 250 lawyers were arrested (Fewsmith 2022, 146–148).

Xi's efforts to centralize power, impose discipline on the party, and quell signs of an emergent civil society reached a climax at the 19th Party Congress in 2017. The important development at that congress was the declaration that the party, "whether north, south, east, west, or center," ruled "everything." Although this had always been true, it flew in the face of post-Mao trends and suggested that Xi really had inaugurated a new era in party history. As if to underline that it was a new era, the National People's Congress (NPC) meeting in spring 2018 changed the state constitution by removing the article that limited the president to two terms. The presidency was the least important of Xi's three titles – being general secretary of the party and chairman of the CMC were obviously more important – but removing this constraint on lifelong tenure raised the question of whether Xi really intended to stay on for a third, and possibly fourth, term. It was that question that hung over China's political system until the 20th Party Congress finally convened in October 2022.

The 20th Party Congress

Elite politics in China are normally carefully orchestrated to reach the foreordained conclusion and thereby make that conclusion seem both inevitable and deserving of public support. Accordingly, a build-up to the 20th Party Congress was kicked off by the party's adoption of a history resolution. There was much speculation about what might be contained in the new resolution. Perhaps there would be some new interpretation of party history that would keep observers busy trying to understand its importance. In the end, when the resolution was finally made public, there was no great revelation. On the contrary, the message of the resolution was one of patriotism: Never forget the original intention, always remember the mission (勿忘初心，牢记使命). But there was no historical explanation of that original intention, much less how it had been distorted at times in the party's past ("Resolution of the CPC Central Committee on the Major Achievements and Historical Experience of the Party over the Past Century" 2021).

So, why did the party adopt a new history resolution? One explanation the resolution gave was to "resolutely uphold Comrade Xi Jinping's core position in the Party Central Committee and in the Party as a whole and to uphold the Central Committee's authority and its centralized, unified leadership to ensure that all Party members act in unison." This was a somewhat long-winded way of saying that the resolution was there to support Xi Jinping and to legitimize his bid for a third term.

Having kicked off Xi's campaign, almost nothing went right over the following year. The economic goal for the year was set at 5.5 percent, but with Xi's "zero-Covid" policy, particularly the two-month lockdown of Shanghai, economic growth flagged significantly.

There could be little doubt that Xi's zero-Covid policy was politically contentious; in April the center sent vice premier and Covid czar Sun Chunlan (孙春兰) to Shanghai to emphasize to party secretary Li Qiang (李强) that the zero-Covid policy needed to be upheld. On May 5, Xi presided over a Politburo Standing Committee meeting that emphasized the importance of upholding the "dynamic zero Covid" policy. The meeting emphasized that resoluteness meant success; laxness would bring about serious economic harm. Li Qiang, a member of the Politburo (PB) who would be promoted to the Politburo Standing Committee (PBSC) at the 20th Party Congress and premier at the NPC meeting in March 2023, did so, provoking serious conflict with Shanghai's residents. China's economy eked out a mere 0.4 percent growth in the second quarter (Wang 2022).

Although party congresses are always occasions for the rumor mill to crank up, the run up to the 20th Party Congress seemed particularly rife. Perhaps because there was significant resistance to Xi's third term or perhaps because some hoped to stir up such resistance, rumors seemed particularly plentiful and particularly outrageous. In May, *Newsweek* carried an article about burgeoning rumors that Xi Jinping's health was in decline (Feng 2022). In late September, shortly after Xi returned from a trip to Central Asia, rumors spread that Xi had been detained in a coup (*Hindustan Times* 2022).

There really was no reason to accept such rumors; after all, Xi had dominated the 19th Party Congress five years earlier and there was little reason to think that those put into office by Xi then would now turn against him. And the History Resolution adopted only a year before had confirmed Xi's dominance of elite politics. Indeed, when the Congress finally met in Beijing on October 16, Xi Jinping read his political report, "Hold High the Great Banner of Socialism with Chinese Characteristics and Strive in Unity to Build a Modern Socialist Country in All Respects," which took some three hours, and it became evident that Xi had succeeded in securing a third term for himself.

As at all party congresses, the report opened by detailing the successes of the CCP over the preceding five years before getting into at least somewhat more substantive issues. The report declared the need to further integrate Marxism with "China's fine traditional culture," further turning its back on the iconoclastic slogan "strike down Confucius' shop" that accompanied the party's founding (so much for the slogan "Never forget the original intention").

No doubt the section that attracted the most attention was that on national security. As pointed out earlier, Xi has focused on the survival of the CCP, so everything from ideology, party discipline, civil society, "peaceful evolution," relations with the outside world, and all areas that would fall under traditional notions of national security, such as military construction, fall under the category of "security." As David M. Lampton has pointed out, China has always seen domestic and external security as closely connected, and Xi did not see China's traditional bureaucracies as meeting China's needs.

Therefore, the Third Plenum of the 18th Central Committee announced in November 2013 that China would establish a National Security Commission (国家安全委员会). Its first meeting was on April 15, 2014. Xi Jinping stated that:

> The aim of the establishment of the Council [sic, Commission] is to better handle new developments and new tasks in the realm of national security, and build a national security system which is centralized, integrated, highly efficient, and authoritative, so as to improve leadership over the work of national security
>
> (Lampton 2015).

Since then, the Security Commission has played an important role in thinking about the relationship between domestic and foreign policy, so the emphasis on security contained in Xi's political report was neither new nor surprising. Xi justifies this emphasis on security by saying that "national security is the bedrock of national rejuvenation" (Xi 2022b).

Xi declares that China will improve the social governance system based on collaboration, participation, and shared benefits noted in the "Fengqiao model (枫桥模式)." The Fengqiao model originated in 1963 as part of the Socialist Education Movement. It was based on the idea of mobilizing the masses to supervise and reform the "enemies of the people" (the four types of people – landlords, rich peasants, counterrevolutionaries, and evil elements). Thus, the Fengqiao model was based on mass mobilization, not government organs (Fengqiao). Although China began turning away from legal institutions some time ago, the Fengqiao model, even if applied more in rhetoric than in practice, seems to be a sharper turn than might have been expected (Fengqiao jingyan).

External security is closely related to domestic security, and Xi's work report accordingly promised to "more quickly elevate our people's armed forces to world-class standards." More specifically, he vowed to establish a strong system of "strategic deterrence," increase the proportion of "new domain" forces – an apparent reference to space weapons – and speed up the development of "unmanned, intelligent combat capabilities." With an eye seemingly on the experience of Xu Caihou and Guo Boxiong, the report promised to "strengthen party building across the board" and to ensure that the armed forces "will always obey the party's command." "We will improve the institutions and mechanisms," it went on, "for implementing the system of ultimate responsibility resting with the chairman of the Central Military Commission" (Xi 2022a).

Given the increase in military activity in the Taiwan Straits area over the previous year, it is not a surprise that Xi made a very strong statement on Taiwan, namely that "resolving the Taiwan issue and realizing China's complete reunification is, for the party, a historic mission and an unshakable commitment." The report continued to call for peaceful reunification but also, as usual, said, "we will never promise to renounce the use of force" (Ibid).

When the congress ended on October 22, the proceedings were overshadowed by the strange scene of seeing former general secretary Hu Jintao being escorted off the stage. What caused this drama has been much debated; PRC media ascribed it to a medical issue. Whether or not that was the case, what will stick in the minds of many viewers was the reaction – or rather the lack of reaction – of the other leaders on the presidium. As Hu was escorted behind the many leaders on the stage, all of them, with the exception of premier Li Keqiang, who Hu patted on the shoulder, stared fixedly ahead. One would think that regardless of whether there was a medical or political issue involved, China's political leadership would express some concern. But nothing. One has to wonder: if China's elite don't show concern for one of their own, how can they empathize with China's people?

Personnel

A new Central Committee of 205 people was named on the last day of the congress, October 22, and the following day the first plenary session of the new Central Committee met to select a new Politburo, Politburo Standing Committee (PBSC), Secretariat, Central Discipline Inspection Commission (CDIC), and Central Military Commission (CMC). The make-up of the PBSC made headlines, as well it should have, because all seven members were political allies of Xi Jinping. It is normal for associates of the General Secretary to make up a majority of the PBSC, but no previous PBSC in the reform era has reflected such a concentration of power (see Table 8.1). When the new lineup was finally unveiled, it was Shanghai Party secretary Li

Table 8.1 Politburo Standing Committee

Name	Age	Position	Relationship with Xi (if any)
Xi Jinping 习近平	69	General Secretary	
Li Qiang 李强	63	Premier	Served as Xi's chief of staff, 2004–2007, when Xi was party secretary (PS) of Zhejiang
Zhao Leji 赵乐际	65	Head, NPC	Headed Organization Dept. in Xi's first term, then CDIC
Wang Huning 王沪宁	67	Head, CPPCC	Holdover on PBSC
Cai Qi 蔡奇	66	Head of Secretariat	Worked as propaganda head in Zhejiang when Xi was party secretary
Ding Xuexiang 丁薛祥	60	Executive Vice Premier	Worked as Xi's personal secretary starting in 2013. Head of General Office since 2017
Li Xi 李希	66	Head, CDIC	Friend since mid-1980s

Source: Assembled by the author using data extracted from *Zhongguo gongchandang diershijie lingdao jigou* (2022)

Table 8.2 The Rest of the Politburo

Name	Age	Position	Relationship with Xi (if any)
Ma Xingrui 马兴瑞	63	Party Secretary, Xinjiang	Technocrat with no known ties to Xi
Wang Yi 王毅	67	Director, CCP Central Committee Foreign Affairs Commission	China's foreign minister under Xi, 2013–2022
Yin Li 尹力	60	Party Secretary, Beijing	Public health official; executive Committee of WTO. Appointed governor of Sichuan in 2016 and PS of Fujian in 2020.
Shi Taifeng 石泰峰	66	Head, United Front Work Department; member, Secretariat	Worked as Xi's subordinate in Central Party School, 2007–2012
Liu Guozhong 刘国中	60	Vice Premier and State Councilor	Shaanxi governor, then party secretary
Li Ganjie 李干杰	58	Secretariat	Technocrat, Minister of Environmental Protection
Li Shulei 李书磊	58	Head, Propaganda Department; Secretariat	Worked under Xi at Central Party School
Li Hongzhong 李鸿忠	66	Vice Chair, NPC Standing Committee	PS, Tianjin, Politburo from 2017
He Weidong 何卫东	66	Vice Chair, CMC	No known relationship
He Lifeng 何立峰	67	Vice Premier	Worked in Fujian with and under Xi
Zhang Youxia 张又侠	72	Vice Chair, CMC	Family friend
Zhang Guoqing 张国庆	58	Vice Premier	No known relationship
Chen Wenqing 陈文清	62	Secretariat, Head, Politics and Law Commission	No known relationship
Chen Jining 陈吉宁	58	Party Secretary, Shanghai	No known relationship
Chen Min'er 陈敏尔	62	Party Secretary, Tianjin	Worked under Xi in Zhejiang
Yuan Jiajun 袁家军	60	Party Secretary, Chongqing	Technocrat; no known relationship
Huang Keming 黄坤明	66	Party Secretary, Guangdong	Worked under Xi in Fujian and Zhejiang

Source: Assembled by the author using data extracted from *Zhongguo gongchandang diershijie lingdao jigou* (2022)

Qiang walking just behind Xi, indicating he would be named premier. Originally people anticipated vice premier Hu Chunhua (胡春华) would be named premier, but Hu, a close associate of former party secretary Hu Jintao, was not even named to the Politburo. All previous premiers in the reform era have served first as vice premier, but Li Qiang has not. Similarly missing from the leadership lineup and from the Central Committee was vice premier Wang Yang. Many expected him to be retained despite his being 68; after all, Xi Jinping is 69. Since the 15th Party Congress in 1997, the party had followed the norm of "seven up, eight down" (七上八下, meaning that someone aged 67 or younger can stay on the Politburo, but those 68 or above should retire). Many observers had taken this as a rule, even though it had been adopted to justify the retirement of Li Ruihuan in 1997. In any case, the dismissal of Hu Chunhua made clear that the CCP was not as institutionalized as many had thought.

The idea of naming a PBSC composed of Xi associates also violated the party tradition of using cadres from the "five lakes and four seas" (五湖四海), i.e., the idea that the party cadres should be chosen without regard to faction. Although regularly violated, party leaders often included leaders from different wings of the party to make a show of their inclusiveness. Such a practice may also have played a role in allowing leaders to think that even if they were passed over at one time, they, or their followers, had a chance of joining the pinnacle of power in the future. For Xi, there was no soothing the egos of losers.

The rest of the Politburo was also top-heavy with Xi associates as well as some technocrats, mostly from the aerospace industry. Technocrats have the advantage (from Xi's point of view) of not being well networked in the party, hence dependent on Xi.

The Secretariat is a body responsible for overseeing the implementation of policies decided upon by the Politburo and/or its Standing Committee. Normally, the

Table 8.3 The Secretariat

Name	Age	Position	Other position?
Cai Qi 蔡奇	66	Head of General Office	Head of Secretariat
Shi Taifeng 石泰峰	66	Head, United Front Work Department	Head of CASS
Li Ganjie 李干杰	58	Politburo	Former PS of Shandong; Minister of Environmental Protection
Li Shulei 李书磊	58	Minister of Propaganda	Head of Central Commission on Building Spiritual Civilization
Chen Wenqing 陈文清	62	Head, Politics and Law Commission	No other position
Liu Jinguo 刘金国	67	Deputy head, CDIC	Head, State Supervision Commission
Wang Xiaohong 王小洪	65	Minister of Public Security	Deputy head of Politics and Law Commission

Source: Assembled by the author using data extracted from *Zhongguo gongchandang diershijie lingdao jigou* (2022)

170 *Joseph Fewsmith*

Table 8.4 Central Military Commission

Name	Position	Age	Previous position or ties with Xi
Xi Jinping 习近平	Chairman	69	
Zhang Youxia 张又侠	Vice chairman	72	His father fought with Xi's father in the revolution
He Weidong 何卫东	Vice chairman	66	Former head, Eastern Theater
Li Shangfu 李尚服 (later removed)	Member	65	In 2017 replaced Zhang Youxia as head of CMC Armaments and Development Division
Liu Zhenli 刘震理	Member	59	Head of Ground Forces, 2021–2022
Miao Hua 苗华	Member	68	Was based in Xiamen when Xi was provincial party secretary
Zhang Shengmin 张升民	Member	65	In 2017 he became head of CMC's discipline inspection commission, replacing Du Jincai, who was closely associated with Xu Caihou and Guo Boxiong

Source: Assembled by the author using data extracted from *Zhongguo gongchandang diershijie lingdao jigou* (2022)

head of the General Office is on the Secretariat, so there may still be some shuffling of posts. Similarly, there is usually only one person with law-and-order responsibilities, but as of now, there are two (Chen Wenqing and Wang Xiaohong). So, again, there may be some reshuffling.

Finally, Xi has reshuffled the CMC, retaining 72-year-old Zhang Youxia.

When looking at the rest of the Central Committee, we can observe some evolution in the Chinese political system. First, the number of women and minorities continued to decline. Of the 205 full members, there are only 10 women and only four minorities. Considering that two of these people were both minorities and female, representation was even less.

Although Hu Chunhua, former head of the Communist Youth League (CYL), was retained on the Central Committee, he was, as mentioned earlier, removed from the Politburo, and then lost his position as vice premier when the NPC met in March 2023. Similarly, although Lu Hao (陆昊), former first secretary of the CYL, was continued on the Central Committee, his responsibilities have now shifted away from the CYL. He served as governor of Heilongjiang, then as Minister of Natural Resources, and, starting in 2022, as head of the Development Research Council. He Junke (贺军科) was appointed head of the CYL in 2018. At only 53 years of age, he is one of the two youngest members of the Central Committee – the other being Yin Yong (殷勇), also born in 1969, who is now mayor of Beijing. Being so young means that they both have a chance to be elevated to a higher position at the next party congress, or even the one after that.

Looking at the composition of the Politburo and Secretariat tells one a great deal about elite politics, but one can dig deeper by looking at the composition of the Central Committee as a whole. It is, however, much more difficult to trace personal relations down to the provincial party secretary or governor level. One way the CCP traditionally tried to balance wings of the party at this level was by appointing a committee to select members of the Central Committee. For instance, prior to the 13th Party Congress in 1987, a seven-person committee was appointed. It was headed by Bo Yibo and included Yang Shangkun (杨尚昆), Wang Zhen (王震), Yao Yilin (姚依林), Song Renqiong (宋任穷), Wu Xiuquan (伍修权), and Gao Yang (高扬). Of course, Deng Xiaoping had the final say.

For the 19th and 20th Party Congresses, a committee was appointed but the membership was not revealed. From the outcome, one can assume that Xi Jinping's views carried considerable weight. There are only three ways for someone to make the Central Committee – be retained from the previous Central Committee, be elevated from the Alternate membership on the Central Committee, or be appointed directly to the Central Committee, usually because of promotion to a position, such as provincial party secretary, that qualifies for Central Committee membership. Because promotions to positions qualifying for membership in the Central Committee require higher-level patronage, they often reflect the political preferences of the party leader. If the number of those appointed directly increases significantly, it is likely because the party leader has greater influence.

If the thesis that the political processes in China were institutionalized were correct, one would expect the number of people to be promoted from the Alternate list to increase over time, but in general, this has not been the case. The one time a substantial number of people were elevated from Alternate status was in 1985, when the party held a rare Party Representative Meeting. The Party Representative Meeting was very similar to a Party Congress except that it did not convene party delegates, which usually number over 2,000, and it did not promote anyone to the Central Committee who was not already an Alternate member of the Central Committee. At that meeting, 55 members who were Alternates were elevated to full membership (26 percent of the 210 members of the Central Committee). This meeting was thus able to drop members of the 11th Central Committee and increase the number of supporters for Deng Xiaoping.

After this meeting, the number of members elevated from Alternate status varied from a low of 10 (6 percent of the new 13th Central Committee) in 1987 to 57 (28 percent of the 18th Central Committee) in 2012. Normally, however, the number elevated from Alternate status to Full membership was about 20 percent. At the 20th Party Congress, 39 people were promoted from Alternate membership to Full membership – 19 percent. Overall, only 58 people were retained from the 19th Central Committee.

If one adds the number retained from the 19th Central Committee and the number promoted from Alternate membership, one sees that 97 members of the new Central Committee were retained or promoted in an "institutionalized" process, meaning that 108 members (53 percent) were selected directly onto the Central Committee. Normally, about a third of each new Central Committee is appointed directly; to jump to 45 percent (19th Central Committee) and 53 percent at this recent Congress means there was a 72 percent turnover. Normally, there is roughly a 50 percent turnover, so the degree of change is unusually large. This is surprising given that Xi had an outsized influence on the makeup of the 19th Central Committee only five years ago. At that congress, 59 percent were new members, already a historic high, but the recent congress was significantly higher.

If we look at one particular group within the Central Committee – the military – we can see the same trends. There are 41 members of the PLA on the new Central Committee, 44 if one counts the three members of the People's Armed Police (PAP), now under direct control of the military. Thirty-four of them are new (83 percent), including six (15 percent) promoted from Alternate membership. So, 68 percent were appointed directly, a very high percentage. Such a high turnover rate in a military leadership that was revamped only five years ago suggests that Xi is still trying to remove the influence of Xu Caihou and Guo Boxiong and build confidence in a new military elite. If one looks at the ages of the military members of the Central Committee, it appears that there will again be sweeping changes at the next party congress.

The State Council

Under China's system of dual governance, China's legislature, the National People's Congress (NPC), and the advisory group, the Chinese People's Political Consultative Conference (CPPCC), meet in the spring to fill out membership in the state system. The most important position, at least symbolically, is the president. Then there is the State Council, headed by the premier and vice premiers. In 2023, the first session of the Fourteenth NPC and Fourteenth CPPCC met in Beijing from March 4 to March 13. Although it was clear from the order in which the leaders emerged at the end of the 20th Party Congress that Li Qiang would be named premier, that and other positions were only revealed officially at the NPC meeting. Other important acts included the reading of the Government Work Report and other reports and speeches by Xi Jinping and other leaders.

On the opening day of the NPC, Xi Jinping was unanimously elected president for his third term. It will be recalled that it was at the NPC meeting in 2018 that the constitution was amended to remove term limits on the presidency, allowing Xi to continue in that position. Politburo Standing Committee member Zhao Leji (赵乐际) was then elected head of the People's Congress, and former vice premier Han Zheng (韩正) was elected vice president, taking over from Wang Qishan (王岐山) (*Renmin ribao*, March 11). The following day, Li Qiang was elected premier (*Renmin ribao*, March 12). Although Li Qiang and Xi Jinping are close allies, the choice of Li to serve as premier was still out of the ordinary. Li's career has been entirely at the local level, although his most recent posting as party secretary of Shanghai certainly gave him a great deal of economic experience. Still, as mentioned earlier, he is the first premier in the reform era not to have served first as a vice premier. Li, raised in Rui'an, next to Wenzhou, and later serving as party secretary of Wenzhou, appears more market-oriented than Xi, which may help him as China needs to revive the economy after three years of Covid shutdowns, but he certainly will not deviate from Xi's instructions.

The following day, March 12, the rest of the State Council was named. Those promoted included four vice premiers – Ding Xuexiang (丁薛祥), who will serve as executive vice premier, and He Lifeng (何立峰), Zhang Guoqing (张国清), and Liu Guozhong (刘国忠). As noted, Ding Xuexiang has long been a close associate of Xi's, and He Lifeng is also a long-time confidant. Zhang spent many years in the armaments business at Norinco, rising to be chief executive. In 2013 he entered politics as deputy party chief of Chongqing. Later he became deputy party secretary of Tianjin and then, in 2020, party secretary of Liaoning (Baidu). Liu Guozhong rose through Heilongjiang provincial party ranks until 2013 when he became deputy head of the All-China Federation of Trade Unions and, in 2020, governor and then party secretary of Shaanxi province (Baidu).

Five people were named as state councilors: Li Shangfu (李尚服), Minister of Defense (later removed); Wang Xiaohong (王小红), Minister of Public Security; Wu Zhenglong (吴政隆), chief secretary of the State Council; Shen Yiqin (谌贻琴), Guizhou party secretary; and Qin Gang (秦刚), Foreign Minister (later removed). This group presents an interesting coming together of trusted associates and aerospace technocrats. Wang Xiaohong has known Xi Jinping since the early 1990s when Xi was party head in Fuzhou and Wang was deputy head, then head, of public security in the city (*Financial Express*).[1] Wang has followed Xi up the chain of command ever since. Particularly strange was the appointment of Chen Yiqin as State Councilor. She is not a member of the Politburo and is only the party secretary of Guizhou, a poor province in the southwest. Her primary qualification appears to be working under Li Zhanshu, one of Xi's close allies, for several years. Similarly, the appointment of Wu Zhenglong appears to be due to the influence of Li Qiang; Wu was governor of Jiangsu when Li was party secretary. Qin Gang, China's newly appointed foreign minister (later removed), is said to be close to Xi Jinping, which this appointment attests to. Perhaps the most interesting appointment as State Councilor is that of Li Shangfu, a member of the CMC and Minister of Defense. Li's father was a long-marcher and high-ranking PLA officer in the railway force. He is an expert in missile technology, serving for many years at the Xichang Satellite Launch Center. In 2014 he served as deputy director of the General Armaments Department and then, three years later, became director of the CMC Equipment Development Department. However, Li was removed in October, apparently for corruption.

In other appointments, China moved to reassure markets, both domestic and foreign. Yi Gang (易纲), the respected head of the People's Bank of China, was reappointed to a second five-year term. Yi Gang is close to former vice premier Liu He (刘鹤), who has been in charge of economic policy for the last decade; however, Yi Gang was later removed. Similarly, Liu Kun (刘琨), who was appointed Minister of Finance in 2018, was retained in his position, and Hou Kai (侯凯) was kept on as auditor-general. So, in the financial arena, China has opted for continuity.

Party Over State

At the 19th Party Congress in 2017, Xi Jinping declared, "the party leads everything – north, south, east, west, middle." Consistent with that approach, the party

174　*Joseph Fewsmith*

issued a decision on March 17 calling for the reorganization of the party and state structures to further centralize control in the party. The most important of these changes is the organization of the Central Financial Commission to take over from the State Council's Financial Stability and Development Commission, and the creation of a Central Science and Technology Commission, which will take control over the development of science and technology. The centralization of science and technology seems particularly problematic, because centralization rarely promotes innovation.

Nationalism

Aside from personnel announcements, the two meetings set a firm, perhaps even aggressive, tone. Xi Jinping, speaking to the CPPCC and the Federation of Labor and Commerce, declared that the previous five years had been "extremely abnormal" (极不寻常) (Renmin ribao, March 8). Western countries, led by the United States, he said, "had carried out comprehensive containment, encirclement, and suppression, giving our development unprecedented difficulties and challenges" (Renmin ribao, March 8).[2] Speaking at a press conference the following day, foreign minister Qin Gang warned, "If the United States does not hit the brake, but continues to speed down the wrong path, no amount of guardrails can prevent derailing and there surely will be conflict and confrontation" (Renmin ribao, March 8). It was highly unusual for Chinese leaders to call out the United States by name.

Given this aggressive tone, the personnel changes that followed only three months later were shocking. The foreign minister, Qin Gang, disappeared in June and was dismissed in July (Johnson). His dismissal was apparently related to an extramarital affair he had had that resulted in a child. But curiously, he has not been removed as State Councilor as of this writing (October 2023). Shortly after Qin's disappearance, the recently appointed head of China's rocket forces, Li Yuchao (李玉超), was removed from office and replaced by Wang Houbin (王侯斌), previously the deputy head of the navy. At the same time, Liu Guangbin (刘广彬), the political commissar of the rocket forces was replaced by Xu Xisheng (徐西盛), political commissar for the air force of the Southern Theater Command (Dan De Luce; Kathrin Hille). These dismissals, with rumors of more to come, are unprecedented and apparently related to corruption. That their replacements came from outside the rocket forces suggests an effort to break up the networks that are often a hotbed for corruption (Wuthnow). What is uncertain as of this moment is whether this shakeup reflects an increasingly autocratic Xi Jinping or whether Xi sees the military as less than loyal.

Implications

Looking at the 20th Party Congress and the first session of the 14th NPC makes it increasingly clear that Xi Jinping intends to rule in a personalistic manner, reversing the norms that Deng Xiaoping set in motion four decades ago. This concentration of power does not mean that all norms have been jettisoned; indeed, most retirements at the party congress were consistent with the age norms we have become accustomed to. But Xi violated norms when it suited him. He violated age norms (Xi, Zhang Youxia), factional balance (Hu Chunhua), precedent (Li Qiang never serving as a vice premier), promotion of personal allies (the PBSC), and institutional norms (the turnover rate). Deng's famous 1980 speech on the reform of party and state structures stressed that Mao's errors were rooted in the over-concentration of power, the failure to separate party and state, the lack of intra-party democracy, and the ignoring of expert opinion. Xi has reversed all of these concerns. In his efforts to concentrate power, Xi has clearly moved China into a post-reform era.

These conclusions raise interesting and important questions. If Xi's power was as consolidated as it appeared to be after the 19th Party Congress, why did he feel the need to make such sweeping changes in the composition of the 20th Central Committee? More particularly, why did he feel a need to fill out the PBSC with his close associates? This seems to say something about Xi's own characteristics as a leader, namely that he is only comfortable with those that he knows well. If that is the case, it certainly says something about the range of views that will be heard at the highest level and hence the direction of policy making. China has a Leninist party, but even within that framework power can be concentrated in the leader or dispersed at least somewhat throughout the party. In trying to reverse what Xi perceived as the "weakening" and "hollowing out" of the party, Xi has concentrated power in his own hands, thus weakening the party as an organization. As a result, the CCP has veered toward personalism in a way not seen since Mao. But there is an important difference between Mao and Xi. Mao, for better or worse, was a charismatic leader who could lead China to disaster without destroying the party; should Xi make similar policy errors (though hopefully not as enormous as the Great Leap Forward and the Cultural Revolution), the consequences for China and the party, and perhaps the outside world, are likely to be regime-shattering.

As noted here, part of Xi's personalistic rule was his decision to pack the Standing Committee with his political allies. Although the PBSC has traditionally included a majority of the leaders' allies, Xi's decision to pack the body with all allies suggests that there will be less discussion of policy options. One hopes that the decision to reverse course on Covid policy is not a harbinger of the policy-making process of the future. It seems that the leadership was developing a plan to open the country step-by-step when protests broke out. Confronted by such protests, Xi and the leadership suddenly reversed policy, telling people that they should take care of their own health. Certainly, the government demonstrated that it was capable of making rapid decisions (because they were all like-minded?), but it also demonstrated that it could be careless – ignoring the plans that were underway and that they could disregard the lessons learned in other countries. To reopen the country quickly in mid-winter, before the approaching Lunar New Year and without an extensive vaccination program in place, seemed to exemplify bad planning and disregard for the health of the citizens. Why did the new decision-making structure perform so poorly? And will that become a characteristic of the new leadership?

The rapid reversal of policy certainly allowed Covid to spread throughout the country, bringing about a large if uncertain amount of illness and death. It also brought about widespread cynicism. Even citizens who had been willing to trust the government through three years of zero-Covid lockdowns had to wonder what the sacrifice was all about if the policy could be tossed out so rapidly.

The 20th Party Congress, however unintentionally, also created greater uncertainty about military policy. Xi remade the military elite at the 19th Party Congress and did it again only five years later at the 20th Party Congress. This degree of change is likely to make the military highly responsive to the party leadership, specifically to Xi's decision-making. This does not necessarily mean that Xi will be careless in his policy choices, but the examples of other personalistic regimes offer good reason to be cautious. As Jessica Weeks put it, "in personalistic regimes in which leaders have eliminated rivals and consolidated power into their own hands, conflict initiation depends on the whims of those paramount leaders" (Weeks 2012). Tai Ming Cheung is equally cautious, seeing in Xi's personalization of power a serious difficulty in passing on power and institutionalization (Cheung 2022). Of course, the Chinese political system has long resisted institutionalization, and Xi's rule seems likely to reinforce that trend (Fewsmith 2022).

Notes

1 Financial Express, "Wang Xiaohong: Meet China's and Xi Jinping's New Spy Master," *Financial Express*, February 28, 2018.
2 *Renmin ribao*, March 8, 2022.

References

Bandurski, David. 2013. "Inside the Southern Weekend Incident." *China Media Project*. January 7. http://chinamediaproject.org/2013/01/07/insidethesouthern-weekly-incident.

Buckley, Chris. 2013. "Vows of Change Belie Private Warning." *New York Times*. February 15.

Cheung, Tai Ming. 2022. *Innovate to Dominate: The Rise of the Chinese Techno-Security State*. Ithaca, NY: Cornell University Press.

Feng, John. 2022. "Xi Jinping Health Rumors Swirl as China's Covid Battle Continues." *Newsweek*. May 17. www.newsweek.com/china-xi-jinping-health-aneurysm-rumors-zero-covid-1707184.

Fengqiao Jingyan. "The Fengqiao Experience." https://zh.m.wikipedia.org/zh-hans/%E6%9E%AB%E6%A1%A5%E7%BB%8F%E9%AA%8C#:~:text=%E2%80%9C%E6%9E%AB%E6%A1%A5%E7%BB%8F%E9%AA%8C%E2%80%9D%E4%BE%BF%E6%98%AF,%E6%9D%80%E4%B8%80%E6%89%B9%E2%80%9D%E7%9A%84%E5%81%9A%E6%B3%95%E3%80%82.

Fewsmith, Joseph. 2022. *Rethinking Chinese Politics*. Cambridge: Cambridge University Press.

Financial Express. 2018. "Wang Xiaohong: Meet China's and Xi Jinping's New Spy Master." February 28. www.financialexpress.com/world-news/wang-xiaohong-meet-chinas-and-xi-jinpings-new-spy-master/1083301/.

Hindustan Times. 2022. "Is Xi Missing? Rumours of Military Coup in China Explained." September 26. www.hindustantimes.com/world-news/china-coup-xi-jinping-missing-xi-jinping-news-china-coup-news-xi-jinping-house-arrest-xi-jinping-house-arrest-news-is-xi-jinping-missing-rumours-of-military-coup-in-china-explained-101664123317118.html.

Lampton, David M. 2015. "Xi Jinping and the National Security Commission: Policy Coordination and Political Power." *Journal of Contemporary China* 24(95): 759–777.

Mulvenon, James. 2015. "Hotel Gutian: We Haven't Had That Spirit Here Since 1929." *China Leadership Monitor* 46(Winter). www.hoover.org/sites/default/files/research/docs/clm46jm.pdf.

"Resolution of the CPC Central Committee on the Major Achievements and Historical Experience of the Party over the Past Century." 2021. *Xinhua*. November 16.

Wang, Yue. 2022. "China's Second Quarter GDP Plunges to Less Than 1% on Covid Hit." *Forbes* July 15. www.forbes.com/sites/ywang/2022/07/15/chinas-second-quarter-gdp-growth-plunges-to-less-than-1-on-covid-hit/?sh=4534cacc1a0c.

Weeks, Jessica. 2012. "Strongmen and Straw Men: Authoritarian Regimes and the Initiation of International Conflict." *American Political Science Review* 106(2). May: 326–347.

Xi, Jinping. 2022a. "Hold High the Great Banner of Socialism with Chinese Characteristics and Strive in Unity to Build a Modern Socialist Country in All Respects." www.fmprc.gov.cn/eng/zxxx_662805/202210/t20221025_10791908.html.

Xi, Jinping. 2022b. "Jianchi zongti guojia anquan quanguan" [Overall View of Upholding Comprehensive National Security]. In *Xi Jinping guanyu zongti guojia anquan quanguan lunshu tibian* [Selections from Xi Jinping on an Overall View of Upholding Comprehensive National Security], ed. Zhonggong Zhongyang dangshi he wenxian yanjiuyuan. Zhongyang wenxian chubanshe: Beijing.

Zhongguo gongchandang diershijie lingdao jigou. 2022. "The 20th Central Leadership Organization of the Communist Party of China." www.gov.cn/guoqing/2022-10/23/content_5720988.htm.

9 The Evolving Leadership in Xi's PLA

Factionalism, Weak Coalition, or Military Preparedness?

Victor C. Shih

Strengthening military preparedness has been the hallmark of Xi Jinping's defense policy. Even early in his administration, he called on the PLA to "strengthen comprehensive construction of forces and strengthen preparation for military struggle." (People's Daily 2013). At the 3rd plenum of the 18th Central Committee in the fall of 2013, he further ordained a wide-ranging reform of the PLA. After over two years of negotiations with senior officers of the PLA, deep reform measures were announced in 2016 which saw the abolition of two military regions, as well as the subsuming of traditionally powerful PLA departments under the Central Military Commission in the name of increasing command effectiveness (Wuthnow and Saunders 2016). Yet, the literature on authoritarian politics suggests that reshuffling the military may not serve the goal of military preparedness alone, since a part of or the entire military typically make up an important member of the support coalition for the dictator (Acemoglu et al. 2010; Wintrobe 1998). Thus, for the dictator, the reshuffling of leaders in the military may instead aim at firming up support within the regime, or at least reducing threats to himself from the military. Military preparedness may become a secondary concern.

In this chapter, I examine the change in the composition of the top leadership in the PLA from 2016 to 2022 to assess whether reshuffling at the top level was geared more toward improving military preparedness or toward reducing threats to the dictator from within the military. By and large, changes in the top PLA leadership since 2016, defined as officers who served at the full military region (*dajunquji* 大军区级) commanding CMC departments, branches, or theater commands, do not suggest that coup-proofing has been the main concern of the party leadership. Instead, there is some evidence that improving military preparedness has been a major objective of the leadership turnovers in the PLA, as suggested by the extant literature (Wuthnow and Saunders 2019).

Military Preparedness and the Guardianship Dilemma

For theorists of realism in international relations, power projected by a country's military is a key, perhaps the key, to determining winners and losers in global politics. As Mearsheimer points out, "The balance of power is mainly a function of the tangible military assets that states possess"(Mearsheimer 2007). For global leaders

DOI: 10.4324/9781003257943-10

with foreign policy ambitions or ingrained distrust of international rivals, they likely would want to appoint senior officers who have the most experience and/or skill in military affairs, since they are, as Huntington puts it, "the active directing element of the military structure"(Huntington 1981, 3). For Huntington, professional officers incorporate a combination of military expertise, responsibility to the organization they serve, and "corporateness," which is "a shared sense of unity" with fellow officers (Huntington 1981, 7). For a rapidly modernizing military such as the PLA, both actual combat experience and command experience in "tip of the spear" frontline units would contribute to these characteristics.

For the PLA specifically, it has placed modernization as its primary objective since the founding of the People's Republic. At the 2022 20th Party Congress, for example, Xi Jinping echoed his earlier speeches and called on the military to "realize the 100-year objective of building up the military in a timely manner; accelerate the building up of the people's army into a first rate one in the world" (Xi 2022). Political disunity within the party has delayed modernization efforts through long periods of the party's history (Fravel 2019). However, after a wide-ranging purge in the military and the eradication of rival factions both in the military and in the party, Xi had consolidated power more than any Chinese leader since Mao by 2016 (V. Shih 2022). Thus, according to the framework set forth by Fravel (2019), Xi was poised to restructure the military and its officer corps to realize the defense modernization objectives starting around 2015.

At the same time, for both democracies and authoritarian regimes, a key challenge is a potential coup launched by the most organized armed forces in those countries, the military (Acemoglu and Robinson 2006). Thus, preventing a coup while maintaining military effectiveness has been a subject of much research over the years (Acemoglu and Robinson 2006; Acemoglu et al. 2010; McMahon and Slantchev 2015). For authoritarian regimes without a strong sense of constitutional rule, the leadership must rely on means beyond legal constraints on the military. Several perspectives have gained prominence in recent years.

First, the dictator can reduce overall resources available to the military so as to weaken it (McMahon and Slantchev 2015). This of course has the drawback of reducing the military's capacity to deal with external threats. This is especially not very feasible if the leadership also would like to expand a country's foreign policy influence, which may require the credible threats provided by an effective military. In terms of personnel arrangements in the military, the dictator can pursue factionalism whereby officers who historically demonstrated loyalty to the dictator are selectively rewarded with appointments to powerful positions (Walder and Dong 2011; Whitson and Huang 1973). This disincentivizes officers in the dictator's faction from joining potential coup plots. The dictator also can reduce threats to himself by placing ostracized, inexperienced, or even ignorant officers in charge of senior positions in the armed forces (Egorov and Sonin 2011; Gregory 2009; Shih 2022). The sheer incompetence and small networks of these individuals reduce the chance of coups and help prolong the rule of the dictator. Again, placing such individuals in positions of responsibility in the military likely will undermine its effectiveness.

Fortunately, for dictators in institutionalized regimes, such as Leninist regimes, the formal institutions invest a great deal of appointment power in the hands of the dictator (Svolik 2012). Dictators can reshuffle the top officers of the military in order to maximize their objective at the moment. Thus, one can get a sense of the dictator's main objective by examining the characteristics of the officers holding senior positions at the moment. Although this falls short of strict hypothesis testing, clear changes in key characteristics of top officers in the military are indicative of shifting priorities on the part of the dictator. For one, unlike changing the content of speeches or writing, personnel reshuffling for those in key positions can affect the quality of policy outcomes and thus is a credible signal.

In the following analysis, I will assess whether Xi is pursuing one of the three strategies outlined here by changing the key characteristics of the PLA's top officers. Based on the literature, Xi may be pursuing a *factional* strategy in the military in order to ensure that the top echelon of the military is controlled by officers who had more to gain with him in power than without him in power (Nathan 1973; Pye 1995). If that were the case, one would expect a higher share of top-level officers who had shared work history with Xi over time. Second, Xi could be pursuing a *coalition of the weak* strategy in the military in order to minimize potential challenges to his power (Shih 2022). According to Shih (2022), Mao reduced threats to his power by appointing either highly compromised or weakly networked officers to the most senior positions in the PLA in the twilight of his life. Xi also could be doing this by placing officers with exceptionally small networks in senior positions over time. Finally, Xi perhaps is focused on military modernization in order to achieve major foreign policy objectives and thus seeks to maximize *military professional expertise* in the PLA officer corp. If that were the case, one would see richer combat or command experience among those holding the most senior positions in the PLA (Wuthnow and Saunders 2016). The following analysis provides some indications for the empirical implications set forth here, although this analysis does a better job at eliminating possibilities instead of pinpointing the exact motivation for Xi's military appointments.

The Military Leadership and Elite Data

The People's Liberation Army (PLA), formerly the Red Army of the Proletariat and Peasants, has been an important organ of the Chinese Communist Party (CCP) since the birth of the Red Army in 1927. Since the earliest days of the Red Army, it has been placed under the control of one or a committee of civilian officials, while the rest of the military is placed under the command of a pyramidal, Leninist structure. Prominent civilian officials like Mao, Zhou Enlai, Zhang Guotao, and Deng Xiaoping rotated through key military positions prior to 1949 as the CCP military underwent multiple rounds of reorganization to adapt to the latest challenges posed by the party's military struggle against the KMT and Japanese forces. After the formation of the People's Republic, the PLA settled into a command structure modeled after the Soviet military. At the top of this pyramidal command structure sat the major departments, branches, and military regions of the PLA, and the analysis in the rest of this chapter focuses on the heads of these major parts of the PLA.

In this structure, the highest authority of the PLA is the Central Military Commission (CMC), chaired by a senior party figure and is responsible for formulating military policies, determining military strategies and objectives, and commanding the armed forces (Cheung 2001). CMC members include heads of PLA departments and branches, as well as other civilian leaders at times. Prior to 2016, several sprawling and relatively autonomous departments of the PLA ran different aspects of the military. Most important, the General Staff Department (GSD) conducted military operations, developed military strategies, and formulated military plans, which also includes military intelligence. These core functions made GSD extremely powerful. The General Political Department (GPD) maintained the ideological and political purity of the PLA and ensured the loyalty and discipline of the troops and officers. These functions also allowed the GPD authorities to dispense justice in the military, which made it powerful. Meanwhile, the General Logistics Department (GLD) provided logistical support to the PLA, including equipment procurement, transportation, supply, medical care, and engineering. Importantly, the GLD could audit itself for procured military equipment and supplies, which provided ample opportunities for corruption (Wuthnow and Saunders 2019).

Beyond these core departments, other departments, such as the General Armament Department and the General Training Department, were constituted and disbanded throughout the history of the PLA. In addition to the army, other branches of the military, the navy and the air force, were formed soon after the formation of the People's Republic in 1949. The Second Artillery Force of the PLA, China's missile force, was formed officially in 1966, which was followed in 2016 by the formation of another new branch, the PLA Strategic Support Force (Xiang 2006).

Finally, the PLA is also divided into geographical military regions (MRs). After spending a few years subduing major resistance to CCP rule, the military in 1955 divided mainland China into 13 major military regions: Beijing, Shenyang, Jinan, Lanzhou, Nanjing, Wuhan, Fuzhou, Guangzhou, Kunming, Chengdu, Neimenggu, Tibet, and Xinjiang (Whitson and Huang 1973). Over the next three decades of restructuring, the number of MRs were reduced to seven in the 1980s: Beijing, Shenyang, Jinan, Lanzhou, Nanjing, Guangzhou, and Chengdu. Most of the senior officers in the PLA today "grew up" under the 7-MR system and have networks that are tied to these military regions. In 2016, the military reform inaugurated by Xi further shrank the seven MRs into five theater commands, Central, Northern, Eastern, Southern, and Western Theater Commands (Wuthnow and Saunders 2019). The formation of the theater commands aimed at integrating the command of land, sea, and air forces within their jurisdictions to a much greater extent than had been the case under the MR system (Wuthnow and Saunders 2019). This approach to military reorganization follows the model of the US military, presumably because China sees the US as its biggest potential rival (Wuthnow and Saunders 2016).

This analysis focuses on the commanders and, in the case of the theater commands, the political commissars, of the major departments, branches, and theater commands of the PLA. These officers are all at the full military region-level and constitute the most powerful officers in the PLA. The vast majority of them are in the Central Committee as full or alternate members. In the case of the CMC vice

182 *Victor C. Shih*

chairmen, they also are in the Politburo, among the three dozen or so most powerful politicians in China. Major shifts in the characteristics of officers at this level would be suggestive of Xi Jinping's policy or political objectives since appointment of officers at this level would require his consent, if not active appointment.

The biographical and factional data for these officers come from CCP Elite Biographical Data compiled by Shih et al. (2020), augmented by PLA officers compiled by Mattingly (2022) and newly coded officers. The data contain basic demographic information on some 600 officers at the army (*jun* 军) level or above, as well as their work history, to the extent that this information is available. As detailed here, factional and network information is derived on the basis of overlaps in these officers' work history.

Factionalism and Weak Coalitions

In this section, I assess whether military region-level officers were appointed in the post-2016 period according to a factional logic or a coalition of the weak logic. Although Xi is not a career military officer, his career as a local leader, especially as party secretary of cities and provinces, has afforded him many opportunities to work with the military. In the 1980s and the 1990s, because Xi was the party secretary of Ningde and Fuzhou respectively, he also automatically served as the first secretary of the party committees of the Ningde Military Sub-District and the Fuzhou Military Sub-District ("Xi Jinping zai Fujian gongzuo qijian ceng tiyan dang paoshou" 2014). In both Fujian and in Zhejiang, he served on the Nanjing Military Region Mobilization Committee, where he broke bread with senior officers of the Nanjing Military Region (MR). Of course, as party secretary of Zhejiang and later Shanghai, he served as the first secretary of the Zhejiang Provincial MR and of the Shanghai Garrison, respectively ("Xi Jinping zai Fujian gongzuo qijian ceng tiyan dang paoshou" 2014). In other words, since the 1980s, when Xi began his work in Fujian, he has had consistent and frequent interaction with officers in the Nanjing Military Region, which encompassed Fujian, Zhejiang, Jiangsu, and Shanghai. Officers who served in the Nanjing Military Region in the 1988 to 2007 period are therefore classified as members of his faction. To be sure, he likely made enemies in the Nanjing MR in this period as well, but by 2016, three years into the anti-corruption campaign, his enemies in the Nanjing MR would have been purged already.

As one can see in Table 9.1, among top officers at the military region-level commanding the major CMC departments, branches, and theaters, Xi followers made up 40% of the officers (11 out of 27) in 2016 and 30% in 2022 (8 out of 27). This is a significant drop and suggests that the appointment of top-level officers had become slightly less factional in the post-2016 period. To be sure, slightly less factionalized does not mean that the military is no longer factionalized. Both vice-chairmen of the CMC remained members of his faction. Zhang Youxia, Xi's childhood friend, was reappointed CMC Vice Chairman in 2022 despite being well above the formal retirement age of 65. The new CMC Vice Chairman, He Weidong, served in the 31st Group Army based in Xiamen while Xi had been a local leader

The Evolving Leadership in Xi's PLA 183

Table 9.1 Key Military Region-Level Officers and Their Factional Ties with Xi, 2016 Versus 2022

Key Positions	Name 2022	Ties with Xi in 2022	Name 2016	Ties with Xi in 2016
CMC Chair	Xi Jinping (习近平)		Xi Jinping (习近平)	
CMC Vice Chair	Zhang Youxia (张又侠)	Yes	Xu Qiliang (许其亮)	Yes
CMC Vice Chair	He Weidong (何卫东)	Yes	Fan Changlong (范长龙)	
CMC Staff	Liu Zhenli (刘振立)		Fang Fenghui (房峰辉)	
CMC Political	Miao Hua (苗华)	Yes	Zhang Yang (张阳)	
CMC Logistics	Zhang Lin (张林)		Zhao Keshi (赵克石)	
CMC Armament	Xu Xueqiang (许学强)	Yes	Zhang Youxia (张又侠)	Yes
CMC Training	Wang Peng (王鹏)	Yes	Zheng He (郑和)	Yes
Navy Commander	Dong Jun (董军)		Wu Shengli (吴胜利)	Yes
Navy PC	Yuan Huazhi (袁华智)		Miao Hua (苗华)	Yes
Airforce Commander	Chang Dingqiu (常丁求)		Ma Xiaotian (马晓天)	Yes
Airforce PC	Guo Puxiao (郭普校)		Yu Zhongfu (于忠福)	Yes
Missile Commander	Li Yuchao (李玉超)		Wei Fenghe (魏凤和)	
Missile PC	Xu Zhongbo (徐忠波)		Wang Jiasheng (王家胜)	
Army Commander	Li Qiaoming (李桥铭)		Li Zuocheng (李作成)	
Army PC	Qin Shutong (秦树桐)	Yes	Liu Lei (刘雷)	
Strategic Support Commander	Ju Qiansheng (巨乾生)		Gao Jin (高津)	
Strategic Support PC	Li Wei (李伟)		Liu Fulian (刘福连)	
Central Theater Commander	Wu Ya'nan (吴亚男)		Han Weiguo (韩卫国)	
Central Theater PC	Xu Deqing (徐德清)		Yin Fanglong (殷方龙)	Yes
Northern Theater Commander	Wang Qiang (王强)		Song Puxuan (宋普选)	
Northern Theater PC	Liu Qingsong (刘青松)		Chu Yimin (褚益民)	

(*Continued*)

Table 9.1 (Continued)

Key Positions	Name 2022	Ties with Xi in 2022	Name 2016	Ties with Xi in 2016
Western Theater Commander	Wang Haijiang (汪海江)		Zhao Zongqi (赵宗岐)	Yes
Western Theater PC	Li Fengbiao (李凤彪)		Zhu Fuxi (朱福熙)	
Eastern Theater Commander	Lin Xiangyang (林向阳)	Yes	Liu Yuejun (刘粤军)	Yes
Eastern Theater PC	He Ping (何平)		Zheng Weiping (郑卫平)	
Southern Theater Commander	Wang Xiubin (王秀斌)	Yes	Wang Jiaocheng (王教成)	
Southern Theater PC	Wang Jianwu (王建武)		Wei Liang (魏亮)	Yes

Source: Author

there. Meanwhile, Miao Hua, another long-time stalwart of the 31st Group Army, was rotated from the navy political commissar position to the traditionally powerful position as the head of the CMC Political Department. Others with Nanjing MR experience, like Lin Xiangyang and Wang Xiubin, also achieved full MR-level positions. Clearly, after the first five years of his rule, Xi had left a deep imprint on the senior ranks of the PLA, much more so than the consolidation that Jiang Zemin or Hu Jintao had been able to achieve (Ji 2001).

However, more than in 2016, the top officers in 2022 were drawn from the "5 lakes and the 4 seas" of the other military regions and branches. The new head of the CMC staff department, Liu Zhenli, spent the bulk of his career in the 38th Army in the Beijing Military Region and had no history with Xi until both took up senior positions in Beijing after 2010. Meanwhile, the heads of strategic forces, including the Missile Force and the newly created Strategic Support Force, are career specialists in their branches with no apparent link to Xi Jinping. This decline in Xi followers in the top echelon of the PLA is striking when compared with the complete domination by Xi followers in the civilian branches of the government. At the 2022 20th Party Congress, nearly all of the Politburo Standing Committee members had a shared history with Xi. This was far from the case in the PLA.

Beyond factionalism, Xi also might be pursuing a "coalition of the weak" strategy in the military in which the highly compromised or thinly networked take up senior positions. On both counts, it does not seem like Xi has engaged in this strategy in the first place, nor has he moved in that direction between 2016 and 2022. We examine two simple metrics. First, given that former CMC vice-chair Xu Caihou was the highest-level PLA officer arrested during the anti-corruption campaign, Xi might cultivate a weak coalition in the PLA by systematically promoting former faction members of Xu Caihou's faction into senior positions in the military. According to the logic I have laid out elsewhere (Shih 2022), placing such compromised figures in senior military positions would reduce the chance of a coup. Second, Xi can place thinly networked officers into senior level positions, which would make it difficult for any particular officer in the military to mobilize a potential coup (Shih 2022).

By 2016, Xu had been arrested and had died of cancer, while scores of his followers had been arrested. Still, there were three officers at the full MR-level with work ties to Xu Caihou in 2016. Of the three, Zhu Fuxi, who overlapped with Xi for over a decade in the Nanjing MR, likely was an informant that Xi had sent into the General Political Department to obtain information on Xu's corrupt dealings. Meanwhile, Song Puxuan had the misfortune of overlapping with Xu at the Jinan MR while Xu served a short stint there to bolster his credentials before further promotions. He likely was not a real member of Xu's faction. The only plausible member of Xu's faction in 2016 was Zheng Weiping, who overlapped with Xu at the General Political Department. However, Zheng had rotated out of the GPD to the National Defense University by the time Xu had obtained real power in the GPD in the early 2000s.

In 2022, three MR-level officers had past ties with Xu: Xu Zhongbo, Wu Ya'nan, and Wang Jianwu. Two of them overlapped with Xu during his brief stint at the Jinan MR. Wu Ya'nan overlapped with Xu earlier on in their careers in the Shenyang MR, which might leave him vulnerable to charges of being a Xu crony. Still, given that only one officer in each period had had a credible tie with Xu, it seems unlikely that Xi is systematically placing compromised officers into senior positions in order to reduce potential challenges from within the military.

Beyond compromised officers, Xi also could have appointed thinly networked officers to minimize the threat of challenges, as Mao did by appointing Zhang Chunqiao to head the General Political Department after the 10th Party Congress (Shih 2022). As Table 9.2 shows, however, this does not seem to be the case across most of the key MR-level positions. In 2016, MR-level officers on average had 128 total ties with the 500 army- or above level officers in the database, which include currently active officers (post-2018) and officers active in the post-17th Party Congress period (2008–2018). MR-level officers in 2016 still had an average network size of 80 active officers in the post-2018 period, signifying considerable staying power of their networks. Among full MR-level officers in 2022, they on average had a total network size of close to 118 officers with 82 officers still in active service after 2018.

Table 9.2 Mean and Standard Deviation of the Number of Current and Total Ties MR-Level Officers Had with Army-Level or Above Officers, 2016 Versus 2022

	2022		2016	
	Current Ties	Total Ties	Current Ties	Total Ties
Mean	82.11	117.74	80.07	128
Standard Deviation	35.61	48.41	28.81	48.42

Source: Author

186 *Victor C. Shih*

This simple exercise shows that the MR-level officers in both 2016 and in 2022 had dense networks with other senior officers. The high density of their networks is partly due to the construction of the data, which assumes that officers who served in the same MR, PLA department, or non-army branch in the past were in the same network. Given the limited number of MRs and branches, officers, especially those with service in multiple MRs, were bound to have large networks. The much larger number of provinces and ministries among civilian officials reduces the expected size of their networks to some extent.

One can see the dynamics of how career paths could affect the network size of senior officers. For example, Liu Qingsong, the political commissar of the Northern Theater, has a total network of 221 officers, of whom 167 were still in active service after 2018. The enormous size of his network stemmed from his multifaceted career, which saw him serve in three different MRs across both the navy and the air force. Likewise, Xu Xueqiang has a sizable network due to his long service in the air force, the Nanjing MR, and the National Defense University. Among the least-networked officers, Li Yuchao and Ju Qiansheng are both officers who have served only in one narrow and technical branch of the military through most of their careers, the Second Artillery (Missile) Force and the Electronic Warfare Department of the General Staff Department, respectively. Of course, the limited number of missile and strategic support officers in the data set also constrains the network size of senior officers in these branches.

Taking all of these factors together, it does not seem like Xi is cultivating a weak coalition in the PLA, neither in 2016 nor today. Among senior MR-level officers,

Table 9.3 The Most and Least Networked MR-Level Officers Active in 2022

Position	Name 2022	Current Network	Total Network
	Most Networked		
Northern Theater PC	Liu Qingsong (刘青松)	167	196
CMC Armament	Xu Xueqiang (许学强)	137	
Eastern Theater Commander	Lin Xiangyang (林向阳)	128	178
Southern Theater Commander	Wang Xiubin (王秀斌)	116	164
Central Theater PC	Xu Deqing (徐德清)	111	144
	Least Networked		
CMC General Staff	Liu Zhenli (刘振立)	38	65
Navy PC	Yuan Huazhi (袁华智)	36	54
CMC Logistics	Zhang Lin (张林)	32	50
Strategic Support Commander	Ju Qiansheng (巨乾生)	32	55
Missile Commander	Li Yuchao (李玉超)	16	22

Source: Author

only Liu Zhenli seems to have an unusually small network for an army officer. This likely is due to the relative under-representation of officers from the Beijing MR in today's PLA. Despite having a relatively small network, Liu was nonetheless put in charge of the traditionally powerful General Staff Department of the CMC. This specific appointment may have been motivated by a coalition of the weak logic. Otherwise, senior PLA officers either had dense networks or had small networks due to their specialization in areas which benefited from the command of specialists.

Improving Military Preparedness

The preceding discussion shows that Xi has appointed senior officers according to the factional logic to some extent, although there is little evidence of him putting in place a coalition of the weak in the senior ranks of the PLA. Is there any evidence that Xi has favored officers with command experience which strengthens the military preparedness of the PLA? The emerging literature on promotion of PLA officers has addressed this question by examining whether officers with real battle experience in Korea or Vietnam enjoyed faster promotions (Mattingly 2022; Mulvenon 1997). Indeed, among full MR-level officers, the number of them with combat experience during the Sino-Vietnam conflict has increased from two in 2016 to five in 2022. This may reflect Xi's preference for officers with real frontline experience, but ultimately, as the officer corps rejuvenated and as officers from other branches obtained senior positions, there is a limit to the dominance by veterans of the Vietnam conflict in the upper echelons.

For younger generations of officers, they either served on the front in the last year of static warfare with Vietnam or had no real battle experience. For them, the more relevant experience may be command of units which increasingly undergo extensive training for future conflicts. In recent years, the PLA has embarked on an intensive military equipment modernization, as well as operational modernization that seeks to increase the types and geographical range of PLA operations (Chase et al. 2015). As an important part of this effort, the PLA has engaged in a rising number of military exercises involving a larger number of units across branches, sometimes even involving foreign military units (Chase et al. 2015).

In the army, units that participate in these training exercises tend to be units in the group armies (*jituanjun* 集团军) (Chase et al. 2015). Indeed, even in the 1980s and the 1990s, the bulk of senior PLA officers in the army had extensive enlisted or command experience in the group armies because these units were expected to bear the brunt of the fighting should conflicts arise (Mulvenon 1997). In the navy, units attached to the major fleets, including the Northern Fleet, Eastern Fleet, or Southern Fleet, took part in all of the naval exercises and protection missions (Saunders 2020). Meanwhile, air force units attached to the military regions, now theaters, undertake training exercises and patrol missions (Wuthnow and Saunders 2016). Thus, for the future battle effectiveness of the PLA, command experience in the frontline units of group armies, navy fleets, and MR air force may have more relevance than experience sitting in trenches in Yunnan some four decades ago. Increasing the share of

188 *Victor C. Shih*

officers with command experience over frontline units also would be consistent with Fravel's prediction that military modernization takes place in the PLA when the party leadership is unified, which certainly is the case after 2016 (Fravel 2019).

As such, I also count the number of those with frontline command experience in group armies, naval fleet, or MR air force units among full MR-level officers in 2016 and in 2022. There are two major limitations to this approach. First, data about the careers of different officers remain uneven, with granular data for some officers available and not for others. This introduces some variation to the data which does not reflect the actual experience of officers. Looking at the data in Table 9.4, however, there do not seem to be too many outliers on the high side, and taking them out does not change the conclusion much. Second, even when some officers served in a frontline unit, their role may have had little to do with military command and instead focused on propaganda or logistics. Still, when these units were mobilized for major exercises, non-combatant officers presumably still must learn to play their parts during war preparation.

Table 9.4 Full MR Commanders, Their Branch, and the Number of Fighting Unit Commands, 2016 Versus 2022

2016	Branch	Number of Frontline Unit Commands	2022	Branch	Number of Frontline Unit Commands
Fan Changlong (范长龙)	Army	2	**Liu Qingsong** (刘青松)	Air Force	7
Chu Yimin (褚益民)	Army	2	**Yuan Huazhi** (袁华智)	Navy	6
Zhao Keshi (赵克石)	Army	2	**Wang Xiubin** (王秀斌)	Army	5
Zhang Yang (张阳)	Army	4	**He Weidong** (何卫东)	Army	4
Zhu Fuxi (朱福熙)	Army	2	**He Ping** (何平)	Army	4
Wu Shengli (吴胜利)	Navy	4	**Lin Xiangyang** (林向阳)	Army	6
Liu Fulian (刘福连)	Army	3	**Zhang Youxia** (张又侠)	Army	4
Zheng Weiping (郑卫平)	Army	2	**Chang Dingqiu** (常丁求)	Air Force	4
Liu Yuejun (刘粤军)	Army	3	**Li Fengbiao** (李凤彪)	Air Force	4
Song Puxuan (宋普选)	Army	3	**Dong Jun** (董军)	Navy	4
Liu Lei (刘雷)	Army	2	**Wu Ya'nan** (吴亚男)	Army	4
Zheng He (郑和)	Army	3	**Liu Zhenli** (刘振立)	Army	4
Xu Qiliang (许其亮)	Air Force	8	**Wang Qiang** (王强)	Air Force	2

2016	Branch	Number of Frontline Unit Commands	2022	Branch	Number of Frontline Unit Commands
Han Weiguo (韩卫国)	Army	5	**Li Yuchao** (李玉超)	Missile	0
Gao Jin (高津)	Missile	0	**Li Qiaoming** (李桥铭)	Army	5
Zhao Zongqi (赵宗岐)	Army	3	**Miao Hua** (苗华)	Army	9
Wang Jiasheng (王家胜)	Armament	0	**Wang Jianwu** (王建武)	Army	3
Yin Fanglong (殷方龙)	Army	1	**Zhang Lin** (张林)	Logistics	0
Wei Liang (魏亮)	Army	4	**Qin Shutong** (秦树桐)	Army	7
Wang Jiaocheng (王教成)	Army	3	**Xu Zhongbo** (徐忠波)	Army	6
Yu Zhongfu (于忠福)	Air Force	14	**Xu Deqing** (徐德清)	Army	5
Li Zuocheng (李作成)	Army	4	**Wang Peng** (王鹏)	Army	3
Fang Fenghui (房峰辉)	Army	1	**Ju Qiansheng** (巨乾生)	Strategic Support	0
Ma Xiaotian (马晓天)	Air Force	4	**Wang Haijiang** (汪海江)	Army	1
Wei Fenghe (魏凤和)	Missile	1	**Li Wei** (李伟)	Army	3
Zhang Youxia (张又侠)	Army	4	**Xu Xueqiang** (许学强)	Air Force	4
Miao Hua (苗华)	Army	9	**Guo Puxiao** (郭普校)	Air Force	5
Average		3.4	**Average**		4.03

Source: Author

Examining Table 9.4, this metric of military experience provides some information on the relative experience of the PLA leadership in 2022, compared to 2016. On average, MR-level officers had 4.03 frontline command experience, compared to 3.4 in 2016. To be sure, some outliers, such as Yu Zhongfu with 14 frontline commands, arose due to data issues. Still, in general, officers with a low number of command experiences indeed had careers which focused on non-combatant roles in rear echelon units, such as military region headquarters or the major PLA departments in Beijing. For example, in the 2016 group, officers like Fang Fenghui and Yin Fanglong had careers either in political departments at the various levels or in second-tier provincial military units. CMC member and head of the General Staff Department Fang Fenghui was a classic case in point. Although he served a brief stint in the 21st Group Army, his career was mainly in units in the

Xinjiang Provincial MR and subsequent high-level administrative appointments in the Guangzhou Military Region and the Beijing Military Region before taking the helm of the General Staff Department in 2012.

Compared to the 2016 cohort, fewer officers at the MR-level in the 2022 cohort had a dearth of command experience of frontline units, except for the few specialists in logistics (Zhang Lin), missile (Li Yuchao), and electronic warfare (Ju Qiansheng). The only exception is Wang Haijiang who, despite relatively less experience in group army commands, had extensive experience commanding local units in Xinjiang and Tibet, which likely earned his promotion to the command position in the Western Theater. Thus, it seems that command experience in frontline units, as well as battle experience in the distant past, have become important pre-requisites of senior command positions in the PLA. Again, this suggests that Xi is able to focus on relevant experience rather than politics in appointing officers to high-level positions in an effort to modernize the military.

Discussion

For a rising power like China which fears preemptive strikes by an established power, it seems sensible for the leadership to focus on military preparedness, both in terms of equipment procurement and appointment of officers (Allison 2017). This is especially the case if the party leadership is unified (Fravel 2019). Yet, for leaders of authoritarian regimes, they always must guard against potential challenges to their power, especially from those who control the guns. Despite a Leninist party structure and the political commissar system, which help communist dictatorships control the military, dictators in these regimes still must use additional measures to guard against potential challenges from the military, including placing faction members and weak figures in senior positions.

Examining high-level appointments in the 2016–2022 period, there is clear evidence that Xi has sought to control the military through factionalism, although that tendency weakened by 2022. Meanwhile, there is little evidence that Xi is pursuing a weak coalition strategy in the military. Additionally, as suggested by the general IR literature and the literature on the PLA, he has appointed more officers with combat and command experience of frontline units in senior PLA positions. Moreover, specialists, instead of loyalists, have been placed in command of strategic branches of the PLA, such as the missile forces and the strategic support forces. For a military that intends to become equal to or surpass the US military, this pattern of appointment suggests that the party leadership is focused on achieving results. For countries that are wary of the rising military effectiveness of the PLA, this pattern may provide further grounds for concern.

References

Acemoglu, Daron, and James A. Robinson. 2006. *Economic Origins of Dictatorship and Democracy*. Cambridge: Cambridge University Press.

Acemoglu, Daron, Davide Ticchi, and Andrea Vindigni. 2010. "A Theory of Military Dictatorships." *American Economic Journal: Macroeconomics* 2010(2): 1–42.

Allison, Graham T. 2017. *Destined for War: Can America and China Escape Thucydides's Trap?* Boston, MA and New York: Houghton Mifflin Harcourt.
Chase, Michael S., Jeffrey Engstrom, Tai Ming Cheung, Kristen Gunness, Scott Harold, Susan Puska, and Samuel K. Berkowitz. 2015. *China's Incomplete Military Transformation: Assessing the Weaknesses of the People's Liberation Army (PLA)*. Santa Monica, CA: Rand Corporation.
Cheung, Tai Ming. 2001. "The Influence of the Gun: China's Central Military Commission and Its Relationship with the Military, Party, and State Decision-Making System." In *The Making of Chinese Foreign and Security Policy in the Era of Reform*, ed. D. M. Lampton. Stanford, CA: Stanford University Press.
Egorov, Georgy, and Konstantin Sonin. 2011. "Dictators and Their Viziers: Endogenizing the Loyalty-Competence Trade-Off." *Journal of the European Economic Association* 9(5): 903–930.
Fravel, M. Taylor. 2019. *Active Defense: China's Military Strategy since 1949*. Princeton, NJ: Princeton University Press.
Gregory, Paul R. 2009. *Terror by Quota: State Security from Lenin to Stalin: An Archival Study*. New Haven, CT: Yale University Press.
Huntington, Samuel P. 1981. *The Soldier and the State: The Theory and Politics of Civil-Military Relations*. Cambridge, MA: Harvard University Press.
Ji, You. 2001. "Jiang Zemin's Command of the Military." *China Journal* 2001(45): 131–138.
Mattingly, Daniel C. 2022. "How the Party Commands the Gun: The Foreign-Domestic Threat Dilemma in China." *American Journal of Political Science*. https://doi.org/10.1111/ajps.12739, Corpus ID: 253066569.
McMahon, R. Blake, and Branislav L. Slantchev. 2015. "The Guardianship Dilemma: Regime Security through and from the Armed Forces." *American Political Science Review* 109(2): 297–313.
Mearsheimer, John J. 2007. "Structural Realism." *International Relations Theories: Discipline and Diversity* 83: 77–94.
Mulvenon, James. 1997. *Professionalizatin of the Senior Chinese Officer Corps*. Rand Monograph Report, Issue.
Nathan, Andrew. J. 1973. "A Factionalism Model for CCP Politics." *The China Quarterly* 53: 34–66. http://links.jstor.org/sici?sici=0305-7410%28197301%2F03%290%3A53%3C34%3AAFMFCP%3E2.0.CO%3B2-P.
People's Daily. 2013. "习近平：要着力拓展和深化军事斗争准备" [Xi Jinping: We Must Work Hard to Expand and Deepen Preparation for Military Struggle]. *People's Daily*. February 7.
Pye, Lucian. 1995. "Factions and the Politics of *guanxi*: Paradoxes in Chinese Administrative and Political Behavior." *The China Journal* 34: 35–53.
Saunders, Phillip C. 2020. "Beyond Borders: PLA Command and Control of Overseas Operations." Strategic Forum 306. Washington, DC: Institute for National Strategic Studies, National Defense University.
Shih, Victor. 2022. "Beyond the 20th Party Congress: Elite Autonomy in the Politburo Standing Committee under Two Scenarios." In *The Party Remakes China: What to Watch for after the 20th Party Congress*, eds. H. Doshay and L. Guang. 21st Century China Center. https://china.ucsd.edu/_files/2022-report-20th-party-congress.pdf.
Shih, Victor, Jonghyuk Lee, and David Meyer. 2020. *The Database of CCP Elite*. San Diego, CA: Institute of Global Conflict and Cooperation.
Shih, Victor C. 2022. *Coalitions of the Weak: Elite Politics in China from Mao's Stratagem to the Rise of Xi*. Cambridge: Cambridge University Press.
Svolik, Milan W. 2012. *The Politics of Authoritarian Rule*. Cambridge: Cambridge University Press.
Walder, Andrew G., and Guoqiang Dong. 2011. "Local Politics in the Chinese Cultural Revolution: Nanjing under Military Control." *Journal of Asian Studies* 70(2): 425–447.

Whitson, William W., and Chen-hsia Huang. 1973. *The Chinese High Command; a History of Communist Military Politics, 1927–71*. New York: Praeger.
Wintrobe, Ronald. 1998. *The Political Economy of Dictatorship*. Cambridge: Cambridge University Press.
Wuthnow, Joel, and Phillip C. Saunders. 2016. "China's Goldwater-Nichols? Assessing PLA Organizational Reforms." *Joint Forces Quarterly* 82 (July).
Wuthnow, Joel, and Phillip C. Saunders. 2019. "Large and In Charge: Civil-Military Relations under Xi Jinping." In *Chairman Xi Remakes the PLA: Assessing Chinese Military Reforms*, eds. P. C. Saunders, A. S. Ding, A. Scobell, A. N. D. Yang, and J. Wuthnow. Washington, DC: NDU Press.
Xi, Jinping. 2022. "在中国共产党二十次全国代表大会上的报告." Zai zhongguo gongchandang ershici quanguo daibiao dahui shang de baogao [Report at the 20th Party Congress of the Chinese Communist Party). Beijing.
"Xi Jinping zai Fujian gongzuo qijian ceng tiyan dang paoshou" ("习近平在福建工作期间曾体验当炮手") [When Xi Jinping Worked in Fujian, He Had the Experience of Being an Artillery Soldier]. 2014. *Xinhua*. August 1.
Xiang, Shouzhi. 2006. 向守志回忆录 *Xiang Shouzhi Huiyilu [The Memoir of Xiang Shouzhi]*. Beijing: People's Liberation Army Publisher.

10 The BRI Under Xi Jinping

Fragmented Authoritarianism Beyond Water's Edge

Andrew Mertha

In 2016, during a break from interviewing ex-Khmer Rouge soldiers on the Thai-Cambodian border, I remember having a chat with my driver. "Are the roads in China as poorly made as the ones the Chinese build in Cambodia?" he asked me. On its face it was a simple question, but one that nonetheless has proven hard to shake. What is interesting to me is not how poorly-made the roads are, nor is it the suggestion that China is somehow shortchanging Cambodia. Rather, it is in the phrase "in China" (denoting the notion of "*as in* China"). It suggested to me that what China is exporting abroad is not simply its technical know-how, or its domestic overcapacity, or its economic diplomacy. It was also the germ of the argument I make here: that the PRC is also exporting, or externalizing, its own domestic structures and processes in attempting to meet its problem-solving challenges and project completion responsibilities on the international stage, in full view of the world.

But what are these domestic structures and processes? Xi Jinping has been heralded as the strongest Chinese leader since Mao. It is true that he has centralized a number of key institutions under his tenure and has curtailed a great deal of malfeasance within the government and the Party. And yet, the enduring Chinese notion of "those at the top have their policies and those of us at the bottom have our countermeasures" (上有政策下有对策) remains a fact of life. On that same trip, I was meeting informally with some government- and Party-adjacent interlocutors in Guiyang, and I asked them what the impact was so far of Xi Jinping's anti-corruption campaign. The response I got was that five-star hotels were removing two of their stars so that cadres could still have official (and reimbursable) meals at those venues despite the Central injunction that such meals must be limited to three-star hotels and below. And it does not stop there.

In this chapter, I unpack and marry the insights gleaned from these anecdotes to demonstrate a broader analysis of Chinese state behavior barely touched upon in current scholarly analyses and all but unknown in the elite policy discourse in Washington.

Context

In the past fifteen years or so, we have seen a dramatic shift outward in terms of Chinese influence-generating mechanisms, from the development of a blue water navy, something that in the early 2000s remained an open question, a fork in the road (Robert Ross, personal communication with author). In more recent years, China's building up of its man-made offshore atolls has raised tensions in the region. Washington's decision not to unduly contest this development only appears to add to China's invulnerability. China's export of its surveillance technology through the "Safe Cities" (安全城市) program is just one more dimension of this dramatic repositioning of China (Greitens 2020). Nor are these developments only in the security arena. What is, in fact, truly breathtaking is the scope and vision of China's outward-oriented investment to create markets, global infrastructure linkages, and gain access to strategic and rare commodities and natural resources. The Belt and Road Initiative (BRI) is among the latest and most dramatic, the breathless scope of which has captured the imagination – and outward-oriented investment – of multiple sets of actors in China. But others, like observers I spoke to in Uzbekistan who had no incentives to praise Chinese efforts, nonetheless spoke approvingly of the Xinjiang-Kazakhstan high-speed railway project as a significant provider of commerce – and public goods in general – to the region.[1]

Given all this, it is not altogether unreasonable to conclude that China is inexorably on the trajectory of a rising power, with very little drag on its global ambitions. Such a conclusion would lend itself to a particular set of policy prescriptions, and indeed, has fueled much of the hawkish rhetoric in Washington DC that Beijing is ready to "eat our lunch."

Certainly, we have seen China's approach to its own international behavior shift dramatically since the founding of the People's Republic in 1949. In the late Mao Zedong era, Chinese aid and cooperation to developing countries was intended to leverage China's international standing, particularly among the non-aligned movement and recently decolonized states. The first two decades of the reform era under the leadership of Deng Xiaoping and Jiang Zemin were critical to mitigating China's previous international isolation (as well as in the aftermath of 1989), which amounted to multipolarity (多极化) combined with "biding time and building capabilities" (韬光养晦). During the Hu Jintao era, we saw the emergence of what would eventually become BRI within the context of mitigating a negative international position over human rights and security transforming into actively pursuing Beijing's own purposeful agenda (that is, trade, investment, cooperation) via the policy of "Making a Difference" (有所作为).

But what is the *"Xi Jinping difference"*? Xi has transformed China's "Going Out" (走出去战备) strategy into the "Belt and Road Initiative" (BRI) and made it one of the key pillars of his turn toward the strategy of "Major Power Diplomacy" (大国外交), in which China seeks to secure (or return to) a more central role in global affairs. This has given rise to any number of debates over China's intentions, from "debt trap diplomacy" to the "Thucydides Trap." This has been reinforced by a continuous casting aside of strategic reassurance from Beijing in favor of a more confident and aggressive posture in which Xi Jinping's "China Dream" has been recast as the "China Threat" in the corridors of power in Washington DC. Even in sober analyses that showcase Beijing's deft handling of global financial challenges, from the Global Financial Crisis of 1997 to the current turn to multilateral debt relief (Bräutigam and Huang 2023), the reaction is the same: China is an unstoppable rising power and thus, by definition, a – indeed, *the* – long-term global threat.

And yet, as is often the case, we are getting it wrong, or at least forming a woefully incomplete picture. In March 2023, two *New York Times* articles perfectly described the complexities and challenges faced by Xi both domestically and globally. In "China's Cities Are Buried in Debt, but They Keep Shoveling It On," journalist Li Yuan provides a sober analysis of unsustainable domestic debt spending:

> As part of the ruling Communist Party's all-in push for economic growth this year, local governments already in debt from borrowing to pay for massive infrastructure are taking on additional debt. They're building more roads, railways and industrial parks even though the economic returns on that activity are increasingly meager. In their struggle to find the money to fund their new projects, and the interest payments on their old ones, cities are cutting public services and benefits.
>
> (Li 2023)

Just one day prior, Li's collogue, Keith Bradsher, wrote on "After Doling Out Huge Loans, China Is Now Bailing Out Countries," in which he argues:

> New data show that China is providing ever more emergency loans to countries, including Turkey, Argentina and Sri Lanka. China has been helping countries that have either geopolitical significance, like a strategic location, or lots of natural resources. Many of them have been borrowing heavily from Beijing for years to pay for infrastructure or other projects.
>
> (Bradsher 2023)

This eerie domestic/global parallel, I argue, goes far deeper than being an eyebrow-arching coincidence. Rather than the Beltway echo chamber and across the public – and increasingly, scholarly – discourse over China, I see equally inexorable constraints faced by Beijing. But these are not simply international constraints, although that is certainly part of the story (just not part of mine). Specifically, it is *domestic* Chinese institutions and their attendant pathologies – the politics embedded in its domestic bureaucratic and institutional landscape – that is increasingly becoming a key factor in explaining China's international behavior.[2] My thesis in this chapter is that the effectiveness of Chinese foreign investment and aid – and the influence that comes with it – is only as good as the domestic institutions that manage the relationship.[3] And not only is the lion's share of those Chinese institutions domestic-facing, but they are also increasingly subnational.

The Literature

This view extends beyond other approaches that we have seen on BRI (一带一路) strategy. But before that, it is worth looking at the existing literature. Much of the research on China's "Going Out" focuses on drivers and determinants of Chinese

OFDI. Political economy and international business scholars have regarded government support as a main driver of Chinese OFDI. Using the political economy perspective, scholars examine why and how the Chinese government stimulates OFDI (Deng 2004; Luo et al. 2010). Chinese firms have benefited significantly from government support at critical stages in their international efforts and their asset acquisition (Wang 2002; Warner et al. 2004). China's considerable foreign exchange reserves also facilitate government support, leading to rising state-controlled investments (Cheung and Qian 2009). State influence is evident in that most of China's OFDI is conducted by SOEs, accounting for approximately 80 percent of Chinese cumulative investment stock (UNCTAD 2013). In recent years, Chinese private enterprises have also emerged as important players in OFDI, but Chinese SOEs still dominate the majority of Chinese OFDI.

The dramatic rise in Chinese OFDI has sparked intense political, economic, and developmental debates in the global community regarding the role of state support in Chinese OFDI (Sauvant et al. 2010; Yeung and Liu 2008). Some scholars argue that the sharp growth of Chinese investment as a result of the Chinese state's "Going Out" strategy aims to serve its national development priorities (Song et al. 2011). Empirical studies show that the Chinese government succeeds in utilizing SOEs to achieve its strategic objectives and increases political and economic influence abroad (Bräutigam and Tang 2011; Jiang 2009). Chinese governmental support creates relative advantages for Chinese SOEs (Alon 2010; Liang et al. 2014; Wei et al. 2015), and China's well-developed regional institutions have a positive effect on Chinese OFDI (Liu et al. 2014; Liang et al. 2014).

Industry factors also shape the process of Chinese OFDI. Luo et al. (2011) report that industry structure uncertainty and firm-specific advantages increase the degree of Chinese OFDI. Yiu et al. (2007) find that Chinese firms with higher technological capabilities pursue more international venturing when home industry competition is stronger. Yang and Stoltenberg (2014) report that increased absorptive capacity and increased industry openness make Chinese MNCs more likely to engage in strategic-asset-seeking OFDI. Firm-specific factors also seem to be related to institutional factors. Wang et al. (2012) suggest that government involvement influences the level of OFDI, although not all firms possess equal abilities to internalize government-related advantages. Huang and Chi (2014) report that Chinese private firms are increasingly active in market- and strategic asset-seeking OFDI because of the unfavorable environment they face at home and the different resources they possess.

In addition to what is driving Chinese OFDI, much of the literature focuses on the adverse impact on the recipient country. Zadek et al. (2009), for example, argue that China's non-involvement policy keeps Chinese businesses away from "intervening in African countries' internal affairs" and therefore, they are less willing to address issues such as corruption, transparency, and human rights, even where these become potential business risks. Others warn about the negative impact of Chinese investments in countries ruled by weak or authoritarian regimes and the linkage between Chinese investment and authoritarian survival in the developing world. In particular, the "Angola model" of loans-for-oil allows countries to circumvent governance and transparency requirements by other investors or donors (Alden and Alves 2008; Lombard 2006; Moss and Rose 2006; Peh and Eyal 2010; Taylor 2007). Still others find that the lack of transparency of Chinese companies' operations and Chinese aid policy may cultivate corruption in less-developed countries (Peh and Eyal 2010). Chinese development financiers, such as the China EXIM Bank, also do not report their own activities in the same way as the other similar agencies, and the bank does not place reporting demands on its clients (Moss and Rose 2006). Yet it is unclear what it is about China that allows this to happen.

The literature also identifies that Chinese investors are willing to finance projects in countries with poor investment environments which lack traditional investors and donors (Cissé 2012; Corkin et al. 2008; Urban et al. 2013). Zhang Youyi has written particularly persuasively that first mover advantage in securing overseas BRI deals forces latecomers to undertake ever-riskier investments, demonstrating an alarming degree of risk-acceptance (Zhang 2017). Research also highlights concerns with the quality of Chinese services, especially in the ICT and construction sectors (Corkin et al. 2008; Dalton 2014; Gagliardone and Geall 2014; Konjin 2014; Marshall 2011). There is also concern over China's potential control over major aspects of the host countries' economy, especially in land-related investments (Hinkley 2011; Onphanhdala and Suruga 2013) as well as over competition between Chinese goods and local industries (Kubny and Voss 2010; Shen 2015).

Much has also been written on China's investments in developing countries that are concentrated in areas that are environmentally sensitive, focusing on concerns (and in some cases open protests) over Chinese investments in mining, infrastructure, forestry and agricultural projects (Gallagher 2010; International Rivers 2012; Martínez Rivera 2013; Mol 2011; Onphanhdala and Suruga 2013). Case studies on Chinese state-owned petroleum companies operating in a national park in Gabon (for example, see Bosshard 2008; Corkin et al. 2008; Deutsch 2010; Kong 2011; Mol 2011; Munson and Zheng 2012) and on key sectors such as forestry, where Chinese businesses have been implicated in illegal logging and not meeting environmental and social safeguards (Global Witness 2009; Al-Aameri et al. 2012; Roque 2009), abound. Similar problems are highlighted in fisheries where illegal fishing contributes to the degradation of coastal areas (Jansson and Kiala 2009; Roque 2009). A key issue raised is that China imposes lower environmental benchmarks on its aid and investment projects than multilateral institutions or Western companies (Bräutigam and Tang 2009; Mol 2011; Munson and Zheng 2012; Sautman and Yan 2009; Van Dijk 2009). Of particular concern is the lack of firm guidelines governing environmental impact assessments and providing for them to be verified and reviewed for accuracy and completeness (Munson and Zheng 2012). Examples of problematic environmental impact assessments (EIAs) have been documented in Argentina (Martínez Rivera 2013), Australia (Validakis 2014), and Cambodia (Grimsditch 2012).

Finally, and closer to the approach I take here, the literature on Chinese domestic constraints abroad is very good; there just simply isn't very much of it. And among what does exist, there is little consensus as to what the key variables or levels of analysis should be. Gill and Reilly (2007) use a principal-agent framework that is elegant but does not capture the multidimensionality of the interactions among relevant actors. Meidan et al. (2009) provide an excellent analysis of energy policy, but it is highly sector-specific. Corkin et al. (2008) argues persuasively that the Ministry of Commerce (MOFCOM) is very much ascendant at the expense of the Ministry of Foreign Affairs (MoFA), while Zhang and Smith (2017) argue precisely the opposite. Jones and Zou (2017) argue that state versus state-owned enterprise relations are governed by weak oversight but potentially underestimate Party control, especially under Xi, leaving us unsure about the balance of forces at work shaping foreign policy outcomes.

It is worth spending time on this last point. In the 1980s Zhao Ziyang sought to provide more opportunities for independent action for the government but was swimming against the tide and was swallowed up by the events of 1989, and Jiang Zemin sought – unsuccessfully – to bring the government under increased Party control (although he was extraordinarily successful in bringing a significant chunk of Chinese society into the Party). Xi Jinping has made no bones about the fact that he wants the Party not only to dominate the government but to take on key roles and functions that have traditionally – at least throughout the reform era – been under increasing government control, such as the economy. Under Xi, there has been an increase in Party leadership small groups (LSGs), quasi-formal coordinating mechanisms that involve top leaders. These Party-specific (as distinct from government-based) LSGs have some subtle differences with their government counterparts. First, Xi sits atop many of them, raising questions about his bandwidth and the leading groups' ability to undertake decisive action. Second, they have veered into replicating if not micromanaging some of the traditional, government-based policy-specific bureaucratic clusters. Finally, in some cases they represent the culmination of years, even decades, of jockeying to create such an organ, such as the National Security LSG (中央国家安全领导小组), which has since – along with the Comprehensively Deepening Reform LSG (中央全面深化改革领导小组) – solidified and institutionalized into a CCP Commission (委员会).

These and other recent additions – including the Public Security Comprehensive Management Commission (中央社会管理综合治理委员会), the Commission for Guiding Cultural and Ethical Progress/Building Spiritual Civilization (中央精神文明建设指导委员会), and the Central Cyberspace Commission (中央网络安全和信息化委员会) – appear to represent several things. First, as noted, they solidify and make more permanent the somewhat temporally defined leadership small groups and thus underscore their deep importance in Xi's approach to governance. The National Security Commission is an example of this. Second, they do appear to extend traditional Party functions into a new age. They also provide a way to enshrine Xi Jinping's own political priorities. And finally, they extend into the government sphere more so than we have seen in the recent past.[4]

Anticipating the next section, by grafting these institutions onto existing ones, Xi is further complicating an already complex system, establishing new political cleaves and potential for bureaucratic turf wars, and allowing for more liminal spaces within which actors can carry out their own goals and priorities without regard to those of Beijing.

My Argument

As already noted, my argument is that the effectiveness of Chinese foreign investment – and the influence that comes with it – is only as good as the institutions that manage the relationship. But what does this mean? What institutions are we talking about? There are several pieces upon which this argument is built. Many observers of China on the international stage consciously or unconsciously adopt assumptions of China being a unitary rational actor. Others, referenced in the previous section, disaggregate the state to the firm or to the sector. I would like to disaggregate even further.

A Good Deal of Chinese Politics is Fragmented

The Chinese government apparatus extends into the most arcane policy areas and is replicated at every level of the Chinese state, with some exceptions at the very bottom of the system. Each policy area has its own bureaucracies and each of these has its own particular structure, administrative rank, formal and informal power bases, institutional history, corporate culture, and idiosyncratic approach to reaching its organizational goals. Bureaucratic competition over power and influence is baked into the system, which is characterized by bargaining and consensus-building when it is working at its best, but is at least just as often defined by knock-down drag-out infighting, bureaucratic fragmentation, and institutional inertia and atrophy.

Who governs the BRI strategy? Like most policy in China, it is coordinated by several key national-level actors. The Ministry of Commerce (MOFCOM) supervises all foreign economic relations, including trade, investment, aid, and Chinese businesses' overseas conduct. MOFCOM is the statutory body on economic development and the caretaker of Chinese companies overseas, so economic interests are prominent when it makes decisions on foreign aid and investment projects. MOFCOM readily forms alliances with Chinese companies when a conflict among economics, diplomacy, and China's global image arises. MOFCOM's Department of Foreign Aid (DFA) has fourteen divisions (three on Africa, two on Asia, one on western Asia, Northern Africa and Eastern Europe, one on Latin America, and one on the South Pacific), and a general office and a staff of 70. MOFCOM also has a Department of International Trade and Economic Affairs (DITEA) that manages inbound grant aid from traditional donors and UN agencies (bilateral aid to China or trilateral aid with China being one of the cooperative entities); this must go through DITEA before approaching the ministries.

But there are obvious areas of overlap with other agencies, which are loathe to subsume themselves under MOFCOM's lead. The Ministry of Foreign Affairs (MoFA) is responsible for China's diplomatic relations and thus has a strong interest in – yet no control over – overseas SOEs. MoFA is the statutory body of China's foreign relations, tasked with building positive external relations and supporting domestic development and stability. For MoFA, political relations trump short-term economic gains. Therefore, MoFA will place more emphasis on whether aid and investment projects serve for broader political and diplomatic ties. The Ministry of Finance (MoF), on the other hand, allocates funding to be disbursed by China's ministries. Foreign aid project proposals need to be circulated to MoF for approval. In terms of direct funding, MoF covers the gap between the commercial and concessional interest rate for Chinese policy banks' concessional loans that help Chinese firms go out.

In addition, there are the state-owned banks. The China Export-Import Bank (EXIM bank) supports trade by providing credit and insurance and, like MOFCOM, supports overseas Chinese business deals by providing aid and concessional funding. Its concessional loans, an increasingly important vehicle to implement the "Go Global Strategy," made up more than half of China's aid in the period from 2010–2014. China Development Bank also funds large-scale infrastructure projects, while the China Export Credit and Insurance Corporation (Sinosure), provides export credit insurance, often as a form of subsidy. Other key participants include the National Development and Reform Commission (NDRC), which is responsible for: authorizing state investment in projects over US$30 million; price-setting for certain scarce/vital commodities and services; licensing; strategic restructuring; and industrial and climate change policy. The State Council's State-owned Assets Supervision and Administration Commission (SASAC) is the largest shareholder of SOE stock, and thus also seeks to maximize profit (and SASAC is at the same administrative rank as MoFA, MoF, and MOFCOM, as well as – for that matter – provincial governments.)

And as noted, another wrinkle is that under Xi Jinping, a growing number of new Chinese Communist Party (CCP) organizations have emerged and have increasingly encroached upon policy areas traditionally – and firmly – under government jurisdiction. This additional layer is intended to cut through much of the institutional and agency slack that exists within the system but may well have the effect of further contributing to it. The most relevant of these is the Comprehensively Deepening Reform Leadership Small Group, announced at the 3rd Plenary Session of the 18th Central Committee in November 2013, subsequently enshrined as a commission (Chinese Communist Party 2013). It has a breathtakingly wide scope, denoted by its constituent subgroups – Economy and Ecology (经济体制和生态文明体制改革), Cultural System Reform (文化体制改革), Democratic and Legal Reform (民主法治灵活改革), Social System Reform (社会体制改革), Party Building System Reform (党的建设体制改革), and Legal Professional Inspection System Reform (律师监察体制改革).

The CDRLSG's main task is to determine policy guidelines for reforming the economic, political, cultural, social, ethical, and party-building systems in order to address long-term reform issues, as well as to guide reform-related bodies of the CCP at central and local level and supervise the implementation of reform plans. It was initially charged with pushing policies past the bureaucracy to assist Xi in consolidating his power over China's vast government apparatus, the State Council, usually the domain of the Premier.

Each of these institutions has its own priorities and mandates, which can conflict with their partner institutions. Moreover, as articulated responsibilities are often vague, there is plenty of room to excessively liberally (or conservatively) interpret a given institution's scope of action. In practice, this means that the Department of

Foreign Aid within MOFCOM does not coordinate with MoFA; Chinese embassies and consulates report to MoFA, but the Economic Counsellor's Office, formally under the Embassy, reports directly to MOFCOM; MoFA visits to recipient countries are replicated or shadowed by MOFCOM with little meaningful coordination; and the China Exim Bank is under the Ministry of Finance but works closely with MOFCOM; indeed, it facilitates "development financing" that enhances MOFCOM via purchases of Chinese goods. Meidan et al. (2009, 596–597), for example, identify eleven different ministerial-level agencies that influence Chinese energy policy, and eleven with some jurisdiction over maritime affairs. Zhang and Smith (2017) count 33 agencies (led by MOFCOM, MoFA, and MoF) among the foreign aid *xitong* (系统), or "cluster of policy-relevant bureaucracies."

All Politics is Ultimately Local

The PRC has under its direct control 22 provinces, four provincial-level municipalities (Beijing, Shanghai, Tianjin, and Chongqing), and five autonomous regions (Tibet, Xinjiang, Guangxi, Ningxia, and Inner Mongolia) that have a significant number of a particular non-Han Chinese minority, Tibetan, Uyghur, Zhuangzu, Huizu, and Mongol, respectively. Chongqing became a provincial-level municipality when it separated out of Sichuan in 1997. Prefecture-level (地级行政区) units include seven actual prefectures (five in Xinjiang, one in Tibet and one in Heilongjiang), 293 prefecture-level cities, 30 autonomous prefectures (containing a large minority population, such as in the autonomous regions listed as well as provinces like Yunnan, Guizhou, and Sichuan), and seven leagues (or *meng*, which are the prefecture-level units in Inner Mongolia).

Of the 2,851 county-level administrative units, 1,355 are counties proper and the rest are a combination of 117 autonomous counties (自治县, counties with one or more designated ethnic minorities, analogous to autonomous regions and prefectures), 360 county-level cities (县级市, which are similar to prefecture-level cities, covering both urban and rural areas), 913 urban districts (市辖区 or 地区, formerly the subdivisions of urban areas, consisting of built-up areas only), and 49 banners (旗, which are the same as counties except in the name, a holdover from earlier forms of administration in Mongolia), three autonomous banners (自治旗), one forestry area (林区, a special county-level forestry district located in Hubei), and one special district (特区, a special county-level division located in Guizhou province.

Below the county, there are some 41,039 township-level units in China, consisting of 13,749 actual townships (乡), 1,098 ethnic townships (民族乡), 19,322 towns (镇), 6,686 subdistricts (街道, or 街, small urban areas), two county-controlled districts (县辖区, that are being dismantled), 181 Sum (肃穆, townships unique to Inner Mongolia) and one ethnic Sum (民族肃穆), also located in Inner Mongolia.

Two important points become salient at this juncture: first, China's state structure is replicated throughout this impossible mosaic, and second, each of these localities and administrative levels has its own set of priorities and goals that can – and often do – vary not only with each other's, but most importantly and starkly with *Beijing's*, as the next section will demonstrate.

Most of Chinese Subnational Politics is Decentralized

So how do we square these national-level institutions – already in conflict with each other – with the overwrought subnational governing apparatus sketched out in the previous section? How is China governed? Specifically, how are binding requirements enacted, and what are the more propitious areas to work around, dilute, ignore, and even undermine a national policy at the local level? There are four things to consider when seeking an answer: distinction, salience, direction, aggregation. The first has to do with authority relations in China. Simplifying considerably here, there are two sorts of these authority relations, binding "leadership relations" (the shorthand is 领导关系); and non-binding, consultative "professional relations" (业务关系). Thus, the first consideration is to *distinguish* between these two types of relations.

The second dimension has to do with understanding the *salience* of these two sets of relations. Any administrative (read: government) unit in China can have any number of relationships – of non-binding, professional relations – even with higher-ranked units; however, it can only have binding, leadership relations with one single unit. The latter is the superior that the administrative unit in question must answer to, which is useful, especially when it is exposed to simultaneously conflicting orders.

The third dimension has to do with the *direction* of these critical leadership relations. If they are vertical in nature – that is, if a national-level ministry (部) can issue binding orders to its functional counterpart at the provincial level (the next administrative level down from the Center) and so on, all the way down the administrative hierarchy to the county level – it has centralized leadership relations or, in the Chinese vernacular, "leadership down a line" (条上领导). If, on the other hand, this ministerial counterpart at the provincial level – often a bureau (局 or 厅) – is established to follow its binding orders from the government at the same administrative level (in this case, the provincial government) and not from its national-level functional counterpart (ministry), such a relationship is called "leadership across a piece" (块上领导) within the corridors of power in China (Lieberthal and Oksenberg 1988; Lieberthal 1996). The direction of these authority relations is determined by concomitant direction of budgetary revenue through the mechanism of 编制, or the allocation system of budgets and personnel (Brødsgaard 2002).

The fourth and final component is the *aggregation* of these horizontal and vertical sets of leadership relations throughout the bureaucratic mosaic described in the previous section. If these sets of relations were relatively evenly or symmetrically distributed, it would be somewhat indeterminate as to whether China – in the aggregate – is a centralized state or a decentralized one. Luckily, the distribution is highly asymmetrical. Most observers of China, if tasked with determining whether China is highly centralized or decentralized, would almost certainly say that China, as a top-down authoritarian regime with little room for deviating from national commands and priorities, tilts far in the direction of centralized leadership relations. In fact, the opposite is true. The Chinese system is overwhelmingly decentralized in nature and has been going back to the Mao era. Of course, there are some caveats: the system has become more centralized under Xi Jinping, and the CCP has always provided the necessary backbone to government decentralization. On the first point, it remains unclear to what degree the tendency to push back on central dictates has been diluted since 2012. The impressionistic evidence suggests the answer is "not so much." This is due in part to the second point, which is complicated by the fact that promotion for subnational cadres has often been tied to local successes in which output figures suggest conformity with central government policy mandates even if the means to achieve them often break the spirit and the letter of the mandate in the first place.

This is important because the vast majority of the economic (and political) actors involved in BRI are *subnational* ones. After a period of painful consolidation (抓大, "grasping of the strong"), the reduction of national-level state-owned enterprises (SOEs) under SASAC has led to a manageable number of just under 100 SOEs, often in strategic sectors. These are powerful players in China's domestic politics. In China's political system, the directors of large SOEs are interchangeable with those commonly rotated into high-ranking political positions such as provincial governors and ministers. Aside from personnel connections to the Party-state, large SOEs are favored to implement China's foreign aid and government-to-government projects because they are state companies and generate revenue for the government, and because they have the resources to implement the projects. Private companies that win projects, such as Huawei, are large enterprises with strong state links. Moreover, some 900 provincial-level SOEs are owned and supervised by provincial governments' SASAC equivalents. The rest – around 112,000 smaller firms – are owned by lower-level administrations. Furthermore, as suggested by the previous discussion, provincial and municipal MOFCOM offices have regulatory authority over all companies registered at that same administrative level; the actual ministry – MOFCOM – does not! This is significant because provincial level SOEs make up 88% of all Chinese firms investing abroad,[5] and even, as in the case of Heilongjiang's "Three Bridges, One Island" (三桥一岛), developed their own local international policies. Even more to the point, subnational governments "interpret" (or ignore) often-vague central regulations, according to local conditions and interests.[6] Lest we think that this applies only to "traditional" Chinese SOEs, differences between local SOEs and private enterprises is negligible, certainly less than the difference between central and local SOEs (Jones and Zou 2017).

The result of all this functional, spatial, and administrative level-based fragmentation has been spelled out by Lieberthal, Oksenberg, Lampton, and others – sluggishness, a focus on extensive and ongoing negotiations, local veto power, policy incoherence, and so on (Lieberthal and Oksenberg 1988; Lampton 1988; Mertha 2008) – but more generally it falls under a dynamic that has described the key dynamic of Chinese politics for centuries, if not millennia: "those at the top have their policies, we at the bottom have our countermeasures." The difference today is twofold and significant. First, as China extends its investment overseas, domestic politics no longer stops at the water's edge, escaping the scrutiny of China's extensive supervisory infrastructure, thus contributing to a widening of informational asymmetries favoring subnational actors (Dimitrov 2022), and thus Beijing has far less ability to rein it in (under a command economy, the plan was the tool to mitigate local tendencies to thwart Beijing, while under reform it has been domestic-based cadre promotion mechanisms). Moreover, this is different from the dynamics that more recent scholarship describes, in which localities exploit opportunities at Beijing's expense through coherent strategies (Wong 2018). Instead, we see something of a "wild West" environment, more akin to the early days of reform, but far less cautious.

Second, these outcomes do not simply have consequences inside China, as Min Ye (2019)'s excellent work makes clear; they have consequences for China's relations with third-party countries as well as for the internal politics of the countries themselves. Thus, fragmented authoritarian governance itself is being exported abroad. The consequences, however, are potentially even more destabilizing, given that in China, domestic actors are all conversant with the rules, norms, language, and tools of the game, and are thus constrained by the others' knowledge of them; this is demonstrably not the case abroad, or if it is, it tends to dovetail with inefficient, rent-seeking, non-democratic norms of a given target country. This – far more than the vague articulation of some generic "third Chinese way" – is what the actual "China model" looks like.

Case Studies

How does all this look in practice? It is difficult to be systematic, given the dearth of information that is currently available. Nonetheless, there is enough data to allow us to derive some potentially illuminating hypotheses, even if we cannot yet adequately *test* them. What these cases do suggest is that the overused paradigm case of "debt trap diplomacy" in the case of the Sri Lankan port of Hambantota is far from the only instance of Chinese foreign engagement going off the rails. Unlike the Hambantota case,[7] the ones listed – Nicaragua, Myanmar, Ghana, and Cambodia – also underscore some of the non-strategic (at least as a part of China's foreign policy goals at the national level) origins, drivers, and effects of China's fragmented foreign policy (Abi-Habib 2018). Finally, these are all negative cases, the representativeness of which must remain unknowable at present – we simply do not have the data to confirm either way – but which are numerous enough to substantially inform the conventional wisdom of China's unfettered rise, as well as Chinese rhetoric that describes success after success in a series of inevitable "win-win" outcomes.

Nicaragua: "Covert" BRI?[8]

These threats to the coherence and stability of Beijing's foreign policy are not simply the result of errant entrepreneurs or desperate county governments involved in destructive but ultimately niche activities under the radar. The HKND canal project in Nicaragua is a case in point. The same year that Chinese-Ghanaian relations were reaching their nadir, a private Chinese company revealed its plans for an extraordinarily ambitious construction project, a shipping canal to rival the Panama

Canal, but located in Nicaragua and able to accommodate ships with greater tonnage. With a price tag estimated between $40 and $50 billion, the project was slated to include several free trade areas, two ports, tourism zones, airports, and facilities for power generation and transmission.

The developer, the Hong Kong-Nicaragua Development Corporation (HKND), was in charge of the project with a number of high-profile Chinese SOEs as partners, including the China Railway Construction Corporation for design work; the China Gezhouba Group, which is charged with "making equity investments in the project"; the Changjiang Institute of Survey, Planning, Design and Research; and "subsidiaries of the central SOEs China Communication Construction Group and China Airport Construction Group Corporation are responsible for the port and airport components, respectively." Despite all this, the Chinese government has denied any link to the project.

In Nicaragua itself, there has been significant opposition to the proposal, particularly surrounding the lack of transparency on a project with the scale and potential for disruption of the HKND canal. The canal would run through Lake Nicaragua, which is the source of drinking water for the whole country. It would also disrupt the integrity of several national parks. In rural residential areas, it would necessitate significant population resettlement. Yet amidst all this, a detailed project description was delayed until preliminary work on the project was already underway before any environmental assessment had been conducted.

Indeed, this non-transparency has been matched by questions surrounding the investors' ability to see the project through. HKND had no experience in infrastructure construction of such a grand scale, and it was unclear how it would be able to raise the amount of financing necessary for such an undertaking (suggesting that the Chinese state *had* to be involved). Perhaps as an example of "protesting too much", "in December 2014 a spokesperson from China's Foreign Ministry stated: 'the Chinese company's engagement in the Nicaragua project is an act of itself and has nothing to do with the Chinese Government.'" (Chu 2014; Miller 2014).

As it turned out, these fears were justified. Without being able to peer into the black box of the HKND-led consortium, it nonetheless appeared that China severed the cord by pressuring its SOEs to abandon the project when its finances came under scrutiny. The project itself was abandoned in 2020 and HKND's CEO Wang Jing unceremoniously vacated his short-lease office in Hong Kong's IFC Building, leaving no forwarding number or address (Schmidt 2018). Although unrealized, and perhaps showing Beijing's ability to rein in a project of such visibility, the HKND story is one that leaves a black mark on China's policies in the region (although ironically, and likely because it was abandoned, not Daniel Ortega's Nicaragua).

Myanmar: BRI as a Force for Destabilization

Although the situation in Nicaragua was nipped in the bud, the situation in Myanmar – also born from a lack of oversight – has been nothing short of disastrous for China (Chan 2017). November 2008 saw China's State Council approve the National Development and Reform Commission's (NDRC) recommendation to move forward on the ambitious Myitsone dam project in Myanmar. But an environmental impact assessment had not been conducted prior to approval. Eventually, the Changjiang Institute of Survey, Planning, Design and Research (CISPDR) was tasked with coming up with an EIA, which it promptly subcontracted to Myanmar's Biodiversity and Nature Conservation Association (BANCA). "BANCA's preliminary report, hastily drafted in October 2009, concluded that while damage caused by six other Irrawaddy Project dams could be mitigated, those associated with the Myitsone dam could not." As a result, BANCA's recommendation was for canceling the Myitsone project and concentrating on the construction of smaller dams and additional mitigation. The Chinese entity responsible for the project, the Yunnan International Power Investment Company (CPI) ignored this, starting construction in December 2009, three months before CISPDR had finalized the EIA (Jones and Zou 2017, 752). CPI also failed to consider growing and vocal opposition to the Myitsone dam which had been ongoing for the previous half-decade from actors within the Kachin state, falsely reporting that BANCA had approved the project.[9]

> CPI continued to violate rules even as Chinese regulators recognised the growing danger. MOFCOM's 'Notice on Issuing Overseas Security Risk Early Warning and Information Release System on Foreign Investment Cooperation' (2010) requires SOEs to minimise risks and losses if warned by MOFCOM (MOFCOM 2010). In June 2011, MOFCOM explicitly warned CPI that rising societal opposition in Myanmar could lead to the company being targeted by the country's government. CPI ignored the warning (Jiang 2009). Nonetheless, MOFCOM did not suspend the project, as it is empowered to do when due-diligence rules are violated.
>
> (Jones and Zou 2017, 753)

The negative effects of Myitsone onto Myanmar's domestic politics were direct and consequential.

As Myanmar slowly moved in the direction of post-military rule, its rulers sought to include and empower its armed ethnic minorities by establishing them as "border guard forces." Prior to that, however, activists within the Kachin state had rallied around opposing the Myitsone dam as a way of mobilizing support, arguing that it debased sacred lands while forcing unwanted relocation of the population living within. As Jones and Zou (2017) relate:

> This movement gradually became part of a powerbase for a group of mid-ranking Kachin Independence Army (KIA) officers disillusioned with their co-opted leaders... The KIA's "young Turks" seized control of the KIO/KIA, re-launching its anti-government insurgency (Brenner 2015). Opposition to the Myitsone dam thus contributed indirectly but significantly to renewed civil war in Myanmar.
>
> (Jones and Zou 2017, 753)

The effect was not simply to significantly destabilize Myanmar's domestic politics; it severely damaged the bilateral relations between the two countries and undermined China's international messaging as a better alternative to conditional Western foreign aid and investment. And the dam remains unbuilt.[10]

Jones and Zou (2017, 753) conclude that in the Myitsone dam case:

> a leading SOE, pursuing profit with reckless disregard for China's wider 'national interests', systematically violated Chinese regulations on overseas investments. Reflecting the Chinese state's fragmentation and uneven internationalisation, oversight within the Chinese-style regulatory state was weak and ineffective, despite the presence of authoritarian controls.

But as the next case demonstrates, this internationalization of Chinese domestic fragmentation gets even more granular.

Ghana: BRI Contributing to Transnational Worker Unrest

As BRI provides secure market access, new actors and entities complicate the situation with "large state-owned firms, often in collaboration with national agencies or subnational governments [seizing] economic opportunities." As they "expand to new markets, increase natural resource extraction, and establish competing manufacturing sites," they also attract "many migrant entrepreneurs . . . with little or no connection to or support from large firms or the national government," but who nonetheless can have a significant impact on Beijing's relations with a particular country or region (Hess and Aidoo 2016, 321).

Ghana provides a fascinating window into the internationalization of the dynamic of in-country migration in China except that it has now been extended beyond China's borders. Of note is the 2013 *galamsey*[11] controversy involving illegal gold mining by Chinese actors in the West African country. What is particularly interesting about their findings is that much of the origin of this fraught relationship can be traced back to a single county, Shanglin (上林), in the Guangxi Zhuang Autonomous Region, itself a major subnational player in BRI.[12]

As Hess and Aidoo tell the story, Shanglin county is the home of migrant workers who had worked in gold harvesting in China's Northeast during the 1990s. When those facilities closed, they returned home to a local economy that had little use for their professional skills. In the early 2000s, several of them ended up in Ghana where they amassed a considerable fortune, returning to Shanglin as millionaires. The inevitable gold rush saw a ballooning of Chinese prospectors in West Africa. Some seven years after the first returnees started spreading the news in Shanglin county, West Africa had 50,000 Chinese expatriates, two-thirds of whom came from Shanglin, and with active support by their local government:

> county government officials encouraged the growth of the overseas mining industry by assisting prospective miners in acquiring passports and travel documentation, ignoring some of the dubious lending practices surrounding the mining ventures, and helping coordinate the export of mining equipment to Shanglin miners in Ghana.
>
> (Hess and Aidoo 2016, 316)

The problem was that such mining was illegal in Ghana. Moreover, use of heavy machinery and toxic chemicals (particularly mercury) not only underscored that the Chinese were outcompeting their Ghanian counterparts who focused more on artisanal mining, but also contributed to the considerable negative environmental and health effects of their *galamsey*.

Unsurprisingly, resentment against the Chinese escalated into armed attacks, culminating in the shooting deaths of two Ghanaians by Chinese miners over a land dispute in Ashanti (Chinese social media was already replete with photos of Chinese workers killed or injured by Ghanaians). The Chinese miners sought help from the Chinese Embassy in Accra but were turned away because their visas and paperwork, secured by the Shanglin county government on the miners' behalf, were not the "proper working documents" (Hess and Aidoo 2016, 317).

As tensions escalated further, in May a fourteen-person delegation of representatives from the Guangxi Autonomous Region government (including its foreign affairs office) met with Ghanaian officials. The latter demanded that the Chinese engaged in illegal mining leave the country immediately, while the Guangxi delegation proposed to provide "technology transfers" and provide "sensitivity training" to Shanglin residents. Demonstrating some tone-deafness, the Chinese delegation criticized Ghanaian authorities for failing to protect the Chinese who had been engaged in illegal activity. None of this succeeded in preventing a crackdown which began the following month.

As the action proceeded, protests erupted in Shanglin, forcing the county and provincial authorities to send another delegation, this time also including officials from the commerce and public security offices to negotiate the release of Chinese taken into custody as well as arrange for the repatriation of some 4,500 Chinese miners. The result is that

> Chinese involvement in galamsey in Ghana has . . . been complicit in threatening Chinese foreign policy priorities in Ghana, soiling China's image, and consequently straining efforts at fostering Sino-Ghanaian relations. Collectively, their actions have not only impacted Sino-Ghanaian engagements but have also raised questions about Beijing's already critiqued foreign policy agenda in Africa.
>
> (Hess and Aidoo 2016, 314)

It is difficult to imagine a darker or more intractable and uncontrolled set of outcomes in the internationalization of China's domestic politics, but, as is often the case, Cambodia provides exactly that.

Cambodia: BRI's "Black Hands"

In a far cry from its headier days as an offloading area for arms to communist forces in South Vietnam and as a showcase for Cambodia's oil refining capabilities, the port city of Sihanoukville (Preah Sihanouk, also known as Kampong Som) had, by the 21st century, turned into a sleepy, sleazy destination for Western backpackers, drug addicts, and "death-pats." A few years later, however, it became a destination for Chinese investment in real estate and casinos, as an offshoot of China's BRI initiatives in the region, including high-speed rail, hydropower, and other infrastructure development (in addition to China's even less transparent strategic presence, such as the Ream naval base).[13] Sihanoukville is Cambodia's only deep-water port, making it an important BRI hub in the region (Inclusive Development International 2020; Ellis-Petersen 2018).

The Chinese population in Cambodia rose from 80,000 in 2013 to a quarter million in just six years, with 80 percent of them living in Sihanoukville. But it isn't simply Chinese entrepreneurs who are establishing themselves there; they have been joined by criminal organizations that are rooted in the Chinese mainland:

> Most of the criminal enterprises in Sihanoukville relocated from mainland China after the Chinese government adopted a draconian national security law that sought to crack down on criminal syndicates and gangsters. With its weak law enforcement, Sihanoukville became a safe haven in which these non-state actors could thrive.
>
> (Rim 2022)

As can be imagined, there have been a number of negative effects brought on by a situation in which the Chinese now make up 20 percent of the port city's population, made even more significant by the asymmetries of income favoring the Chinese in terms of economic and political influence. Social cleavages between the Chinese haves and the Cambodian have-nots have led to increasing tensions that the government seems unwilling or unable to quell. It has also led to a reinforcement of Cambodian leader Hun Sen's well-established authoritarian tendencies. And the kind of dependency that is likely to result is one that a small, vulnerable country like Cambodia cannot control like it had in the past (Mertha 2014).

In 2022, reports began to circulate that things had taken an even darker turn. Chinese-owned and -operated call centers based in Cambodia had transformed residential apartment complexes into heavily guarded and barbed-wired detention centers for indentured servants made up from unwitting victims recruited from China, Taiwan, Malaysia, Vietnam, Thailand, and elsewhere. These people were trained to operate global Internet financial scams from their cramped apartments and held indefinitely and incommunicado until a lucky few were able to escape and tell their stories.

When contacted, the Chinese Embassy in Phnom Penh claimed ignorance, which, while disingenuous, was also likely to be at least partially true, as many of these operations were established and continued far outside the established channels of diplomatic communication and/or fell through the cracks of China's political landscape. Stories of such forms of gangsterism are not uncommon in China and in locations on its periphery (like Hong Kong and Macau). The Cambodian experience demonstrates that BRI has facilitated opportunities to export these networks and project them ever further from their original source (Ye Yuan 2022; Pedroletti 2022; Yang Mei 2022). Human trafficking originating from China has mushroomed in Southeast Asia more generally (Podkul and Liu 2022).

Conclusion

To borrow a distinction from Charles Lindblom (1977) between "thumbs" and "fingers" in explaining political institutions, recasting the target of inquiry, the argument I have made in this chapter lacks the precision as well as the determinacy that a "fingers"-based approach promises. But given the open-endedness of the empirical phenomena under review, phenomena that are imprecise, irregular, unpredictable, and otherwise stochastic – by their very nature – a "thumb"-like framework is a better fit than is a "finger"-like theory or set of hypotheses. The point here is precisely that China's international behavior, when taken to include subnational actors operating abroad, is by its very nature unpredictable. What is important is such unpredictability is not a strategic master plan of nine-dimensional chess by foreign policy elites in Beijing, but rather the result of China's rough-and-tumble domestic political ecosystem being internationalized, as it extends beyond the water's edge and is grafted onto and allowed to shape politics on a global scale.

This has implications for the way in which we must study China in the present day as well as highlighting the importance of the assumptions we make about China in the policy world. In the case of scholarship, this creates a challenge for the study of China as it lays bare the artificiality of the sub-disciplinary distinctions between comparative politics and international relations. Scholars of Chinese domestic politics, that is, through the lens of comparative politics, must now grapple with an ever-complex reality in China where incentives, opportunities, sanctions, and institutional pathologies have an international dimension that is no longer sufficient to relegate to the periphery of one's argument or analytical approach. For the international relations scholar, it requires eschewing theoretical elegance by delving into the messy realm of domestic political structures and processes in China and examining how they can and do work at cross purposes with the best-laid plans of foreign policy elites in Beijing and global structural shifts. Much like Kenneth Waltz (1979)'s protestations that he was looking at *balancing*, not actual, historical *balances* of power, we must be content with how Chinese foreign policy behavior can upset the apple cart in a somewhat less-than-satisfying degree of determinacy.

For policymakers, looking at China's international behavior through the framework suggested here complicates the assumptions of intentionality that we ascribe to Beijing. Of course, intentions, insofar as they match up to goals, are the drivers of politics. But the question becomes: *whose* intentions? How do the intentions of various national and subnational actors reinforce or alternatively undermine one another, how do they work at cross-purposes and even undermine each other, and how much of what Chinese actors do in these target countries is not only in opposition to Beijing's international relations policy goals but is invisible to the elites charged with the actual crafting of China's foreign policy? Finally, what does such a framework tell us about Chinese state capacity? In this reading, China appears less than an international juggernaut and more like a Hobbesian Leviathan scaled up to the global level, suggesting that Xi is either unwilling or unable to alter this domestic fragmentation as it spills out beyond China's water's edge.

Notes

1 Interview Tashkent, February 22, 2023.
2 For a useful guide on the "paradiplomatic turn" in a non-China context, see Hess and Aidoo (2016)
3 This is an insight I developed in my work on China's foreign assistance to Democratic Kampuchea in the 1970s. See Mertha (2014) and Mertha (2015).
4 Johnson et al. (2017); and Alice Miller, China Leadership Monitor.
5 Gill and Reilly (2007); see also Garcia and Guerreiro (2022).
6 Tim Summers sees Yunnan as an "influencer" rather than as a spoiler. See Summers (2021).
7 www.nytimes.com/2018/06/25/world/asia/china-sri-lanka-port.html.
8 Grimsditch (2015).
9 According to Jones and Zou, "CPI's claims were not checked despite extremely high-level political involvement in Sino-Myanmar hydropower development" (Jones and Zou 2017, 753).
10 https://thediplomat.com/2019/03/myanmars-myitsone-dam-dilemma/.
11 "Galamsey, derived from the phrase "gather them and sell," is a local Ghanaian parlance that means illegal small-scale, gold mining in Ghana. Such workers are known as galamseyers or *orpailleurs* in neighboring Francophone nations. Galamseyers are people who perform illegal gold mining independent of mining companies, digging small working pits, tunnels, and sluices by hand" https://en.wikipedia.org/wiki/Galamsey.
12 Li (2019). On Yunnan province's role in BRI, see Summers (2021). On Hainan Province's influence of foreign policy, see Audrye Wong (2018).
13 Lampton et al. (2020); See also Nakashima and Cadell (2022).

References

Abi-Habib, Maria. 2018. "How China Got Sri Lanka to Cough Up a Port." *New York Times*. June 25. www.nytimes.com/2018/06/25/world/asia/china-sri-lanka-port.html.
Al-Aameri, Nour, Lingxiao Fu, Nicole Garcia, Ryan Mak, Caitlin McGill, Amanda Reynolds, and Lucas Vinze. 2012. "Environmental Impacts of China Outward Foreign Direct Investment: Case Studies in Latin America, Mongolia, Myanmar, and Zambia." Master of International Affairs (MIA) Capstones. Texas A&M University George Bush School of Government and Public Service. https://oaktrust.library.tamu.edu/handle/1969.1/152080.
Alden, Chris, and Christina Alves. 2008. "History & Identity in the Construction of China's Africa Policy." *Review of African Political Economy* 35(115): 43–58. https://doi.org/10.1080/03056240802011436.
Alon, Titan. 2010. "Institutional Analysis and the Determinants of Chinese FDI." *Multinational Business Review* 18(3): 1–24. https://doi.org/10.1108/1525383X201000013.
Bosshard, Peter. 2008. "China's Environmental Footprint in Africa." SAIS Working Papers in African Studies. https://sais.jhu.edu/sites/default/files/China%27s-Environmental-Footprint-in-Africa.pdf.
Bradsher, Keith. 2023. "After Doling Out Huge Loans, China Is Now Bailing Out Countries." *New York Times*. March 27. www.nytimes.com/2023/03/27/business/china-loans-bailouts-debt.html#:~:text=lent%20%2468.6%20billion%20to%20countries,%2D%20and%20middle%2Dincome%20countries.
Bräutigam, Deborah A., and Yufan Huang. 2023. "Integrating China into Multilateral Debt Relief: Progress and Problems in the G20 DSSI." China Africa Research Initiative. Briefing Paper No. 9, April. www.econstor.eu/handle/10419/271579.
Bräutigam, Deborah A., and Xiaoyang Tang. 2009. "China's Engagement in African Agriculture: 'Down to the Countryside'." *The China Quarterly* 199: 686–706.
Bräutigam, Deborah A., and Xiaoyang Tang. 2011. "China's Investment in Africa's Special Economic Zones." In *Special Economic Zones: Progress, Emerging Challenges,*

and Future Directions, eds. T. Farole and G. Akinci. Washington, DC: The World Bank. https://deborahbrautigam.files.wordpress.com/2013/04/2011-brautigam-chinese-investment-in-special-economic-zones.pdf.

Brenner, David. 2015. "Ashes of Co-Optation: From Armed Group Fragmentation to the Rebuilding of Popular Insurgency in Myanmar." *Conflict, Security & Development* 15(4): 337–358.

Brødsgaard, Kjeld Erik. 2002. "Institutional Reform and the Bianzhi System in China." *The China Quarterly* 170: 361–386.

Chan, D. S. W. 2017. "Asymmetric Bargaining between Myanmar and China in the Myitsone Dam Controversy: Social Opposition Akin to David's Stone against Goliath." *The Pacific Review* 30(5): 674–691.

Cheung, Yin-Wong, and Xingwang Qian. 2009. "The Empirics of China's Outward Direct Investment." CESifo Working Paper, No. 2621, Center for Economic Studies and Sifo Institute (CESifo), Munich.

Chinese Communist Party. 2013. "中共中央关于全面深化改革若干重大问题的决定" [Decision of the Central Committee of the Communist Party of China on Some Major Issues Concerning Comprehensively Deepening the Reform]. November 5. www.gov.cn/jrzg/2013-11/15/content_2528179.htm.

Chu, Daye. 2014. "Billionaire Confident on Future 278-km Canal." *Global Times*. August 5. www.globaltimes.cn/content/874471.shtml.

Cissé, Daouda. 2012. "Chinese Telecom Companies Foray into Africa." *African East Asian Affairs 69: The second wave of Chinese investment in Africa – Agriculture and the Service Sector*. 16–22. https://doi.org/10.7552/69-0-94.

Corkin, Lucy, Christopher Burke, and Martyn Davies. 2008. "China's Role in the Development of Africa's Infrastructure." SAIS Working Papers in African Studies. https://sais.jhu.edu/sites/default/files/China%27s-Role-in-the-Development-of-Africa%27s-Infrastructure.pdf.

Dalton, Matthew. 2014. "Telecom Deal by China's ZTE, Huawei in Ethiopia Faces Criticism." *Wall Street Journal*, January 6. www.wsj.com/articles/SB10001424052702303653004579212092223818288.

Deng, Ping. 2004. "Outward Investment by Chinese MNCs: Motivations and Implications." *Business Horizons* 47(3): 8–16. https://doi.org/10.1016/S0007-6813(04)00023-0.

Deutsch, James. 2010. "Partnering with SINOPEC in Loango National Park, Gabon." Wildlife Conservation Society. https://abcg.org/files/documents/0e7e53d4-982a-43f3-b652-3029f0f8fe8a.pdf.

Dimitrov, Martin. 2022. *Dictatorship and Information: Authoritarian Regime Resilience in Communist Europe and China*. New York: Oxford University Press.

Ellis-Petersen, Hannah. 2018. "'No Cambodia Left': How Chinese Money Is Changing Sihanoukville." *Guardian*. July 31. www.theguardian.com/cities/2018/jul/31/no-cambodia-left-chinese-money-changing-sihanoukville.

Gagliardone, Iginio, and Sam Geall. 2014. "China in Africa's Media and Telecommunications: Cooperation, Connectivity and Control." The Norwegian Peacebuilding Resource Centre. www.files.ethz.ch/isn/179376/7880fd6b12b93bdd18eddcbd4f4e207f.pdf.

Gallagher, Kevin. 2010. "China and the Future of Latin American Industrialization." Issues in Brief 18. https://hdl.handle.net/2144/22726.

Garcia, Zenel, and Phillip Guerreiro. 2022. "Provincial Players in China's Belt and Road Initiative." Policy Forum. Asia and the Pacific Policy Society. www.policyforum.net/provincial-players-in-chinas-belt-and-road-initiative/.

Gill, Bates, and James Reilly. 2007. "The Tenuous Hold of China Inc. in Africa." *The Washington Quarterly* 30(3): 37–52. https://doi.org/10.1162/wash.2007.30.3.37.

Global Witness. 2009. "A Disharmonious Trade: China and the Continued Destruction of Burma's Northern Frontier Forests." www.globalwitness.org/en/archive/disharmonious-trade-china-and-continued-destruction-burmas-northern-frontier-forests/.

Greitens, Sheena Chestnut. April 2020. "Dealing with Demand for China's Global Surveillance Exports. Brookings. www.brookings.edu/wp-content/uploads/2020/04/FP_20200428_china_surveillance_greitens_v3.pdf.

Grimsditch, Mark. 2012. "China's Investments in Hydropower in the Mekong Region: The Kamchay Hydropower Dam, Kampot, Cambodia." World Resource Institute. https://data.opendevelopmentmyanmar.net/library_record/china-s-investments-in-hydropower-in-the-mekong-region-the-kamchay-hydropower-dam-kampot-cambodia.

Grimsditch, Mark. 2015. "The Role and Characteristics of Chinese State-Owned and Private Enterprises in Overseas Investments." *Friends of the Earth US*. 23–25.

Hess, Steve, and Richard Aidoo. 2016. "Charting the Impact of Subnational Actors in China's Foreign Relations: The 2013 Galamsey Crisis in Ghana." *Asian Survey* 56(2): 301–324. https://doi.org/10.1525/as.2016.56.2.301.

Hinkley, Bobbie. 2011. "Chinese Company Push for Western Australia Farmland." *Farm Land Grab*, August 12. www.farmlandgrab.org/post/view/19067-chinese-company-push-for-.

Huang, Xueli, and Chi Renyong. 2014. "Chinese Private Firms' Outward Foreign Direct Investment: Does Firm Ownership and Size Matter?" *Thunderbird International Business Review* 56(5): 393–406.

Inclusive Development International. August 2020. "Reassessing China's Investment Footprint in Cambodia." Briefing Paper. www.inclusivedevelopment.net/wp-content/uploads/2020/08/2020_IDI_Briefing-on-Chinas-Footprint-in-Cambodia-Update.pdf.

International Rivers. 2012. "The New Great Walls: A Guide to China's Overseas Dam Industry." https://archive.internationalrivers.org/resources/the-new-great-walls-a-guide-to-china%E2%80%99s-overseas-dam-industry-3962.

Jansson, Johanna, and Carine Kiala. 2009. "Patterns of Chinese Investment, Aid, and Trade in Mozambique." Briefing Paper by the Centre for Chinese Studies, Prepared for World Wide Fund for Nature (WWF).

Jiang, Wenran. 2009. "Fueling the Dragon: China's Rise and Its Energy and Resources Extraction in Africa." *China Quarterly* 199: 585–609. https://doi.org/10.1017/S0305741009990117.

Johnson, Christopher K., Scott Kennedy, and Mingda Qiu. 2017. "Xi's Signature Governance Innovation: The Rise of Leading Small Groups." www.csis.org/analysis/xis-signature-governance-innovation-rise-leading-small-groups.

Jones, Lee, and Yizheng Zou. 2017. "Rethinking the Role of State-Owned Enterprises in China's Rise." *New Political Economy* 22(6): 743–760. https://doi.org/10.1080/135634 67.2017.1321625.

Kong, Bo. 2011. "China's Quest for Oil in Africa Revisited." SAIS Working Papers in African Studies. https://sais.jhu.edu/sites/default/files/BoKongWP1-11_1.pdf.

Konjin, Peter. 2014. "Chinese Resources-for-Infrastructure (R4I) Swaps: An Escape from the Resource Curse?" South African Institute for International Affairs. www.africaportal.org/publications/chinese-resources-for-infrastructure-r4i-swaps-an-escape-from-the-resource-curse/.

Kubny, Julia, and Hinrich Voss. 2010. "The Impact of Chinese Outward Investment: Evidence from Cambodia and Vietnam." Deutsches Institut für Entwicklungspolitik (DIE) Discussion Paper 16. www.econstor.eu/bitstream/10419/199351/1/die-dp-2010-16.pdf.

Lampton, David M. 1988. *Paths to Power: Elite Mobility in Contemporary China*. Ann Arbor, MI: University of Michigan Press.

Lampton, David M., Selina Ho, and Cheng-Chwee Kuik. 2020. *Rivers of Iron: Railroads and Chinese Power in Southeast Asia*. Berkeley, CA: University of California Press.

Li, Mingjiang. 2019. "China's Economic Power in Asia: The Belt and Road Initiative and the Local Guangxi Government's Role." *Asian Perspective* 43(2): 273–295.

Li, Yuan. 2023. "China's Cities Are Buried in Debt, But They Keep Shoveling It On." *New York Times*. March 28. www.nytimes.com/2023/03/28/business/china-local-finances-debt.html#:~:text=China%20has%20long%20pursued%20growth,spending%20—%20and%20cutting%20essential%20services.

Liang, Hao, Bing Ren, and Sunny Li Sun. 2014. "An Anatomy of State Control in the Globalization of State-Owned Enterprises." *Journal of International Business Studies* 46: 223–240.

Lieberthal, Kenneth. 1996. *Governing China: From Revolution through Reform*. New York, NY: Norton.

Lieberthal, Kenneth, and Michel Oksenberg. 1988. *Policy Making in China*. Princeton, NJ: Princeton University Press.

Lindblom, Charles E. 1977. *Politics and Markets: The World's Political-Economic Systems*. New York, NY: Basic Books.

Liu, Xiaohui, Jiangyong Lu, and Amon Chizema. 2014. "Top Executive Compensation, Regional Institutions and Chinese OFDI." *Journal of World Business* 49(1): 143–155.

Lombard, Louisa. 2006. "Africa's China Card." *Foreign Policy*. April 11. https://foreignpolicy.com/2006/04/11/africas-china-card/.

Luo, Yadong, Qiuzhi Xue, and Binjie Han. 2010. "How Emerging Market Governments Promote Outward FDI: Experience from China." *Journal of World Business* 45(1): 68–79.

Luo, Yadong, Hongxin Zhao, Yagang Wang, and Youmin Xi. 2011. "Venturing Abroad by Emerging Market Enterprises: A Test of Dual Strategic Intents." *Management International Review* 51(4): 433–459.

Marshall, Andrea. 2011. "China's Mighty Telecom Footprint in Africa." New Security Learning. https://ela-newsportal.com/china's-mighty-telecom-footprint-in-africa/.

Martínez Rivera, Sergio. 2013. "China y América Latina y el Caribe: una visión ambiental heterodoxa de su intercambio comercial." En, Yolanda Trápaga (coordinadora). América Latina y El Caribe – China. Recursos Naturales y Medio Ambiente. RED ALC-CHINA, UDUAL, UNAM, Cechimex, México, 139–154.

Mei, Yang. 2022. "柬埔寨西港：中国犯罪集团的乐园" (Sihanoukville, Cambodia: The Paradise for Chinese Organized Crime Groups). Radio France Internationale. January 17. www.rfi.fr/cn/%E4%B8%AD%E5%9B%BD/20220117-%E6%9F%AC%E5%9F%94%E5%AF%A8%E8%A5%BF%E6%B8%AF-%E4%B8%AD%E5%9B%BD%E7%8A%AF%E7%BD%AA%E9%9B%86%E5%9B%A2%E7%9A%84%E4%B9%90%E5%9B%AD.

Meidan, Michal, Philip Andrews-Speed, and Ma Xin. 2009. "Shaping China's Energy Policy: Actors and Processes." *Journal of Contemporary China* 18(61): 591–616. https://doi.org/10.1080/10670560903033885.

Mertha, Andrew. 2008. *China's Water Warriors: Citizen Action and Policy Change*. Ithaca, NY: Cornell University Press.

Mertha, Andrew. 2014. *Brothers in Arms: Chinese Aid to the Khmer Rouge, 1975–1979*. Ithaca, NY: Cornell University Press.

Mertha, Andrew. 2015. "International Disorganization: Fragmentation and Foreign Policy in Sino-Cambodian Relations, 1975–1979." *Issues & Studies* 51(1): 129–163.

Miller, Matthew. 2014. "China's 'Ordinary' Billionaire behind Grand Nicaragua Canal Plan." Reuters. May 4. www.reuters.com/article/us-china-canal-insight-idUSBREA4309E20140504.

Ministry of Commerce (MOFCOM). 2010. "对外投资合作境外安全风险预警和信息通报制度" [Notice of the Ministry of Commerce on Issuing the Overseas Security Risk Early Warning and Information Release System of Foreign Investment Cooperation]. http://images.mofcom.gov.cn/hzs/accessory/201009/1283734181713.pdf.

Mol, Arthur P. 2011. "China's Ascent and Africa's Environment." *Global Environmental Change* 21(3): 785–794.

Moss, Todd, and Sarah Rose. 2006. "China ExIm Bank and Africa: New Lending, New Challenges." Center for Global Development. www.files.ethz.ch/isn/38231/2006_11_06.pdf.

Munson, Patrick, and Ronghui Zheng. 2012. "Feeding the Dragon: Managing Chinese Resource Acquisition in Africa." USAID Asia, Vermont Law School, US-China Partnership for Environmental Law.

Nakashima, Ellen, and Cate Cadell. 2022. "China Secretly Building Naval Facility in Cambodia, Western Officials Say." *Washington Post*. June 6. www.washingtonpost.com/national-security/2022/06/06/cambodia-china-navy-base-ream/.

Onphanhdala, Phanhpakit, and Terukazu Suruga. 2013. "Chinese Outward FDI in Agriculture and Rural Development: Evidence from Northern Laos." GSICS Working Paper Series 25. https://d1wqtxts1xzle7.cloudfront.net/75939208/2013-25-libre.pdf?1638966429=&response-content-disposition=inline%3B+filename%3DChinese_Outward_FDI_in_Agriculture_and

_R.pdf&Expires=1702485283&Signature=eJp4hQMUN0p6MSJCrbmaO~JoTQBSwuv KQjvjnmojmRgtt3dI9ABMUhxW1ATRFrQ~deZVe52GwH27Ijxx8xYTmPjPr3dPZAcU PWYdCqWhwO42wPD8~1JnjaVDAT4ImPKrP9r17RLygaCnxbf5t00SJzD6hgrVX69N-WZsr4psYmvUP07knWW3-Pdo9xhSkAJNBkGxxYSVPKsRLK7MC-v~KWdpY0f6Ak AuF~n3ZBIWsgQFSDGL18foHhtQdnJq7EUe4iShNrjUkrq~~vaOeJwpwk7KeRIR-UutD-3NP4N2jTKoDjf4mdXf7WgHcaSdSZEhhyAI53QbDgTS1OvWzFKsJ8Fw__&Key-Pair-Id=APKAJLOHF5GGSLRBV4ZA.

Pedroletti, Brice. 2022. "The 'Forbidden Cities' of Chinese Organized Crime in Sihanoukville, Cambodia." *Le Monde*. March 31. www.lemonde.fr/en/international/article/2022/03/31/the-forbidden-cities-of-chinese-organized-crime-in-sihanoukville-cambodia_5979499_4.html.

Peh, Kelvin H. S., and Jonathan Eyal. 2010. "Unveiling China's Impact on African Environment." *Energy Policy* 38(8): 4729–4730.

Podkul, Cezary, and Cindy Liu. 2022. "China Crime Gangs Use Cyber Slaves across SE Asia." *Asia Times*. September 14. https://asiatimes.com/2022/09/china-crime-gangs-use-cyberslaves-across-se-asia/#:~:text=Phony%20job%20ads%20lure%20them,new%20form%20of%20human%20trafficking.

Rim, Sokvy. 2022. "The Social Costs of Chinese Transnational Crime in Sihanoukville." *The Diplomat*. July 5. https://thediplomat.com/2022/07/the-social-costs-of-chinese-transnational-crime-in-sihanoukville/.

Roque, Paula. 2009. "China in Mozambique: A Cautious Approach Country Case Study." South African Institute of International Affairs Occasional Paper 23. https://saiia.org.za/research/china-in-mozambique-a-cautious-approach/.

Sautman, Barry, and Yan Hairong. 2009. "Trade, Investment, Power and the China-in-Africa Discourse." *The Asia-Pacific Journal* 7(52). https://apjjf.org/-Barry-Sautman/3278/article.html.

Sauvant, Karl P., Wolfgang A. Maschek, and Geraldine McAllister. 2010. "Foreign Direct Investment by Emerging Market Multinational Enterprises, the Impact of the Financial Crisis and Recession and Challenges Ahead." In *Foreign Direct Investment from Emerging Markets: The Challenges Ahead*, eds. Karl P. Sauvant, Geraldine McAllister, and Wolfgang Maschek. New York, NY: Palgrave Macmillan, 3–29.

Schmidt, Blake. "Ex-Billionaire Abandons Office in Prime Hong Kong Tower." *Bloomberg*. April 26, 2018. www.bloomberg.com/news/articles/2018-04-26/nicaragua-canal-builder-abandons-office-in-prime-hong-kong-tower?leadSource=uverify%20wall.

Shen, Xiaofeng. 2015. "Private Chinese Investment in Africa: Myths and Realities." *Development Policy Review* 33(1). https://doi.org/10.1111/dpr.12093.

Song, Ligang, Jidong Yang, and Yongsheng Zhang. 2011. "State-Owned Enterprises' Outward Investment and the Structural Reform in China." *Special Issue of China and World Economy* 19(4): 38–53. https://doi.org/10.1111/j.1749-124X.2011.01249.x.

Summers, Tim. 2021. "The Belt and Road Initiative in Southwest China: Responses from Yunnan Province." *The Pacific Review* 34(2): 206–229. https://doi.org/10.1080/09512748.2019.1653956.

Taylor, Ian. 2007. "China's Environmental Footprint in Africa." *China Dialogue*. https://chinadialogue.net/en/pollution/741-china-s-environmental-footprint-in-africa/.

UNCTAD. 2013. "World Investment Report 2013." New York; Geneva: UNCTAD. https://unctad.org/system/files/official-document/wir2013_en.pdf.

Urban, Frauke, Johan Nordensvärd, Deepika Khatri, and Yu Wang. 2013. "An Analysis of China's Investment in the Hydropower Sector in the Greater Mekong Sub-Region." *Environment, Development and Sustainability* 15: 301–324. https://doi.org/10.1007/s10668-012-9415-z.

Validakis, Vicky. 2014. "400 People March in Protest against Shenhua's Watermark Coal Project." *Mining Australia*, June 27. www.australianmining.com.au/news/400-people-march-in-protest-against-shenhuas-watermark-coal-project-2/.

Van Dijk, Meine Pieter. 2009. "Introduction: Objectives of and Instruments for China's New Presence in Africa." In *The New Presence of China in Africa*, ed. Meine Pieter Van Dijk. Amsterdam: Amsterdam University Press, 9–30.

Waltz, Kenneth. 1979. *Theory of International Politics*. New York, NY: McGraw-Hill.

Wang, Chengqi, Junjie Hong, Mario Kafouros, and Mike Wright. 2012. "Exploring the Role of Government Involvement in Outward FDI from Emerging Economies." *Journal of International Business Studies* 43: 655–676.

Wang, Mark Yaolin. 2002. "The Motivations behind Chinese Government-Initiated Industrial Investments Overseas." *Pacific Affairs* 75(2): 187–206.

Warner, Malcolm, Ng Sek Hong, and Xu Xiaojun. 2004. "Late Development Experience and the Evolution of Transnational Firms in the People's Republic of China." *Asia Pacific Business Review* 10(3/4): 324–345.

Wei, Tian, Jeremy Clegg, and Lei Ma. 2015. "The Conscious and Unconscious Facilitating Role of the Chinese Government in Shaping the Internationalization of Chinese MNCs." *International Business Review* 24(2): 331–343.

Wong, Audrye. 2018. "More Than Peripheral: How Provinces Influence China's Foreign Policy." *The China Quarterly* 235: 735–757.

Yang, Xiaohua, and Clyde D. Stoltenberg. 2014. "A Review of Institutional Influences on the Rise of Made-in-China Multinationals." *International Journal of Emerging Markets* 9(2): 162–180. https://doi.org/10.1108/IJoEM-09-2012-0095.

Ye, Min. 2019. "Fragmentation and Mobilization: Domestic Politics of the Belt and Road in China." *Journal of Contemporary China* 28(119): 696–711.

Ye, Yuan. 2022. "In Cambodia, a Network Rescuing Trafficked Chinese Teens Is Unraveling." *Sixth Tone*. July 22. www.sixthtone.com/news/1010752/in-cambodia%2C-a-network-rescuing-trafficked-chinese-teens-is-unraveling.

Yeung, Henry Wai-chung, and Weidong Liu. 2008. "Globalizing China: The Rise of Mainland Firms in the Global Economy." *Eurasian Geography and Economics* 49(1): 57–86. https://doi.org/10.2747/1539-7216.49.1.57.

Yiu, Daphne W., Chung Ming Lau, and Garry D. Bruton. 2007. "International Venturing by Emerging Economy Firms: The Effects of Firm Capabilities, Home Country Networks, and Corporate Entrepreneurship." *Journal of International Business Studies* 38: 519–540.

Zadek, Simon, Chen Xiaohong, Li Zhaoxi, Jia Tao, Zhou Yan, Kelly Yu, Maya Forstater, and Guy Morgan. 2009. Originally published "Responsible Business in Africa: Chinese Business Leaders' Perspectives on Performance and Enhancement Opportunities." Account-Ability and the Enterprise Research Institute, Development Research Centre of the State Council of P.R. China (DRC-ERI), November. Corporate Social Responsibility Initiative Working Paper No. 54. Cambridge, MA: John F. Kennedy School of Government, Harvard University.

Zhang, Denghua, and Graeme Smith. 2017. "China's Foreign Aid System: Structure, Agencies, and Identities." *Third World Quarterly* 38(10): 2330–2346.

11 Chinese Foreign Policy Under Xi Jinping

June Teufel Dreyer

While Xi Jinping is often credited with ushering in China's assertive foreign policy, it did not in fact begin with him. Some have sought to trace the policy and its implied challenge to the liberal internationalist world order back to Mao Zedong's 1949 declaration that "China has stood up," though it is more likely that the chairman meant simply that under communism the newly founded People's Republic of China (PRC) had ended its period of weakness and humiliation by foreign powers. Although Mao implicitly rejected the Westphalian concept of the equality of sovereign states as a capitalist deception, both his words and his actions in the early 1950s indicate a vision of the advent of world communism directed by the Soviet Union. In any case, China, though hardly powerless, had only just emerged from decades of war both external against Japan and domestically against the Chinese Nationalists, and was not strong enough to wage a sustained challenge to the prevailing world order.

More plausible as an antecedent to Xi's current challenge would be Deng Xiaoping as Mao's unofficial successor, advising in 1990 that China "hide our capabilities and bide our time," with the implication that China's strength would in time increase to the point where it could challenge that system. When this time occurred would, however, be contested. After the U.S. apparently accidentally bombed the PRC's embassy in Belgrade in 1999, some Chinese felt that the time had come. Demands for militant counteraction were vociferous; according to the Hong Kong press, there had been anti-American protests against U.S./NATO actions against the former Republic of Yugoslavia (FRY) at military academies across China even before the attack.[1] These became more prominent thereafter.[2]

Although the U.S. embassy in Beijing was quickly besieged by rock-throwing mobs that some believed had been officially encouraged, there were nonetheless evident efforts to restrain the more militant from taking concrete action. Jiang Zemin as Chinese president, party leader and head of the Central Military Commission, appears to have been at the forefront of those favoring restraint. Obviously choosing his words carefully so as not to invite criticisms of cowardice from his domestic enemies, Jiang assured an enlarged meeting of the Politburo's Standing Committee that party and government would never barter away principles. While he made no explicit linkage between the consequences of a militantly anti-U.S.

DOI: 10.4324/9781003257943-12

policy and China's bid to enter the World Trade Organization, Jiang stressed that it was important to continue negotiations on accession to the WTO:

> Our current struggle against the U.S.-led NATO is unlikely to come to a successful end within a short period time, for the United States will continue to resort to sophistry concerning its bombing of the Chinese Embassy in the FRY and . . . we must further retain our rights for taking corresponding actions . . . We must carry out our struggle against hegemonism and power politics, yet we cannot close our door and refuse to deal with certain western countries, like the United States.
>
> Although we know perfectly well that the wolf is going to attack man, we still need to deal with the wolf. That is, we must 'dance with the wolf.' This is the reality we must face and the diplomatic strategy we must adopt. We should develop ourselves and enhance the comprehensive national strength of our country under the condition of simultaneously fighting against and having dealings with hegemonism and power politics.[3]

Jiang vowed to discuss the matter with U.S. President Clinton at an appropriate time.

How conscious this strategy of incrementally increasing power until the proper time for dominance arrived is a matter of conjecture, with some observers seeing a process of experimentation and adjustment to the shifting tide of international forces and others as part of a master plan. Rush Doshi, surely the most articulate exemplar of the latter, sees the strategy of a rising power, in this case China, to displace a hegemon, i.e., the United States, as proceeding in stages: in the first, it is necessary to blunt the hegemon's exercise of control over oneself, and in the second to build forms of control over others. Until the rising power has first blunted the hegemon, efforts to build order are likely to be futile and easily opposed. Having accomplished this, the challenging power must then build forms of control over others, securing the deference of other states through coercive threats, consensual inducements, or rightful legitimacy. After achieving a satisfactory degree of blunting and building in its home region, the challenging power can turn confidently to the third strategy: global expansion. This involves both blunting and building at the global level to displace the hegemon from international leadership.[4]

Whether it was as well thought out as Doshi's paradigm implies, China was by the end of the first decade of the twenty-first century clearly in a position to begin stage three. Doshi traces its inception not to Xi Jinping's ascendance to power but to the early stages of the global financial crisis and U.S. setbacks in Iraq. The former seemed to delegitimize the primacy of American financial capital, the latter to cast doubt on the efficacy of its military power. Doshi points out that although Xi Jinping's predecessor, Hu Jintao, has been regarded as a weak leader, Hu nonetheless introduced stronger language to the political discourse by stating that multipolarity was irreversible and implying that the unipolarity of the United States was fast waning.[5] Hu's words notwithstanding, the concept of multipolarity itself is perhaps better understood as code for weakening U.S. hegemony in the guise of a group effort that never really gained momentum.

Although China did not escape the effects of the financial crisis, its economy continued to grow, as did its military capabilities and its international assertiveness. By 2010, U.S. military leaders were commenting on the increased outspokenness of their Chinese counterparts in international fora.[6]

Xi's ascension to power in 2013 left no doubt that he would continue, and even accelerate, this activist foreign policy.[7] Among other manifestations thereof were an astonishing number of trips abroad, totaling a month each year. In contrast to Hu Jintao, who visited just seven countries in his decade in office, Xi Jinping visited 24 countries in his first four years as leader, including attending nine international conferences.[8] While not explicitly announcing a Xi doctrine of foreign policy, recurrent themes in his speeches, dutifully repeated by the PRC's media, were cooperation for mutual benefit, win-win partnerships, connectivity, and the creation of a community of shared destiny. Sometimes, depending on the venue, this appeared to mean human destiny and sometimes Asian destiny. References to peace and harmony did not, however, preclude the simultaneous rapid expansion of the PRC's military capabilities.

In the following year, Xi proposed a comprehensive national security concept and created a new party entity, the Central National Security Commission, with himself as chair to put the concept into practice. In contrast to America's similarly named National Security Council, which is exclusively devoted to international issues, Xi announced that China's NSC would have broad responsibility for internal matters, including the construction of the rule of law and making it clear that a paramount concern would be social stability, for "only when the nation is safe and *society is stable* can reform and development constantly advance" (italics added).[9] Xi, as other leaders before him have done, tends to conflate internal stability with international issues, frequently implying, implicitly or explicitly, that foreign forces are behind domestic unrest.

In his keynote speech to the Boao Forum in April 2022 Xi introduced a Global Security Concept 2022 (*quanqiu anquan changyi* 全球安全倡议), citing an unnamed ancient Chinese philosopher's observation that "stability brings a country prosperity while instability leads a country to poverty," adding that security is the precondition for development and a Cold War mentality can only wreck global peace.[10]

Xi's Economic Foreign Policy

Economically, the vehicle for achieving these lofty goals was to be One Belt, One Road (OBOR), subsequently renamed the Belt and Road Initiative (BRI). Announced in 2013 soon after he assumed control of the party and state hierarchies, BRI was a fanciful adaption of the ancient silk routes through Central Asia, in this case comprising both a land route through Asia to Europe and a globe-girdling maritime route. In time, a polar silk road and an undersea silk road, the former to take advantage of melting polar ice that would allow for shorter shipping routes and the latter for submerged communications cables, would be added as well. Xi stressed that the initiative would be based on common interests, a win-win venture for the benefit of all in contrast to the Western focus on values.

Premised on the assumption that what kept less developed states less developed was a lack of infrastructure, Chinese expertise and capital would provide the infrastructure. The major vehicle to supply these would be a new bank, the Asian Infrastructure Investment Bank (AIIB), headquartered in Beijing and in which Beijing would be the chief investor. Although the original intent seems to have been as a vehicle for developing countries, the AIIB now has 105 members and prospective members, including many developed states. Despite China declaring that the intent of the AIIB was to supplement rather than supplant traditional international institutions, it is widely considered a rival to the IMF, World Bank, and Asian Development Bank. A BRICS bank intended for Brazil, Russia, India, China, and South Africa and headquartered in Shanghai followed a year later.

In keeping with Xi's avowed commitment to multilateralism, China was active in numerous international and regional fora, and most conspicuously in the United Nations where it was able to place its nationals as heads of more of the UN's specialized agencies than any other country. There they, and nationals of other countries who were recipients of Beijing's generosity, worked to build support for the PRC's positions. This did not always redound to China's credit, or to that of the agencies involved. After maneuvering to get Vice-Minister of Public Security Meng Hongwei appointed head of Interpol in 2016, he was arrested by Chinese authorities two years later and convicted of misusing his position to take over two million dollars in bribes. Meng is currently serving a 13 ½ year prison sentence.[11] The head of the World Health Organization, an Ethiopian national whose country has been a major recipient of Chinese largesse, was widely criticized for stating that there was "no clear evidence of human-to-human transmission" of the coronavirus even as the number of cases was increasing exponentially.[12]

Under Xi, China has also engaged other countries regionally, though the PRC had interacted with several of them well before Xi came to power. China has been a full dialogue partner of the Association of Southeast Asian Nations since 1996 and has been able to use that status to advance China's positions (see section on ASEAN). FOCAC, the Forum on China-Africa Cooperation, was founded in 2000 and has been described as a sometimes-over-the-top spectacle that serves to reinforce China's image of an emerging commercial and diplomatic power in Africa. Seeking to expand China's influence in Eastern Europe, the 16 + 1, later 17 + 1, and now once again 16 + 1 mechanism was founded in 2012. Lastly, signaling Xi's desire to expand China's interests into an area the United States has traditionally regarded as its back yard, the first meeting of the China-CELAC (Community of Latin American and Caribbean States) was held in Beijing in 2015 to push forward "healthy, stable, and sustainable development of [the] China-CELAC relationship" and, like FOCAC, alternates venues among member countries every three years.[13]

The Iron Hand Inside the Velvet Glove

At the same time, Xi implemented sweeping changes in the People's Liberation Army (PLA) to improve its efficiency in combat and, not coincidentally, make it more responsive to the central government, i.e., to Xi himself. These occurred in tandem with the development and deployment of increasingly sophisticated weapons. The navy has launched its third aircraft carrier, this latest featuring state-of-the-art catapults that allow heavier payloads to take off from its decks, and has successfully tested hypersonic weapons that can cover long distances so quickly that the target is unable to defend against them. State media frequently declaim that, although it would prefer peace, China will not hesitate to use force if its red lines, never explicitly defined, are crossed.[14] In 2017, China gained its first overseas military base in strategically located Djibouti, which enhances the PRC's power projection capabilities. Although described by state media as a logistics base meant to support China's part in United Nations Peacekeeping Operations in the area, U.S. military analysts assess that the Djibouti base is now large enough to host aircraft carriers.[15]

Although China denies intent to build naval bases, it is assembling a network of overseas port facilities. Opinion is divided as to whether the motive is to protect its expanding global interests, or is indicating an intent to extend its worldwide military control while moving slowly to avoid provoking too much of a reaction.[16] While never publicly disavowing some of his predecessors' professed aim of creating a multipolar world in which centers such as Europe, Latin America, and Africa are able to counter the power of the American unipole, Xi appears to see the world as a series of interconnected strategic points that can be folded into a China-directed global network.

Under Xi, there has been increasing attention paid to the psychological aspects of war, to attack the enemy's will to resist as opposed to physically destroying them. So-called cognitive warfare has entailed collecting a large amount of detailed personal information on government officials and ordinary citizens and the use of digital means to try to influence elections.[17]

Chinese Foreign Relations in the First Decade of Xi's Reign

It is difficult to assess the strengths and weaknesses of an ongoing scenario, though clearly there have been many setbacks. While some countries declare themselves very pleased with the new railroads and facilities they owe to Chinese help, there are serious complaints from many areas of the world. Not all agreements made result in the promised funding, or the results are unsatisfactory but still must be paid for. Ports can help provide commercial opportunities for developed countries but could also serve as strategic assets for the Chinese military. Abrasive "wolf warrior" diplomacy has alienated many countries, as have United Front tactics aimed at securing support for Beijing's positions whether legally or illegally.

Perhaps surprisingly, some of the complaints came from within the PRC. A study by two Chinese scholars found that the BRI's largesse, coinciding as it has with China's economic slowdown, decreasing fiscal income, and aging population, has resulted in citizens becoming critical of party and government measures that provide aid and investment to foreign countries or offer special privileges to certain groups. Seeing extensive funding being delivered to foreign countries while they perceive their own economic conditions stagnating or deteriorating has engendered resentment.[18]

Will participation in the BRI benefit China but not the participating countries? Is the ultimate aim truly a win-win cooperative effort or an effort to establish China as the international hegemon – if the Silk Roads are fanciful recreations of an imagined past, could not the partnership for mutual benefit be to create Chinese dominance in the style of the comparably creatively imagined *tianxia*, in which the emperor ruled all under heaven?

Since Xi Jinping's policies have impacted different countries in different ways, a brief overview of a selection[19] of these is in order.

Russia

Xi inherited Russian distrust of China dating back to the days of the Willy-Nicky letters of the late nineteenth century, in which the Kaiser and his cousin the Czar discussed the "yellow peril" as a menace to the white race and to Western civilization.[20] More recently, with Chinese power rising and that of Russia contracting, Russians resent being the "little brother" to a country that it had been far more powerful than in the days of the Soviet Union. The disintegration of the USSR had created a power vacuum in the already sparsely populated Russian Far East that led to substantial immigration of Chinese merchants into the area and consequent fears that the area would be taken over by the PRC. The two countries have differences of opinion over the Arctic, which Russia seeks to enclose insofar as possible and China champions freedom of access to all. Putin also sees the Central Asian republics that used to be part of the USSR as its geographic backyard, while China tries to fold them into its Belt and Road Initiative.

In the Xi-Putin era, these frictions have been balanced by a common commitment to authoritarian methods and a sense of danger from the liberal democracies and most particularly by the U.S. Xi and Putin appeared on the reviewing stands of each other's extravagant parades celebrating the 70th anniversary of the end of World War II. In a show of solidarity for the Beijing Winter Olympics, where there was pressure for a boycott due to China's repression in Xinjiang and Hong Kong, Putin appeared in Beijing and the two leaders declared that "friendship between the two states has no limits, there are no 'forbidden areas' of cooperation."[21] At this time, Putin may have attained Xi's acquiescence for an invasion of Ukraine, with Xi asking and Putin assenting to hold off until after the games had ended.

No-limits partnership or not, the invasion put Xi in a difficult position, since it contradicted the PRC's longstanding, even though not always honored, opposition to territorial invasion. China's official reaction can best be described as carefully crafted to avoid either supporting or condemning the invasion, with Xi stating that China had "independently assessed the situation" and calling for all parties to push for a proper settlement, with China willing to play a role in promoting that settlement.[22] While incurring condemnation from several countries for its partnership with a clear aggressor, there were commercial advantages for China, which became the major beneficiary, with India, after Western oil majors and trading houses pulled back due to sanctions. The PRC's crude imports from Russia in May 2022 were up 55 percent from the previous year, obtained at what were described as steeply discounted prices.

United States

Xi's rise to power occurred in the third year of Barack Obama's presidency and attendant ongoing grievances that included American concerns with currency valuation, an imbalance of trade, intellectual property rights (IPR) violations, Taiwan, expansive activities in the South China and East China Seas, and human rights. Already signaling that it was disinclined to cooperate with other powers, China had sent only lower-level delegates to the Copenhagen climate conference in 2009 and seemed intent on stymying initiatives.[23]

The first meeting between Xi and Obama was symbolic of what was to come. Xi, having made his first overseas visit since his inauguration to Russia, next visited Costa Rica, Trinidad and Tobago, and Mexico and was simply stopping by in California on his way back to Beijing – the clear message being that the U.S. didn't matter that much.[24] At a G20 meeting in Hangzhou, Obama was obliged to exit Air Force One through a back door rather than receiving the red carpet treatment accorded to other heads of state while Susan Rice, his national security adviser, was roughly treated by Chinese security personnel.[25] On a state visit to Washington in 2015, Xi publicly pledged not to militarize artificial islands that Beijing was building in the South China Sea even as satellite imagery soon indicated that this was happening.[26] Faced with an economic crisis at home that perhaps diverted his attention from foreign policy, Obama seemed reluctant to press these issues and, in the view of conservatives, allowed himself to be disrespected.

However, in a tacit rebuttal to China's claims over disputed territories in the South China Sea, the administration did respond by pledging to fly and sail wherever allowed to by international law and proceeded to do so. Freedom of navigation operations (FONOPS) that actually began quietly in the Bush administration[27] became more frequent. And the administration reassured Tokyo that it would come to Japan's aid if its territory were to be invaded.

Having vowed to end policies toward China that he regarded as unacceptably weak, the more aggressive stance of Donald Trump failed to produce solutions. Sanctions did not produce results and the trade imbalance actually worsened during his time in office; China continued to consolidate its positions in the South China Sea despite regular patrols by U.S. ships and planes; and China stepped up its pressure on Japan and Taiwan. Supporters of Taiwan who were first buoyed when Trump questioned continued American adherence to the One China Policy were dismayed when shortly thereafter he agreed to Xi's request to honor it.[28] Still, measures were taken to support Taiwan in other ways, such as the enactment of the Asian Reassurance Initiative Act (ARIA) that, inter alia, provided for regular transfers of defensive arms to Taiwan and encouraged the travel of high-level U.S. officials to Taiwan.[29] American warships began to transit the Taiwan Strait more regularly, reaching a high of 13 in 2020.[30]

The Biden administration quietly continued these policies. In an acerbic exchange of views in Anchorage a month after inauguration, Secretary of State Antony Blinken raised "deep concerns" about Chinese cyberattacks, economic coercion, and human rights issues and stated that the U.S. relationship with China would be "competitive where it should be, collaborative where it can be, [and] adversarial where it must be." Chinese State Councillor Yang Jiechi then lectured the U.S. on the need to change its image and stop advancing its own democracy on the rest of the world. Many Americans, he stated, have little confidence in U.S. democracy, whereas the leaders of China have the support of the Chinese people. The results of past confrontation had not served the U.S. well: the only damage was to the U.S., whereas China pulled through and would continue to do so. Moreover, the U.S., not China, was the champion of cyberspying.[31]

Washington's annoyance with Beijing's refusal to condemn Russia's invasion of Ukraine deepened mutual distrust. During the Shangri-La Dialogue in June 2022, Defense Secretary Lloyd Austin described China as engaged in coercive, aggressive, and dangerous actions that threatened to undermine security and prosperity in the Indo-Pacific, while Chinese Defense Minister Wei Fenghe accused the U.S. of being a bully and hijacking countries around the region.[32]

Japan

China is Japan's largest trading partner, with Sino-Japanese relations typically and accurately described as warm economics, cold politics. Historic Sino-Japanese antagonisms have been exacerbated by Xi's activist policies in the East China Sea, where China and Japan dispute ownership of the Diaoyu/Senkaku Islands and drilling and fishing rights to the seas around them, as well as to the South China Sea, through which most of Japan's energy imports come. Xi's ascension to power coincided with the return of activist Shinzō Abe for a second term as prime minister.[33] Scion of a politically prominent family with a history of skepticism about China, he would serve until 2020, becoming Japan's longest-serving postwar prime minister. As Xi Jinping stepped up patrols in and near what Japan regarded as its territorial waters, Abe pressed for, and got, modest increases in the country's defense budget. His advocacy for changes in the country's pacifist constitution, however, failed. Both these efforts annoyed China which, despite far larger annual increases in its defense budget, purported to see the Japanese increases as precursors to a return of the militarism that led to World War II, accompanying these charges by a seemingly endless mantra on the cruelties the Japanese Imperial Army had inflicted on their ancestors. Japan has also championed the formation of collective security arrangements such as the Quad – Australia, India, Japan, and the U.S. – to counter Chinese expansionism. In June 2022, Fumio Kishida became the first Japanese prime minister to attend the annual meeting of the North Atlantic Treaty Organization.

As Chinese pressure on Taiwan for unification increased, so did Japanese anxiety about the effect an annexation would have on its own security,[34] accompanied by efforts to draw close to Taiwan, particularly after the Japan-friendly administration of Tsai Ing-wen's Democratic Progressive Party came to power in 2016. Carefully calibrated small changes toward closer Taiwan-Japan relations have been continued by post-Abe prime ministers, each one eliciting ominous warnings from Beijing about crossing red lines and, frequently, increased visits by Chinese ships to contested waters.

High-level visits between the two states had ceased even before the pandemic, with Xi yet to pay a reciprocal visit for Abe's trip to Beijing in 2018 – that being the first prime ministerial visit to Beijing in seven years. Xi had not traveled outside China for the two and a half years before his fall 2022 visit to a meeting of the Shanghai Cooperation Organization in Uzbekistan, though he has appeared virtually in several fora. Efforts to soothe relations prior to the upcoming 50th anniversary of the normalization of Sino-Japanese diplomatic relations failed, with the date being observed with low-key events sponsored by Japanese business leaders with investments in China and Sino-Japanese friendship organizations.[35]

Polls indicate record lows of regard for each other. An October 2021 bilateral poll showed that almost 91 percent of Japanese replied that their impression of China was "not good," and about two-thirds of Chinese respondents had a negative view of Japan.[36]

Europe

During Xi's first term in office, the European Union, then including the United Kingdom, was China's largest trading partner and China was the EU's second-largest trading partner after the United States. Frictions about human rights and losing jobs to lower-cost industries in the PRC were ongoing, but in general European countries regarded China as a forward-looking technocratic country that would soon become an integral part of the liberal international economic order. Chinese consumers value European brands, with German cars enjoying a high reputation – Volkswagen sells more cars in the PRC than in America or Germany, and prestige cars such as Mercedes are much sought after by China's upward strivers – as are French and Italian luxury items. China was the largest investor in Great Britain, which included a major stake in the controversial Hinkley Point nuclear power station despite concerns over its effect on national security that the Cameron government sought to soothe with what it called significant new safeguards.[37]

Other concerns with national security were evident elsewhere in Europe, where the adoption of Chinese telecom giant Huawei's 5G network aroused intense scrutiny and several countries' decisions not to adopt the system or to put significant monitoring legislation in place. Norway turned down China's request to build a large radar antenna on the Arctic archipelago of Svalbard,[38] and the German government, citing security concerns, withdrew its approval for a Chinese takeover of chip equipment manufacturer Aixtron.[39]

Insulting remarks by Chinese diplomats against the host nations they were posted to undercut Xi's rhetoric on multilateralism and win-win progress through cooperation. Ambassador to Sweden Gui Congyou so regularly disparaged the country's media and public officials that he was summoned by the Swedish foreign ministry more than 40 times in two years. In an expression that became infamous, Gui stated that China "treat[s] its friends with fine wine, but for our enemies we have shotguns." Questioned later about the comment, Gui replied that "Sweden is not important enough to threaten."[40] Lest there be any question of whether Gui was a rogue diplomat acting on his own, the *South China Morning Post* defended him as "only responding to the leadership's calls for a 'fighting spirit' against the Western plot to contain China."[41] In France, the foreign ministry summoned the Chinese ambassador over repeated insults and threats aimed at French lawmakers and a researcher and Beijing's decision to sanction officials across the EU.[42] Were the aim of such salvos to shape European public opinion in favor of Chinese positions, they have had the opposite effect. Still, one study concluded that such verbal abuse may have contributed to self-censorship by European governments.[43]

Another initiative that appears to have backfired is the founding of the 16 + 1, later 17 + 1, and currently again 16 +1 partnership with eastern European states.[44] First formed in 2012, the organization gained an additional raison d'être when a year later Xi Jinping announced his Belt and Road Initiative. The 16/17 would provide China with a gateway to western European markets and the eastern European states, typically far poorer than their western cousins, with loans for infrastructure development – fulfilling Xi's win-win slogan.

A decade on, the results are not merely disappointing, but in some cases counterproductive. Members complained that the 17 + 1 hub and spoke organization meant that they had to deal with Beijing individually rather than coordinating with each other. Rather than seeing consistent investment and infrastructure upgrades, they "received forums; instead of factories they received exchange programs; and instead of exports they received summer camps."[45] A $3 billion dollar project to build a high-speed railway between Belgrade and Budapest has become a symbol of China's failed investment promises,[46] and there were charges that educational partnerships had brought authoritarian malignant interferences in academic freedom.[47] When Lithuania proposed to use the word "Taiwan" rather than Taipei for a representative office, Beijing shut down its embassy and banned the import of not only Lithuanian exports but also of EU products containing parts made in Lithuania, raising hackles in the affected EU countries and confirming EU suspicions that the 16/17 + 1 arrangement was an effort to weaken the unity of the bloc. Disillusioned participants characterized the organization as transformed into a zombie mechanism.[48]

An April 2023 poll conducted by the European Council on Foreign Relations found that in the 11 countries surveyed only 22 percent considered the region's economic relationship with China as bearing more risks than benefits. However, they also displayed considerable caution about the practical aspects of China's economic presence in Europe, for example, whether Chinese companies should be allowed to build and own infrastructure in Europe or buy newspapers, technology companies, and football clubs. On average, a majority would oppose allowing Chinese companies to own infrastructure in Europe, as well as to buy a European newspaper or technology company. Since being asked the same question in late 2020, Europeans have grown somewhat more concerned about China's economic presence in Europe – especially in Italy, the Netherlands, Poland, Spain, and Hungary.[49]

In sum, although Europe remains eager to trade with the PRC, it is increasingly convinced that the policy of *Wandel durch Handel*, that trade would induce positive change in the PRC's authoritarian system, had not worked in practice.

The Koreas

North Korea

Xi has continued his predecessors' efforts to play off the Democratic Republic of Korea, DPRK or North Korea, against the Republic of Korea, ROK or South Korea, with some success. Occasional statements of cordiality notwithstanding, relations are best described as cool. Although the DPRK is heavily reliant on China for both food and fuel, there are limits to how much leverage this gives to Beijing, since it cannot allow the country to disintegrate lest the peninsula be unified under the democratic government of South Korea, which has close ties to the United States. Xi continues to affirm a commitment to unification of the two Koreas, though he is well aware that this would not be in China's best interests but dares not say so since this would have repercussions for his resolve to unify China and Taiwan. Publicly, Xi also affirms a commitment to de-nuclearization of the Koreas while realizing that, since possession of nuclear weapons is Kim's only guarantee of staying in power, it is unrealistic to imagine that any amount of pressure on Kim would persuade him to surrender them.

On ascending to power, Xi did not visit DPRK leader Kim Jong-un or invite him to visit Beijing. Nor did the two exchange the usual ritualized pleasantries on birthdays and anniversaries. Beijing was reportedly unhappy with Kim's brutal execution of his uncle-in-law Jang Song Thaek[50] in 2013 and half-brother Kim Jong-nam four years later, with the latter having lived in exile in Malaysia and supported by the Chinese government. Both had been regarded as friendly to the PRC.[51] Kim also snubbed China by choosing a Russian firm in a $25 billion deal to revamp the DPRK's rail and road system.[52]

Still, larger forces were in play, in this case relations between the DPRK and the United States. Kim did visit Beijing twice before Kim met with then-U.S. president Donald Trump in Singapore in 2018 and visited again afterwards, the last time in 2019, just before the pandemic halted state visits.[53] Privately, some Chinese intellectuals confide that, like it or not, China is stuck with North Korea. Beijing continues to veto efforts to impose further international sanctions on its difficult ally while seemingly turning a blind eye to violations on existing sanctions such as the sale of oil.[54]

South Korea

China is South Korea's largest trading partner, though frictions flare up from time to time. Chinese maps depicting Goguryeo, an ancient Korean kingdom, as part of China rankle patriotic Koreans and when, just prior to becoming party general secretary, Xi praised the heroic accomplishments of the PRC-DPRK during the Korean War, there was widespread anger in the ROK. In November 2013, China unilaterally declared an Air Defense Identification Zone that overlaps South Korean jurisdictional claims, with the Chinese foreign ministry rebuffing several efforts by Seoul to revise the parameters of the ADIZ. Still, early ROK-PRC relations were cordial, with President Park Geun-hye visiting China in June 2014 and Xi, in a rebuff to the DPRK, paying a reciprocal visit in July.

This changed rapidly when, in response to North Korean missile tests, Ms. Park decided to deploy the Theater High Altitude Area Defense system (THAAD). Beijing, believing that THAAD could be used to spy against China, then imposed sanctions against the ROK, including curtailing tourism, retail operations, and imports of Korean television shows and films and cars. While hurting trade, the sanctions also aroused South Korean anger. Park's successor Moon Jae-in made an official visit to Beijing in 2017, agreeing not to extend THAAD, though his replacement by the more conservative Yoon Suk-yeol regards North Korea as more of a threat to be defended against.[55]

Existing Chinese-South Korean grievances escalated on a variety of issues ranging from soft power to security. Anger erupted when, at the opening ceremony for the Beijing Winter Olympics, a woman wearing the traditional Korean hanbok represented one of the PRC's 56 ethnic groups. There were also disputes over who invented the spicy cabbage dish known to Koreans as kimchi, and anger when the South Korean historical drama Joseon Exorcist allegedly used Chinese props that Korean audiences objected to.[56] The proposed construction of a Chinatown had to be canceled. Polling showed that views of China had sunk to an historic low, below even the views of traditional Korean enemy Japan.[57]

India and Pakistan

India has un-demarcated border issues with both China and Pakistan, with all three being nuclear powers. Compounding India's concerns with China are its close relations with Pakistan in what the two sides call an all-weather strategic partnership while at the same time India and Pakistan are in an ongoing state of hostility. China supplies Pakistan with most of its arms, and some believe that Beijing may have aided it to become a nuclear power.

In recent years, China has built bridges and roads in disputed Sino-Indian border areas, leading to periodic skirmishes that in spring 2020 erupted into the deadliest clash in 45 years. In February 2021 the two sides agreed to separate their forces along the Line of Actual Control. However, in October of the next year China's National People's Congress passed a Land Boundary Law which stipulates that the defense of land borders is a military mission, which Indian pundits criticized as the PRC using domestic law as a pretext for international expansionism.[58] China's expanding activities in the Indian Ocean have contributed to Sino-Indian tensions as well. India also resents Chinese influence over Sri Lanka, whose debts to the PRC resulted in its leasing the port of Hambantota to the PRC for 99 years.

India has responded by drawing closer to the United States, with China charging that New Delhi is being used by Washington to the detriment of India's own interests. India has also been increasing its military capabilities. Presence in the Indian Ocean is being reinforced with additional deployments in the Andaman and Nicobar Islands and a naval facility that is under construction in the Agalega Islands of Mauritius. The country's first indigenously constructed aircraft carrier, *Vikrant*, was commissioned in September 2022, diesel-electric submarines are being produced in cooperation with France, and S-400 surface to air missiles have been purchased from Russia. The Indian Army, the world's largest ground force, has been acquiring advanced equipment including main battle tanks, howitzers, and unmanned aerial vehicles.[59]

Tensions notwithstanding, Prime Minister Modi has been loath to antagonize India's third-largest trading partner (second if Hong Kong's trade is added to China's). Bilateral trade reached a high of $125 billion in 2021, with Chinese exports to India exceeding its imports by $28.1 billion.[60] The trade deficit is a sore point with India, eliciting complaints that the country has become a colony of China.[61] Although a founding member of the China-led Asian Infrastructure Investment Bank (AIIB), India has thus far refused to join the BRI, citing concerns with lack of transparency.

Since Pakistan faces the Indian Ocean its strategic importance to China has been enhanced consonant with the PRC's expanding interest in the area. The China-Pakistan Economic Corridor (CPEC), stretching from the Pakistani port of Gwadar to Xinjiang's Kashgar City in northwest China, is a key part of the PRC's Belt and Road Initiative. Construction of the CPEC has faced many difficulties, including Sino-Pakistani differences of opinion on the details and financing of the corridor, opposition from India, terrorist attacks from Baluchi separatists who want to break away from Pakistan, Islamic extremist groups, and Pakistani nationalists who oppose Chinese influence in the country. Several Chinese nationals have been among the victims.[62] Nonetheless, construction continues and is likely to further increase China's influence in Pakistan.

Southeast Asia

China regards Southeast Asia as its backyard and cites a long history of trade relations with the area as the antecedent to its Maritime Belt and Road Initiative. In keeping with the countries of the region's diversities in population, religions, and strategic interests, the influence of China differs, being strongest in Laos and Cambodia, to a lesser though still significant degree with Burma and Thailand, and still less in Singapore, Indonesia, Brunei, the Philippines, and Vietnam. The ten members of the Association of Southeast Asian Nations, divided among themselves, have sought unsuccessfully to negotiate with Beijing over such contentious issues as disputed islands in the South China Sea (SCS), a Code of Conduct in the SCS, and fishing rights. ASEAN's 2012 meeting ended without issuing a joint statement for the first time in its history, with host country Cambodia refusing to put Vietnam's and the Philippines' request to put on the agenda what they regard as Chinese encroachment on islands that they claim.[63]

The regional forum having denied it redress, Manila brought its case to the United Nations Permanent Court of Arbitration (PCA). Beijing, denying that the PCA had jurisdiction over the issue, refused to take part, as it did when in 2016 the PCA backed the Philippines' contention that, to the extent that China had historic rights to resources in the waters of the South China Sea, such rights were extinguished to the extent that they were incompatible with the exclusive economic zones provided for in the United Nations Convention on the Law of the Sea, and that there was no legal basis for China to claim historic rights to resources within the sea areas falling within its self-proclaimed nine-dash line.[64] This turned out to be a Pyrrhic victory for Manila when Rodrigo Duterte, the next president of the Philippines, declared he was willing to ignore the PCA ruling in favor of a joint exploration project with China,[65] and even agreed to honor Chinese passports showing the nine-dash line.[66] The issue may not be over: at the 2020 meeting of the UN General Assembly the mercurial Duterte said that the PCA's award was "now part of international law beyond the reach of passing governments to dilute, diminish, or abandon."[67] And Duterte's successor, President Ferdinand Marcos Jr., has said that the Philippines will not allow his country's rights to be trampled on.[68] In practice, however, the South China Sea remains under China's de facto control save for occasional transits principally by the United States under its vow to defend freedom of navigation in the Indo-Pacific.

China has also obtained access to Cambodia's Ream Naval Base. Although Prime Minister Hun Sen termed a July 2019 report that it had concluded a secret agreement giving China exclusive access to the base as rubbish and that hosting foreign military bases is against its constitution,[69] less than two years later construction began on a Chinese-funded upgrade of the base as part of the two countries' "iron-clad partnership." Chinese ambassador Wang Wentian, denying that the upgrade was aimed at any third party, added that it would be conducive to even closer practical cooperation between the two militaries.[70]

Several Southeast Asia states, including Indonesia, Vietnam, and the Philippines, periodically protest against Chinese fishing boats' presence in their exclusive economic zones, with Indonesia in 2015 going so far as to sink one of them.[71]

Africa

African governments have generally been receptive to Chinese investment, and Chinese companies are major buyers of African mineral and energy commodities; China became Africa's largest trading partner in 2009. While some of these transactions have had positive results and are appreciated, others have not, and result in debts that the governments find difficult to pay back. In some cases, China has agreed to forgive the debts African states have incurred as, for example, when much-touted rail lines fail to be cost-effective. Many Africans have emigrated to the Guangzhou area in search of jobs, where relations have been marked by ugly incidents of discrimination against them, such as being denied entry to the factories where they worked and evicted from their dwellings and refused services in shops and medical facilities after the outbreak of the pandemic.[72] Separately, an investigation by the BBC revealed a video posted on Chinese media showing African children in China chanting racist slogans in Chinese without knowing what they were saying.[73] Beijing's nationalistic *Global Times* has denounced allegations of discrimination as fake news as indeed some, but scarcely all, may have been.[74] State media also cite the 2022 African Youth Survey as indicating that 76 percent of respondents between 18 and 24 years of age believe that China has a positive influence on their lives compared with 72 percent for the United States.[75] In some cases, it appears that African governments who are the recipients of Chinese aid are loath to publicize unfavorable information for fear of jeopardizing relations with Beijing. As a case in point, when a Paris newspaper revealed that the headquarters of the African Union, built by China, had been transmitting data to the PRC since its inception, the organization's authorities took pains to downplay the news.[76]

It should also be mentioned that there have been racial incidents against Chinese nationals in Africa, with their homes and shops being looted by mobs protesting that the immigrants have taken jobs from locals.[77] Chinese nationals have also been kidnapped and held for ransom.[78]

Conclusion

Xi's foreign policy has succeeded in the sense of gaining support for many of China's international positions, whether through economic and financial incentives, clever initiatives, or intimidation. Several countries have welcomed Chinese investment, which has to some extent helped the PRC's economy to keep growing, pandemic notwithstanding. Yet the many manifestations of power projection have led to a sharp drop in the country's image globally and to the image of Xi Jinping specifically.[79] There was a diminution in insulting diplomacy after June 2021 when Xi urged officials to create a more "lovable" China,[80] with external analysts undecided whether this heralded a genuine effort or was simply the latest phase in a *fang-shou* policy of loosening pressure on target countries when it seems to be counterproductive, but only temporarily, since it will be resumed again when conditions are deemed more favorable.

In a sign that the confrontational attitude would continue, when asked by Reuters in October 2022 whether wolf warrior diplomacy had been counterproductive, Vice Foreign Minister Ma Zhaoxu replied stridently that

> We Chinese will not capitulate. We will not sit and do nothing while our country's interests are being harmed. Going forward, Chinese diplomats will continue to overcome all obstacles and always be the devoted guardian of the interests of our country and our people.[81]

This may be standard rhetoric and, should circumstances seem to favor a softer line, that could also be justified by the same "the interests of the country and people" rhetoric.

Xi's Global Security Initiative, introduced in vague terms at the Boao Forum for Asia in April 2022,[82] seems meant to be the foreign policy companion to the BRI. As expanded on in his speech to the 20th Party Congress in October, the Global Security Initiative comprises six commitments, basically repeating the Five Principles of Peaceful Coexistence dating from 1954.[83] It may best be understood as a call for an alternative global security initiative based on China's newly acquired international primacy and a challenge to the U.S.-led world order.

Since then, China has played a more active role in international diplomacy that could erode and further challenge the U.S.-led world order. Its first initiative, brokering a peace agreement between Saudi Arabia and Iran, was successful. Given its reaffirmation of a "rock solid" relationship with Russia and refusal to rule out supplying weapons to Moscow, its second initiative, offering its services to reach a settlement for the Ukraine-Russia conflict, was dismissed as an effort to burnish its image rather than assume a neutral stance.[84]

A third, recent initiative has been to place current/retired Chinese judges on foreign and international courts or tribunals. The retired head of the #4 Civil (foreign-related) Division of the PRC's Supreme People's Court was appointed to the Singapore International Commercial Court[85] and to the Qatar International Court and Dispute Resolution Centre,[86] in addition to two currently serving Supreme People's Court judges and another on the UN Appeals Tribunal and Disputes Tribunal respectively,[87] and a third on the Administrative Tribunal of the International Labor Organization.[88] What influence they will have on shaping international law to Beijing's policy premises remains to be seen: the justices will be in a minority on their respective courts, and, since they will be sitting with outstanding foreign judges, may bring some of the reasoning back to Beijing. How accepting party and government will be of this reasoning is unknown.

A 2022 Pew poll noted that the opinion of China in advanced economies had soured precipitously under Xi. In the United States, 82 percent of respondents that year expressed an "unfavorable opinion" of China, up from 79 percent in 2020. The percentage of those who said they had "no confidence" in Xi to do the "right thing regarding world affairs" was 87 percent in South Korea in 2022, up from 29 percent in 2015. In Britain, the figure increased to 70 percent in 2022 from 44 perent in 2014. In the words of Laura Silver, a lead author of the report, "Across advanced economies, there is very little confidence in Xi's handling of world affairs and very negative views of the country, overall."[89] Apprised of Pew's statistics, foreign ministry spokesperson Wang Wenbin argued that since the poll was conducted among a small number of developed countries it was not representative of the vast number of developing countries that comprise 90 percent of the world's population.[90]

Public perceptions aside, the drop in soft power has been offset by large gains in hard power, and it seems clear that Xi regards the latter as more important. There have been efforts at countering China's expansionism, but they remain cautious and so far inadequate. The Quad suffers from episodic hesitation from India, its largest member, although coordination among the remaining three, Australia, Japan, and the U.S., has improved marginally. The Indo-Pacific strategy to compete with Beijing may at best be described as nascent, and a five-country initiative of Australia, Japan, New Zealand, the UK, and the U.S. to help Pacific Island nations resist Chinese pressure has been characterized as too little, too late.[91]

So far, notwithstanding foreign criticism, nearly all of it from developed countries, Xi has been able to proceed unimpeded largely with the support of less developed states, as symbolized by a fall 2022 victory in the United Nations Human Rights Council that blocked discussion of a UN report that found China's actions in Xinjiang to be crimes against humanity.[92] Roman emperor Caligula is famous for saying let [one's opposition] hate as long as they fear you, and Machiavelli for saying that it is better to be feared than loved if you cannot be both.

How long Xi can sustain these policies in the face of domestic economic downturn and pushback from some countries remains to be seen. Some analysts believe that the power of the PRC has peaked,[93] and that signs of decline are already evident that may make it difficult for a rejuvenated China to remake the world order consonant with Xi's vision.

Notes

1 Lo Ping, "Zhu Rongji's Visit to U.S. and Internal Struggle Within Top Hierarchy," *Tung Hsiang [动向]*, No.164, 15 April 1999, pp. 6–10. FTS19990427001937. According to Lo, a veteran correspondent for the respected Hong Kong magazine *Cheng Ming [Contending* 争名*]*, the demonstrations took place from 22 to 24 March.
2 Willy Wo-Lap Lam, "Urgent U.S. Action Needed to Soothe Beijing and Prevent Collapse of Ties," *South China Morning Post*, 1 May 1999, p. 1. Lam hypothesized that the reason military hardliners were able to gain the upper hand is that Beijing saw patriotism as a means to divert attention from social problems such as unemployment.
3 Yü Ching-Sheng, "Jiang Zemin Repeatedly Expounds China's Domestic and Foreign Policies in Three Internal Speeches Giving a Quick Response and Winning the Support of the Public," *Ching Pao*, July 1, 1999, pp. 24–26, FTS19990703000863. Article is dated 3 June 1999, based on Jiang's speeches prior to that; hence Pan's article of 8 June can be considered a response to Jiang.
4 Rush Doshi, *The Long Game: China's Grand Strategy to Displace American Order* (New York: Oxford University Press, 2021), pp. 3–4.
5 Doshi, p. 166.
6 "Author's Conversations at the U.S. Pacific Command (Re-Named the Indo-Pacific Command in 2018)," February 14, 2011.
7 Xinhua, "Xi Jinping to Lead National Security Commission," *Global Times*, January 25, 2014. www.globaltimes.cn/content/839220.shtml
8 Alfred L. Chan, *Xi Jinping: Political Career, Governance, and Leadership, 1953–2018*. (New York: Oxford University Press, 2022), p. 386. See also "List of International Trips Made by Xi Jinping," https://en.wikipedia.org/wiki/List_of_international_trips_made_by_Xi_Jinping#:~:text=t%20e%20Xi%20Jinping%2C%20the%2018-19th%20General%20Secretary,he%20assumed%20the%20leadership%20on%2015%20November%2C%202012
9 Xinhua, "Xi Jinping to Lead National Security Commission," *Global Times*, January 25, 2014. www.globaltimes.cn/content/839220.shtml
10 CGTN, "Full Text: Xi Jinping's Speech at 2022 Boao Forum for Asia," April 21, 2022. https://news.cgtn.com/news/2022-04-21/Full-text-Xi-Jinping-s-speech-at-2022-Boao-Forum-for-Asia-19ppiaI90Eo/index.html
11 "Ex-Interpol Chief Meng Hongwei Sentenced to 13 Years in Jail," *Deutsche Welle*, January 21, 2020. www.dw.com/en/china-ex-interpol-chief-meng-hongwei-sentenced-to-13-years-in-jail/a-52082404
12 Jules Crétois and Olivier Marbot, "Coronavirus: Tedros Ghebreyesus of WHO Faces Firestorm of Criticism," *The Africa Report*, June 10, 2020. www.theafricareport.com/29554/coronavirus-tedros-ghebreyesus-of-who-faces-firestorm-of-criticism/
13 R. Evan Ellis, "The China-CELAC Summit: Opening a New Phase in China-Latin America-U.S. Relations?" *Strategic Studies Institute*, U.S. Army War College, January 27, 2015. https://ssi.armywarcollege.edu/2015/pubs/article/strategic-insights-the-china-celac-summit-opening-a-new-phase-in-china-latin-america-u-s-relations/
14 The most explicit example of a red line is Taiwan declaring independence. Yet there is considerable ambiguity about the definition of a declaration of independence, which could perhaps be construed as the Taiwan government abolishing its provincial

government apparatus – which the Taiwan government declared to have been "frozen" to avoid further provoking Beijing.

15 John Vandiver, "China's Base in Africa Now Big Enough to Host Aircraft Carriers, AFRICOM Boss Says," *Stars and Stripes*, April 21, 2021. www.stripes.com/theaters/africa/china-s-base-in-africa-now-big-enough-to-host-aircraft-carriers-africom-boss-says-1.670578

16 Kathrin Hille, "China Denies Building Naval Bases But Fear of its Military Reach Grows," *Financial Times*, June 19, 2022. www.ft.com/content/f3687d1d-6cff-407a-917f-994dbd3da120

17 Koichiro Takagi, "New Tech, New Concepts: China's Plans for AI and Cognitive Warfare," *War on the Rocks*, April 13, 2022. https://warontherocks.com/2022/04/new-tech-new-concepts-chinas-plans-for-ai-and-cognitive-warfare/

18 Dongshu Liu, and Li Shao, "Public Opinion Backlash against China's International Expansion," *Journal of Contemporary China*, Vol. 31, No. 135, May 2022, pp. 367, 381.

19 Due to space constraints, not all areas can be included.

20 "Introduction: Willy-Nicky Letters Between the Kaiser and the Czar," *WWI Document Archive*. https://wwi.lib.byu.edu/index.php/Introduction:_Willy-Nicky_Letters_between_the_Kaiser_and_the_Czar

21 "Russia and China Line Up against U.S. in 'No Limits' Partnership," *Reuters*, February 4, 2022. https://timesofindia.indiatimes.com/world/china/russia-and-china-line-up-against-us-in-no-limits-partnership/articleshow/89351575.cms#:~:text=Russia%20and%20China%20line%20up%20against%20US%20in,%2F%20Feb%204%2C%202022%2C%2020%3A31%20IST%20Share%20AA

22 Simone McCarthy, "China Will Support Russia on Security, Xi Tells Putin in Birthday Call," *CNN*, June 16, 2022. www.cnn.com/2022/06/15/asia/china-support-russia-security-xi-birthday-putin-intl-hnk/index.html

23 "Obama Says Disappointment at Copenhagen Justified," *Reuters*, December 24, 2009. www.cnet.com/culture/obama-says-disappointment-at-copenhagen-justified/

24 June Teufel Dreyer, "The Xi-Obama Summit: Much Ado about Very Little," *The Asia Dialogue*, June 10, 2013. https://theasiadialogue.com/2013/06/10/the-xi-obama-summit-much-ado-about-very-little/

25 "China Blames United States, Journalists for Obama Airport Fiasco," *Reuters*, September 5, 2016. www.reuters.com/article/us-g20-china-usa-obama-row-idUSKCN11B138

26 Jeremy Page, Carol E. Lee, and Gordon Lubold, "China's President Pledges No Militarization in Disputed Islands," *Wall Street Journal*, September 25, 2015. www.wsj.com/articles/china-completes-runway-on-artificial-island-in-south-china-sea-1443184818

27 "U.S. Department of Defense Freedom of Navigation (FON) Program," https://policy.defense.gov/OUSDP-Offices/FON/

28 Edward Wong, "U.S. Tries to Bolster Taiwan's Status, Short of Recognizing Sovereignty," *New York Times*, August 17, 2020. www.nytimes.com/2020/08/17/us/politics/trump-china-taiwan-hong-kong.html

29 Congressional Record, S. 2736-Asia Reassurance Initiative Act of 2018, 115th Congress, U.S. Tries to Bolster Taiwan's Status, Short of Recognizing Sovereignty

30 See Ronald O'Rourke, *U.S.-China Strategic Competition in South and East China Seas: Background and Issues for Congress* (Washington, DC: U.S. Government Congressional Research Service, January 26, 2022), p. 45. for a detailed listing of the Taiwan Strait transits and FONOPs. www.crs.gov R42784.

31 "How it Happened: Transcript of the U.S.-China Opening Remarks in Alaska," March 19, 2021. https://asia.nikkei.com/Politics/International-relations/US-China-tensions/How-it-happened-Transcript-of-the-US-China-opening-remarks-in-Alaska

32 Brad Lennon, and Heather Chen, "China Blasts U.S. 'Bully,' Says it Will Fight to the End' for Taiwan," *CNN*, June 12, 2022. www.cnn.com/2022/06/12/asia/us-china-defense-shangri-la-dialogue-intl-hnk-ml/index.html

33 Abe had been prime minister in 2006–2007, resigning due to poor health and returning after his recuperation.
34 Actually, then-head of Japan's defense agency Shin Kanemaru told U.S. Defense Secretary Harold Brown exactly this in 1978, but was promptly silenced lest they jeopardize Tokyo's ongoing negotiations for normalization of Sino-Japanese diplomatic relations.
35 "China Mulls In-Person Event to Mark Normalization of Ties With Japan," *Kyodo*, January 18, 2022. https://english.kyodonews.net/news/2022/01/f10d8e14c977-china-mulls-in-person-event-to-mark-normalization-of-ties-with-japan.html; Editorial, "Return to Origins of Pledge of Friendship/Beijing's Hegemonic Behavior Unacceptable," *Yomiuri*, September 29, 2022. https://japannews.yomiuri.co.jp/editorial/yomiuri-editorial/20220929-61217/
36 Laura Zhou, "In Japan, the View of China Is Gloomier As Perceptions of Threat Grow," *South China Morning Post*, October 21, 2021. www.scmp.com/news/china/diplomacy/article/3153163/japan-view-china-gloomier-perceptions-threat-grow
37 Neno Duplan, "Hinkley Point Nuclear Power Plant: UK Approves Nuclear Plant Deal," *Locus Technologies*, September 15, 2016. www.bbc.com/news/business-37369786
38 "Norway Won't Let China Build Radar," *newsinenglish.no*, September 12, 2014. www.newsinenglish.no/2014/09/12/norway-wont-let-china-build-radar/
39 Maria Sheahan, and Caroline Copley, "Germany Stalls Chinese Takeover of Aixtron, Citing Security Worries," *Reuters*, October 24, 2016. www.reuters.com/article/us-aixtron-m-a-fujian-germany-idUSKCN12O13G
40 "Shotgun Diplomacy: How Sweden Copes With Chinese Bullying," *The Economist*, February 20, 2020. www.economist.com/europe/2020/02/20/how-sweden-copes-with-chinese-bullying
41 Shi Jiangtao, "Why China's Fiercest Wolf Warrior in Sweden Was Just Fighting the Good Fight," *South China Morning Post*, October 12, 2021. www.scmp.com/news/china/diplomacy/article/3152102/why-chinas-fiercest-wolf-warrior-sweden-was-just-fighting-good
42 "France to Summon Chinese Envoy Over Threats, Insults," *Reuters*, March 22, 2021. www.reuters.com/article/us-france-china-idUSKBN2BE2O1
43 Björn Jerdén, and Viking Bohman, "China's Propaganda Campaign in Sweden, 2018–2019," *U Brief*, April 2019. www.ui.se/globalassets/ui.se-eng/publications/ui-publications/2019/ui-brief-no.-4-2019.pdf
44 Originally, the 16 were Albania, Bosnia and Herzegovina, Bulgaria, Croatia, Czechia, Estonia, Hungary, Latvia, Lithuania, North Macedonia, Montenegro, Poland, Romania, Servia, Slovakia, and Slovenia. In 2019, Greece joined, but Lithuania withdrew in 2021.
45 Andreea Brinza, "How China's 17 + 1 Became a Zombie Mechanism," *The Diplomat*, February 10, 2021, unpaginated. https://thediplomat.com/2021/02/how-chinas-171-became-a-zombie-mechanism/#!#:~:text=For%20the%20United%20States,%20the%2017+1%20mechanism%20is,featuring%20a%20plethora%20of%20unfulfilled%20promises%20and%20projects
46 Kafkadesk Budapest Office, "Belgrade-Budapest High-Speed Train: Highway to Rail?" May 15, 2020. https://kafkadesk.org/2020/05/15/belgrade-budapest-high-speed-train-highway-to-rail/
47 Matej Simalcik, and Adam Kalivoda, *China's Inroads into Slovak Universities: Protecting Academic Freedoms From Authoritarian Malign Influence*, Central European Institute of Asian Studies, Bratislava, 2020. https://ceias.eu/chinas-inroads-into-slovak-universities/#:~:text=In%20the%20policy%20paper%20China%E2%80%99s%20inroads%20into%20Slovak,the%20Slovak%20Academy%20of%20Science%29%20with%20Chinese%20entities
48 Brinza, 2021, *op. cit.*
49 Jana Puglierin, and Pawel Zerka, "Keeping American Close, Russia Down, and China Far Away: How Europeans Navigate a Competitive World," *European Council on Foreign Relations Policy Brief*, June 7, 2023. https://ecfr.eu/publication/keeping-america-close-russia-down-and-china-far-away-how-europeans-navigate-a-competitive-world/

50 Paul Liem, "The Execution of Jang Song Thaek," *Korea Policy Institute*, December 31, 2013. www.kpolicy.org/post/the-execution-of-jang-song-thaek

51 Choe Sang-Hun, and Rick Gladstone, "Kim Jong-un's Half Brother Is Reported Assassinated in Malaysia," *New York Times*, February 14, 2017. www.nytimes.com/2017/02/14/world/asia/kim-jong-un-brother-killed-malaysia.html

52 Michelle FlorCruz, "Russia To Revamp North Korea's Rail System, Eyes Mineral Resources," *International Business Times*, October 30, 2014. www.ibtimes.com/russia-revamp-north-koreas-rail-system-eyes-mineral-resources-1716262

53 James Griffiths, and Yong Xiong, "China Hosts Surprise Visit by Kim Jong Un Amid U.S. Tensions," *CNN*, January 8, 2019. www.cnn.com/2019/01/07/china/kim-jong-un-visit-china-intl/index.html

54 Colum Lynch, "It Was Like Having the Chinese Government in the Room With Us," *Foreign Policy*, October 15, 2021. https://foreignpolicy.com/2021/10/15/china-sanctions-north-korea-hardball/

55 "Who is South Korea's New President Yoon Suk-yeol?" *France 24*, May 5, 2022. www.france24.com/en/asia-pacific/20220510-who-is-south-korea-s-new-president-yoon-suk-yeol

56 Greeshma Nayak, "South Korean Drama 'Joseon Exorcist' Sparks Controversy Over Portrayal of Chinese Culture," *Republic World*, March 25, 2021. www.republicworld.com/entertainment-news/web-series/south-korean-drama-joseon-exorcist-sparks-controversy-over-portrayal-of-chinese-culture.html#:~:text=The%20Jeonju%20Lee%20Royal%20Family%20Association%20made%20up,and%20showed%20favoritism%20toward%20China%27s%20Northeast%20History%20Project

57 Gi-Wook Shin, Haley Gordon, and Hannah June Kim, "South Koreans are Rethinking What China Means to Their Nation," Freeman Spogli Institute for International Studies, Stanford University, February 8, 2022. https://fsi.stanford.edu/news/south-koreans-are-rethinking-what-china-means-their-nation

58 Brahma Chellaney, "China's Expansionism Creeps along as West Distracted by Ukraine," *Nikkei Asia*, October 7, 2021. https://asia.nikkei.com/Opinion/China-s-expansionism-creeps-along-as-West-distracted-by-Ukraine

59 Brad Lendon et al., "India's First Homegrown Aircraft Carrier Puts it Among World's Naval Elites," *CNN*, September 2, 2022. www.cnn.com/2022/09/02/asia/india-indigenous-aircraft-carrier-vikrant-commissioned-intl-hnk-ml/index.html

60 Ananth Krishnan, "India's Trade With China Crosses $125 Billion, Imports Near $100 Billion," *The Hindu*, January 15, 2022. www.thehindu.com/business/Economy/indias-trade-with-china-crosses-125-billion-imports-near-100-billion/article38272914.ece#:~:text=Bilateral%20trade%20reached%20%24125.6%20billion%20in%202021%2C%20with,by%2022%25%20from%20the%20pre-pandemic%20figure%20in%202019

61 Shekhar Gupta, "Is India a Colony of China," April 2, 2021, www.youtube.com/watch?v=26rw6UYM3_w

62 (No Author), "Embassy Condemns Suicide Attack Targeting Chinese Nationals in Pakistan, Two Local Children Killed," *Global Times*, August 21, 2021. www.globaltimes.cn/page/202108/1232063.shtml

63 (No Author), "ASEAN Nations Fail to Reach Agreement on South China Sea," *BBC*, July 13, 2012. www.bbc.com/news/world-asia-18825148

64 Press Release, "The South China Sea Arbitration: The Republic of the Philippines v. The People Republic of China," *Permanent Court of Arbitration, The Hague*, July 12, 2016. https://docs.pca-cpa.org/2016/07/PH-CN-20160712-Press-Release-No-11-English.pdf

65 Joyce Balancio, "Duterte Says Willing to Ignore Hague Victory for Joint Exploration Project with China," *ABS-CBN News*, September 11, 2019. https://news.abs-cbn.com/news/09/11/19/duterte-says-willing-to-ignore-hague-victory-for-joint-exploration-project-with-china

66 Pia Ranada, "Duterte Allows Stamping of China Passports With 9-Dash Line Image," *Rappler*, August 6, 2019. www.rappler.com/nation/237165-duterte-allows-stamping-china-passports-ending-philippine-protest-vs-9-dash-line-image/

67 Jelly Musico, "Duterte Affirms Arbitral Ruling on SCS Before UN General Assembly," *Philippine News Agency*, September 23, 2020. www.pna.gov.ph/articles/1116296
68 Nestor Corrales and Tina G. Santos, "Marcos to Assert Hague Ruling Against China's Claim on South China Sea," *Philippine Daily Inquirer*, May 27, 2022. https://asianews.network/marcos-to-assert-hague-ruling-against-chinas-claim-on-south-china-sea/
69 (No Author), "Cambodia Denies Deal to Allow Chinese Forces at Its Naval Base," *Al Jazeera*, July 22, 2019. www.aljazeera.com/news/2019/7/22/cambodia-denies-deal-to-allow-chinese-forces-at-its-naval-base
70 Simone McCarthy, "China and Cambodia Break Ground at Naval Bases in Show of 'Iron-Clad Relations," *CNN*, June 9, 2022. www.cnn.com/2022/06/09/asia/china-cambodia-naval-base-military-intl-hnk/index.html
71 Prashanth Parameswaran, "Why Did Indonesia Just Sink a Vessel from China?" *The Diplomat*, May 22, 2015. https://thediplomat.com/2015/05/why-did-indonesia-just-sink-a-vessel-from-china/
72 Damola Durosomo, "Africans in China are being Evicted from Their Homes and Blamed for Spreading Coronavirus," *OkayAfrica*, April 10, 2020. www.okayafrica.com/africans-in-china-guangzhou-evicted-left-homeless-blamed-for-coronavirus/
73 "How Chinese Vendors are Making Money from Videos of African Children," *France, 24*, April 9, 2020. https://observers.france24.com/en/20200409-how-chinese-vendors-make-money-videos-african-children; Oliver Young, "'Racism for Sale,' Investigation Rekindles Debate Over Exploitation in China-Africa Relationship," *China Digital Times*, June 17, 2022. https://chinadigitaltimes.net/2022/06/racism-for-sale-investigation-rekindles-debate-over-exploitation-in-china-africa-relationship/
74 "Who Is Behind the Fake News of 'Discrimination' against Africans in China?" *Global Times*, April 16, 2020. www.globaltimes.cn/content/1185845.shtml
75 Chen Weihua, "African Youths Make it Clear They Prefer China Over US," *China Daily*, June 17, 2022. www.chinadaily.com.cn/a/202206/17/WS62abb589a310fd2b29e632c3.html
76 Reuters, "China Rejects Claim it Bugged Headquarters it Built for African Union," *The Guardian*, January 18, 2018. www.theguardian.com/world/2018/jan/30/china-african-union-headquarters-bugging-spying
77 Faith Karimi and Lynda Kinkade, "Thousands Flee After South African Mobs Attack Immigrants," *CNN*, April 17, 2015. www.cnn.com/2015/04/16/africa/south-africa-anti-foreigner-attacks/index.html
78 "Five Chinese Kidnapped in Armed Attack on Congo Mine: Embassy," *Global Times*, November 21, 2021. www.globaltimes.cn/page/202111/1239548.shtml
79 Laura Silver, "China's International Image Remains Broadly Negative as Views of the U.S. Rebound," *Pew Research Center*, June 20, 2021. www.pewresearch.org/fact-tank/2021/06/30/chinas-international-image-remains-broadly-negative-as-views-of-the-u-s-rebound/
80 "Xi Jinping Calls for More 'Lovable' Image for China in Bid to Make Friends," *BBC*, June 2, 2021. www.bbc.com/news/world-asia-china-57327177
81 Yu Lun Tian, "China Signals No Let-Up in its Aggressive Diplomacy Under Xi," *Reuters*, September 2022. www.reuters.com/world/china/china-signals-no-let-up-its-aggressive-diplomacy-2022-09-29/
82 (No author), "China's Global Security Initiative," http://ug.china-embassy.gov.cn/eng/xwdt/202205/t20220525_10692409.htm
83 The six commitments of China's Global Security Initiative are.

   1. Staying committed to comprehensive, cooperative, sustainable security
   2. Respecting the sovereignty and territorial integrity of all countries
   3. Abiding by the U.N. charter
   4. Taking seriously the legitimate security concerns of all countries
   5. Peacefully resolving disputes through dialogue
   6. Maintaining security in both traditional and non-traditional domains.

See Pak Niu, "China's Global Security Initiative: Xi's Wedge in the U.S.-led Order," *Nikkei*, November 1, 2022. https://asia.nikkei.com/Spotlight/Asia-Insight/China-s-Global-Security-Initiative-Xi-s-wedge-in-the-U.S-led-order

84 Martin Quin Pollard, "Analysis: China's Role as Ukraine Peacekeeper in Doubt as it 'Deepens' Russia Ties," *Reuters*, February 23, 2023. https://ecfr.eu/publication/keeping-america-close-russia-down-and-china-far-away-how-europeans-navigate-a-competitive-world/

85 www.pmo.gov.sg/Newsroom/Appointment-of-International-Judge-Jan-2023

86 www.zawya.com/en/legal/regulations/qatar-qicdrc-appoints-2-new-international-commercial-law-experts-to-judges-panel-kr1f7d9l

87 https://press.un.org/en/2022/ga12471.doc.htm

88 www.zawya.com/en/legal/regulations/qatar-qicdrc-appoints-2-new-international-commercial-law-experts-to-judges-panel-kr1f7d9l. I am indebted to Dr. Susan Finder of the Supreme Court Monitor for citations 85 through 88.

89 James Pomfret, "Opinion of China in Advanced Economies Sours Precipitously Under Xi – Pew," *Reuters*, September 29, 2022. www.reuters.com/world/china/opinion-china-advanced-economies-sours-precipitously-under-xi-pew-2022-09-29/

90 *Ibid.*

91 Demetri Sevastopulo, "U.S. and Allies Launch Initiative to Help Pacific Island Nations," *Financial Times*, June 25, 2022. www.ft.com/content/8400c75b-36d4-408a-9b58-85872c10739a

92 Yuan Yang, "UN Human Rights Council Blocks Debate on China's Abuses in Xinjiang," *Financial Times*, October 6, 2022. www.ft.com/content/e00c7c4f-f28a-4d6e-b9a4-eb89df8d6d81 Nineteen members of the UNHRC voted against holding a debate on the report, vice 17 in support and 11 abstentions.

93 Hal Brands, and Michael Beckley, *The Danger Zone: The Coming Conflict with China*. (New York: W.W. Norton, 2022) *passim*. The authors caution against complacency, pointing out that a declining power may be tempted to resort to war to arrest its declining prestige.

12 Who Is Blamed for the Pandemic? Survey Findings and Implications for the China Model

Yuen Yuen Ang, Twila Tardif, and Wenjia Song

Acknowledgments: We thank Sofia Hiltner for research assistance and Ann Lin for comments.

Introduction

The COVID-19 pandemic should have been a time when nations united to find common solutions – instead, America and China doubled down on a mutual blame game. Former president Donald Trump and his aides blamed China for covering up the outbreak and causing it to spread to the U.S. ("Remarks by President Trump in Press Briefing" 2020). Blame was sometimes expressed in racist tones: Trump nicknamed the coronavirus the 'Chinese virus' and 'Kung Flu,' for example.[1] Chinese politicians and media outlets lashed back at Washington, accusing it of 'scapegoating' China for its failures. Foreign Ministry spokesman Zhao Lijian claimed on Twitter that the U.S. military could have planted the virus in China. This sparring of words was followed by the mutual closures of consulates, marking a new low in US-China relations.

In blaming each other, both America and China habitually referred to the other as a single homogeneous entity (see the opening quotes) and did not distinguish among leaders, government, and people. In the United States, this "bundled" perception of China has provoked anti-Asian sentiments and crimes. According to the Center for the Study of Hate and Extremism (hereafter CSHE), from 2019 to 2020, anti-Asian hate crimes grew 149%, even though overall hate crimes dropped by 7% (CSHE 2020, 1). 'The first spike [occurred] in March and April amidst a rise in COVID cases and negative stereotyping of Asians relating to the pandemic,' the study noted (CSHE 2020, 1). Pushing back against this disturbing trend, Representative Judy Chu of California emphasized that while the U.S. should condemn the authoritarian practices of the Chinese Communist Party (hereafter CCP), it must 'avoid careless or inaccurate rhetoric that conflates the CCP with all Chinese people and unintentionally puts Asian Americans at risk of violence' (Chu 2020).[2]

Motivated by this politically charged context, we investigate a question that hasn't been explored in previous public opinion surveys: When people blame America and/or China for the pandemic, *who* specifically do they blame – the national leader, the government, or the people? From 21 May-20 June 2020 (the early stage of the pandemic), we conducted a 15-country survey. In total, we surveyed 15,005 respondents from North America (the U.S. and Canada), Europe (Germany, Poland, Russia, Sweden, and Ukraine), Southeast Asia (Indonesia, Malaysia, Philippines, Singapore, Thailand, and Vietnam), the Middle East (Turkey), and Mainland China. Our survey is the first effort to disaggregate attitudes of blame across regions and countries.

To preview, we highlight three findings:

1 On average, more global respondents blame China (56.5%) than the U.S. (49.3%) for the pandemic. (In this chapter, we use the term 'global' in reference to the respondents across all 15 cases in our survey.)
2 Among those who blame the U.S., the most commonly blamed actor is President Trump. Trump is blamed *more* frequently than the U.S. government, Centers for Disease Control (CDC), and state/local governments.
3 Among those who blame China, the most commonly blamed actor is the Chinese government. President Xi is blamed *less* frequently than the Chinese government, the CCP, local government, and the Chinese people.

Our findings highlight a sharp contrast in blame attitudes toward the US and China. For the US, Trump personally received the most blame, whereas for Xi, it was the opposite: respondents in all 15 cases blamed the Chinese government more than they blame Xi personally. Moreover, Chinese respondents blamed Xi even less than they blamed the Chinese people.

Our findings indicate that Xi successfully avoided personal blame during the early stage of the pandemic, despite his personalization of power. This perception likely reflects his regime's effective control of the virus using top-down mobilization methods in contrast to the Trump administration's dramatic politicking and mismanagement. This initial success in 2020 through 2021 bolstered Xi's propagandistic claims about the "institutional advantage" of centralized authoritarian rule. By 2022, however, Xi's insistence on maintaining "Zero-COVID" was no longer compatible with the milder strain of the virus and came at staggering social and economic costs. The mass protests and abrupt ending of Zero-COVID in November-December 2022 may have deflated Xi's popularity and the credibility of his claims about the advantages of top-down controls.

The rest of the chapter proceeds as follows. First, we briefly review existing surveys on COVID-19 and their limitations in measuring blame attitudes. Second, we introduce our survey, how it was conducted, and the relevant survey questions. Third, we describe the key patterns in our survey related to blame attitudes. Fourth, we situate our findings in the broader context of domestic governance under Xi and the US-China ideological competition over whose political system is superior.

Measuring Blame: A Survey of Existing Surveys

For political scientists, the issue of blame strikes at the heart of accountability, i.e., holding officials responsible for public outcomes. Political scientists find that politicians are keener to avoid blame for failures than to claim credit for successes, due to what is known as 'negativity bias.' As Weaver puts it, 'voters tend to be more sensitive to what has been done *to* them than what has been done *for* them' (Weaver 1986, 373). To avoid blame, politicians resort to finding a scapegoat, passing the buck, and circling the bandwagon (i.e., blaming as many people as possible). Under the Trump administration, all of these tactics were dramatically displayed. As President Trump famously declared, 'I don't take responsibility at all' (Oprysko 2020). Instead, he blamed China, the Obama administration, governors, hospitals, Dr. Fauci – everyone but himself (Phillips 2020).

In China, the Xi administration tried to deflect blame by 'redefining the issue.' By March 2020, as the outbreak began to come under control in China while the U.S. was just experiencing the first surge of cases, CCP propagandists quickly reshaped the global narrative of the pandemic by claiming 'total victory' under Xi's 'outstanding leadership.' They flooded the media with messages about the 'institutional advantages' of China's top-down political model, which stood in stark contrast to America's flailing democracy. At a press conference, Zhao Lijian, spokesperson for the Foreign Ministry, pronounced: 'China's signature strength, efficiency and speed in this fight has been widely acclaimed' (Ministry of Foreign Affairs of China 2020).

During COVID, there was a steady stream of surveys that explored various aspects of the pandemic, but few examined the issue of blame (see Table 12.1). Among surveys that did include questions on blame, the general approach was to bundle China (or the U.S.) under one national flag. For example, a YouGov-Economist poll of American citizens in 2020 asked:

Do you think China's handling of the COVID-19 outbreak led to the worldwide pandemic?

Another survey conducted by Boston University had one blame-related question:

Since China could have prevented the COVID-19 virus before it spread to the rest of the world, China should make reparation payments to those harmed by the virus.

Lacking follow-up questions at a fine-grained level, these surveys cannot tell us which particular actors respondents have in mind when they think of 'China' or 'the U.S.'

A few surveys worded their questions specifically about the Chinese/U.S. government or Chinese/U.S. president. For example, a poll by the University of

Table 12.1 Survey Questions on Blame in Existing Surveys

Survey	Sample	Relevant survey questions
Pew Research Center (published July 30), data collected (from June 16 to July 14, 2020)	Around 1,000 U.S citizens	1. U.S. should hold China responsible for the role it played in the outbreak of the coronavirus, even if it means worsening relations with China. 2. The Chinese government's initial handling of the coronavirus outbreak in Wuhan is not at all to blame for the global spread of the virus.
Berkeley IGS Poll: data collected from (April 16 to April 20, 2020)	8,800 California voters	1. To what extent do you think the Chinese government/administration is responsible for the COVID-19 pandemic and shortage of tests and medical supplies? 2. To what extent do you think Chinese individuals are responsible for the COVID-19 pandemic and shortage of tests and medical supplies?
Boston University (April 24 to May 7, 2020)	2,049 U.S. respondents	1. Do you agree/neutral/disagree with the following statement: "The Chinese people should be blamed for the COVID-19 pandemic"? 2. Do you agree/disagree with the following statement: "Since China could have prevented the COVID-19 virus before it spread to the rest of the world, China should make reparation payments to those harmed by the virus"?
YouGov/Economist (May 3, 2020 – May 5, 2020)	1,500 U.S. citizens	1. Do you think China's handling of the COVID-19 outbreak led to the worldwide pandemic? 2. Do you think the U.S. should or should not take some action for the express purpose of punishing China for the COVID-19 pandemic?
Morning Consult (Published on May 8)	Not indicated	1. Who is responsible for the current death toll in the U.S. from the COVID-19 pandemic? (Choices: the Chinese government, Americans who did not socially distance, Americans who traveled internationally, the federal government, governments of other countries, the Trump administration)
The Harris poll (April 3, 2020 – April 5, 2020, weekly poll	1,993 US citizens	1. Should China be required to pay other countries for the spread of the virus or is that not the responsibility of China? 2. Who do you blame more for the spread of coronavirus in the United States? Choice: Chinese/the US government 3. How trustworthy do you think each of the following sources are to provide accurate information regarding the coronavirus outbreak? (Choices: Chinese President, Xi Jinping).

Source: Authors

Chicago Harris School of Public Policy and The Associated Press-NORC Center for Public Affairs Research asked:

> Who do you blame more for the spread of coronavirus in the United States? The Chinese/the US government.

However, in using the term 'the government,' this poll does not distinguish between the government and the top leader, where the former is an institution and the latter is a person. Another poll by Morning Consult disaggregates 'the U.S.' into several actors (e.g., the Trump administration, state governments, scientific community), but in terms of China, it only asked about the Chinese government. Existing surveys also do not ask whether respondents blame the 'government' as compared to 'society or individuals,' except for Berkeley IGS. Last but not least, all of these surveys were limited to American citizens, so they do not provide a cross-national comparison.

Our Survey and Methods

In contrast to existing surveys, our survey was designed to disaggregate blame attitudes and compare responses across diverse regions. We performed an online cross-sectional study in 15 cases, focusing on the social and behavioral effects of COVID-19.[3] We used Qualtrics Panels, an online survey platform that maintains a database of residents of those 15 cases who have volunteered to participate in survey-based research (Table 12.2). For these 15 cases, we used quota sampling

Table 12.2 Number of Respondents in Each Country

Country	Number of Respondents (N = 15005)
United States of America	1159
Canada	1069
China	1342
Germany	1050
Indonesia	1072
Malaysia	941
Philippines	1058
Poland	1057
Russia	475
Singapore	538
Sweden	1056
Thailand	1080
Turkey	1071
Ukraine	1045
Vietnam	992

Source: Authors

methods to target a sample that was 60% female with age representation of the country's demographics. Participants who completed the survey via the Qualtrics panels were compensated in the amount agreed upon when joining the Qualtrics panel. Of the 38,127 people who accessed the landing page and reviewed the consent form, 18,614 (48.8%) completed the survey and spent over 10 minutes on the survey, and 15,005 answered both questions regarding blame of China and the U.S. Our descriptive results focus on these 15,005 respondents. The survey was reviewed and approved by the University of Michigan Institutional Review Board. The results presented here were collected between May and June 2020.

Questions on Blame

Our survey questions on blame asked the following:

If you believe that 'China' should be blamed for the COVID-19 pandemic, who specifically do you blame? (Check all that apply)

(1) The Chinese government
(2) The Chinese Communist Party (CCP)
(3) President Xi Jinping
(4) The Wuhan municipal government
(5) Chinese society and people
(6) I don't blame China

If you believe that 'the U.S.' should be blamed for the COVID-19 pandemic, who specifically do you blame? (Check all that apply)

(1) The U.S. government
(2) The U.S. Centers for Disease Control
(3) President Trump
(4) State and local governments
(5) American society and people
(6) I don't blame the U.S.

From these survey items, we are first able to measure blame in binary terms, between those who 'don't blame [China/the U.S.]' (selected option 6) and those who blame at least one entity from China or the U.S. (selected one or more of options 1–5). We are then able to assess which specific entities from each country people blame for the pandemic.

Who Blames China and the USs?

We first review responses to the survey items about blame for the pandemic. From these items, we are first able to measure blame in binary terms, between those who 'don't blame [China/the U.S.]' and those who blame at least one entity from China or the U.S. We are then able to assess which specific entities from each country people blame for the pandemic. Throughout this article, we use the term 'global' to refer to respondents across all 15 cases.

Who Blames China?

Across all 15 cases, between 20.8% and 75.7% of respondents indicated that they blamed China for the COVID-19 crisis, with a global average of 56.5%. Not surprisingly, Chinese respondents were the least likely to blame China (20.8%). Among American respondents, 61.1% of them blamed China, a proportion close to the global average (56.5%).

Russia, which is one of China's few allies and a nation that Western nations group with China as authoritarian threats, exhibited the second lowest level of blame. Still, 38.9% of Russian respondents blamed China, a level that was almost double that in China. On the other end of the spectrum, Thai respondents exhibited the highest level of blame (75.7%). One possible influence was an online feud that took place in April 2020, two months before our survey was conducted.[4] Sparked by a Thai celebrity's retweet about the virus originating in a Chinese lab, Chinese and Thai netizens launched a spat of words that went viral, prompting the Chinese embassy to warn against 'inflaming and sabotaging the friendship between the Chinese and Thai people' on its Facebook page (Ehrilich 2020).

Except for Indonesia, countries in Southeast Asia exhibited levels of blame above the global average, despite strong economic ties between China and the region. Indonesia's outlier status is consistent with a recent ISEAS survey which finds that among the ASEAN countries, Indonesian elites are most inclined to ally with China if forced to pick sides between the US and China (Tang et al. 2020, 29). Kurlantzick (2006) argued that China has carried out an effective 'charm offensive'

% respondents who blame China for the COVID-19 pandemic

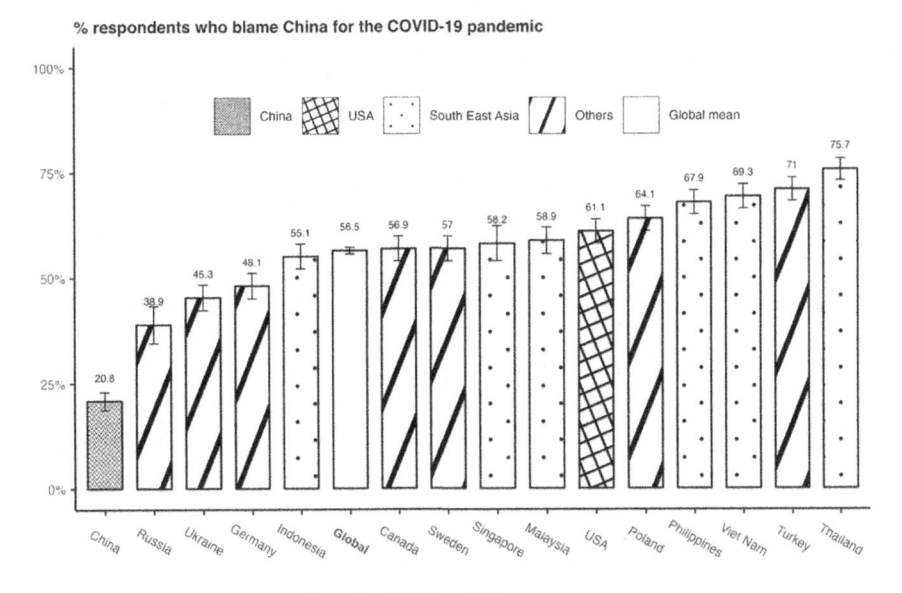

Figure 12.1 "Yes, I Blame China for COVID-19"

Source: Authors

Who Blames the US?

in Southeast Asia, but this effort did not appear to pay off consistently in terms of public opinion during the early stages of the pandemic.

Next, we turn to the US. Across all cases, between 25.9% and 83.1% of respondents blame the US for COVID-19, with a global average of 49.3%, which is approximately 7 percentage points lower than the average for China-blame (56.5%).

Interestingly, whereas Chinese respondents were the *least* likely to blame China for COVID-19 across the surveyed regions, US respondents are *not* the least likely to blame the U.S. Among American respondents, 48.7% blamed the US, close to the global average of 49.3%. This was only moderately lower than the share of Americans who blamed China (61.1%). Among Chinese respondents, however, 61.3% blamed the US, compared to only 20.8% who blamed their own country.

In other words, while the average American respondent was inclined to blame both the US and China, the average Chinese blamed the US considerably more than China. This pattern is consistent with one study of overseas Chinese students, which observed that the students perceived criticizing China as a sign of disloyalty to the nation (Redden 2015).

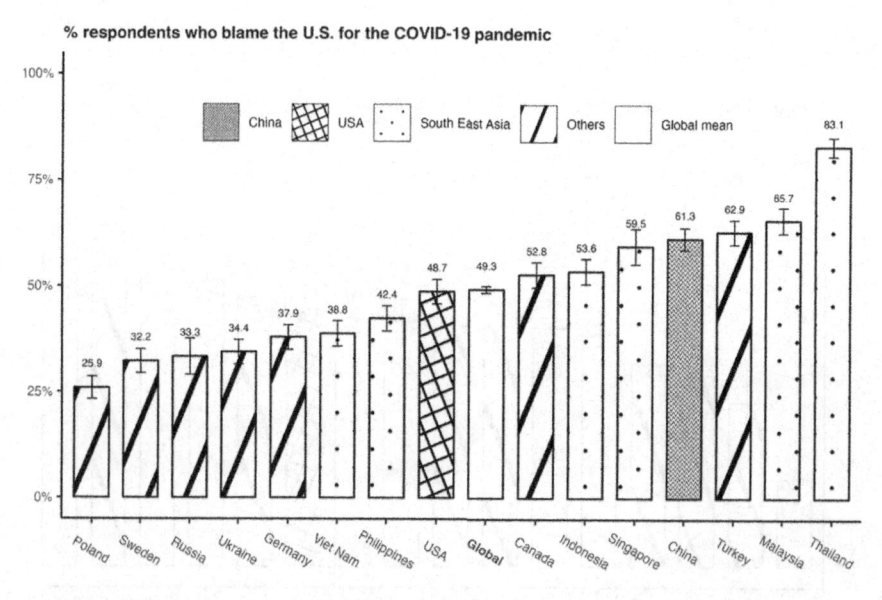

Figure 12.2 "Yes, I Blame the U.S. for COVID-19"

Source: Authors

Other studies also find Chinese citizens sensitive to foreign criticisms, and in several high-profile events, they self-mobilized to punish critical speakers (Weiss 2014, 9).[5]

Global Distribution of Blame

Figure 12.3 illustrates where cases fall in relation to the global average that blame the U.S. and China for COVID-19. Most cases cluster around the global averages. China and Thailand, however, appear to be outliers: the percent of Chinese respondents who blame China is notably lower than the global average and the percent of Thai respondents who blame the US and China is notably higher than the global average for both countries.

In three cases (Malaysia, Thailand, and Turkey), a higher percent of respondents blamed both the U.S. and China more than the global average. Respondents in Germany, Russia, and Ukraine were most inclined to blame neither the U.S. nor China.

Again, China's 'charm diplomacy' in Southeast Asia appears to have mixed effects across the region. If such diplomacy worked, we should expect countries in this region to blame neither the US nor China or blame the US more than China; however, only Indonesia fell marginally into this category. Respondents

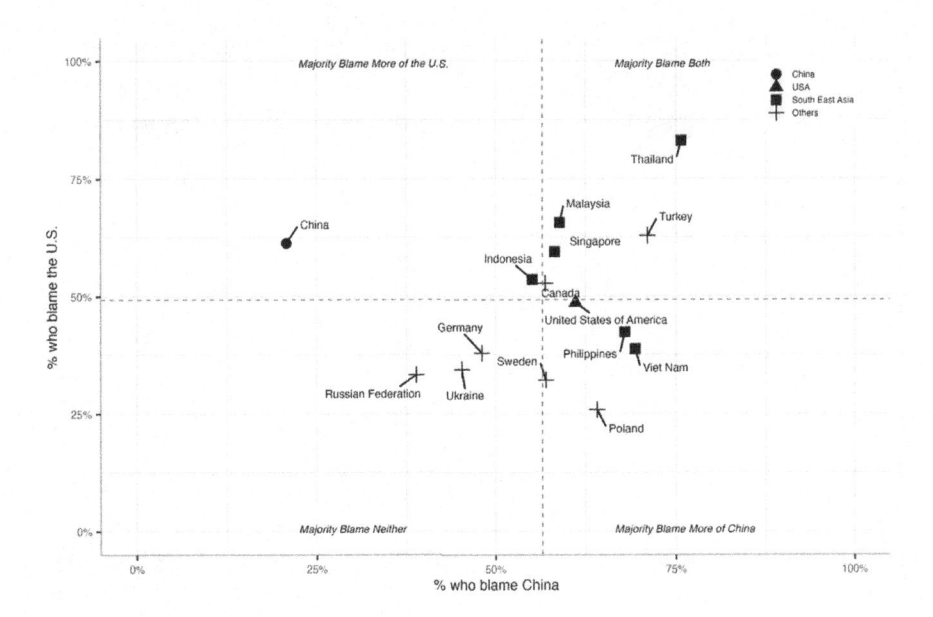

Figure 12.3 Global Distribution of Blame

Source: Authors

248 *Yuen Yuen Ang, Twila Tardif and Wenjia Song*

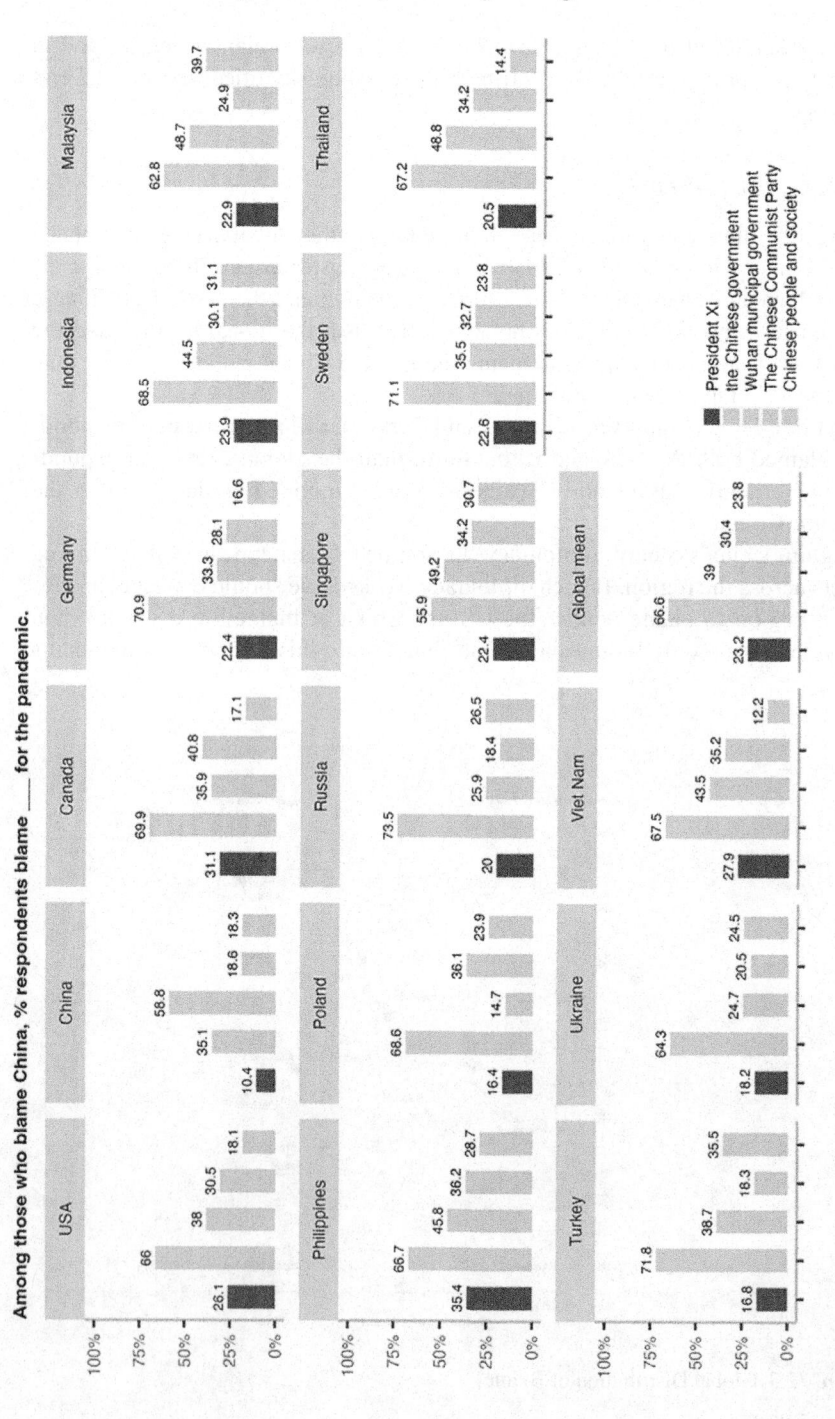

Among those who blame China, % respondents blame ___ for the pandemic.

Figure 12.4 Who in China Is Blamed?
Source: Authors

in Malaysia and Singapore blamed China at a level close to the global average, whereas those in the Philippines, Thailand, and Vietnam all blamed China more than the global average.

Unbundling Blame

Who in China Is Blamed?

Moving on, we unbundle attitudes of blame toward China. In terms of the global average, the most frequently blamed actor is the Chinese government (66.6%), followed by the Wuhan Municipal government (39%), the Chinese Communist Party (30.4%), Chinese people and society (23.8%), and President Xi Jinping (23.2%).

Chinese respondents blame the Wuhan municipal government the most (58.8%), and to a considerably larger extent than the central government (35.1%). This pattern is consistent with several studies on Chinese public opinion, which found that the Chinese public generally trusts the central government more than local governments (Li 2004). This partly reflects the success of Beijing's tactic in shifting blame from the top leader and/or regime to corrupt local officials, so that any problem will be perceived as idiosyncratic rather than systemic.[6] Chinese respondents also blamed the central government (35.1%) more than the CCP (18.6%) even though under Xi, 'the Party leads everything.'

Notably, Chinese respondents blamed Xi the least (10.4%), even though the president had effectively centralized power in his own hands (Economy 2018). When the virus first broke out, Xi took the unusual action of detailing the timeline of his decisions in an editorial in the party magazine *Qiushi*, which prompted fervent debate about what Xi knew and did not know about the outbreak as well as his personal responsibility for it. At a live interview on CCTV in January 2020, Zhou Xianwang, Wuhan's mayor at the time, admitted, 'As the head of a local government, after I receive the information, I can only release it after I am authorized.' His words sparked vigorous commentary about what it seemed to imply: central authorities knew about the severity of the crisis but did not authorize local authorities to inform citizens. Our survey findings suggest that these incidents scarcely dented Xi's image, and he was blamed the least among all the actors.

Indeed, it may seem surprising that Chinese respondents blamed Chinese society and people (18.3%) more than President Xi (10.4%). This level of self-blame was higher than the blame Vietnamese, Thais, Americans, Canadians, and Germans assigned to the Chinese people. A closer look at societal dynamics on the ground suggest that Chinese citizens did blame one another. For example, some non-Wuhan residents insulted Wuhan residents for spreading the virus (*The Paper* 2020). Another common target of blame was Chinese students returning from overseas, whom some netizens blamed for 'bringing the virus home from 10,000 miles away' (People's Daily 2020a).

Across the 15 countries in our survey, Xi was most frequently blamed in the Philippines (35.4%) and Canada (31.1%), and least blamed in China (only 10.4%). American respondents blamed the Chinese government the most (66%), and Chinese society and people the least (18.1%). Xi came in second to last at 26.1%. Americans blamed the

Chinese government (66%) more than Wuhan's government (38%) or the CCP (30.5%). This finding could reflect the general habit of lumping political actors into one category, as discussed earlier. Americans who do not know the distinction between the government, the party, and the leader may instinctively blame 'the Chinese government.'

Who in the US Is Blamed?

On average across cases, those who blamed the US for the pandemic most frequently blamed President Trump (55.3%), followed by the US government (49.5%), U.S. Centers for Disease Control (CDC) (24.3%), American society and people (18.4%), and state and local governments (16.6%).

Similarly, US respondents were most likely to blame President Trump (59%), a rate slightly higher than the global average, followed by the US government (44.3%). Americans blamed state and local governments the least (16.3%), marginally less than the rate of blame on American society and people (20.9%).

By comparison, Chinese respondents did not blame Trump (51.6%) the most. Instead, they expressed the highest level of blame for the US government (59.2%), more so than U.S. respondents (44.3%) and the global average (49.5%). Chinese respondents blamed American people (14.7%) less than American respondents blamed the Chinese people (18.1%).

Notably, whereas Xi received little blame relative to other actors, Trump was the most blamed actor in 8 out of 15 countries. The three countries most critical of him were Canada (75.5%), Germany (70.1%), and Malaysia (70.1%), whereas the three countries that blamed him the least were Vietnam (29.6%), Ukraine (32.8%), and Russia (36.7%).

Who Is Blamed Most?

Across all cases, a significantly greater percentage of respondents blamed President Trump (55.3%) than President Xi (23.2%). Respondents blamed both the US and Chinese governments, though a greater percentage blamed the Chinese government (66.6%) than the US government (49.5%). More respondents also blamed the Chinese people (23.8%) than the American people (18.4%).

Figure 12.6 compares blame attitudes between US and Chinese respondents only. Notice that Trump was highly blamed by US respondents (59%), whereas Xi was little blamed by Chinese respondents (10.4%). US respondents were more likely to blame the national government (44.3%) than their Chinese counterparts (35.1%), while Chinese respondents were slightly less likely to blame the people and society (18.3%) than their US counterparts (20.9%). Consistent with global patterns, President Trump was the most blamed actor in the US, whereas the Chinese government was the most blamed actor in China.

Mainland China, Taiwan, and Hong Kong

In addition to the 15 countries earlier discussed, we also collected responses from Taiwan and Hong Kong (see Table 12.3). We find that blame attitudes differed across mainland China, Taiwan, and Hong Kong.

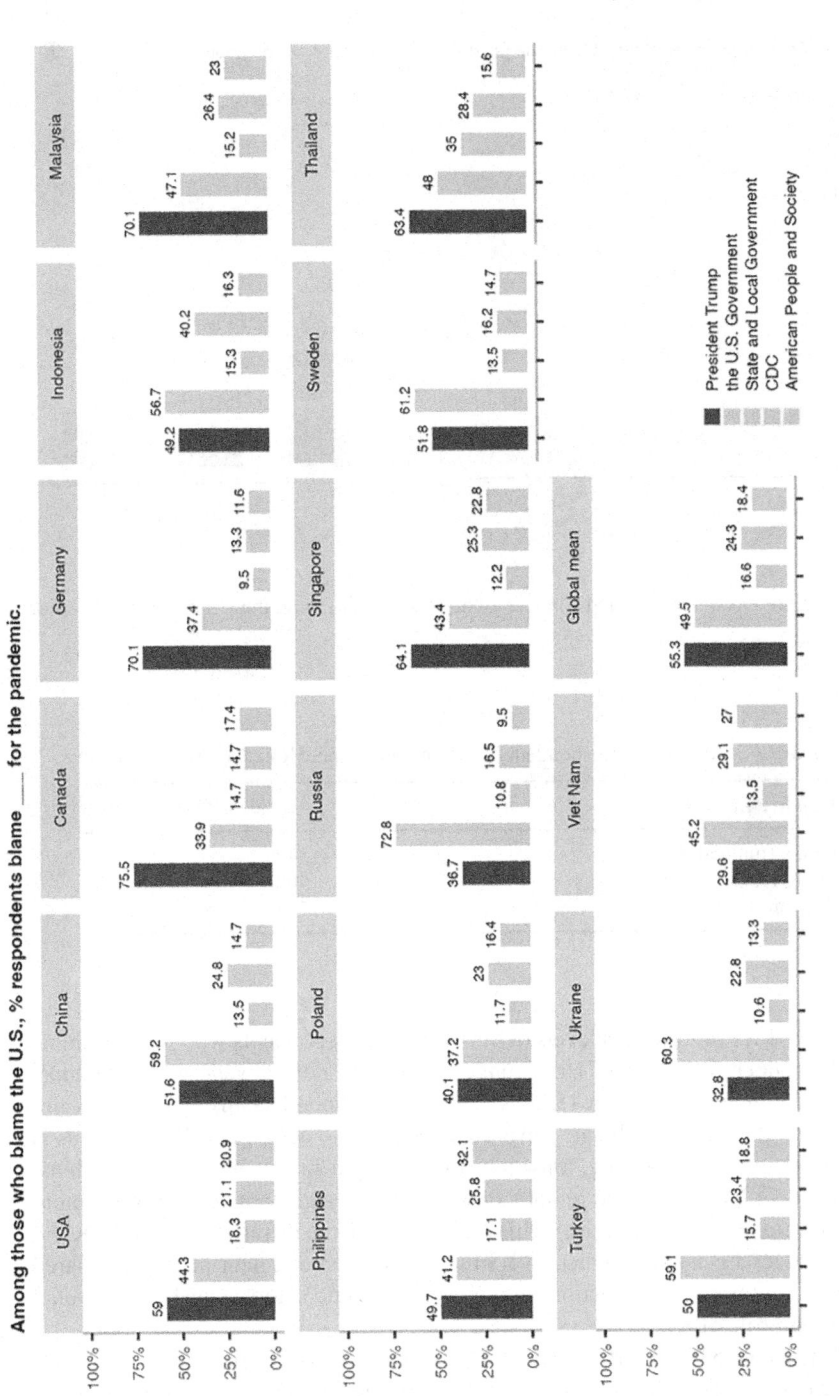

Among those who blame the U.S., % respondents blame _____ for the pandemic.

Figure 12.5 Who in the US Is Blamed?

Source: Authors

Do Americans and Chinese blame the government, the leader, or the people?

US respondents:
- The U.S. Government: 44.3
- President Trump: 59
- American People and Society: 20.9

Chinese respondents:
- The Chinese Government: 35.1
- President Xi: 10.4
- Chinese People and Society: 18.3

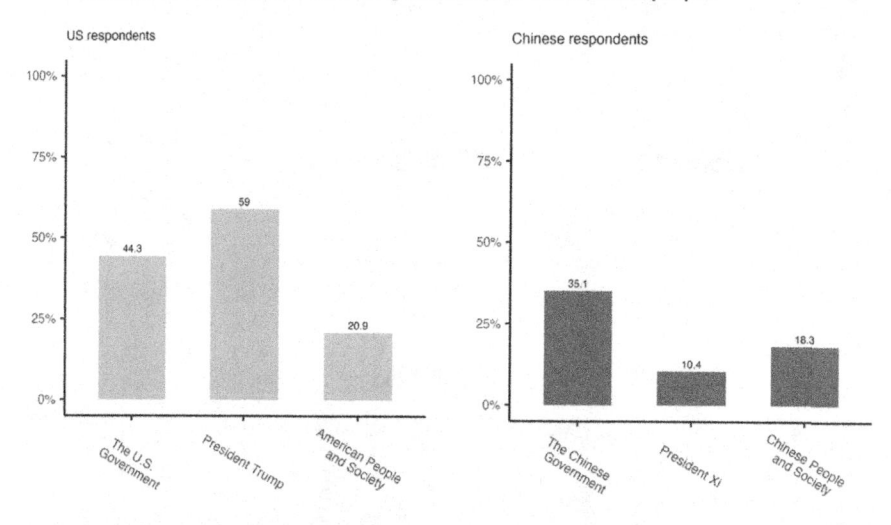

Figure 12.6 Do Americans and Chinese Blame the Government, the Leader, or the People?
Source: Authors

Table 12.3 Number of Respondents in Mainland China, Hong Kong, and Taiwan

Country/Region	Number of Respondents
China (mainland)	1342
Hong Kong	568
Taiwan	757

Source: Authors

Figure 12.7 summarizes levels of blame among respondents who 'blame China' for the pandemic. 64.6% of Hongkongers and 77.9% of Taiwanese blame China, more than the global average (57.8%). Moreover, respondents from Taiwan exhibited the highest level of blame toward China (77.9%) across all 17 cases. This is not surprising given the long, fraught history between Taiwan and mainland China.

President Xi was blamed in both Taiwan (38.1%) and Hong Kong (36%), more than the global average (24.6%). This high rate of blame in Taiwan and Hong Kong could reflect a generally higher level of knowledge among their public, compared to other countries, of distinctions among Chinese state actors as well the personal power and role of Xi.

Hong Kong (53.7%) and Taiwan (48.1%) respondents also blamed the CCP at levels higher than the global average (32.4%). By comparison, mainland Chinese respondents blamed both the CCP (18.6%) and Xi (10.4%) less, despite presumably knowing more about Xi's and the Party's central role in politics (in China, both President Xi's

Who Is Blamed for the Pandemic? 253

Among those who blame China, % respondents blame ___ for the pandemic.

China overall:
- Mainland China: 20.8
- Hong Kong: 64.6
- Taiwan: 77.9
- Global mean: 57.8

President Xi:
- Mainland China: 10.4
- Hong Kong: 36
- Taiwan: 38.1
- Global mean: 24.6

the Chinese government:
- Mainland China: 35.1
- Hong Kong: 54.8
- Taiwan: 70.8
- Global mean: 66.4

Wuhan municipal government:
- Mainland China: 58.8
- Hong Kong: 53.1
- Taiwan: 31.2
- Global mean: 39.1

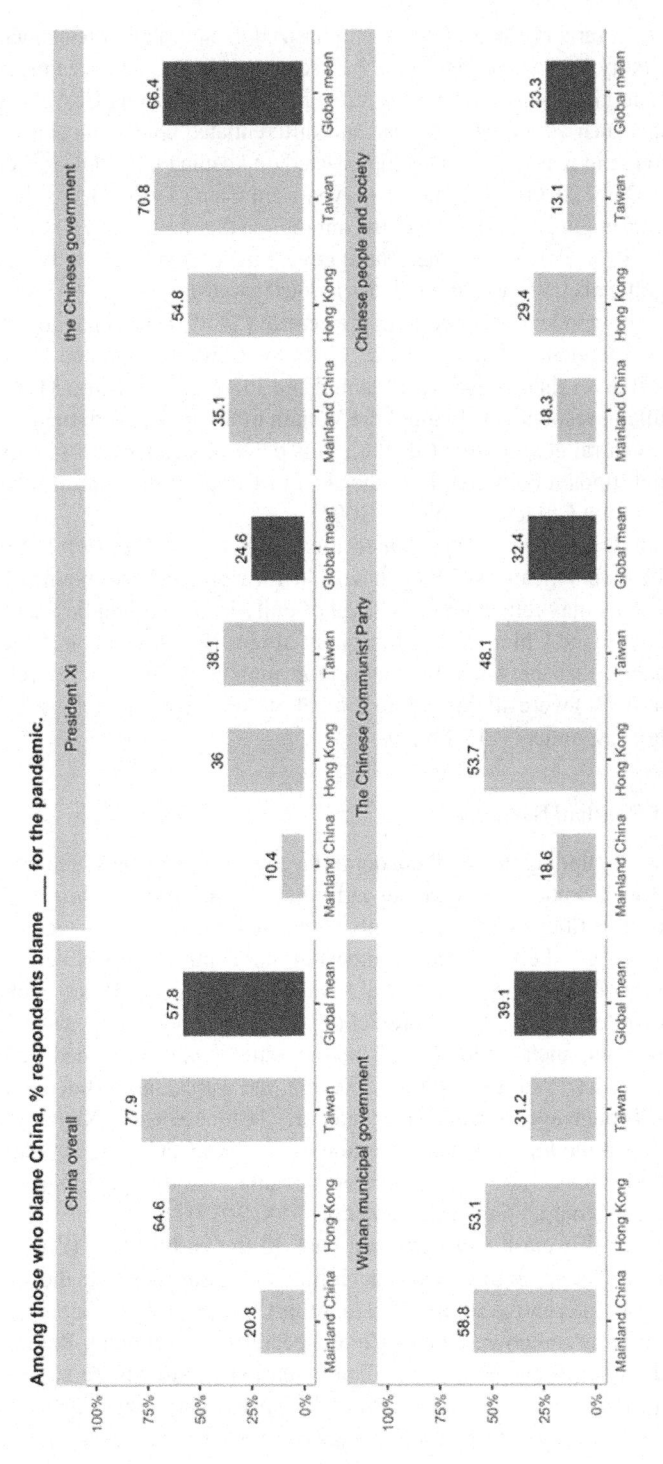

The Chinese Communist Party:
- Mainland China: 18.6
- Hong Kong: 53.7
- Taiwan: 48.1
- Global mean: 32.4

Chinese people and society:
- Mainland China: 18.3
- Hong Kong: 29.4
- Taiwan: 13.1
- Global mean: 23.3

Figure 12.7 Who in China Is Blamed by the Respondents from Mainland China, Hong Kong, and Taiwan?
Source: Authors

and the Party's overarching leadership are emphasized in almost all official documents after the 18th Party Congress). This could be because since 2020, the central government appeared to give local governments flexibility in implementing COVID policies through slogans such as 'practice precise and differentiated epidemic-control strategies,' even though in reality the leadership insisted on keeping COVID cases close to zero (People's Daily 2020b; translation retrieved from China Daily 2020). Thus, Chinese respondents might have been under the impression that when COVID restrictions were too strict, it was not because the central government forced them to be strict but because local officials failed to tailor policies to local contexts.

Hong Kong respondents blamed both the central (54.8%) and local government (53.1%) for the pandemic, whereas twice as many Taiwanese blamed the central government (70.8%) than those who blamed the local government (31.2%). By contrast, mainland respondents blamed the Wuhan municipal government (58.8%) more than the central government (35.1%). This pattern is consistent with existing literature which finds a consistently higher level of trust in the central than local governments among Chinese people (Li 2004).

Respondents from Hong Kong blamed the Chinese people (29.4%) at a level higher than the global mean (23.3%), whereas in Taiwan, much less blame (13.1%) was assigned. This may reflect a higher level of daily intermingling between Hong Kongers and mainland Chinese, which brought about friction and competition for jobs and housing, than between Taiwanese and mainland Chinese. Interestingly, mainlanders (14.7%) were slightly more critical of the Chinese people and society than Taiwanese respondents (13.1%).

The Clash of Political Systems?

What do our survey findings tell us about domestic governance under Xi and US-China competition? In this section, we zoom out and situate our findings on a broad canvas.

US-China competition is waged not only on economic and technological but also ideological fronts. On the ideological dimension, the competition has been framed as an epic battle of two opposing political systems. As President Biden declared at his first press conference in 2021: 'I predict to you, your children and grandchildren are going to be doing their doctoral thesis on the issue of who succeeded, autocracy or democracy, because that is what is at stake, not just with China' (Biden quoted in Sanger 2021). Though avoiding the term 'autocracy,' Chinese leader Xi made a similar proclamation at the Fourth Plenary Session of the 19th CPC Central Committee: "Institutional advantage is a nation's greatest advantage, and competition between systems is the core competition between nations" (Xi 2019).[7]

The origins of this clash can be traced back to the early 2000s (Zhao 2017). In 2004, Joshua Cooper Ramo wrote an influential essay positing the "Beijing Consensus" as an alternative to the "Washington Consensus."[8] As Scott Kennedy described, 'Virtually unknown among China specialists at the time, Ramo's tract took the field by storm and drew immediate attention from Chinese scholars and officialdom' (2010, 467). Western observers disagreed on whether there was such a consensus. While some like Kurlantzick (2008) claimed that Ramo's thesis was widely accepted in China, Kennedy pointed to a range of discussions within China rejecting the existence of a Beijing consensus.

Perceptions changed after 2008, the year the U.S. financial crisis exploded and Beijing hosted the Olympics. Among Chinese policy elites, the idea that China has a system superior to the West gained greater credibility as the merits of the American capitalist system were called into question. Still, throughout the 2010s, the Chinese leadership was careful not to formally adopt the term "China model," which originated in the West, not in Beijing. Under Hu-Wen, the official stance was that all nations should follow their own path, and that the Chinese model, if there was one, is too unique to be replicated elsewhere (People's Daily 2009). Despite this cautionary tone, celebratory terms such as "the China miracle" and "China's golden age" became popular amid a rising tide of confidence (Zhao 2017).

Xi's rise to power in 2012 marked a sharp turning point. In 2011, China overtook Japan to become the world's second-largest economy. This soon coincided with a sense of democracy in crisis in the West, triggered by Trump's election and Brexit in the UK in 2016 (Rose 2018). Breaking from Deng Xiaoping's tradition of "lying low" and "never taking the lead," Xi (2017) projected greater desire in becoming a global power. At the 19th Party Congress in 2017, he proclaimed, 'China is blazing a new trail for other developing countries to achieve modernization. It offers a Chinese solution (*zhongguo fang'an* 中国方案) to solving the problems facing mankind.' Yet, despite projecting more confidence, Xi never defined the "Chinese solution," and at another speech only two months later, he insisted that 'China will not export the Chinese model' (China Daily 2017).

What this historical overview goes to show is that the "Beijing consensus," "China model," or "Chinese solution," whatever it may be called, was never an actual blueprint that leaders in Zhongnanhai pre-planned and executed – but rather a contested and politicized branding of China's political-economic system vis-à-vis the Western-liberal ideal. The popular impression of the "China model" as rapid growth through top-down, authoritarian planning was in fact divorced from reality. As Ang (2016) showed, the Chinese development experience is better characterized as "directed improvisation" – 'the mixture of top-down direction from Beijing and bottom-up improvisation among numerous local governments – that enabled a locally tailored pattern of development' (UNDP 2018).

When COVID-19 broke out in 2020, US-China ideological competition reached a boiling point. Beijing and Washington jostled over whose political system was better equipped at handling the pandemic, which had stakes not only for soft-power competition but also for domestic legitimacy. Initially, the CCP and Xi himself were intensely criticized for covering up the outbreak, to the point that Xi made the unusual move of publishing his timeline of decisions in *Qiushi* (the journal of the CCP Central Committee). But his leadership quickly turned around public opinion by curbing the virus through a combination of mass testing, mass quarantine, and city-wide lockdowns – methods that could only be accomplished in China's authoritarian system. From 2020 through the end of 2022, COVID case and death counts were very low in China (among the lowest in the world) and visibly high in the United States.[9] Xi's team packaged this success, backed by statistics, as solid evidence of the "institutional advantage" of the

CCP's top-down mobilization, i.e., it could channel the entire nation's efforts toward a single goal – in this case, eliminating COVID – without being distracted by political contestation (Xinhuanet 2022).

Our survey results showed that this political messaging worked in May-June 2020: Xi received little personal blame for the outbreak, whereas Trump was intensely blamed not only in the US but also around the world. For political scientists, this may seem paradoxical. Dictatorships are normally more personalist than democracies,[10] so the Chinese leader should have been more personally blamed than the US leader. Moreover, Xi had steadily dismantled Deng's norms of institutionalized, collective leadership and concentrated power in his own hands, so he should have been blamed more than the CCP or Chinese government.

One key explanation for this paradox is that Trump had created a political anomaly: a 'personalist democracy' with authoritarian characteristics (Frum 2017; Frantz et al. 2021). Trump's bombastic personality, wild tweets, and reality TV antics, along with his brazen disregard for democratic norms and bureaucratic autonomy, drew both attention and blame to himself during the pandemic. Next to Trump, Xi appeared aloof and "presidential," thus those who were not aware of Xi's personalization of power would blame the CCP and government more than the leader himself. Put differently, Trump may be considered a blessing for Xi personal's popularity, even though the Trump administration took an overtly combative stance toward China.

Yet Xi's initial success later became a primary source of his regime's political crisis.[11] In 2020, the virus was novel and dangerous, and no vaccine was available. In that context, China's strategy of strict mass containment worked wonders, impressing even skeptics (Zi 2021; Ip 2022). By 2021, as vaccines became available and more people contracted the virus and recovered, countries learned to live with the virus. China was the sole exception: Xi remained attached to "zero-COVID," channeling vast quantities of personnel and resources toward containment. This approach became obsolete, even absurd, with the emergence of the highly transmissible but milder Omicron variant. Ignoring this reality, local governments did not want any cases to emerge on their watch. Accordingly, their response was to enforce relentless blanket lockdowns, spray disinfectants in the streets, and quarantine people who had been exposed but had no symptoms. The absurdity of these measures makes sense only when one understands that their true goal is not protecting public health but rather meeting a political target: keep the numbers at zero.

On November 25, 2022, a deadly residential fire broke out in the city of Urumqi, where rescue efforts were apparently delayed by barricades commonly used to block residents from leaving their homes during lockdowns. For many people in China, this was the last straw. 'If it's not me this time, it could be me next time,' one viral post on social media read. The next day, protests erupted across multiple cities, with people taking to the streets and demanding an end to harsh lockdowns. Many held up pieces of blank white paper, protesting wordlessly against censorship. A few others went beyond criticizing public health restrictions, taking aim at autocratic rule: 'We don't want COVID tests! We want freedom!' a group of demonstrators in Shanghai chanted, repeating words from an earlier lone protestor who unfurled a banner on a bridge in Beijing.

This is perhaps the first time that Chinese citizens have rallied together to resist a national policy – and they successfully prompted the authorities to change course. At a meeting on December 2 with European Council President Charles Michel, Xi reportedly told the audience that 'after three years of COVID he had an issue because people were frustrated. It was mainly students, or teenagers in university' (Bermingham 2022). Shortly afterward, China quickly lifted COVID controls. Because the policy ended with little preparation, however, Chinese residents struggled with surging infections and shortage of medicine. In the coming months and years, China will likely face a long, tough road to economic recovery.

We highlight two key takeaways on domestic governance. First, Xi has made Zero-COVID a core part of his argument about the "institutional advantage" of centralized authoritarian rule. The failure of Zero-COVID – both in terms of the socio-economic damage it wrought and its abrupt end – has damaged Xi's narrative and likely his own popularity. If our survey were repeated in November-December 2022, it is unclear whether Xi would remain the least blamed actor for the pandemic. But even if Xi's image has taken a hit, this does not mean that he is at risk of losing power. With his predecessors (Jiang Zemin and Hu Jintao) and rival factions (e.g., Community Youth League) gone and a post-2022 cabinet stacked with his loyalists, Xi's grip on power will remain secure.

Second, the failure of Zero-COVID precisely demonstrated the gap between the top-down mobilization model championed by Xi's propagandists and the actual "China model" that enabled economic success during the reform era. Besides delegating authority, another core ingredient of adaptive governance under Deng was his emphasis on encouraging and giving honest feedback. As Deng said at his historic speech launching reform and opening in December 1978, the problem under Mao was that people sought only to be politically correct and no longer dared speak the truth. "Seeking truth from facts," Deng stressed, was necessary for effective governance. Xi's insistence on maintaining zero cases stood in opposition to Deng's principles of pragmatism and flexibility. His regime's suppression of dissent and free speech prevented the leadership from hearing the voices of the people – until people were forced to take to the streets.

What does this mean for the clash of political systems, if there is one? It is temptingly simplistic to see the world in black-and-white terms, with America showcasing democracy in its best form and China under CCP rule representing autocracy in its worst form. In this binary portrayal, the "good" will defeat the "evil" and save the world. Reality, however, does not fit this simplistic picture. As Susan Shirk pointed out, the period from 2016 to 2020 saw the 'coincidence of the election of a personalistic autocratic American President, Donald Trump, with China's rule by Xi Jinping, its most personalistic autocrat since Mao Zedong' (Shirk 2022, 235). Trump demonstrated that authoritarian forces can corrupt a mature democracy, whereas Xi has departed from the institutionalized, pragmatic version of autocracy Deng installed. In terms of COVID control, neither America nor China are glowing models for other countries; both failed at different times, in different ways, for different reasons. Both America and China must first prevent themselves from becoming a worse version of their respective political system.

Notes

1. In a more overtly racist example, Republican Senator John Cornyn of Texas said: 'China is to blame. Because the culture where people eat bats and snakes and dogs and things like that' (Shen-Berro 2020). In this comment, he also incorrectly cited China as the source of MERS and the swine flu. In fact, the latter originated in the US in 2009.
2. Likewise, Josh Rogin argued in *The Washington Post* that the coronavirus should be called the 'CCP virus,' not the Chinese virus, because 'that's more accurate and offends only those who deserve it' (Rogin 2020).
3. This survey is part of the interdisciplinary project 'People and Pandemics' at the University of Michigan.
4. However, we note that Thai respondents also blamed the US the most. It appears that the Thais are inclined to blame both superpowers.
5. For example, after President Nicolas Sarkozy publicly contemplated a boycott of the Beijing Olympics in 2008, nationalist Chinese protested against France.
6. For example, central authorities have portrayed and attacked corruption as a problem of bad individual officials, rather than as a feature of the political system (Ang 2014).
7. In Chinese, Xi's words are: 制度优势是一个国家的最大优势，制度竞争是国家间最根本的竞争
8. Ramo defined the "Beijing consensus" as a development model with technological innovation as its core, that is equitable and sustainable, and is unique. Kennedy (2010) refuted each of these points.
9. According to Johns Hopkins University's Coronavirus Resource Center, as of June 2022, China had only one death per 100,000 people, compared with three hundred per 100,000 people in the United States.
10. Geddes et al. (2014) classified autocratic regimes into personalist and non-personalist types, but no such distinction was made among democracies, which were all placed in one category. Other political scientists apply the term 'personalist dictatorships' to characterize regimes such as Iraq under Saddam Hussein and China under Mao Zedong (Colgan and Weeks 2015; Blaydes 2018).
11. This section is adapted from Yuen Yuen Ang (2022), "The Problem with Zero," by permission of Foreign Affairs (online issue, 2 December 2022). Copyright (2022) by the Council on Foreign Relations, Inc. www.ForeignAffairs.com.

References

Ang, Yuen Yuen. 2014. "Authoritarian Restraints on Online Activism Revisited: Why 'I-Paid-A-Bribe' Worked in India But Failed in China." *Comparative Politics* 47(1): 21–40. www.jstor.org/stable/43664341.

Ang, Yuen Yuen. 2016. *How China Escaped the Poverty Trap*. Ithaca: Cornell University Press.

Ang, Yuen Yuen. 2022. "The Problem with Zero: How Xi's Pandemic Policy Created a Crisis for the Regime." *Foreign Affairs*. December 2. www.foreignaffairs.com/china/problem-zero-xi-pandemic-policy-crisis (accessed February 18, 2023).

Bermingham, Finbarr. 2022. "Chinese President Xi Jinping Believes 'Frustrated Students' Are behind COVID-19 Protests, EU Officials Say." *South China Morning Post*. December 2. www.scmp.com/news/china/diplomacy/article/3201901/chinese-president-xi-jinping-believes-frustrated-students-are-behind-covid-protests-eu-officials-say (accessed February 15, 2023).

Blaydes, Lisa. 2018. *State of Repression Iraq under Saddam Hussein*. Princeton, NJ: Princeton University Press.

Center for the Study of Hate and Extremism. 2020. *FACT SHEET: Anti-Asian Prejudice March 2020*. California State University, San Bernardino. www.csusb.edu/sites/default/files/FACT%20SHEET-%20Anti-Asian%20Hate%202020%203.2.21.pdf (accessed June 30, 2021).

China Daily. 2017. "Highlights of Xi's Speech at World Political Party Dialogue." *China Daily*. December 1. www.chinadaily.com.cn/china/2017-12/01/content_35161658.htm (accessed February 1, 2023).

China Daily. 2020. "Word of the Day: Precise and Differentiated Epidemic Control Strategies." *China Daily*. February 28. https://cn.chinadaily.com.cn/a/202002/28/WS5e58682e-a3107bb6b57a2dfb.html (accessed February 15, 2023).

Chu, Judy. 2020. "Member Toolkit on Combating Xenophobia amidst the Coronavirus Pandemic." Congressional Asian Pacific American Caucus (CAPAC). July 27. https://chu.house.gov/sites/chu.house.gov/files/documents/Anti-Asian_Bigotry_Dear_Colleague_Toolkit.pdf (accessed June 30, 2021).

Colgan, J. D., and Weeks, J. 2015. "Revolution, Personalist Dictatorships, and International Conflict." *International Organization* 69(1): 163–194. doi: 10.1017/S0020818314000307.

Economy, Elizabeth. 2018. *The Third Revolution: Xi Jinping and the New Chinese State*. Oxford: Oxford University Press.

Ehrlich, Richard. 2020. "China, Thai Netizens in a War of Viral Words." *Asia Times*. April 16. https://asiatimes.com/2020/04/china-thai-netizens-in-a-war-of-viral-words/ (accessed June 30, 2021).

Frantz, Erica, Andrea Kendall-Taylor, Carisa Nietsche, and Joseph Wright. 2021. "How Personalist Politics Is Changing Democracies." *Journal of Democracy* 32(3): 94–108. doi: 10.1353/jod.2021.0036.

Frum, David. 2017. "How to Build an Autocracy." *The Atlantic*, March 2017. www.theatlantic.com/magazine/archive/2017/03/how-to-build-an-autocracy/513872/ (accessed February 15, 2023).

Geddes, Barbara., Joseph Wright, and Frantz Erica. 2014. "Autocratic Breakdown and Regime Transitions." *Perspectives on Politics* 12(2): 313–331. doi: 10.1017/S1537592714000851.

Ip, Greg. 2022. "Zhong guo dong tai qing ling zheng ce dui qi ta guo jia you he jie jian yi yi" [What Are the Lessons of China's Zero-Covid Policy for Other Countries?]. *The Wall Street Journal*, February 18. https://cn.wsj.com/articles/中国-动态清零-政策对其他国家有何借鉴意义-11645074674 (accessed February 15, 2023).

Kennedy, Scott. 2010. "The Myth of the Beijing Consensus." *Journal of Contemporary China* 19(65): 461–477. https://doi.org/10.1080/10670561003666087.

Kurlantzick, Joshua. 2006. "China's Charm Offensive in Southeast Asia." *Current History* 105(692): 270–276. https://doi.org/10.1525/curh.2006.105.692.270.

Kurlantzick, Joshua. 2008. *Charm Offensive: How China's Soft Power Is Transforming the World*. New Haven, CT: Yale University Press.

Li, Lianjiang. 2004. "Political Trust in Rural China." *Modern China* 30(2): 228–258. https://doi.org/10.1177/0097700403261824.

Ministry of Foreign Affairs of the People's Republic of China. 2020. "Foreign Ministry Spokesperson Zhao Lijian's Regular Press Conference on March 5, 2020." March 5. www.fmprc.gov.cn/mfa_eng/xwfw_665399/s2510_665401/t1752564.shtml (accessed October 1, 2021).

Oprysko, Caitlin. 2020. "'I Don't Take Responsibility at All': Trump Deflects Blame for Coronavirus Testing Fumble." *Politico*. March 13. www.politico.com/news/2020/03/13/trump-coronavirus-testing-128971 (accessed July 1, 2021).

The Paper. 2020. "Jingqing tongbao dalian yinanzi zai weixin pengyouquan ruma wuhanren yibei yifa juliu" [Police Briefing – A Man in Dalian Who Verbally Assaulted People from Wuhan on His WeChat Has Been Detained]. *The Paper*. February 2. www.thepaper.cn/newsDetail_forward_5737593 (accessed October 7, 2021).

People's Daily. 2009. "Can Chinese Model Be Replicated." *People's Daily*. September 18.

People's Daily (Comments) (*renmin ruiping*). 2020a. "Shuo tamen qianli toudu diyiming henbuheshi" [Accusing Them (Overseas Students) of Bringing the Virus Back Home Is Very Inappropriate]. *People's Daily*. March 18. https://wap.peopleapp.com/article/5287160/5193663 (accessed July 1, 2021).

People's Daily. 2020b. "Renmin ribao pinglunyuan zai yiqing fangkong changtaihua tiaojianxia jiakuai huifu shengchan shenghuo zhixu" [Commentators from *People's Daily*: Accelerating Work and Production Resumption in an Orderly Manner Based on the Conditions of Regular Epidemic Prevention and Control]. *People's Daily*. March 30. http://opinion.people.com.cn/n1/2020/0330/c1003-31652822.html (accessed February 15, 2023).

Phillips, Amber. 2020. "Everyone and Everything Trump Has Blamed for His Coronavirus Response." *The Washington Post*. March 31. www.washingtonpost.com/politics/2020/03/31/everyone-everything-trump-has-blamed-his-coronavirus-response/ (accessed July 1, 2021).

Redden, Elizabeth. 2015. "Patriotism Abroad." *Inside Higher Ed*. January 21. www.insidehighered.com/news/2015/01/21/study-examines-how-overseas-chinese-students-respond-criticism-their-country (accessed July 1, 2021).

"Remarks by President Trump in Press Briefing." 2020. https://trumpwhitehouse.archives.gov/briefings-statements/remarks-president-trump-press-briefing-august-10-2020/.

Rogin, Josh. 2020. "Don't Blame China for the Coronavirus-Blame the Chinese Communist Party." *The Washington Post*. March 13. www.washingtonpost.com/opinions/global-opinions/dont-blame-china-for-the-coronavirus-blame-the-chinese-communist-party/2020/03/19/343153ac-6a12-11ea-abef-020f086a3fab_story.html (accessed 30 June 2021).

Rose, Gideon. 2018. "Is Democracy Dying?" *Foreign Affairs* 97(3). www.foreignaffairs.com/issue-packages/2018-04-16/democracy-dying.

Sanger, David. 2021. "Biden Defines His Underlying Challenge with China: 'Prove Democracy Works'." *New York Times*. March 26. www.nytimes.com/2021/03/26/us/politics/biden-china-democracy.html (accessed February 25, 2023).

Shen-Berro, Julian. 2020. "Sen. Cornyn: China to Blame for Coronavirus, Because 'People Eat Bats'." *NBC News*. March 18. www.nbcnews.com/news/asian-america/sen-cornyn-china-blame-coronavirus-because-people-eat-bats-n1163431 (accessed June 30, 2021).

Shirk, Susan L. 2022. *Overreach: How China Derailed Its Peaceful Rise*. Oxford, NY: Oxford University Press.

Tang, S. M. et al. 2020. *The State of Southeast Asia: 2020*. Singapore: ISEAS-Yusof Ishak Institute. www.iseas.edu.sg/wp-content/uploads/pdfs/TheStateofSEASurveyReport_2020.pdf (accessed February 15, 2023).

UNDP. 2018. "The Real China Model: What Other Developing Countries Should Learn from China". United Nations Development Programme. September 13. www.undp.org/cambodia/press-releases/real-china-model-what-other-developing-countries-should-learn-china. (accessed February 15, 2023).

Weaver, R. Kent. 1986. "The Politics of Blame Avoidance." *Journal of Public Policy* 6(4): 371–398. doi: 10.1017/S0143814X00004219.

Weiss, Jessica Chen. 2014. *Powerful Patriots: Nationalist Protest in China's Foreign Relations*. New York, NY: Oxford University Press.

Xi, Jinping. 2017. "Secure a Decisive Victory in Building a Moderately Prosperous Society in All Respects and Strive for the Great Success of Socialism with Chinese Characteristics for a New Era." (speech, 19th National Congress of the Communist Party of China). *Xinhuanet*. October 18. www.xinhuanet.com/english/download/Xi_Jinping's_report_at_19th_CPC_National_Congress.pdf (accessed February 15, 2023).

Xi, Jinping. 2019. "Uphold and Improve the Chinese Socialist System and Modernize State Governance." (speech, the second full assembly of the Fourth Plenary Session of the 19th CPC Central Committee). October 31. *Qiushi (CPC Central Committee Bimonthly)*. https://en.qstheory.cn/2022-01/28/c_696684.htm (accessed February 15, 2023).

Xinhuanet. 2022. "Zhong guo kang yi cheng xiao zhang xian zhong guo zhi du li liang" [The Effectiveness of China's Fighting against the Pandemic Demonstrates China's Institutional Strength]. *Xinhuanet*. May 6. https://news.cctv.com/2022/05/07/ARTIGPLhGsmz3a58dqSl9PfE220507.shtml (accessed February 15, 2023).

Zhao, Suisheng. 2017. "Whither the China Model: Revisiting the Debate." *Journal of Contemporary China* 26(103): 1–17. https://doi.org/10.1080/10670564.2016.1206277.

Zi, Peng. 2021. "Xin guan yi qing zhong guo qing ling zhi zhan de zheng zhi jing ji hong li she hui dai jia he wei lai bian shu" [Covid-19 Pandemic: The Political-Economic Benefits of the Zero-Covid Battle, Its Cost on the Society and Future Changes]. *BBC Chinese*. October 4. www.bbc.com/zhongwen/simp/chinese-news-58759145 (accessed February 15, 2023).

13 Implications of the Reformation of China's Demographic Structure

Wang Feng

Emerging from the global Covid-19 pandemic, a new economic and political landscape awaits China. As the pandemic began winding down in 2022, China entered another new era: an era of population decline. The population contraction which began in 2022 will in all likelihood be sustained and irreversible. Once home to a quarter or even over a third of all humanity (Lee and Wang 1999), China by the end of the current century could see its population size shrink by as much as 45 percent in less than 80 years, and its share of the global population dwindle to no more than 10 percent (United Nations 2022). Such a population decline, aside from those due to wars, famines, and pandemics, is unprecedented in Chinese history. Pundits and critics are quick to proclaim that with this population decline, China's era of economic growth, and moreover the "China century," are over. Whether these pundits and critics are right is a debatable question, but certainly China's transition to an era of population contraction presents vexing new economic and social challenges for the Xi Jinping leadership, problems which – as outlined here – Xi has tried to mitigate by enacting policies to encourage couples to have more children.

China's onset of population decline coincides with the end of the country's age of abundance. For four long decades, since the late 1970s, China has seen one of the most transformative economic growth periods in its own, and the world's, history. Per capita income, in constant 2015 USD, rose 25 times, from $431 in 1980 to $11,188 in 2021.[1] Once a country where most of the population lived on the margins of subsistence, China today is a land of material abundance and comfort. After decades of double-digit hyper economic growth, and with the end of rural to urban migration, economic growth slowed significantly over the past decade.

A major driving force of China's age of abundance was a demographic one: the presence of a large reservoir of young and hard-working laborers. On the eve of China's economic take-off, the country had already accomplished its demographic transition, a historical transformation from high to low death and birth rates. By the end of the 1970s, life expectancy for the Chinese population was approaching 70, gaining nearly 25 years since 1950. The total fertility rate, a measure of the number of children expected for each woman in her lifetime, was not much above the replacement level of 2.1. At 2.3 children per woman in 1980, before the nationwide enforcement of the one-child policy, fertility was less than half the level of 1970 (Wang 2011). This demographic transition opened a historical time

DOI: 10.4324/9781003257943-14

window: reduced fertility and a population yet to age resulted in a population age structure that had the most favorable dependency ratio, a ratio between the dependent population (young and old) and the working-age population.

On the eve of China's economic takeoff, the country had an abundant supply of young labor. What China had, however, was not just cheap labor, but also high-quality labor, a vast force that was already largely literate and comparatively healthy (Wang 2024). The vast labor supply trapped in the Chinese countryside – by China's one-country, two systems, institutional arrangements – was composed of people who were hungry and eager to improve their lives, and willing to sustain decades-long exploitation and discrimination in order to achieve these goals. One only needs to recall the fear of overpopulation prior to China's economic reforms to appreciate the critical roles of institutions. As the market-based economy took root, the population transformed from being burdens needing employment under the failed socialist planned economy to energetic and enthusiastic producers and consumers. But four decades into China's age of abundance, as the pace of economic growth slowed significantly, the rural surplus labor supply is largely exhausted.

The fear of population decline is often articulated in simplistic and exaggerated terms. It is based on a model of population- or labor-driven economic growth, a model that the world has gotten quite used to for the last seven decades. The post-WWII world witnessed an unprecedented population explosion. Population size more than tripled in seven decades, from 2.5 billion in 1950 to close to 8 billion by 2020.[2] Yet, against the deepest Malthusian fears, these decades of the fastest population growth were also the ones with the fastest economic growth era in world history. Per capita income level rose five-fold if not more, from $3,351 in 1950 to $15,212 by 2018, controlling for inflation.[3]

Should China's leaders and people be afraid of the country's decline? Can China, and the world, adapt to a new era of global demographics featured by population aging and decline, just as they adapted to the era of population explosion? To explore such questions, one must move beyond simple numbers, numbers of total population or labor force size, or even simple dependency ratios. The answers can only be found first by an assessment of the sources of the population decline, and by an appreciation of the changes within the population, in terms of educational attainment and health status, and more crucially, in the social fractures of the population. Rather than fixating on the population number, one must look into the institutional conditions that have allowed past economic successes and that will in the future present challenges.

An Irreversible Decline

Transition to Ultra Low Fertility

The Chinese government in 2015 announced the end of the country's one-child per couple birth control policy, three and half decades after its national enforcement began. Yet, the much-delayed lifting of this most restrictive birth control policy did not result in an anticipated and feared baby boom. Instead, after only a one-year increase in the number of births in 2016, annual birth numbers embarked on a continuous decline. The number of births in 2018 was almost 20 percent down from that in 2016, lower than the number in 2015. In 2021, reported at 10.6 million, the birth number collapsed: it was 36 percent below that of 2015, and 44 percent below 2016.[4] China saw in 2021 the lowest number of annual births recorded in six decades, since the devastation of the Great Leap Forward famine that sent the annual number of births below the number of deaths.

The rapid reduction in birth numbers, more than halving from 23.9 million in 1990 to merely 10.6 million in 2021, was in part driven by a population echoing effect, namely the smaller sizes of childbearing age population, a result of the declining birth cohort sizes after the late 1980s. At the last peak, China registered close to 25 million births in 1987. A decade later, by 1997, that number shrank by one-fifth, to barely over 20 million. Shrinking annual birth numbers then turn into small cohorts of young people of marriage and childbearing ages two decades later. So, a major source of the collapsing birth numbers can be traced back to the 1980s and 1990s.

Aside from such an age composition effect, the major driving factor of low birth number is low fertility. The fertility level, often measured by the number of births a woman may have in her lifetime, declined after the early 1980s, especially after the early 1990s. Beginning in 1992, the fertility level nationwide for the first time dropped to the replacement level of 2.1 births per couple and it has never recovered above that level. It is notable that in the first decade of the one-child policy era, overall fertility did not decline noticeably (Figure 13.1). It was not until the early

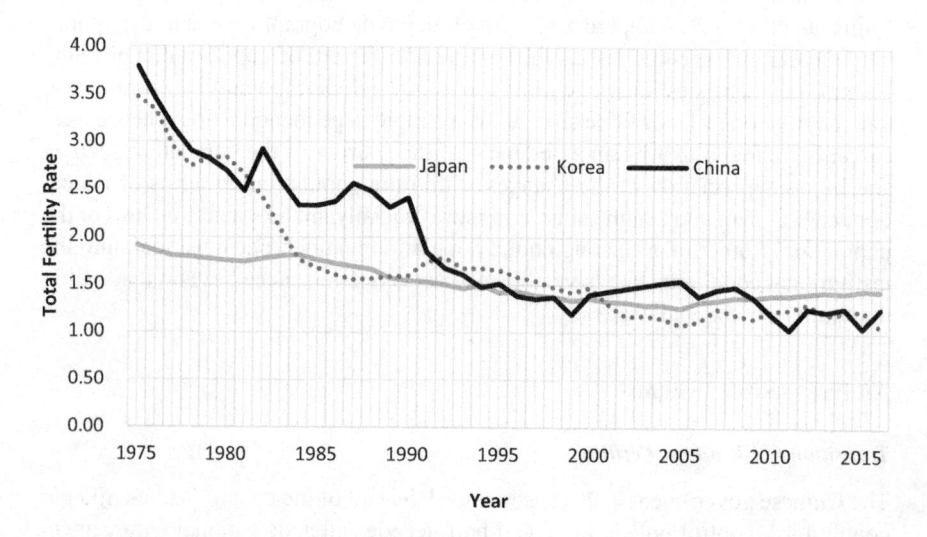

Figure 13.1 Convergence to Very Low Fertility

Source: Generated by the author using data presented in Tsuya et al. 2019

1990s when the policy was more strictly enforced, and more importantly, when a large number of young people in rural China started to migrate out of villages, that fertility for the first time dipped to the below-replacement level.

China since the early 1990s has converged with its East Asian neighboring countries Japan and South Korea to form one of the lowest fertility regions in the world. By the turn of the 21st century, all three populations had a fertility level of around 1.5 or fewer births per woman, a level that is at least 25 percent below the replacement level (Figure 13.1). All three countries, though with different political systems and policy contexts, share a similar history of a Confucian cultural tradition, a period of rapid economic growth, and a strong gender inequality regime biased against women. The common descent to very low fertility in these societies therefore can be traced to the similar cultural and social characteristics (Tsuya et al. 2019). In the case of China, the sustained low fertility after lifting the one-child policy makes it abundantly clear that this policy was not the main driving force for low fertility.

China entered the era of below-replacement fertility with a characteristic difference from both Japan and South Korea. While all three societies reached and stayed at the below-replacement fertility level, this low fertility was an outcome of different structures. Women in China, at least up to the mid-2000s, almost uniformly formed a marriage union and had one child, a homogeneous demographic behavior not observed in either Japan or South Korea. Unlike in China, where almost all women had at least one birth, as shown by the "parity progression ratio" from a woman's own birth to her birth of the first child (Figure 13.2, China B-1), roughly 10 percent of women in Japan never had a birth (a parity progression ration of 900

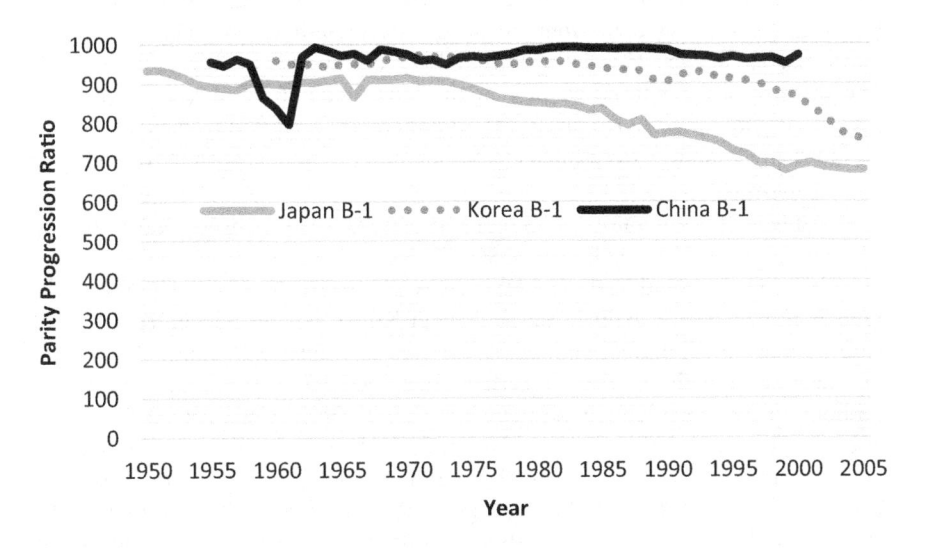

Figure 13.2 Parity Progression Ratios from Birth to First Child

Source: Generated by the author using data presented in Tsuya et al. 2019

per 1000). Starting in the mid-1970s, the share of women with no birth started to increase consistently. By the mid-2000s, the numbers in Figure 13.2 reveal that about 30 percent of women in Japan would stay childless. Up to c. 1980, parity composition in South Korea resembled that of China, with a level above 90 percent. That homogeneity in childbearing in South Korea started to change as well. By the mid-1990s, around 10 percent of women would be childless in their lives. By 2005, that share rose to almost 25 percent.

Staying Away from Marriage

The homogeneous march toward marriage and childbearing, a salient feature of the Chinese demographic system in the past, may soon fade into history. One of the most notable social changes in the past two decades is in the marriage institution. In the last several decades, especially since 2000, both the marriage age and share of unmarried individuals have risen sharply. In the two decades after 1990, mean age at marriage for men and women rose by a full two years, from less than 24 to 26 for men, and from 22 to 24 for women. That increase was only the start of a continued trend of delayed marriage. In contrast to the rise in marriage age in the 1970s resulting from the government requirement of late marriage, the new wave of late marriage is a result of individual choice rather than "collective synchronization" (Cai and Wang 2014).

The more drastic change is in the share of never-married young people at a late age. For men, the share of never-married in their late 20s more than doubled between the two decades of 1990 and 2010, from 17 to close to 36 percent. By 2020, more than half of men aged 25 to 29 (53 percent) remained single, a share that was about three times larger than in 1990. In 2020, at ages 30 to 34, one in five men was still single, up from one in 16 back in 1990. For women, the share of never-married at ages 25 to 29 rose from 4 percent in 1990 to 33 percent in 2020. The share of never-married women among those aged 30 to 34 rose nearly fivefold, from 2 to 9 percent (Figure 13.3). The share of unmarried women aged 25 to 29 in urban China was even higher, reaching nearly 30 percent by 2010 and over 40 percent by 2020.

A rising share of unmarried young people in itself is part of the reason for the rising marriage age, but it also expresses its own significance: continued postponement of marriage could lead to a higher share of never-married and childless individuals in China, just as in Japan and South Korea. Such a phenomenon is still entirely new for China but perhaps will not be new for much longer. Late or no marriage has already occurred in certain other societies sharing a similar cultural tradition of universal female marriage as in China (Retherford et al. 2001; Jones 2007; Raymo et al. 2015; Cheng 2020). In South Korea, for instance, the share of never-married women aged 35 to 39 more than quadrupled from 4 to 19 percent between 2000 and 2015. In Japan, where such a change took place earlier, the share more than doubled between 1990 to 2005, from 8 to 18 percent, and further increased to 25 percent by 2015. For men, the share reached 35 percent. Should such a percentage persists to even later cohorts, more than one-third of Japanese

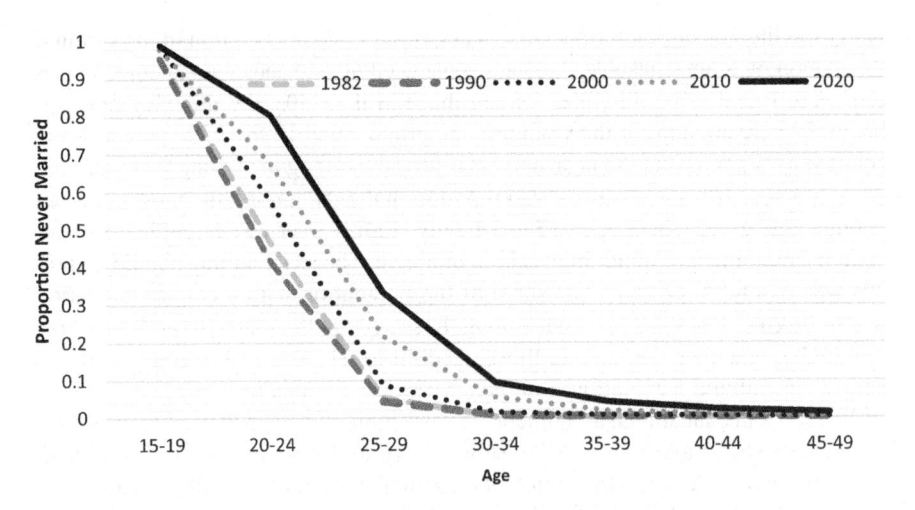

Figure 13.3 Proportion of Women Who Never-Married by Age, China, Selected Years
Source: Generated by the author using Chinese census tabulations

men in the future would never get married (Tsuya et al. 2019). Postponing marriage or abandoning it entirely is even more pronounced in Taiwan, where nearly 30 percent of women aged 35 to 39 were never married in 2020, more than tripling the share of 1995. For men, it was more than four in ten.[5]

It's Not All About a Number: New Faces of the Chinese Population

Four decades into China's age of abundance, the faces of China's population are not just older, but they also display other features previously unseen in Chinese history. Efforts and investments made during the past decades, especially after the late 1990s, have produced a new generation of young Chinese people who are the best educated in Chinese history. With increasing material abundance, population health also continued to improve, creating a generation of elderly Chinese people that is by far the healthiest in China's history. Extended life span at older ages, however, also contributes to a shift in the composition of causes of deaths, with chronic non-communicable diseases rising to become the dominant causes, causes that are much harder and more expensive to treat. And in contrast to four decades ago, when the overwhelming majority of the Chinese population still resided in the countryside, China by the early 2010s became an urbanized society, with the majority of the population living in cities. All of these new features contribute to the new face of the Chinese population.

The Most Educated Generation

Four decades ago, when the first post-Mao population census was taken, the picture that emerged was one of a population that was already largely literate, a critically important characteristic for China's subsequent economic transformations.

Increased literacy during the socialist years, despite the interruption of the Cultural Revolution, was unmistakable. Among people aged 60 and above at the time, 80 percent were found to be illiterate. Among those in their 30s, the illiteracy rate was below 30 percent, and for the youngest age group, aged 15 to 19, 90 percent were counted as literate.[6] Yet the near-universal literacy among the young was just that: basic literacy. The same census also reported that even among the most educated younger age group, those aged 15 to 19, only slightly over 40 percent had an educational attainment of junior high school or above. The share among people in their 30s was barely 20 percent. The share of the population with a college education was miniscule: less than 1 percent among those aged in their late 20s and early 30s. The highest number was among those aged 40 to 44, who had attended colleges before the Cultural Revolution. But that share was still a paltry 2 percent.

Increases in educational attainment, as best signified by expansion at the college level and higher, have been nothing short of extraordinary, or even revolutionary. In slightly over a decade's time after 1998, annual enrollment in colleges rose more than sixfold, from about 1.08 million in 1998 to 6.6 million in 2010.[7] By 2020, annual enrollment in tertiary education further increased to 9.68 million.[8] With an annual birth number dropping to a new low of 10.6 million in 2021, China reached virtual tertiary education enrollment saturation. Even without further expansion, everyone born in the early 2020s will be able to enroll in a higher educational institution when they reach the appropriate age.

Vast improvements in educational attainment can be appreciated by comparison across age groups and over the decades. As plotted in Figure 13.4, the share of the population with a college education was around 10 percent among those aged 45 to 49 in 2020. Among the youngest age group, those aged 20 to 24, the share was five times, with over half of all in this age group already attaining a tertiary education.

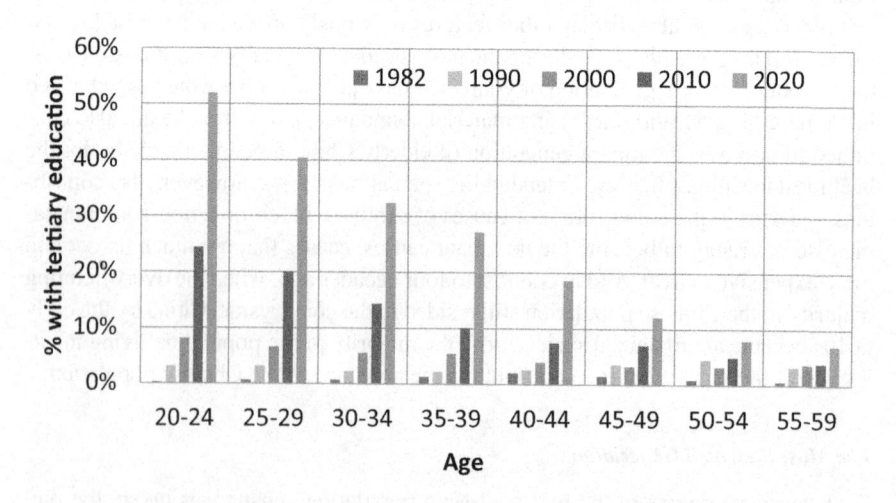

Figure 13.4 Four Decades of Educational Expansion in China, 1982–2020

Source: Generated by the author using Chinese census tabulations from 1982, 1990, 2000, 2010, and 2020

Four decades ago, in this age group, the share with a college education was less than 0.25 percent. Even a decade earlier, in 2010, the share was less than 25 percent. By 2020, more than a third of the young people in their prime working age (20 to 34) already had a tertiary school education. Such a rapid shift in the educational level of the young population has transformed the Chinese economy and society in numerous fundamental ways, from work and income, to consumption, and to participation in social and political affairs.

A Healthier Nation, With Two Faces

As China ascended from a low-income to an upper-middle-income society in a time span of forty years, its population's health profile further converged with those of the high-income countries. This convergence has come with two faces: one in the general health level of the population, and the other in the disease profiles. As China's life expectancy further increased, approaching the expectancies seen in high-income societies, its composition of causes of deaths also shifted. This composition is now dominated by deaths from non-communicable diseases, resembling the pattern seen in other high-income and aging populations.

Four decades ago, following three decades of rapid mortality decline, life expectancy at birth in China reached the high 60s (66.84 in 1980), a level that was still about seven years shorter than in the United Kingdom (73.68 in 1980), France (74.05), and the United States (73.61), and nine years below Japan (76.09). These gaps largely persisted until the turn of the century. By 2020, however, China had further closed the gap in overall population health level with the world's leading high-income countries of large populations. China only lagged about four years behind the United Kingdom (77.13 versus 81.37), 5.5 years behind France (82.66), and 7.5 years behind Japan (84.65). With its per capita income still several times below that of the United States, China in 2020 was coming closer to the United States in terms of overall population health level, with a life expectancy at birth difference of only 1.72 years (77.13 versus 78.85).[9]

Life expectancy is not only getting longer at birth in China, but also at the beginning of old age. As in neighboring Japan and South Korea, life expectancy in China at the age of 65, which demographers normally consider to be the cut-off point for the beginning of old age, nearly doubled between 1950 and 2020, from 9.1 years to 17.7 years. Older people living longer, in a way analogous to younger people receiving more and better education, can be highly beneficial for the economy. Not only can older people work for many more years, contributing productively to society, but they will also inevitably consume more, contributing to aggregate economic demand.

China's age of abundance has brought with it another face of health improvement. With rapid changes in nutrition and lifestyle, and with accelerating population aging, new challenges are also on the horizon, or indeed have already arrived. Along with the abundance in food supply, the meaning of malnutrition is being redefined, from undernutrition to excessive, unhealthy eating. With the influx of dairy products, processed foods, and sweetened soft drinks and snacks, recent generations of Chinese children are growing up with new health risks they will have to face later in life.

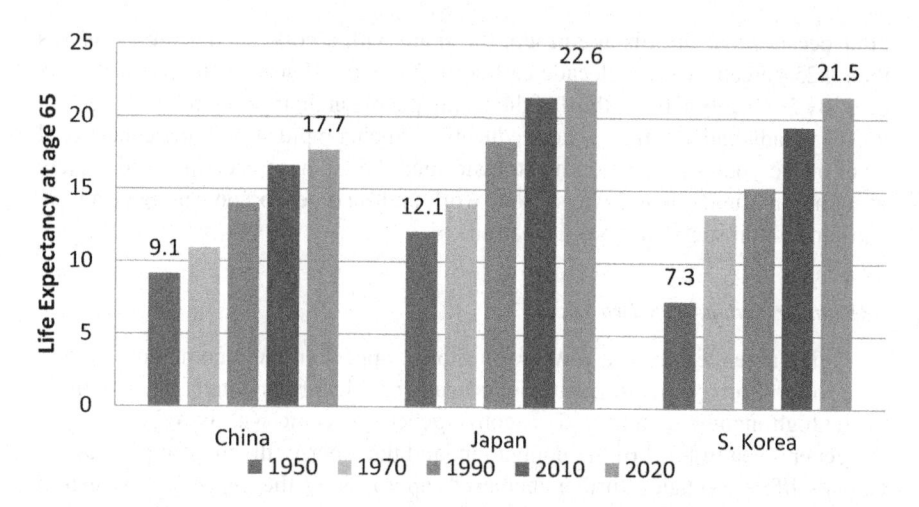

Figure 13.5 Life Expectancy at Age 65, China, Japan, and South Korea
Source: Generated by the author using data extracted from the UNDP World Population Prospect 2022

In contrast to the earlier generations, whose early-life health risks were mostly attributable to lack of nutrition, those who were raised during China's age of abundance face a whole different type of early-life adverse health risk. While the overall number of overweight and obese people in China is still relatively low compared to the numbers in some Western countries, the rate of increase in China is stunning. Between 1985 and 2000, the share of overweight school children aged 7 to 18 increased 28 times, and obesity by 4 times, with the increases particularly pronounced among boys. National surveys revealed that in 1985, fewer than 2 percent of boys and girls were overweight or obese. By the early 2000s, however, the obesity rate shot up to 12.9 percent among boys 7 to 9 years of age, and 9.1 percent among those 10 to 12 in Chinese cities. Combined overweight and obesity prevalence rose to 25.4 percent for boys and 17 percent for girls aged 7 to 9, and rose 17 and 14.3 percent among 10 to 12 year old boys and girls, respectively (Ji et al. 2004). In four decades, over the period of rising material abundance, the term of malnutrition has acquired a new meaning in China. By the early 2010s, 244.5 million or 23.2 percent of adults aged 18 and over had clinical hypertension, while another 435 million or 41.4 percent had pre-hypertension, based on the Chinese national guidelines.[10]

Changes in causes of death foretell challenges to health care and the inevitable attendant increases in costs associated with health care. The three main causes that make up the majority of non-communicable diseases (NCDs) – cancer, cardiovascular diseases, and cerebrovascular diseases – are already on the rise. These diseases are chronic and require much higher cost outlays for treatment and care, consequently draining resources from working-age cohorts. In 1990, these three types of NCDs accounted for about 60 percent of all deaths among the urban population and 45 percent among the rural population. The share increased to 66 percent and 52 percent for urban and rural China respectively by 2000, and to 69 percent and 66 percent in 2010. By 2020, deaths resulting from these non-communicable diseases combined accounted for about 70 percent of all deaths, for both urban and rural populations. Not only have these non-communicable disease deaths risen to account for seven deaths in 10, but the rural population also caught up to converge with the urban population, with the same share of deaths resulting from these NCDs.

This increase in the share of non-communicable disease deaths is due to two sources: increased incidences among the population of such diseases, and importantly, changing population age composition. As cancer and in particular cardiovascular and cerebrovascular diseases are more likely to develop later in life, an older population is also more likely to have an increased incidence of these illnesses, resulting in more deaths. With the number of elderly people continuing to increase, an even higher share of deaths in the future will also be likely to result from these non-communicable diseases.

In addition to a population that is much more educated and healthier, the other most transformative demographic face is undoubtedly China's vast urbanization. Entering the second decade of the twenty-first century, China for the first time began to have more people counted as urban than rural. By the decade's end, more than 60 percent of China's population was counted as urban. It took China only 30 years (1980–2010) to increase its share of the urban population from 20 to 50 percent, a process that took Japan 35 years, from 1920 to 1955, and the United States 60 years, from 1860 to 1920.[11] In two decades alone, between 2000 and 2019, 367 million people, more than the entire population of the United States, became new urban residents in China. Nearly three-quarters of them, 274 million, became urban residents due to changed household registration status. Most of these new urban residents, however, dwell in townships and small to medium-sized cities; large cities were still mostly off-limits to them.

A Fractured Land

As China enters a new era of sustained population decline, a decline that could shave its total population size by as much as 45 percent before the end of this century, the demographic challenges are not just unprecedented but also seem extremely daunting. Along with population decline, China will see a further aging of its population. One measure of the age structure of the population, the median population age, reveals this scenario in striking terms. In 2022, the median age of China's population was 38.2 years. By 2050, this number is projected to rise to 50.7 years, meaning that over half of the population will be above the age 50 by the middle of this century. Perhaps even more stunningly, 30 percent of the population will be over the age of 65.[12]

Yet it would be a distortion to say that the challenges China faces in the decades to come are, strictly speaking, in its population numbers. As explained earlier in this chapter, China's demographic changes are by no means simply quantitative, such as the shrinking population size and the increasing share of the elderly. Such quantitative changes can arguably be ameliorated by qualitative changes, including the increased educational levels of younger people and the healthier lives older people can now lead. What China faces are economic and ultimately political challenges, among them the imperatives to transform the nation's economic growth model; complete urbanization; and provide social benefits that are compatible with those of an upper-middle income society. All of these challenges are critical for the governing party's political legitimacy and the country's social stability.

Unfinished Urbanization

In the three decades from 1990 to 2020, China finally transformed from a predominantly rural to a predominantly urban society. In 2011, for the first time in Chinese history, more people lived in an urban area than in a rural area. The share of the population classified as having an urban residence type rose from 26 percent in 1990 to 64 percent in 2020 (Figure 13.6). China today is unmistakably an urbanized society.

Yet, China's urbanization is not finished. It is unfinished not because 35 to 40 percent of the population was still formally classified as rural. Rather, it is unfinished because China has not just one but three concurrent types of urbanization. Along with the officially published statistics on urbanization, which are based on residence (residential, middle line, Figure 13.6), there are two other urbanization indicators: one social, defined by a person's type of household registration (bottom line, Figure 13.6); and the other economic, by the type of employment, whether in or outside the farming sector (top line, Figure 13.6). Not all residents classified as urban have the same social status.

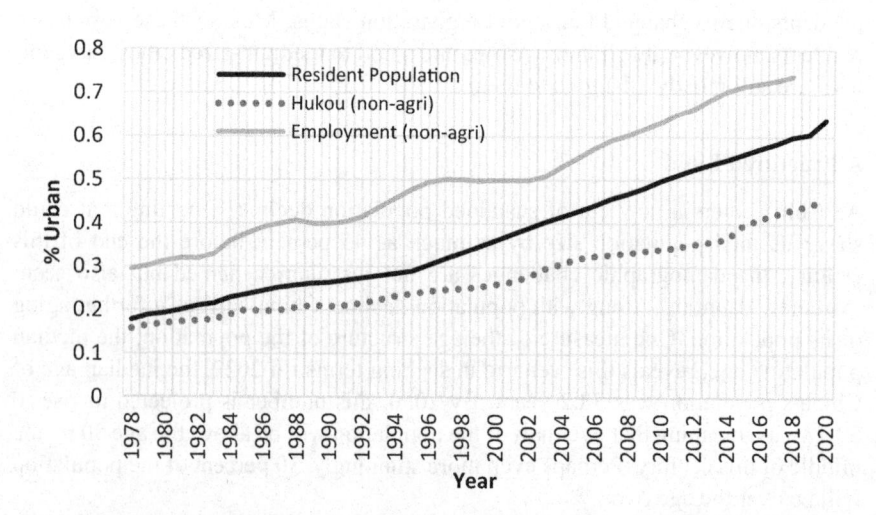

Figure 13.6 Three Urbanizations in China, 1978–2020

Sources: Residential urban: SYB 2019 Table 2–1, Employment, SYB 2019, Table 4–2, Hukou, 《中国卫生和计划生育统计年鉴》, 1978–2014, and annual statistical communique, National Bureau of Statistics. 2020: https://finance.sina.com.cn/china/gncj/2021-05-11/doc-ikmxzfmm1763811.shtml

Some analysts exaggerate the number of Chinese people who remain to be urbanized, or in other words, the remaining labor force available for transfer from the countryside to the cities. By the late 2010s, the number of people employed in urban China already surpassed the number in rural areas.[13] Nationwide, as measured by employment type, nearly 75 percent of the labor force was reported to be employed in the non-farming sector. The share of China's labor force employed in farming had already dropped sharply over three decades: from 70 percent in 1979, to 50 percent in 2000, 37 percent in 2010, and only 24 percent in 2018 (Figure 13.6, top line). China by 2020 did not have 40 percent of the population living in non-urban areas, as suggested by residence type, but instead only 25 percent. These were the people who remained to be urbanized.

For China, the true challenge no longer lies in whether a person is classified as agricultural or non-agricultural. Nor is it in how to further increase the share of the urban population, drawing from the dwindling share of the labor force that is still in its countryside. The true challenges now center on how to "digest" the hundreds of millions of city residents who suffer from having only a secondary citizenship status. As of 2020, 376 million Chinese were still counted as "floating population," people living in areas different from those where they have their household registration. Some 261 million new urban residents still did not have a "non-agricultural" or urban household registration status as of 2020. That is more than one in four and one in five persons in China, respectively.[14]

Most of the more than 250 million Chinese people who did not have an urban residential household status in 2020 and yet still lived in cities found it difficult or impossible to access social benefits. Among such migrants were 135 million laborers working in Chinese cities,[15] double the size of the employees in state or collectively owned organizations (60.87 million), and twice the size of those in limited liability companies (65.55 million). As of 2021, policy changes dictated that cities with population sizes up to 3 million must allow newcomers to register locally without restrictions. The state, however, still deemed it necessary to continue residential designation in cities with population sizes greater than five million. To qualify for household registration status changes in these cities, migrants are judged by a point system modeled on those countries such as Canada or Australia use for international migration.[16] Combined, with over 210 million residents in 19 cities, these super-large cities encompassed about one quarter of all Chinese urban residents in 2020.[17] Rural migrants who dwell in these large cities are still formally considered to be outsiders, and are not entitled to the same social services as residents with a local registration status.

Haves and Have-Nots

Just as urban working populations are stratified by their social status, so are the elderly populations stratified by their major sources of income and support. The Chinese census conducted in November 2020 collected information on main sources of living by age, with the categories of "labor income," "pension," "other family member," and "other." For elderly in cities (accounting for 41 percent of the population aged 15 and over by the census definition), between 65 to 80 percent above the age 60 reported "pension" as the main source, and except for those over the age of 85, no more than 20 percent relied on other family members (Figure 13.7).

For the elderly population in rural areas, the picture looks almost like the complete opposite. More elderly people continue working to a much older age on average, with over a third of the rural elderly under age 70 reporting that they rely on their own labor income as their main source of support, compared with only 5 to 10 percent after age 65 in cities. At age 65, fewer than 10 percent of the urban elderly relied on their own labor income, compared with nearly half (47 percent) of the rural elderly.

For those in the countryside, the main source of economic support reported was from other family members. At age 65, 31 percent of rural elderly reported relying on other family members, at age 75, over 50 percent, and at age 80, over 60 percent. The comparable numbers for urban elderly at these ages were 16, 17, and 20 percent. The share relying on pensions among the rural elderly was around 10 percent (Figure 13.8).

Such a contrasting profile of sources of living among the urban and rural elderly, along with the social divide among populations residing in cities, reveals the depth of continued inequality in quality of life and life chances. These are major challenges the country must address in the years and decades to come. Such long-lasting inequalities are largely legacies of China's socialist planned economy era (Whyte 2010) (Chan 2012). Four decades of rapid economic growth and social benefits expansion have left such social gaps wide open.

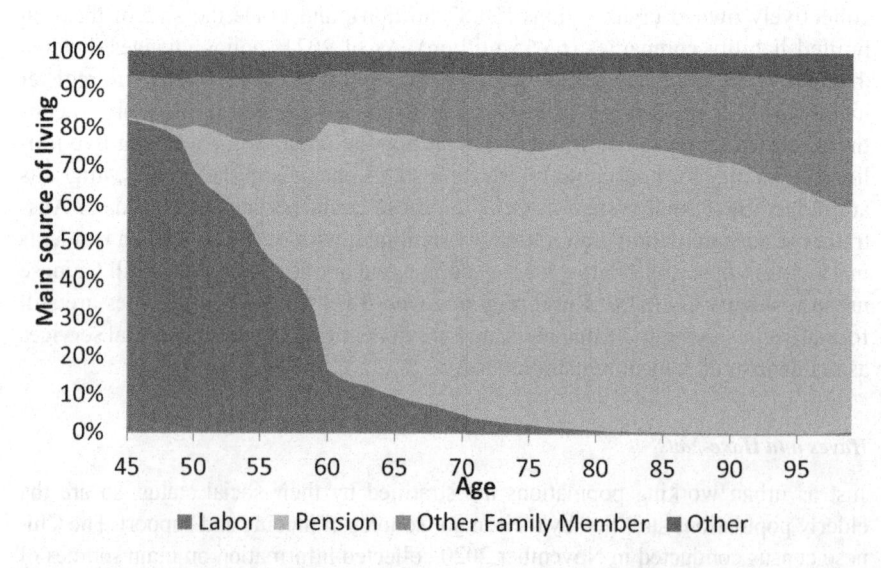

Figure 13.7 Shares of Population by Main Source of Living, Urban China, 2020

Source: Generated by the author using China 2020 census tabulations

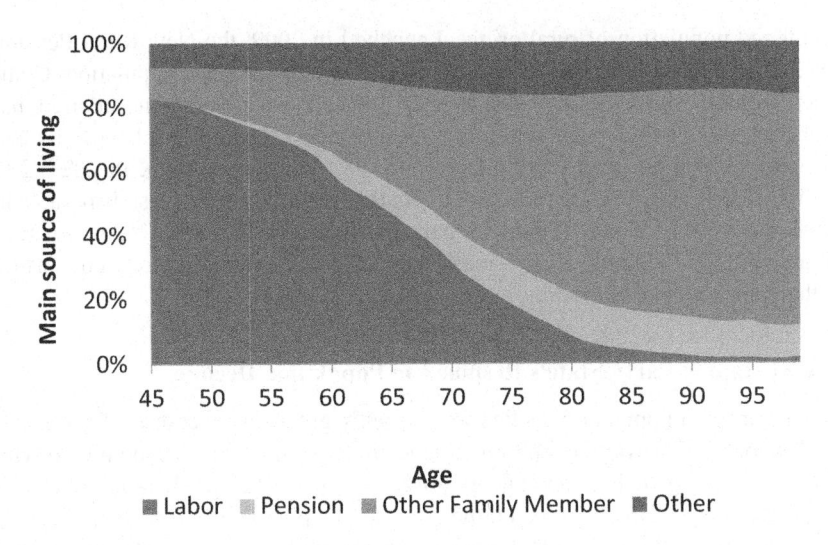

Figure 13.8 Shares of Population by Main Source of Living, Rural China, 2020

Source: Generated by the author using China 2020 census tabulations

In future decades, as the parents of only children (most of whom are in urban areas) move into their more advanced years, in their 70s and 80s, China's only-child generation will start to experience increasing pressure to take care of their aging parents with failing health, while working and trying to raise children. The prospect of being in such a position, squeezed between the pressure of supporting older parents and their own children, is probably already a contributing factor to the very low fertility rate in China. Many young couples have evidently already decided to stop childbearing after having just one child, or else to not have a child at all.

For the elderly population in the countryside, the prospect waiting for them could be even more precarious. Employment opportunities in cities have attracted the younger population to move away from the countryside, making rural China a much older place than the cities. China's 2020 census tabulated only 10.8 percent of the population classified as in cities aged 65 and over. Within the rural population, the share aged 65 and over was 17.7 percent.[18] As rural elderly people move into their even older ages, they will no longer be able to rely on their labor for self-support but must turn to other sources of income to survive. Many of their children, as profiled in the prior section, are migrants in cities without a permanent local status that entitles them to full social benefits, including pensions. These migrant laborers, like their full rights-bearing urban counterparts, are also caught between on the one hand, sustaining their own lives and supporting their children in the cities, and on the other hand, providing a source of material support for their aging parents.

In the first two decades of the twenty-first century, especially 2000–2010, fast income growth and the rapid increase in state coffers allowed expansion of social benefits programs such as health care and pensions to cover the previously uncovered population of rural origin. Launched in 2009, the New Rural Pension Scheme has since expanded to cover a large share of the rural population. Combined with other pension schemes, by 2021 the Chinese government reported that over one billion people were now under the coverage of some sort of pension plan, an increase of more than tenfold from only 98.5 million in 1993. In 2021, 290 million elderly people were receiving a monthly payment.[19] Yet, vast disparities in pension payout level still exist, with gaps of 10 times if not more.[20] As shown in Figure 13.8, in 2020 only a very small share of rural elderly could rely on pension as the main source of support.

The Xi Jinping Party-State's Response to Population Decline

China's onset of population decline was instantly greeted by a chorus of doomsayers. The pessimists were quick to pronounce the end of China's economic growth, or even China's growing global geopolitical influence. Such predictions are overly simplistic and are largely based on the premise of a population-growth driven economic development model. That model may indeed be valid in certain times and places, based on the experiences in some parts of the world during the last half century, including China. Yet it takes little knowledge of economics to know that labor is only one of the key ingredients of economic output. And even labor is not just a number. Whereas China's economic boom in the past several decades indeed benefited from a large reservoir of hard-working labor, in particular the vast flows of rural migrants to cities, it was institutional changes that made the feared "surplus labor" during the planned economy era into a productive labor force.

For more than a decade, since about the time of the 2010 census, policymakers and academics alike in Beijing have been addressing the need to move away from a resource-extensive and export-oriented economic growth model. With rising income and living standards, the once-low-cost Chinese labor and other resources that propelled Chinese products to the global market are no longer that cheap. With the onset of a shrinking young labor force and rampant environmental pollution, such a resource-extensive growth model becomes both unsustainable and increasingly costly and unacceptable to the public. Continued economic growth will have to rely more on technological innovation and on domestic consumption. Such a shift seems logical, given both the shifting demographic profile and vastly increased income wealth level following decades of rapid economic growth. Demographically, China is not simply entering an era in which its labor force will continue to shrink in size, but it is also witnessing the arrival of a young labor force that is the best educated in Chinese history, as explained earlier.

Unlike his predecessors, who were slow to recognize China's shifting demographic landscape and who were indecisive in taking actions, lifting the decades-old strict birth control policy was clearly on Xi Jinping's mind when he assumed the top leadership role in November 2012. Xi took action early and swiftly, often against fierce internal bureaucratic resistance. In March 2013, only months into Xi's reign and with the first government reorganization under his watch, the State Population and Family Planning Commission, a ministerial-level government entity specifically created and expanded to carry out birth control, was merged into the newly formed State Health and Family Planning Commission.[21] To effect this merger took political courage, as birth control had been a "basic state policy" for decades and there was clearly strong bureaucratic resistance from the organization to be abolished.

This reorganization was only the first of several actions to follow. In November 2013, when the first (and perhaps the last) ambitious economic reform agenda under Xi was announced following the Third Plenum of the 18th Party Congress, relaxing the one-child policy also made the list. At the end of reform agenda number 46, out of a long list of 60, was a sentence stating that couples in which one parent is an only child would be allowed to have two children.[22] Of that long list of an ambitious reform agenda, only this change, along with item number 34 (ending "reform through labor"), received the most public support and media attention.[23] Two years later, in November 2015, again surprising many observers, the party-state finally lifted the one-child policy entirely. Xi's awareness and decisiveness in shifting the direction of birth control could in part be due to his own governing experiences preceding his ascendance in Beijing. In both Zhejiang province (2002–2007) and in Shanghai, where Xi served prior to his move to Beijing, low fertility and population aging were already social and policy concerns prior to the nationwide policy changes.

Yet, unlike lifting birth control policies, the transition to a new economic model needs more than a desire or even a plan. It requires political courage and wisdom, and it requires new adaptation. Population aging is increasingly a global new reality, and there are more unknowns than knowns concerning how societies can adapt to this new era (Mason et al. 2022).

The list of unknowns is long: Are China's educational institutions capable of preparing a new generation of creative and independent minds? Are there economic and social support institutions for young people to innovate? Will positions in government agencies and state-owned enterprises continue to be the top job choices attracting young people? Will rural migrants in cities be better integrated in their destinations? What changes will there be to reduce the pervasive gender inequality so that women can play more important economic and political roles and face less stress in marriage and childbearing? And will the government be able to increase social benefits coverage in health care and pensions (and to make them more equal), so that the ordinary person can save less and spend more for an economy that is driven by consumption?

In contrast to Xi's swift moves to end the one-child policy, most of the other reform agenda items announced over a decade ago have been long forgotten. Many are arguably being reversed. Instead of relying on a more vibrant society, a strong government controlling hand has returned. Instead of making hard decisions such as raising the retirement age, or addressing the deep-rooted gender inequality structure, or moving to control skyrocketing housing prices in big cities, the government has resorted to familiar and outdated practices. Having failed to anticipate that there would be no baby boom after the one-child policy was lifted, and then confronting the reality of a continued sharp decline in annual birth numbers, the

278 *Wang Feng*

party-state announced a "three-child" policy in 2021.[24] But such a policy is still reminiscent of the one-child policy era, when the government believed it was in the driver's seat in dictating people's reproductive choices.

The challenges associated with China's historical demographic shift are daunting. A new economic growth model in the era of population decline is essential for sustaining increased living standards. It is also essential to render the state the fiscal capacity to provide basic social benefits such as health care and pensions for an aging population. These fiscal challenges are daunting. Between 2007 and 2020, public spending on health care as the share of GDP already more than doubled from 1.3 percent to 4 percent, and pension spending rose from 2.2 percent of GDP to 5.4 percent. Combined, these expenditure items accounted for more than a quarter of all government spending.[25] Public spending on education, after rising from 2.9 percent of GDP in 2007 to 3.9 percent in 2012, dropped slightly to 3.6 percent in 2020 as the number of school-age children declined. In 2015, the combined public spending on education, health care, and pensions accounted for about 10 percent of GDP.

A fiscal stress test for the Chinese state is on the horizon. One study has projected that population aging alone could drive such public spending up to 20 percent of the GDP by 2040, and to 23 percent by 2050. To increase per capita benefit levels commensurate to those of an upper-middle class society – which is a social and political imperative for maintaining policy legitimacy – could increase the GDP share of public spending much faster, to 32 percent of GDP by 2050. In the absence of substantial government revenue increases, such a share would imply that the entire government revenue would have to be used for such public spending, mostly in support of the aging population (Cai et al. 2018). Mounting pension and health care expenditures at a time of reduced economic growth rates and dwindling government revenue increases will present one of the constant political challenges in the decades to come.

With the onset of population decline, China has embarked on a path of demographic no-return. China's share of the world's population stood at more than one-third of all humans alive merely two centuries ago. By 2022, it had already shrunk to less than one-fifth, or 18 percent. The most striking projection, based on a recently updated UN projection, suggests that by the end of this century, China could have as little as 7 percent of the world's total population (United Nations 2022). Such a scenario seems inconceivable at the moment but is highly likely to unfold. Regardless of the pace of decline and the share in the world's demographic total, however, China's population decline has arrived and will continue. Based on the experiences of population-declining societies elsewhere, there is little evidence that fertility can be increased to reverse the trend of population decline (Shen et al. 2020). The end of population growth nevertheless is by no means an automatic end of economic growth. What should be feared is not a smaller and older population. The challenges lie in adaptation.

Notes

1 Source: https://data.worldbank.org/indicator/NY.GDP.PCAP.KD?locations=CN.
2 Source: https://ourworldindata.org/world-population-growth.

3 In International $ with 2011 prices. Source: https://ourworldindata.org/grapher/maddison-data-gdp-per-capita-in-2011us-slopechart?country=~OWID_WRL.
4 Annual birth numbers up to 2020 are calculated from China Statistical Yearbook 2021, Tables 2.1 and 2.2. Birth number for 2021 is reported in www.xhby.net/index/202202/t20220228_7442473.shtml. Accessed April 27, 2022.
5 I am indebted to Yen-hsin Alice Cheng for sharing these statistics on Taiwan.
6 A person was counted as being illiterate or semi-illiterate in the census if the person could not read up to 1,500 Chinese characters, could not read, or could not write a simple note. Those who had not attended school but could read more than 1,500 Chinese characters, could read newspapers and popular books, and could write a simple note, were classified as having a primary school educational attainment.
7 China Statistical Yearbook 2010, Table 20–7. The enrollment number includes both four-year university and three-year vocational colleges. In 2010, 3.1 million of the 6.6 million enrolled were in the three-year institutions.
8 China Statistical Yearbook 2021, Table 21–7.
9 Data from https://data.worldbank.org/indicator/SP.DYN.LE00.IN. Accessed April 25, 2022.
10 www.ahajournals.org/doi/full/10.1161/CIRCULATIONAHA.117.032380
11 United States Census Bureau, "Urban and Rural Areas," www.census.gov/history/www/programs/geography/urban_and_rural_areas.html. Urbanization level in Japan was reported at 18 percent in 1920.
12 According to projections by the United Nations Population Division. World Population Prospect 2022. Median variant assumption.
13 In 2018, 434.19 million were employed in cities, compared with 341.67 million in rural areas. SYB 2019, Table 4–1
14 Shares calculated from China 2020 census reports. https://finance.sina.com.cn/china/gncj/2021-05-11/doc-ikmxzfmm1763811.shtml. Accessed 06/09/2021.
15 www.stats.gov.cn/tjsj/zxfb/202004/t20200430_1742724.html.
16 An example to illustrate this point-system is in Zhang (2012).
17 https://en.wikipedia.org/wiki/List_of_cities_in_China_by_population. Accessed March 15, 2021.
18 Calculated from China's 2020 census tabulations, Tables A0105a (for cities) and A0105c (for the countryside). City population accounted for 40.8 percent of the total, and rural accounted for 36.2 percent. The remainder are classified as in "townships."
19 Source: www.gov.cn/xinwen/2021-08/05/content_5629682.htm.
20 Source: https://news.sina.com.cn/c/2023-03-13/doc-imyktfsz5542850.shtml. Also, see (Cai et al. 2018).
21 www.economist.com/china/2013/03/16/monks-without-a-temple.
22 www.dangjian.com/shouye/zhuanti/zhuantiku/dangjianwenku/quanhui/202005/t20200529_5637913.shtml.
23 www.nytimes.com/2013/11/16/world/asia/china-to-loosen-its-one-child-policy.html.
24 www.gov.cn/zhengce/2021-07/21/content_5626255.htm.
25 Share of public spending as GDP estimated by the IMF for 2020 was 35.4 percent (www.statista.com/statistics/236299/public-spending-ratio-in-china/).

References

Cai, Yong, and Feng Wang. 2014. "4 (Re) Emergence of Late Marriage in Shanghai: From Collective Synchronization to Individual Choice." In Deborah S. Davis and Sara L. Friedman (Eds.), *Wives, Husbands, and Lovers*. Stanford, CA: Stanford University Press, 97–117.

Cai, Yong, Feng Wang, and Ke Shen. 2018. "Fiscal Implications of Population Aging and Social Sector Expenditure in China." *Population and Development Review* 44(4): 811–831. www.jstor.org/stable/45174458.

Chan, Kam Wing. 2012. "Migration and Development in China: Trends, Geography and Current Issues." *Migration and Development* 1(2): 187–205. https://doi.org/10.1080/21632324.2012.739316.

Cheng, Yen-hsin Alice. 2020. "Ultra-Low Fertility in East Asia." *Vienna Yearbook of Population Research* 18: 83–120. www.jstor.org/stable/27041932.

Ji, Cheng-ye, Jun-ling Sun, and Tian-jiao Chen. 2004. "Dynamic Analysis on the Prevalence of Obesity and Overweight School-Age Children and Adolescents in Recent 15 Years in China." *Zhonghua liu xing bing xue za zhi = Zhonghua liuxingbingxue zazhi* 25(2): 103–108.

Jones, Gavin W. 2007. "Delayed Marriage and Very Low Fertility in Pacific Asia." *Population and Development Review* 33(3): 453–478. www.jstor.org/stable/25434630.

Lee, James, and Feng Wang. 1999. *One Quarter of Humanity: Malthusian Mythology and Chinese Realities, 1700–2000*. Cambridge, MA: Harvard University Press.

Mason, Andrew, Ronald Lee, and Members of the NTA Network. 2022. "Six Ways Population Change Will Affect the Global Economy." *Population and Development Review* 48(1): 51–73. https://doi.org/10.1111/padr.12469.

Raymo, James M., Hyunjoon Park, Yu Xie, and Wei-jun Jean Yeung. 2015. "Marriage and Family in East Asia: Continuity and Change." *Annual Review of Sociology* 41(1): 471–492. https://doi.org/10.1146/annurev-soc-073014-112428.

Retherford, Robert D., Naohiro Ogawa, and Rikiya Matsukura. 2001. "Late Marriage and Less Marriage in Japan." *Population and Development Review* 27(1): 65–102. https://doi.org/10.1111/j.1728-4457.2001.00065.x.

Shen, Ke, Feng Wang, and Yong Cai. 2020. "Government Policy and Global Fertility Change: A Reappraisal." *Asian Population Studies* 16(2): 145–166. https://doi.org/10.1080/17441730.2020.1757850.

Tsuya, Noriko O., Minja Kim Choe, and Feng Wang. 2019. *Convergence to Very Low Fertility in East Asia: Processes, Causes, and Implications*. 1st ed. New York, NY: Springer.

United Nations, Population Division. 2022. "World Population Prospects – Population Division – United Nations." https://population.un.org/wpp/.

Wang, Feng. 2011. "The Future of a Demographic Overachiever: Long-Term Implications of the Demographic Transition in China." *Population and Development Review* 37: 173–190. www.jstor.org/stable/41762404.

Wang, Feng. 2024. *China's Age of Abundance: Origins, Ascendance, and Aftermath*. Cambridge: Cambridge University Press.

Whyte, Martin King. 2010. "One Country, Two Societies: Rural-Urban Inequality in Contemporary China." www.amazon.com/Martin-King-WhytesOne-Country-Societies/dp/B00422JDLE/ref=sr_1_15?dchild=1&keywords=Martin+Whyte&qid=1624667534&s=books&sr=1-15.

Zhang, Li. 2012. "Economic Migration and Urban Citizenship in China: The Role of Points Systems." *Population and Development Review* 38: 503–533.

Index

Note: Page numbers in *italics* indicate figures, **bold** indicate tables in the text, and references following "n" refer notes.

Abe, Shinzō 224; trip to Beijing 225
"absolute leadership" 17, 19, 30, 163
absolute poverty 126, 136n3
ACT (American College Testing) 47
Advanced Manufacturing Industry Investment Fund 114
Africa: 2022 African Youth Survey 230; Chinese foreign relations with 230–231
aging (of Chinese population) 263, 269, 271, 277, 278; *see also* demographic structure, implications of reformation of
AI *see* artificial intelligence (AI)
Aidoo, Richard 207
AIIB *see* Asian Infrastructure Investment Bank (AIIB)
Alibaba 71, 96–98, 119; Alipay 75, 76; Ant Financial Group 73, 76, 97; Taobao 75, 91
All-China Federation of Trade Unions 173
Amazon 97
AMD 119, 120
Anbang 71, 72
Ansell, Christopher 155
Ant Financial Group 73, 76, 97
artificial intelligence (AI) 96, 110, 114, 117–120
ASEAN *see* Association of Southeast Asian Nations (ASEAN)
Asian Infrastructure Investment Bank (AIIB) 220, 229
Associated Press-NORC Center for Public Affairs Research 243
Association of Southeast Asian Nations (ASEAN) 220
Austin, Lloyd 224
authoritarian legality 17

authoritarian political system 2, 5; fragmented authoritarianism 193–211
autonomous mass organizations 25

Baidu 96–98, 119; Baidu Tieba 87; Baidu Wiki 84
BANCA *see* Biodiversity and Nature Conservation Association (BANCA)
Bangguo, Wu 18
BBS *see* Bulletin Board Services (BBS)
Beijing Consensus 254, 255, 258n8
Beijing Municipal Government: microblog service providers, real-name registration rules for 91, 95
Belt and Road Initiative (BRI) 10, 193–211, 221, 222, 229; Cambodia 208–209; context 193–195; Ghana 207–208; literature 195–198; Myanmar 205–207; Nicaragua 204–205
Benkler, Y. 87
Biodiversity and Nature Conservation Association (BANCA) 206
births, annual 264, 268
BIS *see* Bureau of Industry and Security (BIS)
Blinken, Antony 223–224
Bo Xilai 70, 162–163
Bo Yibo 163, 171
Bradsher, Keith 3; "After Doling Out Huge Loans, China Is Now Bailing Out Countries" 195
BRI *see* Belt and Road Initiative (BRI)
Buckley, Chris 5
Bulletin Board Services (BBS) 89
Bureau of Industry and Security (BIS) 120
Bush, George H. W. 56

Index

CAC *see* Cyberspace Administration of China (CAC)
cadre-police 29
Cai Feng 132
Cai Xia 142
Cambodia: Belt and Road Initiative 208–209; BRI projects 10
Canada: Internet-related expenditures 91
Cantoni, Davide 61
capitalism 54–55; as exploitative system 6, 54, 60; party-state 7, 67–79
capitalist democracy 55–57
CASS *see* Chinese Academy of Social Sciences (CASS)
CATL *see* Contemporary Amperex Technology Co. Limited (CATL)
CCDI *see* Central Commission for Discipline Inspection (CCDI)
CCP *see* Chinese Communist Party (CCP)
CDC *see* Centers for Disease Control (CDC)
censorship 86, 88, 90–91; self-censorship 91
Center for the Study of Hate and Extremism (CSHE) 239
Centers for Disease Control (CDC) 240, 250
Central Commission for Discipline Inspection (CCDI) **22**, 23–26, 32
Central Cyberspace Commission 198
Central Economic Work Conference (2022) 78
Central Financial Commission 174
Central Leading Group for Comprehensively Deepening Reform 153
Central Leading Group for Cybersecurity and Informatization (CLGCL) 93, 94
"Central Leading Small Group for Comprehensively Deepening Reform" 146–147
Central Military Commission (CMC) 161, 163, 166, 170, **170**, 181, 182, 187
Central Organization Department 32
Central Political Legal Commission (CPLC) 21, **22**, 23
Central Science and Technology Commission 174
Chan Kam Wing 131, 134
Changjiang Institute of Survey, Planning, Design and Research (CISPDR) 205, 206
Chaohu City Mass-Volunteer Integration *150*
Chaohu City New Era Civilized Practice Center 150

charismatic authority 143
Chen, Albert H. Y. 19
Chen Jianfu 19
Chen Ling 109
Chen Shengluo 61
Chen Wenqing 21
Chen Yixin 21
Chi Renyong 196
Chicago Harris School of Public Policy 243
China Airport Construction Group Corporation 205
China Banking and Insurance Regulatory Commission 76
China Communication Construction Group 205
China Development Bank 200
China Export Credit and Insurance Corporation (Sinosure) 200
China Export-Import Bank (EXIM bank) 197, 200
China Gezhouba Group 205
China Internet Investment Fund 96
China Internet Survey (CIS) 84, 86–87, 99n1
China Minsheng Investment Group (CMIG) 72
China Network Information Center (CNNIC) 84, 92, 99n1
China–Pakistan Economic Corridor (CPEC) 229
China Railway Construction Corporation 205
Chinese Academy of Governance 32
Chinese Academy of Social Sciences (CASS) 126, 127, 130, 133, 134
Chinese Communist Party (CCP) 13, 33, 86; 20th Party Congress 2, 4, 8, 9, 21, 26, 83, 92, 136, 142, 161–176, 179, 184; bodies, issuance of legal norms by 31; control over financial resources 12; Elite Biographical Data 182; general secretary's five-year term 1; leadership 30; 2019 "Implementation Outline for Citizen Moral Construction in the New Era" 154; Propaganda Department 32, 89, 98, 145, 152, 154; 2021 "Propaganda Work Regulations" 154; Secretariat 169–170, **169**; and state institutions, merger of 32–33; *see also specific entries*
Chinese People's Political Consultative Conference (CPPCC) 172
CIS *see* China Internet Survey (CIS)

Index 283

CISPDR *see* Changjiang Institute of Survey, Planning, Design and Research (CISPDR)
"civilized" state-building, Xi Jinping-style 145–148
civil society 9, 144, 161, 162, 164, 165
CLGCL *see* Central Leading Group for Cybersecurity and Informatization (CLGCL)
Clinton, Bill 218
CMC *see* Central Military Commission (CMC)
CMIG *see* China Minsheng Investment Group (CMIG)
CNNIC *see* China Network Information Center (CNNIC)
Collier, Andrew 134
Commission for Guiding Cultural and Ethical Progress/Building Spiritual Civilization 198
common prosperity 3, 7, 12, 58, 59, 70, 73–74, 77, 78, 125, 135
Communist Party of the Soviet Union (CPSU) 162
Comprehensively Deepening Reform Leadership Small Group 198, 200
constitutionalism 5, 19, 31, 33–34, 67
Contemporary Amperex Technology Co. Limited (CATL) 116, 117
Corkin, Lucy 198
court system reforms 26–30; current status of 29–30; funding reforms 28–29; judge quota reform 27
Covid-19: attribution of blame for the pandemic 239–257, **242**, **243**, *245–248*, *251–253*, **252**; death rate 5; lockdown 2, 76, 77, 144, 155, 165, 176, 255, 256; protests against Zero-Covid 4, 77; shock of 76–78; zero-Covid policies 1–5, 10, 77, 154, 165, 176, 240, 256, 257
CPI *see* Yunnan International Power Investment Company (CPI)
CPLC *see* Central Political Legal Commission (CPLC)
CPPCC *see* Chinese People's Political Consultative Conference (CPPCC)
CPSU *see* Communist Party of the Soviet Union (CPSU)
CSHE *see* Center for the Study of Hate and Extremism (CSHE)
Cultural Revolution 18, 49, 62n5
Cultural System Reform 200

Cyber Power strategy 93
Cyberspace Administration of China (CAC) 90, 93–96, 99n3
Cyber Super-Power strategy 93, 96

Dalian Wanda 71, 72
debt trap diplomacy 194
decentralized subnational politics 202–204
"Decision on Major Issues Concerning Comprehensively Deepening Reforms" 68
demographic structure, implications of reformation of 11–12, 262–279; educational attainment 267–269, *268*; haves and have-nots 273–276; healthier nation 269–271, *270*; staying away from marriage 266–267, *267*; transition to ultra low fertility 263–266, *264*, *265*; urbanization 272–273, *272*; *see also* aging (of Chinese population)
Deng Guoying 134
Deng Xiaoping 3, 161, 174, 187, 194, 217, 255, 256; as "architect of the reform program" 7; on capitalism 55; on general secretary's five-year term 1; on infrastructural state-building 146; personality cult 142
Department of Foreign Aid (DFA) 199, 200–201
Department of International Trade and Economic Affairs (DITEA) 199
DEPA *see* Digital Economy Partnership Agreement (DEPA)
DFA *see* Department of Foreign Aid (DFA)
dibao (minimum livelihood norm) 126–130, 132, 133, 135, 136n3, 136n8, 137n20, 137n26
Didi (China's Uber) 74, 97
Digital Economy Partnership Agreement (DEPA) 78
Dikötter, Frank 142–143
Ding Xuexiang 173
DITEA *see* Department of International Trade and Economic Affairs (DITEA)
Document No. 9 164
Doshi, Rush 218
Douban 84
"double designation" 24–25
"Double Reduction" policy 74
DreamMore 75
Du Weigong 134
"dual circulation" policy 79

EDA *see* electronic design automation (EDA)
education 107, 267–269, *268*; levels 129, 269, 272; patriotic 6–7, 145; *see also* political education
EIAs *see* environmental impact assessments (EIAs)
electric vehicles (EVs) 116–117
electronic design automation (EDA) 115
Electronic Warfare Department 186
environmental impact assessments (EIAs) 197, 206
Europe, Chinese foreign relations with 225–226
European Union 14, 96, 107
Evergrande 71, 72
EVs *see* electric vehicles (EVs)
Ezubao 76

factionalism 180, 182–187, **183–184**
Fang Fenghui 189
fang-shou policy 68, 231
farmers 130–132
Feng Yuting 134
"Fengqiao model 166, 168
fertility rate of Chinese women 262–265, 275, 277, 278
Five Principles of Peaceful Coexistence 231
FONOPS *see* freedom of navigation operations (FONOPS)
foreign policy 11, 217–233; economic 209–210
Fosun 71, 72
Four Wind Power Project 54
fractured land 271–276
Fravel, M. Taylor 179, 188
Freedom House 83
freedom of navigation operations (FONOPS) 223
Fu Hualing 27, 29, 30
funding reforms 28–29

Gansu MIC fund 114
Gao Bonan 134
Gao Yang 171
Gaokao 6, 44, 45, 49, 51, 52, 55, 59–62, 135; design and content of 47–48
gender inequality 15n2, 265, 277
General Administration of Press and Publications 99n4
General Armament Department 181
General Data Protection Regulation (GDPR) 96

General Logistics Department (GLD) 181
General Political Department (GPD) 181, 185
General Staff Department (GSD) 181, 187
General Training Department 181
Germany: Internet-related expenditures 91
Ghana: Belt and Road Initiative 207–208; BRI projects 10
Gill, Bates 197–198
Ginsburg, Tom 19, 30
GLD *see* General Logistics Department (GLD)
Global Financial Crisis of 1997 194
Global Security Initiative 231, 237n83
Go Global Strategy 200
"Going Out" strategy 196
Google 91, 97
GPD *see* General Political Department (GPD)
Great Firewall of China 83
Great Leap Forward 49, 175, 264
"grey rhinos" 72
gross domestic product (GDP) 3, 67, 106, 107, 112, 278
GSD *see* General Staff Department (GSD)
Guangdong Province: Department of Transportation 98
guardianship dilemma 178–180
Gui Congyou 225–226
"Guiding Opinion on Establishing New Era Civilized Practice Center Pilots" 147
Guo Boxiong 163, 172
Guo Guangcheng 72
Guo Shengkun 29–30

Han Zheng 172
Hart, G. 56
He Junke 170
He Lifeng 173
He Weidong 182
He Xin 21
Hess, Steve 207
Hezhong Zeyi 154
HKND *see* Hong Kong-Nicaragua Development Corporation (HKND)
HNA 71, 72
Hong Kong: attribution of blame for the pandemic 250–254; Covid-19 death rate 5; youth mobilization in 44
Hong Kong-Nicaragua Development Corporation (HKND) 204, 205
Hou Kai 173
Hu Chunhua 169, 170, 175

Huabei 76
Huang Haifeng 143
Huang Keming 155
Huang Xueli 196
Huawei 71, 109
Hu Jintao 3, 4, 8, 12, 83, 84, 98, 99, 109, 110, 161, 163, 256; Internet governance strategies 87–93; on political education 46; on poverty 126; socialist or civilized "harmonious society" 146; vision of the Internet 87–88
Hun Sen 209, 230
hukou (household registration) 128, 129, 131, 132
Huntington, Samuel P. 179

IC Megaproject 115
IDDS *see* Innovation-Driven Development Strategy (IDDS)
imperialism 51–54; Western 51, 60
India, Chinese foreign relations with 228–229
indigenous innovation 106, 109, 110
inequality 11, 12, 55, 70, 72, 274; gender 15n2, 265, 277
initial public offerings (IPOs) 69, 73, 74, 76
Innovation-Driven Development Strategy (IDDS) 106, 110, 112
institutional structure 89–90, 93–94
"Integrated Media Centers" 8, 144, 148, 151, 155; "civilizing" role of 152–154; "platformization" function of 153
International Olympic Committee 36n31
Internet governance 8, 9, 83, 84; censorship 90–91; company instruments 91–92, 97–98; definition of 87; under Hu Jintao 87–93; institutional structure 89–90, 93–94; licensing 90; political information flows 84–87; state instruments 90–91, 94–96; users in China, 2000–2021 85; under Xi Jinping 8, 84, 92–98
Internet Information Management Bureau 89
Internet-Plus Plan/Internet + plan 93, 106, 114
IPOs *see* initial public offerings (IPOs)
irrational investments 71

JAC 116
Jang Song Thaek 227
Japan: Chinese foreign relations with 224–225; Japanese Imperial Army 224; Japanese National College Entrance Examination 47

Jefferson, Gary 108
Jiang Renai 108
Jiang Zemin 3–4, 92–93, 161, 163, 194, 198, 217, 256; on "civilized" state-building 146; negotiations on accession to the WTO 218; political education 46
Jiebei 76
Jones, Lee 198, 206, 207
JPSC *see* Judges and Procurators Selection Committee (JPSC)
Judges and Procurators Selection Committee (JPSC) 28

Kachin Independence Army (KIA) 206
Kai-Fu Lee 118
Kennedy, Scott 254
Key Technologies R&D Program 105
Khrushchev, Nikita 142
KIA *see* Kachin Independence Army (KIA)
Kim Jong-un 227
Kishida, Fumio 224
Kurlantzick, Joshua 245, 254

laid-off workers and staff 132–133
Lampton, David M. 165
leadership small groups (LSGs): Party 198
Legal Professional Inspection System Reform 200
legal system 17–37; Central Commission for Discipline Inspection 24–26; court system reforms 26–30; institutions, ranks of 22–24, **22**; judicial independence 17, 19, 31, 35; in Mao era 18; National Supervisory Commission 24–26; political-legal system 20–22; in post-Mao era 18–20
Lei Feng 50, 148
Lei Zhenhuan 30
Li Keqiang 3, 167
Li Qiang 165, 172, 175
Li Shangfu 173
Li Xi 26
Li Yishuang 30
Li Yuan: "China's Cities Are Buried in Debt, but They Keep Shoveling It On" 195
Li Yuchao 174, 186, 190
Liebman, Benjamin L. 19
Lin Xiangyang 184
Lindblom, Charles 210
Liu Ernest 30
Liu Guangbin 174
Liu Guozhong 173

Liu Kun 173
Liu Qingsong 186
Liu Zhenli 184
Lu Hao 170
Luo Jiali 48
Luo Yadong 196

Ma, Jack 73, 99, 107
Ma Xiaojuan 134
Ma Zhaoxu 231
Made in China 2025 (MIC 2025) 9, 79, 93, 106, 107, 110, 112–119, **113**; artificial intelligence 117–119; electric vehicles 116–117; Roadmap of Major Technical Domains for Made in China 2025 114; semiconductors 114–116; Strategic Cooperation Agreement between China Development Bank and MIIT 114
"Major Power Diplomacy" strategy 194
"Making a Difference" policy 194
Mann, Michael 144
Mao Zedong 68, 161, 194, 217; legal system 18; "little red book" 143; personality cult 142; on political education 46
"March of Saving China" 46
"March of the Volunteers" 46
Mattingly, Daniel C. 182
McKinsey Global Institute 91
Mearsheimer, John J. 178
Medium-and-Long-term Plan (MLP) for Science and Technology (2006–2020) 106, 109, 110
Meidan, Michal 201
Meng Hongwei 220
Mercedes 225
Miao Hua 184
Michel, Charles 256
micro, small, and medium enterprises (MSMEs) 69; Covid-19, impact of 76, 77; in Xi era 74–76
MII *see* Ministry of Information Industry (MII)
MIIT *see* Ministry of Industry and Information Technology (MIIT)
military leadership 180–182
military preparedness 178–180; improving 187–190, **188–189**
military promotions: coalition of the weak logic 182–187, **186**; factional logic 182–187, **183–184**; improving preparedness logic 187–190, **188–189**
Miller, Alice 143

Minimum Livelihood Guarantee 126
Ministry of Civil Affairs 127, 133, 135
Ministry of Commerce (MOFCOM) 198, 199, 203; Department of Foreign Aid (DFA) 199, 200–201; Department of International Trade and Economic Affairs (DITEA) 199
Ministry of Culture 90, 145
Ministry of Electronic Industry 89
Ministry of Finance (MoF) 21, 96, 199–200
Ministry of Foreign Affairs (MoFA) 198, 199, 201
Ministry of Industry and Information Technology (MIIT) 91
Ministry of Information Industry (MII) 89, 94
Ministry of Posts and Telecommunications 89
Ministry of Public Security (MPS) 2, **22**, 23, 35n12, 90, 94
Ministry of Science and Technology (MOST) 96, 106, 118
Ministry of State Security 35n12
Minzner, Carl F. 17, 19, 30, 35
Miura, Satoshi 155
"mixed ownership" reforms 67, 69–70
MLP *see* Medium-and-Long-term Plan (MLP) for Science and Technology (2006–2020)
Moon Jae-in 228
multilateralism 220
Myanmar: Belt and Road Initiative 10, 205–207

Nanjing Massacre 52
National Bureau of Statistics (NBS) 77, 127
National College Entrance Exam (NCEE) *see Gaokao*
National Conference on Science and Technology 109
National Defense University 185, 186
National Development and Reform Commission (NDRC) 200, 205
National Emerging Industries Investment Guiding Fund 114
National IC Fund 115
nationalism 174
National New-type Urbanization Plan (2014–2020) 131
National Patent Development Strategy (2011–2020) 108
National Security Commission 68, 166, 198, 219

National Security Education 44
National Security LSG 198
National Supervisory Commission (NSC) **22**, 23–26, 32, 36n16, 36n18, 219
Naughton, Barry 105, 109
NBS *see* National Bureau of Statistics (NBS)
NCDs *see* non-communicable diseases (NCDs)
NCEE *see* National College Entrance Exam (NCEE)
NDRC *see* National Development and Reform Commission (NDRC)
negativity bias 241
"New Era Civilized Practice Centers" 8, 144, 146, 148–151, 155
New Normal 68, 136
Newsweek 165
Ng Kwai Hang 21
Nicaragua: Belt and Road Initiative 10, 204–205
Nio Inc. 117
non-communicable diseases (NCDs) 270–271
North Korea, Chinese foreign relations with 227
NSC *see* National Supervisory Commission (NSC)
Nvidia 119, 120

OFDI *see* outward foreign direct investment (OFDI)
Office of the Party Central Committee 146
One Belt, One Road (OBOR) *see* Belt and Road Initiative (BRI)
one-child policy 11, 262, 263, 265, 277, 278
outward foreign direct investment (OFDI) 196
Overholt, W. 13–14, 15n4; *The Rise of China: How Economic Reform Is Creating a New Superpower* 13

Pakistan, Chinese foreign relations with 228–229
PAP *see* People's Armed Police (PAP)
Park Geun-hye 227, 228
"Party member parenting" programs 149
Party/state and law/politics distinctions 5–6, 30–33
party-state capitalism 7; international backlash to 78; private economy under 67–79
patents 107–109

patriotic education 6–7, 145
PBSC *see* Politburo Standing Committee (PBSC)
Peerenboom, Randall 19
peer-to-peer (P2P) online lending platforms 75, 76
People's Armed Police (PAP) 172
People's Bank of China 21
People's Daily 164
People's Liberation Army (PLA) 163, 172, 220; leadership 178–190; Second Artillery Force 181; Strategic Support Force 181
Pettis, Michael 15n3
Pils, Eva 19
PLA *see* People's Liberation Army (PLA)
platform power (of Chinese tech giants) 92, 96–98
PLCs *see* political-legal committees (PLCs)
Politburo Standing Committee (PBSC) 3, 9, 23, 26, 163, 165, 167–169, **167**, **168**, 172, 175, 217
political education 44–59; alternatives to 51–57; capitalism 54–55; capitalist democracy 55–57; *Gaokao* 44, 45, 49, 51, 52, 55, 59–62; propping up the Party 49–51; Xi Jinping effect in 57–59
political information flows 84–87
political-legal committees (PLCs) 19–21, 30, 31
political legitimacy as complex 60
political systems 17–37; clash of 254–257
poverty: abolition of 7, 125–126; absolute 126, 136n3; alleviation of 8; measurement 126–128; relative 126, 127, 129, 136n5, 136n6; urban 125–137
private economy 67–79; common prosperity 73–74; MSMEs in Xi era 74–76; perceived threats to stability, management of 73–74; private sector conglomerates, risk management of 71–72
production 107–109
publications 107–109
public opinion guidance 88, 89, 95
public opinion supervision 88
Public Security Comprehensive Management Commission 198
Putin, Vladimir 222

Qihe County Integrated Media Center 153
Qin Gang 173, 174
QQ 84, 87
"quota reform" 27

Rachman, Gideon 142
ranks of legal system institutions 22–24, **22**
Reilly, James 197–198
relative poverty 126, 127, 129, 136n5, 136n6
revenue-maximization 112
rise of China/China's rise concept 3, 12–14, 15n3, 15n4, 58, 204
risk management 68; of private sector conglomerates 71–72
Rosenberg, E. 51
Rosenberg, J. 51
rule of law 6, 17, 19, 24, 31, 219
Russia, Chinese foreign relations with 222

"Safe Cities" program 194
SAIC-GM-Wuling 117
Samsung 115
sanwu 128–130, 137n12
SARFT *see* State Administration for Radio, Film, and Television (SARFT)
SASAC *see* State-owned Asset Supervision and Administration Commission (SASAC)
SAT (Scholastic Aptitude Test) 47
SCIMC *see* State Council Information Management Commission (SCIMC)
Second Artillery (Missile) Force 186
securitization 2, 72
SEI *see* Strategic Emerging Industries (SEI) initiative
self-censorship 91
semiconductors 9, 78, 110, 114–116, 119, 120, 121n16
Sesame Credit 76
17 +1 partnership 226
Shaanxi MIC 2025 Fund 114
Shanghai Cooperation Organization 225
Shen Yiqin 173
SIIO *see* State Internet Information Office (SIIO)
Sina 86, 98; Sina Weibo 87
16 +1 partnership 226
Smith, Graeme 198, 201
Snowden, E. 68
socialism 44, 47, 52, 53, 55; market, with Chinese characteristics 67
social media platforms: political information flows 84–87; used by Internet users *86*; Xi Jinping partnership with 83–99
Social System Reform 200
SOEs *see* state-owned enterprises (SOEs)

Song Puxuan 185
Song Renqiong 171
Southeast Asia: Chinese foreign relations with 229–230
Southern Weekend incident 164
South Korea: Chinese foreign relations with 227–228; Theater High Altitude Area Defense system (THAAD) 208
sovereign wealth funds (SWFs) 69
SPC *see* Supreme People's Court (SPC)
Special Constructive Funds 114
Special Plan of the Development of Intelligent Manufacturing Science and Technology for the 12th FYP 118
Spiritual Civilization Steering Committee 146
SPP *see* Supreme People's Procuratorate (SPP)
State Administration for Radio, Film, and Television (SARFT) 32, 89, 99n4
State Administration of Civil Service 32
State Administration of Press and Publications 32, 99n4
State Bureau of Film 32
State Council Information Management Commission (SCIMC) 89
State Intellectual Property Office 108
State Internet Information Office (SIIO) 89, 90, 93, 95, 99n3
State Leadership Group of Informatization 90
State-owned Asset Supervision and Administration Commission (SASAC) 69, 70, 200, 203
state-owned enterprises (SOEs) 67–70, 79, 111, 196, 203
State Population and Family Planning Commission 276–277
State Security Law: Article 4 32; Article 44 31–32; Article 63 32
Stevenson, Alexandra 3
Stoltenberg, Clyde D. 196
Strategic Emerging Industries (SEI) initiative 106, 109, 110
Strategic Support Force 184
subnational politics as decentralized 202–204
Sun Hongshan 21
Sun Ying 27, 29, 30
Supreme People's Court (SPC) **22**, 23, 26
Supreme People's Procuratorate (SPP) **22**, 23, 26
SWFs *see* sovereign wealth funds (SWFs)

Taiwan 166, 223; attribution of blame for the pandemic 250–254; Covid-19 death rate 5
Tan Yeling 105, 109
Taobao 2P2 lending platforms 75, 91
technology companies 83–99; MIC 2025 112–119
technology policy (2012–2022) 105–120; education 107; institutional constraints 111–112; patents 107–109; production 107–109; publications 107–109; state's reaction to continuing constraints on technological development 109–110
tekun 128, 130
"Ten Articles on WeChat" 95
Tencent 96–98, 119; Tenpay/WeChat Pay 75; WeChat 84, 87, 95, 97, 98, 150, 153, 155
Tesla 117
Third Plenum, Eighteenth Party Congress decision 68, 134, 166, 277
"three-child" policy 278
"3+1+1" work model 153
Thucydides Trap 194
Tiananmen Square movement 52–53
Tibet: unrest in 68
Tieba 84
TikTok 78, 97
Trans-Pacific Partnership 78
Trump, Donald 10, 223, 227, 239, 240, 250, 256
Tsai Ing-wen 224
Tsinghua Unigroup 115, 116
Tsinghua University 115, 118
TSMC 115
Twitter 97

Umbrella Movement (2014) 44
United Nations Human Rights Council 232
United Nations Peacekeeping Operations 221
United States (U.S.) 1, 9, 12, 14; artificial intelligence 118, 119; Asian Reassurance Initiative Act (ARIA) 223; attribution of blame for the pandemic 250; Centers for Disease Control (CDC) 240, 250; Chinese foreign relations with 223–224; Constitution 18; democracy 56–57; elections, role of money in 56; hegemony 218; imperialism 52; Internet-related expenditures 91; National Security Council 219; patents 108; as primary threat 51–54; protectionism 54; publications 107, 108

urbanization 11, 128, 131, 137n30, 271, 272–273, *272*
urban poor, living conditions of 133–134
urban poverty: causes of 128–129; groups and investment 129–133; misunderstanding of 125–128; policy 134–135

Volkswagen 225

Waltz, Kenneth 210
Wandel durch Handel policy 226
Wang Chengqi 196
Wang Houbin 174
Wang Jing 134, 205
Wang Kai 133
Wang Qishan 172
Wang Shengjun 21
Wang Xiaohong 23, 173
Wang Xiubin 184
Wang Zhen 171
weak coalitions 180, 182–187, **185**, **186**
Weber, Max 143
WeChat 84, 87, 95, 97, 98, 150, 153, 155
Weeks, Jessica 176
Wei Fenghe 224
Weibo 84, 95, 98, 99n4, 153
Wendel, Frederick C. 48
Wen Jiabao 8, 12, 88
Whyte, Martin 61
WIPO 108, 118
wolf warrior diplomacy 221, 231
World Bank: on poverty 125
World Trade Organization (WTO) 15n3, 69, 218
World Values Survey 143
WTO *see* World Trade Organization (WTO)
Wu Xiuquan 171
Wu Zeying Zena 61
Wu Zhenglong 173

Xiang Junbo 71–72
Xiao Yaqing 115
Xichang Satellite Launch Center 173
Xi Jinping: Belt and Road Initiative 10, 193–211; on collapse of CPSU 162; on common prosperity 3, 7, 12, 58, 59, 70, 73–74, 77, 78, 125, 135; "comprehensive national security concept" 2; effect in political education 57–59; foreign policy 11, 217–233; on general secretary's five-year term 1; Global Security Initiative

231, 237n83; *The Governance of China* 143; "Hold High the Great Banner of Socialism with Chinese Characteristics and Strive in Unity to Build a Modern Socialist Country in All Respects" 165; Internet governance strategies 8, 84, 92–98; law and political system 17–37; "Made in China 2025" policy 9, 79, 93, 106, 107, 110, 112–119; obsession with security 14; partnership with technology companies and social media platforms 83–99; personality cult 8, 142–144, 155; on political education 46, 50; on private economy 67; sense of insecurity 68; technology policy (2012–2022) 105–120; theories of 7; Thought 8, 47, 59, 142–156; vision of the Internet 92–93; zero-Covid policies 4, 5; *see also specific entries*
Xi Jinping Thought 8, 47, 59, 142–156; "civilized" state-building 145–148; impact assessment 154–156; Integrated Media Centers, "civilizing" role of 152–154; volunteering to construct 148–151
Xinjiang: unrest in 68
Xpeng 117
Xu Caihou 163, 172, 184, 185
Xu Qiliang 163
Xu Xisheng 174
Xu Xueqiang 186
Xu Zhongbo 185

Yang Guobin 144
Yang Jiechi 224
Yang Shangkun 171
Yang Xiaodu 26
Yang Xiaohua 196
Yao Yilin 171
Ye Xiangqun 133
Yi Gang 173
Yin Fanglong 189
Yin Yong 170
Yiu, Daphne W. 196
Yoon Suk-yeol 228
Youku 84
Yu Tao 133
Yu Zhongfu 189
Yu'e Bao 76, 97–98
Yunnan International Power Investment Company (CPI) 206

Zadek, Simon 196
zero-Covid policies 1–5, 10, 77, 154, 165, 176, 240, 256, 257
Zhang Denghua 198, 201
Zhang Guoqing 173
Zhang Lin 190
Zhang Qianfan 19
Zhang Taisu 19, 30
Zhang Youxia 170, 175, 182
Zhao Lijian 239
Zhao Weiguo 115, 116
Zhao Ziyang 6, 31, 161, 198
Zhihu 86
Zhongnanhai 3, 255
Zhou Yongkang 21, 23
Zhu Rongji 4
Zou Yizheng 198, 206, 207

Made in the USA
Columbia, SC
27 August 2024